Praise for
The *Five Ages* of Humanity

~~~~~~~~~~~

"Dear Gerald Heard -- I have now had time to read your new volume, which you very kindly sent me, and I have found it wonderfully rich, full of brilliant insights, and a great pleasure to read."
   —**Professor Joseph Campbell,** commenting on *The Five Ages of [Humanity]*, from a letter he wrote to Gerald Heard on Dec. 29, 1963

"I hope this new reissue of Gerald Heard's *The Five Ages of Humanity* will find many readers. Offering a deeply informed and wide-ranging psychological interpretation of world history, it invites readers to dialogue and at times to respond with challenges and doubts. But there can be no doubt at all about the continued urgency of what Heard saw as the most vital question confronting humanity: whether it can transform its own nature after having so catastrophically increased its power over technology. Yes, such transformation is possible, he argues, stressing how emotion, habits, and choices have influenced the evolution of human consciousness in five stages. What would be needed at our present precarious stage would be psychological changes to foster human potentialities by a therapeutic education that could, in Heard's words 'fully develop both an entire person and a complete society.'" (2022 endorsement)
   —**Sissela Bok, PhD,** moral philosopher, former professor of philosophy at Brandeis University, retired Senior Visiting Fellow at the Harvard Center for Population and Development Studies. Dr. Bok's latest book is *Exploring Happiness: From Aristotle to Brain Science*

"Gerald [Heard]'s *The Five Ages of [Humanity]* [is] where he can be seen as the savant, the repository of the most encompassing cosmology of his generation."
   —**Rabbi Zalman Schachter-Shalomi**, pioneering founder of the Jewish Renewal movement, author of numerous books, and a tireless champion of interfaith dialogue, from 2009

The *Five Ages* of Humanity

(Revised and Retitled Edition of 1964's *The Five Ages of Man*)

60th Anniversary Special Hardcover Edition

"The most important work to date of this challenging and brilliant philosopher, a volume which in scope and daring might be the 'Novum Organum' of the 20th century. ... Heard is admirably suited for this kind of universal, cosmological approach. His learning can be described as immense; his thinking about as untrammeled as is possible to imagine; his eloquence, for the most part, startling."
—**Robert R. Kirsch**, *Los Angeles Times* book review, Jan. 5, 1964

"I applaud this newly reissued edition of *The Five Ages of Humanity*, Gerald Heard's magnum opus, which offers a sweeping and optimistic view of humanity's future." (2022 endorsement)
—**William H. Forthman, PhD**, Professor of Philosophy Emeritus, California State University, Northridge

"A work of scientific art ... *The Five Ages of* [*Humanity*] is, in fact, a systematic literary exposition of one of the chief natural scientific principles of biopsychology, recapitulation. ... It is through the rich, lavish, well-woven and meaningful tapestry of material from biology, history, anthropology, psychology and psychiatry that this remarkable study achieves its effect. The author is as modern as yesterday. ... a beautiful book ..."
—**F. L. Kunz**, *Main Currents in Modern Thought* book review, Jan.-Feb. 1964 issue

"A sweeping vision that is often illuminating, sometimes exciting. His basic concept of a psychological evolution makes sense."
—**Herbert J. Muller**, *The New York Times* book review, January 5, 1964

The *Five Ages* of Humanity

(Revised and Retitled Edition of 1964's *The Five Ages of Man*)

The Psychology of Human History

60ᵗʰ Anniversary Special Hardcover Edition

Gerald *Heard*

Sky Parlor Publications™ · Nevada City, California

Copyright © 1963 by Gerald Heard.
Copyright renewed 1991 by Jay Michael Barrie.
Copyright transferred to The Barrie Family Trust.
This edition Copyright © 2023, 2024 by The Barrie Family Trust.

All Rights Reserved. No part of this book may be reproduced or used in any manner without the prior written permission of the publisher, except for the use of brief quotations in critical articles and book reviews.

Foreword Copyright © 2022 by Thomas Armstrong, PhD.

The digital enhancements and arrangement of the image "Twin Blue Marbles," used on the front cover and in the interior, showing five progressive stages of earth's evolution, was created by John Roger Barrie. Copyright © 2023 by John Roger Barrie.

The bio/dust-jacket photograph of Gerald Heard was taken by Jay Michael Barrie, ca. 1955, Copyright © by The Barrie Family Trust. All other photographs were taken by Jay Michael Barrie, Copyright © by The Barrie Family Trust.

Library of Congress Control Number: 2023938279

ISBN: 979-8-9908834-4-4 (hardcover)

Retitled and revised edition first published May 2023.
60th Anniversary Special Hardcover Edition
first published August 2024.

Cover design and layout by Sky Parlor Publications™.

Sky Parlor Publications™ is a registered trademark
in the United States of America.

Sky Parlor Publications™
P.O. Box 252
Nevada City, CA 95959
skyparlorpublications.com

My thanks to
JAY MICHAEL BARRIE
for his help as collaborator and editor,
and to
THE BOLLINGEN FOUNDATION
whose grant made this work possible

EDITOR'S PREFACE

Beginning in the early 1960s, the ideological map of the Western world erupted. That tumultuous decade started out as an afterthought of the 1950s and ended up upending many of our cultural, social, political, psychological, and spiritual values. Less than two years after astronaut John Glenn orbited the earth, and just over one month after the assassination of President John F. Kennedy, author-historian-lecturer-philosopher Gerald Heard published his monumental final book, *The Five Ages of Humanity*, originally titled *The Five Ages of Man*.

From the 1950s through the 1960s, the philosophical–sociological landscape in America dramatically changed. Freud transitioned to Jung. Frank Sinatra to the Beatles. Uncle Ben to *Mod Squad's* Linc. Betty Crocker to Betty Friedan. Conformity to individualism; order to protest. This was the decade of ideas, of waking up. And, who better to lead the intellectual charge than Gerald Heard.

Summarizing the prevailing historical concepts from multiple disciplines, then adding his theory about the teleological evolution of consciousness, and churning them all in his vast polymathic blender, Heard confidently mapped out heretofore uncharted territories. In what arguably is an early forerunner to the models of consciousness explanation of reality, he produced a broad compendium of incisive analyses, cogent diagnoses, and prescriptive cures for humankind's various dysfunctionalities.

The Five Ages of Humanity was the product of eight years of research. Heard received a two-year fellowship grant from the Bollingen Foundation in the mid-1950s under the auspices of St. Louis' Washington University's Department of Philosophy. This enabled him to undertake the studious investigations that resulted in *Five Ages*.

According to Heard biographer Alison Falby, "the book received a wide and positive reception." Proponents who jumped on the evolution-of-consciousness bandwagon hailed it. A few detractors who defended the fossilized old guard derided it. Heard did what he had so often done throughout his foresightful career: toss a grenade into the established status quo and let the fragments settle where they will. He aimed at moving the discussion forward to the next point on the dial. If some rigid, unproductive dogma lay in the rubble, all the better.

A reader should be prepared for an in-depth intellectual journey, accompanied by a number of epiphanic moments, and perhaps a few instances of head-scratching, as well as an uncanny sense of déjà vu (as if Gerald had a crystal ball), when assimilating the steaming cauldron of ideas that percolate throughout Gerald Heard's magnum opus, his self-described "psychological interpretation of history," *The Five Ages of Humanity*.

~~~~~~~~~~~

I am greatly indebted to Thomas Armstrong, PhD, not only for providing his brilliant, insightful foreword but for so generously making himself available to address occasional issues as they arose. Dr. Armstrong has proven an enormous asset to this project, and I am most grateful for his enthusiastic participation.

It is my good fortune that noted author and attorney Jonathan Kirsch, Esq, kindly agreed to review and advise on certain sections of the book. Mr. Kirsch's father was none other than the late respected author and distinguished literary critic Robert R. Kirsch, who penned his favorable *L. A. Times* book review of *The Five Ages of [Humanity]* nearly sixty years ago. An excerpt from Robert R. Kirsch's erudite, in-depth review graces our endorsements section above. Coming full circle, it is especially meaningful that Jonathan Kirsch and I, the son of Heard's longtime secretary Jay Michael Barrie, are both involved in this project.

Editor and author Rob Bignell provided knowledgeable editing recommendations for a few selected portions of the book. I am especially appreciative to Mr. Bignell for his expert, helpful suggestions.

The Joseph Campbell endorsement is used by kind permission of the Joseph Campbell Foundation. For more information, visit www.jcf.org.

William H. Forthman, PhD, provided his thoughtful endorsement for *Five Ages* in July 2022, one month prior to his passing.

The image of Earth from space, titled "Twin Blue Marbles-West" is made freely available for re-publication by NASA, and is credited to Reto Stöckli, based on data from NASA and NOAA. It is accessible at NASA's Visible Earth website at https://visibleearth.nasa.gov.

~~~~~~~~~~~

Gerald Heard's writing style can at times be challenging, as one navigates many of his trademark compound sentences and run-on paragraphs. With the aim of rendering certain complex sentences more readable, I have added occasional punctuation marks and have made minor layout emendations, including silently correcting a number of spelling, formatting, and factual errors, as well as usage inconsistencies that appeared in the original published edition.

The wording in this edition reflects inclusive and sensitive language wherever possible, and I have silently incorporated gender-neutral wording in Heard's Introduction and in a number of places throughout the remainder of the text. For example, "mankind" is replaced with either "humankind" or "humanity." Reflecting the usage conventions of his time, Heard almost exclusively uses the pronouns "man," "he," "him," and similar gender-based words in nonspecific contexts when he clearly intends a generic application. And so, whenever "man" or "woman," "men" or "women," "he" or "she," "him" or "her," "his" or "hers," or "himself" or "herself" are used as nonspecific pronouns, this usage is not intended to indicate any specific gender.

John Roger Barrie
Literary Executor of Gerald Heard
Nevada City, California
May 12, 2023

EDITOR'S PREFACE
to the 60th Anniversary Special Hardcover Edition

On this date of August 14, 2024, marking the 53rd commemoration of Gerald Heard's passing, we are especially pleased to publish this special hardcover edition of Gerald Heard's monumental tome, *The Five Ages of Humanity*, as 2024 marks the sixtieth-year anniversary of its initial publication year, the exact date of which was January 6, 1964.

Along with encasing the 60th Anniversary edition in this stylish hardcover finish, suitable not only for Gerald Heard aficionados but also for collectors of fine literary works, we have included four rare black-and-white photos from the early 1960s of Gerald Heard with various high-profile individuals: Igor and Vera Stravinsky, Henry and Clare Boothe Luce, and Nancy Wilson Ross.

We have also included images of two pages from the fifty-one leaves of the typewritten *Five Ages of* [*Humanity*] draft manuscript that is stored at the extensive Gerald Heard Papers archival collection at the UCLA Library Special Collections. We have included another item from the UCLA collection: a facsimile of Gerald's handwriting and signature on the page below from a handwritten note that Gerald wrote to reviewer Dr. F. L. Kunz on March 15, 1963, just after he had completed the *Five Ages* manuscript. We are grateful to the staff at UCLA Library Special Collections for their courtesy and assistance in facilitating our use of these images.

Finally, I added a first-ever index, and I judiciously intervened with another round of gentle, minor edits aimed especially at rendering some passages even more readable.

We hope that all readers will enjoy this elegant, enduring edition of Gerald Heard's elegant, enduring classic, *The Five Ages of Humanity*.

John Roger Barrie
Literary Executor of Gerald Heard
Nevada City, California
August 14, 2024

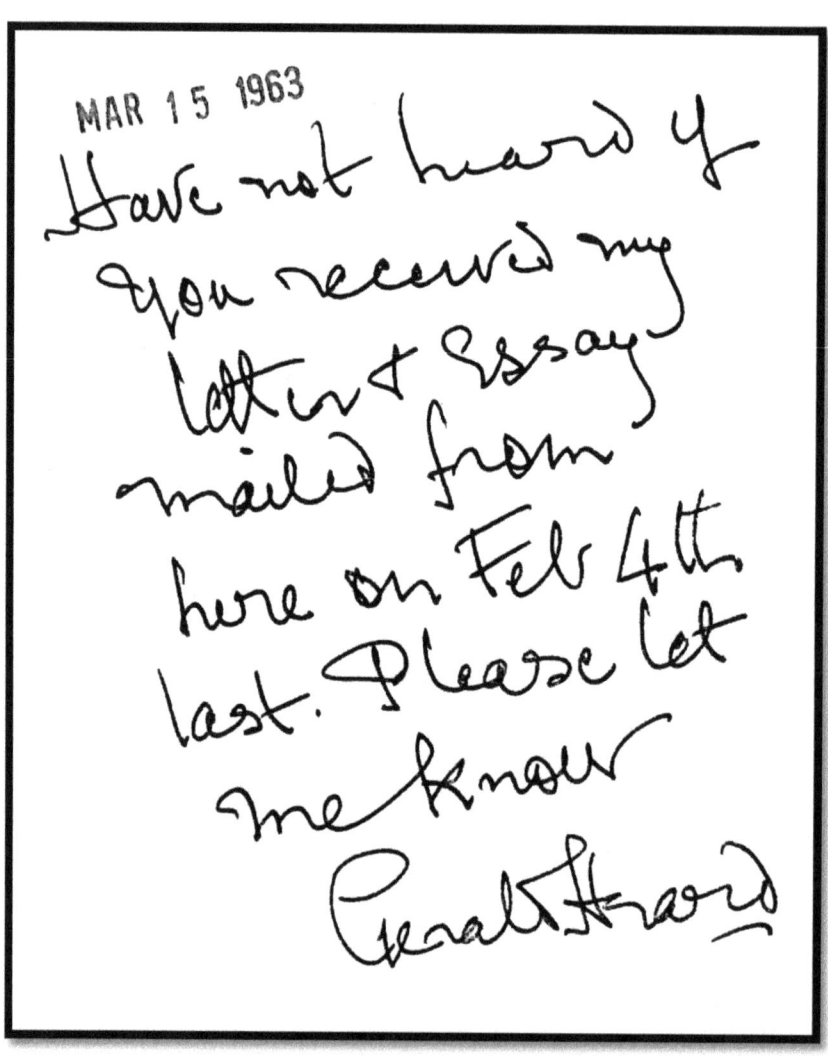

Above: Facsimile of Gerald Heard's March 15, 1963, handwritten note to reviewer Dr. F. L. Kunz, which served as a follow-up to Heard's initial February 4, 1963, typewritten letter. Copyright 2024 The Barrie Family Trust.

The *Five Ages* of Humanity

CONTENTS

Editor's Preface viii
60th Anniversary Edition Editor's Preface xi
Facsimile of Gerald Heard's Handwriting xii
Contents xiii
Foreword by Thomas Armstrong, PhD xv
Publisher's Note xxv
Introduction by Gerald Heard 1

Section I: The Psychological Story of Social Humans
(The Five Crises)

1. The Preindividual (*Coconscious humans*) 15
2. The Protoindividual (*Heroic, self-assertive humans*) 25
3. The Midindividual (*Ascetic, self-accusing humans*) 37
4. The Total Individual (*Humanic, self-sufficient humans*) ... 51
5. The Postindividual (*Leptoid humans*) 75

Section II: The Personal Psychological Story of Humans
(The Five Ordeals)

1. The Ordeal of Birth and Infancy and Its Specific Mental Breakdown (*The Trauma of Birth*) 87
2. The Ordeal of Childhood and Its Specific Mental Breakdown (*Dementia praecox becoming Paranoia*) 97
3. The Ordeal of Adolescence and Its Specific Mental Breakdown (*Schizophrenia*) 115
4. The Ordeal of First Maturity and Its Specific Mental Breakdown (*Manic depression*) 131
5. The Ordeal of Second Maturity and Its Specific Mental Breakdown (*Involutional melancholy*) 139

Section III: The Development of Initiations or Psychophysical Religious Exercises
(*The Five Mysteries*)

    Introduction 157
1. The Initiation of Rebirth (*Earth*) 161
2. The Initiation of Catharsis (*Water*) 177
3. The Initiation of Inspiration (*Air*) 189
4. The Initiation of Illumination (*Fire*) 203
5. The Initiation of Transformation (*Electricity*) 229

60th Anniversary Edition Photographs and Manuscript Drafts... 255

Epilogue
The Psychophysical Future of Humanity (*Evolution resumed*) 261

Appendices
A. The Hybrid Psyche 291
B. On Further Direction of Psychophysical Evolution 301
C. On the Cataclysmic Character of the Successive Epoch Changes 305
D. On the Evidence for an Esoteric Mystery Tradition in the West 307
E. Laboratory Experiments in Limited Environment 333
F. A Note on the Sources of Fear 343

Editor's Afterword 351
Table 1: Gerald Heard's Fivefold Schema, Part 1 353
Table 2: Gerald Heard's Fivefold Schema, Part 2 354
Glossary 355
Bibliography 359
Notes 365
Index 387
About the Author 399

FOREWORD
by Thomas Armstrong, PhD

In an era of specialists, I've always been drawn to interdisciplinary thinkers. Life is simply too rich and complex to be captured through a single lens. For much of my career, I've written about and lectured on Harvard professor Howard Gardner's theory of multiple intelligences, a framework which posits the existence of eight basic human intelligences as opposed to the single lens perspective of I.Q. testing. The theory rests upon research in neuropsychology, cognitive psychology, anthropology, animal studies, psychometrics, semiotics, biography, and developmental psychology. So, how delighted I was when approached by the literary executor of Gerald Heard's work and editor of this volume, John Roger Barrie, the son of Gerald Heard's longtime personal secretary, business manager, and editor Jay Michael Barrie (d. 2001), to write a foreword to Heard's book originally titled *The Five Ages of Man*. This book outdid even Gardner's interdisciplinary focus, integrating findings from developmental psychology, mysticism, mythology, anthropology, animal physiology, sociology, religion, physics, psychiatry, medicine, politics, history, evolutionary biology, biography, and more. It is truly a celebration of ideas, and in this foreword, I hope to acquaint the reader with some of its most powerful arguments and illustrations.

But first let me tell you a little bit about Gerald Heard, because he may be the most significant countercultural intellectual of the twentieth century that you've never heard of (no pun intended!). Active from the 1920s to the 1960s, he was lauded by some of the greatest minds of the modern era. Referring to Heard's frequent BBC radio broadcasts in the 1930s regarding contemporary developments in science, H. G. Wells commented: "Heard is the only man I ever listen to on the wireless [radio]. He makes human life come alive." Novelist E. M. Forster regarded him as "one of the most penetrating minds in England." He was a mentor to Aldous Huxley, author of *Brave New World*, traveling and lecturing with him throughout the United States in the late 1930s, and even sharing mescaline with him in the early 1950s. Huxley called Heard "that rare being—a learned man who [made] his mental home on the vacant spaces between the pigeonholes." Georgia O'Keefe once painted a picture inspired by Heard dancing around a desert tree. Actor and idol James Dean said his favorite book was by Heard (*Pain, Sex and Time: A New Outlook on Evolution and the Future of Man*). Jazz legend Dave Brubeck used to attend his lectures in California and reflected, "Gerald Heard had a brilliant mind ... I can truly say that he broadened my vision of religion and spirituality."

Heard was an early student of the Indian-based philosophy of Vedanta and did much to spread its teachings in the West. He inspired Michael Murphy and Richard Price to found the Esalen Institute (he had established his own proto-Esalen center in the 1940s called Trabuco College where writer Alan Watts, religion scholar Huston Smith, and poet Ezra Pound were visitors). He was one of the earliest gay activists in the United States, writing articles for the first openly gay national periodical—ONE—in the early 1950s, and was far ahead of his time in advocating that homosexuals stop trying to conform to the existing masculine stereotypes of their time and instead celebrate their creative and gender-fluid potentials. In the 1950s, years before the Summer of Love, Heard introduced LSD under supervised conditions for therapeutic and spiritual growth to talk show host Steve Allen, movie director John Huston, U.S. ambassador Clare Boothe Luce, and Bill Wilson, the founder of Alcoholic Anonymous. He was active in politics along a continuum ranging from left-wing pacifism in England in the 1930s to more conservative pursuits in the U.S. in the 1960s. He wrote 38 books, including books on evolution, theology, and philosophy, spiritual guides, pacifist treatises, ghost stories, detective novels, science fiction, and a book about flying saucers! But that's just part of his story, and those who

Foreword

are interested in further exploring his life and work should consult the official Gerald Heard website at geraldheard.com.

And now to the book itself. I think it's important to recognize that this is not simply an abstract compendium of ideas and speculations nor an argument for understanding a single systemized view of reality. *The Five Ages of Humanity* is above all a compassionate and wholly constructive work. Implied in much of what he writes about is a deep concern with the ever-present threat of violence in humankind and the danger of descending into chaos. He doesn't explicitly refer to the possibility of nuclear war or environmental disaster, but readers are advised to keep these and other ills of humanity in the back of their mind as they read the book. Heard begins the book with three simple questions: (1) Can we change our nature? (2) Have we ever done it? and if so, (3) How have we done it? *The Five Ages of Humanity* is an optimistic book in that regard, answering "yes" to the first two questions, and then spending the rest of the book tackling question number three, explaining how human nature has changed in significant ways over the millennia and providing suggestions for how humanity might continue to progress into the uncertain future to forestall any future catastrophe or collapse.

Although Heard is not particularly a systemizer in the way of, say, a Rudolf Steiner, a Jean Gebser, or a Ken Wilber, there is a certain architecture to his book as revealed in its table of contents that merits consideration before readers launch into the book itself. First and foremost, Heard argues that historical consciousness progresses along a course that mirrors a similar pattern in individual development. Although scientists have largely debunked the idea that "ontogeny recapitulates phylogeny," Heard is really doing something quite different. He's not arguing for a schema that connects the evolution of species to human embryology, but rather for a perspective that links the progression of the history of humankind with the way that individuals grow over time from birth to old age. Along with William James, he was one of the first thinkers of the 20th century to use the term "consciousness" in a substantive way, and his unique contribution was to delineate the growth of consciousness on both a collective and individual level. So he was as much concerned with anthropologists like Margaret Mead and

Alfred Kroeber as he was with child development experts such as Jean Piaget and Arnold Gesell.

The core of *The Five Ages of Humanity* consists of the eponymous five ages representing the growth of consciousness over time, which he defined in terms of the extent to which the collective as a whole, and the people within it, have developed a robust and mature manifestation of individuality. In the first age, which he describes as "co-conscious" or "preindividual," the members of a culture live in a kind of *participation mystique* with their rulers and gods (a situation which he wryly refers to as a "hypnocracy"), while on a personal level, the individual infant exists in a state of symbiotic unity with its mother. In the second age, the "heroic" or "protoindividual," the collective breaks free from its thralldom to the rigid elders and idols of the previous age and, as individuals, explode into rebellion, aggression, and rage toward those who would seek to suppress them. Collectively, we have the heroic deeds of the *Iliad*, while at the individual level, one can see the young child bursting the bonds of authority during the "terrible twos."

The third age is referred to as the "ascetic" or "midindividual" level of consciousness which is attained when the hubris of the aggressive warrior leads to a tragic comeuppance that ultimately turns his gaze inward. The result is a descent into feelings of guilt, rituals of expiation, and patterns of deep philosophical reflection. The warriors of the Trojan war become the tragedians of the Periclean Age. The wrath of Achilles gives way to the self-mutilation of Oedipus the King. On an individual basis, this is reflected in the life of rebellious adolescents who long for guidance from their idols but go into a deep funk (spending long hours in their rooms brooding and reflecting in their diaries) after being disillusioned by the adults around them. The fourth stage Heard calls the "humanic" age, where the human being is now a fully formed individual, and the culture expresses itself as a well-articulated polity. This age of consciousness, which Heard terms "first maturity," approximates what we consider to be the so-called "normal" adult human being living in the modern era. According to Heard, this type of consciousness emerged during the Renaissance and is characterized by hyper-rationality, ambition for material success, and acute self-consciousness.

Foreword

During the fifth age of humanity, things begin to get really interesting. He calls this the Leptoid Age (from the Greek *lepsis* "to seize") or the level of the "postindividual." This age, which he viewed as beginning in the early twentieth century, opens up potentials and possibilities that go beyond the limited ego-bound personality of the Humanic Age. Here in this "second maturity," the emphasis is on cooperation not competition, on being part of a "field" of consciousness rather than existing as a separate individual pitted against other individuals. Here dawns the realization that it is impossible to posit the existence of a fixed objective world. Now, alternative forms of consciousness and reality become possible, and humans begin to realize the connectedness of all living beings (Heard presciently uses the term "ecology" in this regard). The hyper-rationalism of the Humanic Age gives way to the body-mind ethos of the Leptoid Age where a new kind of thinking becomes possible that is creative, integral, and far-reaching.

After giving us a picture of the five ages of humanity, both collective and personal, Heard then moves on to the question of pathologies or what he calls "ordeals." These are dangers that lurk beneath the surface of each of these ages where cultures and individuals can self-destruct, fall into an abyss, or reach a dead end. Heard utilizes terms from early to mid-twentieth century psychiatry in naming these pathologies. This section of the book may pose a problem for some readers who could take issue with the specific pathologies he names and the ages to which they are assigned. According to Heard, the pitfall of the Heroic Age (corresponding to childhood) is what he calls "noradrenaline rage," a state that can deteriorate into "paranoia," "homicidal mania," and "dementia praecox." He contrasts this "ordeal" with the Ascetic Age (corresponding to adolescence) where the dangers are "adrenaline self-blame" and "schizophrenia." The ordeal of the Humanic Age is described by Heard as "manic-depression," and that of the "second maturity" or Leptoid Age he refers to as "involutional melancholy."

The use of these terms may raise red flags in the minds of many readers, but it is important at this juncture not to throw out the baby with the bathwater. It's true that our understanding of hormones, neurotransmitters, the structure and function of the brain, and an ever-expanding nosology of psychiatric categories, have far outpaced Heard's own knowledge base, given the times in which he was writing. But what Heard has caught ahold of (and I believe he was way ahead of many scientists in seeing this) was the biological basis of mental illness, and in particular, the role that stress plays (he cites stress research pioneer Hans Selye) in the incidence of psychosomatic illness, depression, and other mental and physical disorders. At a time in the early 1960s when many psychiatrists were pointing the finger at Freudian-based Oedipus and Electra complexes as primary factors responsible for fomenting a person's mental distress, Heard was accurately intuiting the neurochemical origins of their emotional difficulties.

Heard leaves the best for last when he concludes his work with a comprehensive look at possible solutions or "treatments" for these and other ills of humankind. Again, some readers may be shocked by some of his prescriptions, but again we must keep in mind that Heard is an intuitive thinker, and like a metal plate with a moving magnet underneath it that draws metallic filings together in interesting patterns, Heard's mind was a field that drew together a wide range of disparate solutions to bear upon the deep problems he has presented in this book. Using the five elements of nature (earth, water, air, fire, and "aether," which he calls "electricity"), he dips into anthropology, mythology, mysticism, and a wide range of other fields to describe what he calls "initiations" or "mysteries." According to Heard, such interventions have been designed throughout the millennia to purge individuals and cultures of their pathologies so as to bring about an outpouring of energy that can propel them into the next age of consciousness.

Among a wide range of possibilities, he describes the use of ritual burial in different cultures (earth), water rituals such as those involving life-threatening immersion in a river or ocean (water), breath control techniques such as the practice of pranayama in Hindu cultures (air), and rituals that involve walking on hot coals (fire). Regarding the latter, Heard includes a written account of a fire ritual experienced by none other than Joseph Campbell. Finally, for what Heard calls "electricity," he posits among other approaches the awakening of the kundalini or coil of psychic energy seated at the base of the spine as practiced by different schools of Hinduism. Heard may raise eyebrows when he also suggests subjecting individuals in their "second maturity" to electrical shocks (he later modifies this to "surges"), but we should note that scientists are already doing something similar with electroconvulsive therapy, transcranial magnetic stimulation, and similar interventions to treat refractory depression.

Taken as a guide to the human life cycle, *The Five Ages of Humanity* includes a staggering range of progressive ideas and practices for the optimal development of each stage of life from birth to old age. Heard was ahead of his time when he promoted prenatal care and humane methods of childbirth (he cites a pioneer in the field, Grantly Dick-Read). He also writes about the use of regression therapy to help heal the trauma of birth, citing as a major source the psychoanalyst Otto Rank. He points to the importance of early language enrichment and lots of free play experiences to promote optimal infant mental and emotional growth. He advises parents and teachers to encourage children and adolescents to "develop initiative toward new experience, be curious about the anomalies, and feel adventurous toward the enigmatic," suggesting that the child's Heroic Age tendency "to attack" be transmuted into a "wish to investigate."

He anticipated the emergence of "emotional intelligence" and "social and emotional learning" as important cultural priorities. This topic is currently all the rage in today's American and British educational institutions. He was a pioneer in "humanistic psychology," advocating that "therapy can't be a process that simply returns the person to normality." He cautioned that we not put the sick person back into a sick society but seek society-wide educational measures to effect systemic change. He also was ahead of his time (along with pioneers like Stanislav Grof and Humphry Osmond) in suggesting that therapists might consider using psychedelic drugs to alleviate mental suffering. We're now seeing a resurgence of research in this area after a fifty-five-year U.S. government-initiated lacuna which so far has suggested that LSD and psilocybin are powerful agents in treating depression, alcoholism, and end-of-life anxiety.

Heard was also ahead of his time in his advocacy for aging adults. Heard correctly predicted that "we should be prepared for a large new age group of the hearty aged." He understood that this group traditionally has been viewed as expendable by the culture because it has little to contribute to Humanic Age priorities regarding material accumulation. He rightly regarded melancholy as the chief danger for this age group (suicide rates are highest in older adults). He also saw the danger of older adults becoming rigid in their thinking, thus anticipating society's concerns with dementia, an apprehension that wasn't prevalent at the time he was writing the book. He recommended, as have many in the human potential movement, that older adults embrace becoming "seers" and "guides" to the younger generation (anticipating the work of Rabbi Zalman Schachter-Shalomi on "spiritual eldering"), and that they seek to retain their youthful plasticity as they age, thus foreseeing by sixty years the current popularity of the term "neuroplasticity" as an important feature of the developing brain.

In this regard, one of the most exciting aspects of *The Five Ages of Humanity* is the emphasis that Heard gives to the concept of neoteny (a Latin word meaning "holding youth"). He noted that this idea was unknown to the child therapists of his day (and it *still* is largely unrecognized by most people). Neoteny is a developmental idea that refers to the retardation of maturity. A look at the evolution of species suggests that there's more of a tendency for childlike characteristics to be "held" into later development in complex as opposed to more primitive organisms. Harvard paleontologist Stephen Jay Gould once suggested half-humorously that humans are "neotenous apes." A look at a baby chimp reveals very human-like traits. As the chimp matures, these traits are lost. But in human beings, these characteristics are "held" into adulthood. These are *physical* traits of neoteny, but Gould and Princeton anthropologist Ashley Montagu have also pointed to *psychological* characteristics of neoteny which include such childlike traits as flexibility, playfulness, curiosity, imagination, creativity, and wonder. Heard suggested that "the elasticity of wonder is a child factor and always stands in danger of being lost." He advocated for a kind of "neotenic education" that seeks to preserve these childlike qualities in human beings as they age. He suggested that the adult leaders, and in particular the elders of the culture, undergo a neotenic training so that they will be "young at heart" as they guide others.

Foreword

In sum, I'd like to suggest that readers set aside their scruples and simply enjoy this incredible synthesis, this rich feast, this sumptuous festival of ideas. You might keep your smartphone dictionary handy to look up unfamiliar words. Also, it's probably not a good idea to read through *The Five Ages of Humanity* as you would a "beach read." Better to savor it, celebrate its serendipities, and let your mind mold itself gently to its peripatetic pace. Heard tends to digress a lot in this book and double back on things already said in previous sections, and his digressions and repetitions are often among the most interesting things that he has to say. After savoring the chapters, make sure to save room for dessert, that is to say, the appendices, which focus on issues such as fear, mystery traditions, and laboratory experiments in sensory isolation. I'd like to suggest that readers think of this book as an archaeological find, out of print for sixty years, but now retrieved from obscurity and brought to the attention of a new readership. My wish for you is that this book may further the development of your own consciousness into the post-individual future!

~~~~~~~~~~~

About Thomas Armstrong, PhD

Thomas Armstrong, PhD, is the Executive Director of the California-based American Institute for Learning and Human Development, and an award-winning author and speaker who has been an educator for nearly 50 years. More than 1.4 million copies of his books are in print in English on issues related to learning and human development.

He is the author of twenty books, including his groundbreaking nonfiction books on education, neurodiversity, and human development as well as one novel titled *Childless*. He has written for respected magazines, periodicals, and journals. He has appeared on several national and international television and radio programs, including NBC's *The Today Show*, *CBS This Morning*, CNN, the BBC, and *The Voice of America*. Articles featuring his work have appeared in *The New York Times, The Wall Street Journal, The Washington Post, USA Today, Investor's Business Daily, Good Housekeeping*, and many other newspapers and magazines around the country.

Dr. Armstrong has given more than 1,000 keynote addresses, workshop presentations, and lectures on six continents in 29 countries and in 44 states over the past 30 years. His clients have included *Sesame Street*, the Bureau of Indian Affairs, the European Council of International Schools, the Republic of Singapore, and several state departments of education. For more information, visit his website at https://www.institute4learning.com.

PUBLISHER'S NOTE

Sky Parlor Publications is proud to publish *The Five Ages of Humanity*, a revised and retitled edition of the *magnum opus* by Gerald Heard (1889–1971), which was first published on January 6, 1964, as *The Five Ages of Man*.

While his observations and insights remain important and influential, in certain places Heard's prose may strike some contemporary readers as insensitive or off-putting. The present edition contains some revisions that are meant (1) to address his intended meanings; (2) to reflect the incorporation of inclusive and sensitive language wherever possible; (3) to use gender-neutral language in some, but not all instances, as we have attempted to strike a balance between Heard's original writing style and gender-neutral usage; (4) to correct inaccurate information where possible; and (5) to caution the reader against some observations that we now know to be inaccurate. A number of passages are accompanied by an explanatory editor's note located within the text or as an endnote. Wherever the original text has been changed, the change has been made either silently, or else as indicated by ellipses or brackets.

The single most prominent change, of course, is in the title. We believe that Heard meant "Humanity" when he mentions "Man," and we think he would have approved of this change, as well as the other changes we have carefully considered and made.

All third-party quotations in the book also appeared in the first edition and have been used without objection ever since. The publisher continues to rely on the Fair Use Doctrine in using these quotations, many of which are formally referenced or otherwise credited to its author and place of publication.

No sponsorship by or affiliation with the owners of trademarks that are mentioned in passing is claimed or suggested.

DISCLAIMER: The reader is strongly cautioned not to rely on Gerald Heard's observations about the use of regression therapy; hypnosis; yoga; breathing exercises/breath-control techniques; colonic irrigation; firewalking practices; swimming underwater for protracted periods; water-tank immersion using a breathing apparatus; isolation chambers; confined or restrictive environments; ritual burial; use of a stroboscope, soundwaves, and indoles; respiratory psychotherapeutic treatments involving the use of carbon dioxide or other gas mixtures; and any and all similar practices and treatments in these pages. Concerning some of the aforementioned methods, Heard wrote further below that "All these means can be and are being accepted" and that "psychically, they are safe; any physiological risk is nonexistent." Quite to the contrary, there is always a potential risk, even if minimal, in following such advice, and all the methods mentioned by Heard carry a potential risk. The same is true of the additional therapies, practices, and therapeutic agents he mentions in passing or advocates, including but not limited to the use of various psychedelics and pharmaceuticals (including tranquilizing drugs), and treatments involving the use of electric shock/surge therapy; Metrazol therapy; and infrared/shortwave radiation therapy and radiant heat therapy treatments.

Above all, the reader is strongly cautioned to approach *The Five Ages of Humanity* as the brilliant work of a great mind and a great imagination but not as a manual of psychological, spiritual, or medical advice. The practices and treatments mentioned in this book are intended for educational purposes only, and they do not constitute professional advice or act as a substitute for seeking medical advice from a qualified medical, healthcare, psychological, or other professional. As Heard himself notes in one context, "such proposals can only be tentative suggestions, extrapolations from our present convergent lines of knowledge." We believe this observation applies equally to all of Heard's proposals, which should be viewed as hypothetical.

Accordingly, any reader interested in the practices or treatments mentioned in this book should consult appropriate professionals rather than rely on the suggestions that Heard makes, discusses, or advocates in this book. We strongly suggest that you, the reader, must satisfy yourself that you have consulted and followed the advice of appropriate professionals before pursuing anything you find in these pages. For this reason and all the other reasons listed in this Disclaimer, the publisher expressly disclaims any and all liability for injury or loss resulting from the reader's reliance on the contents of this book. Such reliance is solely at the reader's own risk.

The *Five Ages* of Humanity

60th Anniversary
Special Hardcover Edition

INTRODUCTION
by Gerald Heard

The most vital question that confronts humanity today is a threefold one. Can humans, who have so catastrophically changed their power over their environment, change their own nature? Have they ever done so? If they have, how have they done it? Whether we can have any hope of answering this triple question depends on whether, in looking at history, we can discern any overall pattern or process of development.

Alfred North Whitehead, together with many other philosophers and historians of science, has called the one hundred years from 1600 to 1700 the Century of Invention. These were the three generations during which the basic insights were made in regard to the Sciences. But it is a strange fact that, although in that formative period, history, too, was looked on as being a process that could only be understood as a science, later historians have refused so to regard it.

Hugo Grotius (1583–1645) was the founder of International Law. In 1604 he wrote, although he did not publish it, his *De Jure Praedae*. It was the first sketch of his classic *De Jure Belli* which, including *Jus Pacis*, was written in 1625. This book has often been said to have founded a new science, the science of International Law, extracted from consideration of the actual process of history. As Mark Patterson has said, "the law in war" was but a small part of the whole of Grotius' study of those principles which hold people together—principles to which humans' basic nature compels them to return, however often they may behave aberrantly.

THE FIVE AGES OF HUMANITY

Giovanni Vico (1668–1744) develops and enriches these insights into the structure of history and into the cohesive forces that shape its process. By the end of the eighteenth century (and using the cold scientism of Francis Bacon to remove the orthodox prejudices from Grotius' thinking), he could perceive the anthropological basis underlying law. Therefore, as the eighteenth century opened, he was able (from his universal law, *De universi juris uno principio et fine uno*) to arrive at his classic contribution to a philosophy of history, *Principi d'una Scienza Nuova*.

From the fragmentary evidence yielded by the Jewish canonical books and Greek literature, he recognized that humanity had gone through at least three great stages. Primitive tribes have an almost instinctive power to hold together: a power of co-consciousness or group-suggestibility (I have called it hypnocratic; see endnote 71.) This stage is succeeded by the Heroic which, in turn, is followed by the Humanic Epoch. Strangely enough (and, it may be, out of subconscious caution), Vico neglects the Ascetic Epoch.

However, we can see that this is not only a schema of history, an outline of a significant process. This is also an interpretation of history in psychological terms. It shows that there can be a historia[1] of humanity, just as there can be a natural history, a science of the other creatures. But humankind's history is not to be understood in terms of instinct any more than it is to be understood in terms of economics. Though for the first epoch of its history humans were raised by an *unconscious* drive, that drive finally lifted them into intentional development in their efforts to satisfy an inborn wish to understand. Their story is not the result of their reaction to blind forces that work either from within or without. Humanity's story is specifically the winning of an increasing awareness, purpose, intention, and objective. In short, humanity's history is the record of how it has gained in the intensification of consciousness, of self-understanding. It is a psychological story. For the spiral evolution of the psyche is the theme of the human venture. It is the clue to humanity's varied and successive behaviors, to the interpretation of its activities. It is the key to the explanation of its conflicts and its constructs, its orders and revolts, its catastrophes and recoveries, its breakdowns and resumptions.

Introduction

Intensified special studies of history, and indeed the increasing restriction of history to a study in itself that is confined to documents, made historians neglect Vico's magnificent map. Goethe, visiting Naples, was shown the master's work. But the great concept fell barren on that polished mind that was divided into the two facets of natural science and poetry. Edward Gibbon, who can span and compose fifteen hundred years, could only confirm the prejudices of rationalistic taste and mechanistic science: human history is divided between brutal or superstitious ignorance and critical, sophisticated knowledge. There were no alternatives other than the reign of reason or "the triumph of barbarism and religion."

Soon the historian was relieved of the task of having to handle predocumentary data—by the archaeologist. And when, with Boucher de Perthes' discoveries of the Old Stone Age tools (and after a hard struggle that was thoroughly discreditable to the guardians of history), there was disclosed a further and vaster past lying back of the archaeological ages, this awkward revelation was handed to the paleontologist. Then this latest research began to show that here might lie the only basic datum line of history, that in this amazing evidence (again, it was passionately resented by "the custodians of the past"), which had been brought to light by the discovery of the great Paleolithic cave frescoes and bas-reliefs, might be mirrored a different, pre–self-conscious type of mind and level of consciousness. But again, the historian refused to shoulder the obligation. To the anthropologist was left the fascinating and informative task of correlating the surviving Stone Age cultures[2] of Australia with the dawn cultures of Ice Age Europe, and so catch glimpses of the vast process whereby the human mind, as it contracted focus, achieved increasing objectivity.

Now, therefore, the historian is self-confined to their own ever narrower documentation. Naturally, such voluntary myopia denies any general pattern. A tapestry cannot be understood by studying its threads with a magnifying glass. Exchange the glass for a microscope and the higher magnification will only render the design less perceptible. We need a lens with a wider angle, not a more intense focus, if we are to perceive an aeonic process. As it was pointed out by James Anthony Froude, the capable and popular nineteenth-century Oxford historian, it was this very lack of extent and span, not a lack of detail and particulars, that prevented his generation of students of the past from perceiving its vast pattern—a lack which he did not hold was irremediable.

Sir Flinders Petrie was the founding father of predocumentary (or nondocumentary) history, a chronology of culture deduced from a series of artifacts. He had an almost unsurpassed knowledge of Egyptian history, and at the beginning of the twentieth century he did indicate (in his *Revolutions of Civilisation*) that he had detected a process of alternating cycles of order, arrest, revolt, and restored order throughout the millennia of the Nile culture-course and social heredity.

Max Weber, as a Comtist Positivist and influenced by Herbert Spencer, with truly German eruditional pertinacity, collected a vast mass of documentation to establish his thesis that the whole process of history brings humanity to a complete and final rationalism, in the name of which he dismisses religion and metaphysics as irrationalisms. In spite of his immense learning, he (like Sir James Frazer with his vast but fruitless *Golden Bough*) uses it only to establish this utterly inadequate thesis: All religion is magic, and magic is merely humanity's first, fumbling, mistaken effort to make science. All metaphysic is also humanity's false view of things seen through the superstition-clouded minds of the past, and now corrected for good by the critical self-conscious mind of modern humans, who at last are able to see things as they are, have always been, and will be.

Even James Henry Breasted, like Petrie, could not make use of his great insight: the recognition that a new kind of person had appeared almost in one century (the three generations required for a new challenge to be made and a new question to be put, a new answer to be offered and that new answer to be put into practice). Breasted called it "the rise of conscience" (after which we all become individually responsible egos). He did not recognize this phase as a midterm in the condensation of consciousness—that it lay between the phase of the simple-minded, unreflective hero and that of the fully isolated consciousness of the modern Renaissance individual who believes only in the critical, skeptical reason.

And even Karl Jaspers, in his *Vom Ursprung und Ziel der Geschichte*, though he does recognize this the Ascetic phase and its importance (for this doctrine of secession from the going concern is found extending in three lifetimes from Shantung, the peninsula pointing northeast to the Upper China Sea, to Calabria, the peninsula that reaches down into the Western Mediterranean) nevertheless calls it "the axis of time in human history." He can view it only as a fulcrum up to which humankind rises and then, like a child crawling up a teeter-totter, having passed the pivot can now come easily down to ground again. He does not recognize any more than Breasted that the mind, after having reached this middle phase of self-consciousness, condensed even further, and then, and then only, has begun again to re-expand.

Eric Voegelin (see Bibliography, reference 88), in his huge, still unfinished study of history, gives us the philosophy that will rule his work. In the first volumes, and most succinctly in his *New Science of Politics, An Introduction* (88), he takes his stand on that neo-Catholicism which, in one comprehensive excommunication, dismisses all concepts of development, improvement, and resumed epigenesis as heresy, as Gnosticism. And he calls on, as allies, such antipathetic figures as Richard (called contemporaneously "the Judicious") Hooker, the Elizabethan Anglican Divine, and Thomas Hobbes, the designer of the monster state-master Leviathan, the power elite focused in one person, the absolute autocrat.

Indeed, this continued refusal to look at the huge design now exposed to our view is so unreasonable that we are bound to suspect an unconscious prejudice. An unfriendly reception was given by most professional historians to Arnold Toynbee's attractive and inspiring study of history. Also, that compendious historian refused to start his interpretation with the basic platform of human history. He traced only those mesas, benches, and buttes of cultures that rise from that common peneplain. He started at the archaeological level of history, not at its paleontological base. These two facts seem to me to be evidence of a deep unwillingness to face the possibility of a psychological interpretation of history in which the clue to humanity's historia is the evolution of its consciousness.

As it is in the case of the long-rejected results of research into extrasensory perception, this appears to be due to a rare concatenation of forces usually so opposed to each other that, when they combine to deny something, the public is convinced that what they deny needs no further examination; it cannot but be false. The theologians of the Western World have claimed that one of the reasons for the superiority of their religion was that it was historical. But at least since the dismissal of the Alexandrine Fathers (especially Origen, A.D. 185–254), they have been hostile to any information, whether astronomical or biological, which might suggest that their view of the process of history was too narrow because their concept of the developmental emergence of humans was too local and brief. "Ours, the one true religion and therefore the one historical religion," they said, "is being endangered by irresponsible research." For the greater part of the last one hundred years, this slogan allowed the theologians to prevent new historical knowledge from being incorporated into the basis for a growing morality.

On the other hand, the biologists were just as anxious to prevent the public being offered any picture that was less out of date than that of the theologians. Smarting from the reception given to the evolutionary hypothesis of humanity's ascent, they certainly had strong negative motivation to collect and stress all the evidence that might indicate the meaninglessness of creation.

Nevertheless, although most biologists have clung to the belief that almost throughout its course the evolutionary process has been completely blind and fortuitous, and although this belief has been accepted by historians as showing that humanity's story must be as incoherent and pointless as Nature's, some influential biologists have themselves not accepted this deduction. Probably no biologist has been more influential in informing and directing American public opinion on evolution than G. G. Simpson. In his most popular and probably most telling presentation of the present majority view of evolution, *The Meaning of Evolution* (79), he states categorically that man was never intended; he is simply a fluke, the blind consequences of a totally unconscious randoming. Yet in concluding this work, Professor Simpson goes on to assert that no one must say humanity is pure freak or simple brute. On the contrary, humans are incomparable, the intensest appearance of a power form whose essence can only be described by their unique characteristics, by their traits that are found in no other creature. So in humans, there arises

Introduction

"a new form of evolution." Further, this new form can largely overrule the old. This new evolution is social heredity, the ascent and blending of ideas (information, correlation, and supposition). Thus humans can psychically, purposively evolve because of their capacity to choose and to give all manner of answers to outer challenges. And these answers spring far less from built-in reactions than from a capacity to recognize that the situation has altered and that the new here-and-now is the challenge, not old circumstances and the familiar associations. Though design, we are told by Simpson, was never present in life before, with humans and their process it is. Here then is biological authorization for regarding history as significant growth, purposive evolution.

Meanwhile, though the historian as a rule still seems anxiously desirous of denying any process in the history of this unique creature that strives toward goals, the anthropologist is certain now that sequence can be detected. And though it is still described in economic terms (as perhaps it must be first rendered because of our lack of psychological insight into or direct evidence of the psychological changes, the successive alterations in consciousness, which attended the material cultural developments), yet this sequence, even as we have it now in bare outline, can hardly fail to be recognized by any open mind as being symptomatic of an alteration and evolution of ideas.

In studying the progressive shapes and uses of humankind's gear, we see the coagulation of material into patterned, functional forms and objects as the stimuli of the outer world were focused, by an intensifying consciousness, into a ray of ever more powerful intention. W. D. Strong has given six steps of humanity's ascent from the wandering food-gatherer up to what he calls the imperial epochs. Starting [with] humans at the food-gatherer state, he has, of course, in this first phase of necessity included in one basic aeon the six or more epochs of the Paleolithic. His stage two is incipient horticulture. At stage three, the designation has been altered from one that describes development of food production to one that describes a political-social process, the formation of local civilizations. The fourth heading is to describe the flowering of such separate cultural units. Stage five is the time when such units, as they spread, began to coalesce. Stage six is when these coalescences are compulsorily structured into the larger coercive units of empires.

J. H. Steward (82) has indicated that this sequence is shown just as much across the centers of culture-origins in the entire Eurasian land mass as throughout the Americas. Gordon Childe has shown that different rates of development, and the confusion caused by the collision of cultures at different levels, still makes difficult the correlation of at least the cultural growth stages of Europe and the Near East.

When, however, in the study of vertebrate evolution, paleontologists find themselves with a section of the fossil record confused or lacking, they have discovered that owing to the recapitulatory growth process of the fetus in the womb it is possible from embryology to fill these lacunae. And so it can now be done with the cultural evolution of humans and the evolution of consciousness that precipitates those cultural sequences. As Stanley Hall, Cyril Burt, Stanley Hall's outstanding student Arnold Gesell, and many other child psychologists have established, the individual infant, child, and adolescent are recapitulating, in their individual growth phases, the past epochs of humankind's psychosocial evolution. This is, of course, an extension into human history and cultural evolution of the biological principle that has helped in elucidating biological evolution: the principle that ontogeny, the history of the individual's developmental growth, is an epitome of phylogeny, the history of the race's development.

So the individual infant, being in the preindividualized, symbiotic field-relationship with its mother, permits us to understand the pre-critical, pre–self-conscious mind of primitive humans. In turn, the child, being in the protoindividualistic stage that protestingly struggles for independence from the closed circle of infancy's symbiosis, is recapitulating the Heroic Age that smashed the pristine culture and, having destroyed the hypnocracies (the suggestion-imposed consent of the governed), had, when tired of loot, to impose the military dictatorships.[3] These two correlations of what may be called the individual's psycho-ontogeny and the race's psycho-phylogeny are now, we see, recognized by the child psychologists. They permit us to do two things. First, they make it possible for us to help the young with their growth, to help them not to stand in their own light. Second, if we realize that the young are now epitomizing history, it is possible for us to understand the past, to recognize the process and avoid its mistakes (which were tragic enough to have been desperate but vital enough to have been survived), to have hope of the future and co-operative capacity with the present.

The third correlation of humanity's history with the individual's third stage is emerging only today. However, Gesell (30) and his collaborators have in their *Youth: The Years from Ten to Sixteen* now carried on into its third stage the elucidation of the individual's growth. So to the stages of inherent development of the infant and the child they have added that of youth. Applying the particular quality of character that is found to emerge at this third stage of the individual's growth (human psycho-ontogeny), we can see that it is a recapitulation of the age which in history succeeded the Heroic, Protoindividualistic Epoch. This third stage of humans is the Ascetic.

We can, from our knowledge of the inherency of the individual's psychophysical growth process now, recognize the psychosocial forces that brought humans from protoindividualism to midindividualism. We can have still further insight (as we did with infancy and childhood) into our past and also perceive that its formative and directive force was fundamentally psychological, not economic or political. History can not only be elucidated (that is, recognized as having a patterned direction) but also we can recognize the nature of the drive in it as being the growth of consciousness, the intensified awareness of intention.

But if the Preindividualistic, pre–Heroic Epoch of humans is today recapitulated by the infant, the Protoindividualistic Epoch recapitulated by the child, and the Midindividualistic by the adolescent—what then? Neither the race nor the individual has closed its development with the adolescent, Midindividualistic Epoch. The individual goes on into first maturity, and human society went on into the Humanic Epoch that succeeded the Ascetic. Both are marked by correlative psychological symptoms of development, increasing self-consciousness, intensification of individualism.

We can, then, answer the first part of our threefold question. Humans can hope to change themselves constructively because there is a power of unexpended growth in them. They do grow in consciousness, learn from experience, and make sense of an increasing area of awareness. But when that is allowed (as the findings of modern psychoanthropology and of the growth psychology of Gesell and others compel us to allow), we have to face the second part of the question. Let us grant that there is an intense growth vitality in humans, which has made it possible for them to survive the shattering of their primal society by the Heroic explosion and, in turn, the failure of nerve and secession of the Ascetic shrinkage. But does not the evidence show that with every epoch there is an intensification of individualism and so a steady loss of cohesion, of loyalty, and of any sense of any purpose beyond personal and indeed sensory satisfaction?

Two facts contradict this foreboding. When the Ascetic Epoch passed into the Humanic, this meant, and was caused by, a rapid intensification of consciousness. Humanity suffered terribly: for example, from the fiendishly cruel methods of the Inquisition as, increasingly through the fourteenth century, the Church tried to extirpate all heretics and, during the fifteenth and sixteenth centuries, from the ghastly Wars of Religion that at last ended with the Peace of Westphalia in 1648. Nevertheless, and this is the first contradictory fact, although there was great shock, no Dark Age of breakdown ensued between these two epochs. The second fact (as we shall see in Section I, Chapter 4) is that as humans found themselves rapidly subjected to an intensification of self-consciousness, they did, as a historical fact, undertake specific psychological training to counter this contraction. However, these countermeasures were reactionary not progressive. They were of the nature of a parachute, to break a fall rather than, like a helicopter, to bear upward the person who was plummeting earthward under the pull of gravitation. Nevertheless, time was gained, catastrophe was postponed, the loss of loyalty was delayed, shock and disintegration were extended so as to become a sustained strain, a protracted tension, a tautening *angst*, not a paralyzing dismay.

This, then, will deal with the third part of our question. If humans *can* change their nature and if they have done so, then how have they done it? As a hypothesis, I have attempted a correlation

Introduction

among four aspects of humanity's history, each of which divides into five parts. The first aspect is that of the race's history. I see it as five epochs during which, through the contraction of consciousness, humans become first a creature of a spoken tradition; secondly, a being of protest against that stifling tradition; thirdly, a person of self-blame; fourthly, an individual of objectivity; and fifthly, an individual who is objectively aware of their subjectivity.

The second fivefold aspect is that of the five age-stages through which each individual passes to complete their life span today: (i) infancy, (ii) childhood, (iii) adolescence, (iv) first maturity, and (v) second maturity (the veterine).

The third aspect is the delineation of the five dominant symptoms of mental morbidity that mark and indicate the specific disintegration-stress and collapse-states both of each of the historic epochs and of each of the age-stages of the individual life. These are (i) the trauma of birth, the extreme resultant of which is womb-recessionalism; (ii) paranoia;[4] (iii) schizophrenia; (iv) manic-depressive insanity; and (v) involutional melancholy. The allotment of each one of these five types of insanity to one of the five historical social and individual breakdowns will be dealt with in Section II. There we shall deal with the question at some length and try to show that although there are two of these insanities which may, through arrested development of the individual, appear outside its age group, each particular type of mental illness does belong to a specific mental age group.

The fourth fivefold aspect is an account of those five methods and therapies whereby, with increasing purposiveness and self-consciousness, humans have remedied the five psychophysical morbidities that threaten not only their personal sanity but their society's survival. This fourth fivefold aspect of history is complementary to the other three because here we can trace the steps in which humans did devise, in the beginning almost unawarely, those five successive therapeutic psychophysical methods whereby they could remedy both their individual psychoses and also the psychosocial disasters of their successive societies. [These are:]

(I) The rite of burial and resurrection, called the mystery of Earth, recovers the individual from (*a*) the trauma of birth and the inability to develop beyond infantile reactions and a suckling, tethered emotional life; and (*b*) that blind desire for an unmoving, infallible, completely and comprehensively authoritarian society and tradition.

(II) Next, the rite of immersion and catharsis, called the mystery of water, recovers the individual from (*a*) the paranoid overreaction against society, the noradrenaline violence (28) of the child who, in its uninstructed and unguided demand for liberty and the right for approved independence, verges toward dementia praecox; and (*b*) from that desire to join, and in the end lead, a freelance delinquent gang that as freebooters preys on a society for which it has nothing but contempt.

(III) Then there comes the rite of breathing and auditory suggestion, which is called the mystery of air. This aimed at releasing the psyche from fixation at an adolescent level, from an arrest at self-contempt and self-despairing when, facing the unlimited demands of society and the newly confronted unruliness of its own nature, it becomes schizoid. Those who have newly reached puberty must be restored from a disgust with the psychophysique, a loathing that is a hypertrophied development, an unbalanced reaction to self-knowledge and self-criticism that emerged and emerges at that age (individually and racially). The young, then, have to be taught by a psychophysical training (*a*) to tolerate themselves and understand, without disgust or indulgence, their new equipment; and (*b*) to serve without servility or contempt a society wherein the administrators are not persons of superhuman self-denial.

(IV) Next there is the still further tonicity given by intensified use of infrared radiation. This is called the mystery of fire and it is employed to cure the manic-depressive, alternating psychosis to which those in first maturity are subject. This discipline is directed at reducing and healing this exaggerated reaction by rebalancing the individual so that by a new knowledge of the extent of their nature and its unfamiliar capacities, of which they are ignorant, they may (*a*) be led beyond their premature trust in their individualism and discover their paraconscious nature; and (*b*) they may be able to conceive of a society beyond the economic and political structure of today's international anarchy and ideological deadlock.

Introduction

(V) Finally, by what was called the mystery of aether, or the finer fire, those in second maturity may be educated by a psychophysical method or praxis through which (*a*) there is removed for the individual the death phobia; and (*b*) they are given an experience of the essential part they can and must play in constructing that fivefold society which, till now, has not existed and for lack of which social pattern there is, in our society today, neither any place for those veterine in second maturity (therefore they are the prey of their specific and most stubborn mental complaint, involutional melancholy) nor any design whereby death may be significantly incorporated into the life cycle.

Briefly, then, this is the thesis of this book: humankind can train itself, and it has done so with increasing understanding. Although at first this training was implicit in a rite that worked without being consciously comprehended and, next, it was esoteric and a mystery understood only by psychophysical pioneers, today it can become explicitly exoteric, rendered in contemporary terms and applied with scientific exactitude and as a therapeutic education. Such an education can fully develop both an entire person and a complete society. It can produce a constituent able to accept and fulfill their whole personal process and also be the conscious, willing, and developmental unit of a civilization that is creatively run by a common consent and coterminous with a nonviolent humanity.

Section I

THE PSYCHOLOGICAL STORY OF SOCIAL HUMANS

(*The Five Crises*)

1. The Preindividual (*Coconscious humans*)

In the Introduction, we have presented the basis of a faith in the future of humanity. We have given the reasons for believing that, through those exercises, technics, praxes, and education whereby conduct, character, and consciousness can now be developed to total capacity, humanity's behavior may at last be commensurate with its powers.

Now, and first, we must present the outline of human phylogeny. And once this is clear, we may view history as an increasingly accelerated and coordinated process whereby the two sides of man's nature (individual man and social man, man with self-consciousness and man with a preterconsciousness, critical man and creative man) have been kept in reciprocal play until they are perfectly balanced. But this is not all. We may also find in the individual development, in specific human ontogeny, in the process stages of each person's lifetime sequences, the recapitulation and, finally, the extrapolation of humankind's story and destiny.

I - PSYCHOLOGICAL STORY OF SOCIAL HUMANS

Here lies the only real cure for our present discouragement with ourselves. The first discoveries that man had a past, that his present was mainly ruled by that past, that that rulership was largely a mortmain, a dead hand, a husk of prejudices, tabus, misapprehensions, irrational fears, and cowardly dislikes led to dismay. Most historians felt, during those brief times when momentary order permitted an educated leisure in which to study the past, that we clung precariously to a raft of reason (or rather to a quaking sargasso coil of floating sea-wrack) which, between storms, permitted the creamy scum of culture to gather on the surface of a deep that would soon again be churned by the blasts of barbarian violence.

This crude idea that humanity's story begins with barbarism, achieves occasional civilization, and relapses periodically into the barbarian magma out of which it cooled, was, of course, an application to history of the Indian ascetic Sankhya dualistic philosophy of a cosmos perpetually oscillating between *prakriti* and *purusha*, matter and energy, form and flux.

Vico, the seventeenth- and eighteenth-century Neapolitan historian (1668–1744) had perceived, with extraordinary insight aided by studies of epic literature and hints from the Sumerian fragments embedded in the Hebrew Pentateuch, that beside and behind the saga and epic ages lay another epoch that was as different from barbarism as barbarism was alien to civilization. Vico's insight, however, had to wait until this century to become convincing and to wean historians from their taste for melodrama, for self-pitying tragedy. Now, such discoveries as those made by Arthur Evans of the Minoan culture (which was millennially previous to and far more lasting than its successor, the Hellenic, classical Greece), together with those made about the Sumerian and Indus cultures and the Shang Dynasty in China, have made historians realize that there was a protohistory, when man lived in a cultured society compacted largely by coconscious suggestion: a suggestion hypnotically so powerful that I have called this form of government a *hypnocracy*.

And anthropology was able to add confirmation to this discovery. In Central Australia, and later in Papua, tribes were found living a balanced life which, though at the price of the inhibition of experiment and adventure, avoided the self-willed violence of the epic

1. The Preindividual

barbarian. The discovery of these still surviving, food-gathering cultures helped, still further, in the understanding of the prehistoric ages brought to light by the slow studies of flint implements (for example, by Boucher de Perthes' studies of the Chellean flints on the Somme terraces) and the latest studies of the eidetic imagery of the fresco artists in the Dordogne caves (l'Abbé Breuil). Here, there can be no doubt, there was not only another type of culture, but there was another quality of consciousness. Besides the unreflective, boastful violence of the barbarian and the critical constructiveness of the civilized man there was also at least (and back of them both, it is reasonable to surmise) a third type of mind that was precritical but creative, preindividual but considerate.

In short, today we find ourselves to be the first generation able to walk on the floor of history. We are the first civilization that can, at last, see the foundation on which all humankind's cultural development has been reared; that can understand the basic and balanced adjustments to landscape-environment, to fellowship-community that were made by our superanimal ancestor—that speechful, tool-extending and depending, fire-fencing and focusing creature, protoman.

And this fuller, more complete knowledge of our story has produced two further insights. The first is one of the main supports of our hope for and faith in the future of man. This is the fact that the story has accelerated so intensely. Today, our generation can add an epoch to the saga of humankind by the way that each one of us lives out his individual span. The second insight is complementary to the first. The history of humankind is not to be understood as being a survival by violence: drum and trumpet history. Man is man (the supreme animal) because of his teachability, his openness of mind. And this is not only a firm part of his biological structure; it is built up in his entire development. Nor, again, can man be understood (and his story explained) by saying that he is an accident of economy, that all his culture has risen from his physical necessities. It is true that his art and his science have aided his physical survival, but only because he has been fascinated by form and because his curiosity has forced him to pursue knowledge of his environment. Human history, if we are to understand it, is psychological history.

I - PSYCHOLOGICAL STORY OF SOCIAL HUMANS

Humankind's works and his instruments are the silt lines of its mind's currents, the tidemarks of its consciousness. At first it is as slow as the rivulets that ooze from the melting fringes of the glaciers, but it carries, in solution, the rich alluvium of the ice-ground rock. That is to say, the primal community's fluidity-of-response, its capacity to understand its environment and to react to it with a modifying conduct is equaled, and kept within social bounds, by the fact that all its percepts are automatically censored by concepts. In other words, means and meaning are kept in creative play because all individual apprehensions of the outer world are, as it were, seen through the condensing lens made by the apprehensions of the entire tribe. Only those things that make sense can be noticed and remembered. Anomalies do not register—at least not as exceptions that might disturb the rule (36, 39). And, if the Abbeyvillian food-hunting, food-gathering Paleolithic dates from 450,000 B.C., and if the first agricultural society begins at about 10,000 B.C., this means that man's gradual change in consciousness continued for something like 440,000 years.

So, in the first vast epoch of man's history, his religic capacity, his ability to make sense, kept pace with his scanning power, his ability to grasp new facts about his environment. This capacity for making sense was both compositional and censorial. In other words, although man, at this point, rejected data too odd to even up with ordinary experience or to fit in with antecedent probability, the anomaly was not treated with horror, disgust, or contempt. These are later reactions, and they summon such strong resistance because the data can no longer be denied. At the start, the mind of man was like the subhuman, mammal consciousness: it recorded, memorably, only what had been repeated to it often enough. Just as through the night hours the photographic plate that is put into the telescope camera in order to record a star that is invisible to the naked eye gradually soaks up sufficient photons to retain an image, so some natural event brought persistently enough to his attention at last made an enduring impression on the mind of early man. And since man is not only the most curious of the mammals but also the one most inclined to communicate, and because his mind at this point was not wholly inelastic, this gave him sufficient time to bring his

1. The Preindividual

new discoveries to the attention of others and agree with them on an explanation.

However, the elasticity of wonder is a child factor and always stands in danger of being lost. As tradition grows by its successful incorporation of data—an incorporation increasingly expressed in the rigid form of words rather than in the comparatively free medium of responsive behavior—tradition grows self-assured and stiff. The more successful the solutions prove to be, the more they tend to become comprehensively final answers. Provisional responses, apt for the occasion, fossilize into repressive dogmas. Those who have had the most experience, those heartwood *robur* veterans (as the Romans later called such seasoned sergeants) who, because they have survived more dangers and are therefore less inclined to panic, and whose stubbornness makes them invaluable when the younger are alarmed and retreat, have the large vice of their rigid virtue. In a moving world they mistrust movement. They will not give ground, but neither will they open ranks and advance.

On the other hand, the younger members of the tribe, because they are young, tend to grow in curiosity—curiosity that is whetted by each new success of the tribe in extending its exploration farther afield and, thereby, bringing itself up against more and more anomalies. But the failure of the old to give the young an expanded explanation (to set, compose, and frame the newfound data) makes for either subservience or secret doubt. The extension of the lifespan into old age (owing to easier economic conditions) must already have meant, as it means so gravely today, an overwhelming disbalance of the social values in the direction of fear, suspicion, arrest, and reaction. On these grounds alone, the sum of human enterprise and happiness must have been steadily diminished, unless some method was known whereby voluntary death might be brought on among those who had finished their usefulness. Plenty of cases are now known, from the Eskimo to the pygmies of the central forest of Africa, who when conditions are too severe for the tribe to preserve the ailing and costly old, do abandon them.

However, the fissure of the primal mind was postponed and the pressures contained longer, which made the ultimate burst catastrophic when it did come.

This delay seems to have been due, at least in part, to the growth of language, which was also largely responsible for the hardening of the rite into the dogmatic spell. After the first choruses of co-encouragement (more phatic than informative), speech became increasingly instructive but was still used mainly for emotional purposes. However, because of its great success as a descriptive-informative instrument, the word tends to become definatory. The definatory term, sooner or later, becomes definitive, terminal, final. Language, because it became descriptive of separate objects, could not deal with succession (97). Mathematics, with its calculus, is needed for that. So there can be little doubt that the first sense of the-power-holding-things-together, of the-way-things-go (Tao), of the growth process, is pananimistic. It not only *is* everywhere, it is equally, pervasively diffused through one's self and it dilates one's entire physique.

But with words came distinctions, and with distinctions came further specific, localized, and concentrated attentions. The surge of life in the whole body becomes concentrated in the genitals. The lingam and the yoni become the almost obsessional foci of emotion and, indeed, sensation.

Meanwhile, woman comes to be regarded as the specific aspect of fertility. This is due, in large part, to the fact that she advances more slowly toward the exclusiveness of individualism. Physically, she remains less specialized in muscle and skeleton than the male, and her part in the reproductive function involves more of her physique and her psyche. Therefore, reproduction now becomes typified as the abundant power of parturition. In the middle Paleolithic figurines that have been found, we see depicted female physiques that are dilated into ample containers and yielders of plentiful, easy births. They are as faceless and almost as distended as the queen termite.

From such beginnings we can then trace the path of what we find to be fully emerged when the Paleolithic is over and the Neolithic has begun. At this point, with his management of an annual agriculture, man has become aware of time. Now religion has become gynolatrous: that is, the woman's figure is now the object of excitational adoration. The general sensing that all adults are

1. The Preindividual

reproductively charged has concentrated into one specific object of desire and the definite worship of fecundity forms. The dawning capacity to reason led, of necessity, to crude, overdeveloped notions of purpose and cause. There could be only one purpose and reason for a process. The panesthetic psychophysical rapture became increasingly to be regarded solely as a surge for reproduction. Therefore, rites had to be devised to canalize this tide and to prevent its natural diffusedness. *Pari passu,* such an attempt to confine the excitation to one purpose led to the feeling that the power must be confined to the one male organ that served the female's purpose. Hence, gynolatry (worship of woman) inevitably leads to phallolatry (phallic worship).

Then, as the rites become more formalized, they become divided into two: (*a*) the food rites for increasing luck in the hunt and, later on, increase among the kept animals;[5] and (*b*) the sex rites for increasing human fecundity. To define is always to disturb what was, originally, an unquestioning awareness. To give reasons is equally likely to make those who are given such explanations watch to see whether the reason proves to be correct and, if it does not, to suggest another. The hunting magic must have failed often. The sex magic, both by its concentration on the reproductive act and by its tabu against any variation in the theme, must have raised as many questions and caused even more serious breaches of the rules. Departures from the hunting magic might go unnoticed because these deviations would take place out in the wild open. But deviations from the reproductive magic could not long escape inquisition in the close purlieus of the cave.

We shall see in Section III that in tribes which preserved their cohesion, which did not explode in rebel protest but continued intact (such as the Arunta in mid-Australia), there has been a method of keeping at least the leaders in touch with their own dawn or birth consciousness. While in at least one culture (the Indus), which rose to and retained civilization for at least a millennium without being disintegrated by rebellion, there was a method of reducing the fever of revolt. These cases where a ritual was devised that really gave a regressional experience, and relieved—at least among the ruling caste—the mounting pressure of protesting frustration, are certainly rare.

However, such instances are valuable to us because they show that explosive cataclysm, violent psychic mutational revolt, is not invariably necessary. It is true that the Australian tribes have anchylosed, to use the phrase of Moret and Davy in *From Tribe to Empire* (63). They have become hypercomplex, rigid social structures, ruled wholly by their routine-obsessed elders and in which there is no place for growth. And apparently the Indus culture perished from an inanition that may be basically similar (67). Yet each of these cultures had its specific psychophysical method for giving the burgeoning consciousness the capacity to continue some growth, without having to repress and become severed from a past that is now repugnant because it has been wrongly lived through. So, as it will be suggested later, each culture did make some contribution to the problem of educating the total mind.

But in the vast majority of cases, the tribe's pattern of culture, under the pressure of the crystallizing consciousness of its constituents, became definitional and explanatory. And this produced the conviction that every custom and habit must be pruned to fit the utilitarian purpose that the one-track reasoning mind now regarded as being the whole purpose of the behavior. And where this took place the process of constriction continued. Finally, all movement, all variety became impossible. Any experiment and, at last, any alternative explanation became blasphemy. There was nothing left for the growing mind but death or revolt.[6] And as the growing seed bursts the pod, so the pioneers broke their way out and the emptied husk of their society finally collapsed.

Still, although the process was cataclysmic whereby the protoindividual, heroic, self-assertive man emerged and rent the old coconscious social structure, it was slow and diffident. Reformations were repeatedly followed by counterreformations. The old Life religion, the worship of the Yoni and the Lingam, made repeated comebacks. We can trace its stubborn return in Hebraism, for instance, where we see the desert-minded prophets worshiping a sky god and butchering, time and again, the priesthood that worshiped the tree phallus. Elijah massacres them in his day. They are back in the Temple again in time for Hosea to denounce their libidinous rites—rites which, in accordance with the religious custom of the

1. The Preindividual

time, involve his wife who goes up to the national shrine to be fertilized by the holy men, the priesthood who represented the fertility god. Hezekiah and again Jehoshaphat carry out bloody purges. But until the destruction of the Temple by Nebuchadnezzar and the carrying away of the people into Mesopotamia, the worship of fertility continued. This we know from the prophets' denunciations of the latest kings.

Nevertheless, growth is of the nature of the mind of man. Consciousness evolves just as does the brain, the structure that consciousness precipitates. Though the fertility rites continued and gave some outlet to deep racial drives otherwise repressed, the forms were increasingly inadequate. It may be that they could help men not to become wholly sundered from their racial past. But they could not help men to make contemporary answers to a world that was seen, increasingly, in the light of reason and subject to the discipline and censorship of experience and sometimes of experiment. The rites, themselves infected by reason, rationalized their procedures. Therefore, instead of being regarded as psychophysical exercises for altering conduct, character, and consciousness, for reducing egotism by giving a direct sense of belonging to the general life, the rite became magic for giving the individual egotist his personal desires and so confirming his obsession with his private selfishness.

The process of consciousness growth was, therefore, with the rebels. A damaged birth is better than a still one. The heroic outburst was so frustrant and so violent that it obliterated, rather than recovered, resuscitated, and made explicit the procedures that once had given not only solidarity to the tribe but also a comprehension of its environment. Nevertheless, man went on. And so by anguish, endured as agony, he attained at least enough understanding that even when the prestige-image of the hero proved to be inadequate, it could be replaced, in the minds of men, by the ideal figure of the ascetic. In the following chapter, therefore, we trace the rise and fall of the hero: the coconscious tribe's successor.

2. The Protoindividual
(*Heroic, self-assertive humans*)

We must regard the hero as being an inevitable development of consciousness. The critical faculty had to grow and, [because] the coconscious tribe had become negative to all invention and hostile to the capacity for asking questions, it had to grow because of an increasing sense of separateness. Objectivity and detachment could only arise from rejection. Spontaneous revulsion gave the position and status necessary for perspective and proportion. Thus, the Heroic Epoch is such an inevitable reaction to the rigidifying of the coconscious tradition that we find it (together with its characteristic, the saga-epic literature) in all the giant cultures. It was so emphatic, so aggressive that until this century there was no general recognition, among historians, of the pre-Heroic, priest–kingly, coconscious, or hypnocratic culture that lay behind it, from which the hero was ejected and which the hero in turn destroyed. Such a belt of Cimmerian darkness, dividing us from the mild saturnine kings and queens, seemed to be only disaster. No wonder that Hesiod, living under one of the later deluges (that of the Dorian "iron-bearing Kings"), joined and gave classic expression to the chorus that lamented a previous Age of Gold, an aeon of Peace. The sad poets, "praisers of previous ages," in the clash of arms and under the pressure of despots, could not conceive the suffocating tyranny of "custom that lies upon him as a weight heavy as frost and deep almost as life." Nor could he imagine that Man, left alone, can honestly cry, "Better dwell in the midst of alarms than reign in this horrible place." As Professor Charles Edward Spearman, the University College London psychologist, has remarked, "We only know two basic things about the central nervous system of man:—one, that it likes the same stimulant, and the other, that it doesn't." Boredom is the subtle misery with which life nags man into adventure. No doubt the timid would have sacrificed curiosity to security—as they still do today. But there is natural selection in human history, as in all life. The vital welcome risk.

Whether man's history, his psychosocial evolution, [and] the development of his social heredity could have been a gradual process, without spastic mutations, without the cyclic spiral of revolt, destruction, reimposition, and again revolt, we cannot say. It does not seem to have been possible in the past, though it is not impossible now, as this essay hopes to indicate. For up until now man does not seem to have been able to understand, consciously, and to cooperate, deliberately, with the life process that not only has brought him to his superanimal station but is still driving him on to higher achievement, greater powers, and greater comprehension.

The "nothing fails like success" principle suggests that the capacity for comprehension ends in being content with the achieved reaction. This is the weakness of an efficiency that is achieved by specialized response: the more finished it becomes, the less conscious it is of its partiality. The vast achievement of coconscious man—a balanced tradition of technics and psychics—made the powerful become complacent, turned obedience into subservience, and made the entire group lethargic. If man was to progress, he must again raise questions, seek adventure, give hostages to fortune, offer challenges.

In Section II, we shall see how deeply this pattern is etched into our individual characters. Self-consciousness must arise in each, and as the group, naturally, does not welcome this, the individual protects his unwelcomed sense of separateness with the husk of

2. The Protoindividual

egotism. Man's second phase, the Heroic Age, therefore seems chaotic, purposeless, anarchic. Closer examination, however, has shown that it certainly is not. For although man may strangulate off his surface, objective, personal intelligence from his deep racial mind, he never succeeds in separating himself completely from this profound continuum of consciousness. We have proof of that in the reaction of the hero hordes to the original culture. They not only wish to attack it for loot. They are filled with a righteous disgust at its two distinctive communicatory convictions: the pervasiveness of eroticism (the constant interest in glamor, the constant awareness of longing for tactile closeness) and the pervasiveness of magic (the constant interest in spells, in psychological methods of getting one's way, the constant awareness of longing for communion with the nonhuman and the unseen). The hero, because of his sense of separateness, dreads and shuns the seductive caress. He keeps others at arm's length, and when he closes with someone else it is to subdue that one, either by duel or rape. Yet when he has conquered and crushed, he is often seized with remorse. Especially when he has killed, the sense that his own fate is common with that of the victim, whom he has sent only a little ahead of himself into the shades, shakes him with grief.

Thus, the Heroic Epoch is psychologically (and therefore socially) unstable. The rules that it could not but observe seemed, to the protoindividual egotist, to be irrational and, indeed, to endanger a man's safety. Why should an individual spare an enemy or feel any compunction at the death of a rival? David Hume's childish remark, "There is no reason why I should prefer the pricking of my own finger to the death of a hundred human beings," is preanthropological. But it is a natural enough attitude for the first egotist, the hero. And yet, providentially, this self-assertive creature could not act on his inadequate reasoning, which was false in its mistaken premise that each individual is really separate. For, firstly, he is always seeking for praise and fearing shame.[7] These are states of the psyche that indicate the power of a common field of consciousness. True, this rudimentary individualist still projects his inner conflict in rage against all who thwart him. But if his passion becomes complete delusional paranoia, then, when in moments of lucidity he sees that he has lost face, the hero has no way out but to commit suicide.[8] So suicide is always at hand, especially in the Heroic phase that produced Bushido and the Samurai in Japan. And in its grotesque form of hara-kiri we see that, although the Japanese hero begins with boastful exhibitionism of his physical equipment, in the end he is driven to complete contempt for the body. This drive, naturally, is from his repressed nature.

Inevitably, therefore, this shame will turn into guilt, this wounded self-love will lead to self-destructive humiliation. Probably no Heroic Age lasts longer than half a dozen generations. It is too self-degenerative. Of course, there are attempts, more or less convulsive, to revive this outlived pattern of prestige.[9] And from the point of view of epochs, these attempted throwbacks are as significant as the Gothic revival, Palladian architecture, or existentialism. In spite of all their arrogance, cruelty, and destructiveness, they are mere reactions, histrionics, fancy dress, adopted, and temporarily dangerous, because the Humanist house had been left empty, swept, and garnished; the scientific machine had stood ready without a driver in the seat.

The hero, then, becomes increasingly pessimistic, a prey to his own suppressed preterconscious. Gloom becomes his standard feeling tone. And like all paranoics, he attempts to burn this melancholy out of his nature by bouts of homicidal rage. For when he rests, he can foresee for himself (after that bodily death which he knows is hurrying inevitably toward him) only a ghostly life. To him, to whom his body is everything and to whom physical action is the sum of experience, this prospect is frightful in its certain futility. "Better be a poor man's slave than King among the dead." In these words, Homer's Achilles, the paragon of heroes, estimates the common, unavoidable doom of hero and slave alike. Naturally, therefore, rage is the immediate reaction. For, to quote Homer, the primal authority on the heroic predicament, "anger rises in a man's mind like smoke and is sweeter in his mouth than honey." The noradrenaline (see Section II, Chapter 2) not only gets rid of misgiving, in the blaze of animal courage, but it releases so much sugar-for-energy that the palate is flooded with sweetness.

But, inevitably, there follows the letdown of depletion and despair. Hence, after rage on the field, after drinking delight of battle, there follows drunkenness in the evening. Finally, alcohol, which is a depressant and not a stimulant, makes for maudlin self-pity. Then to this depressant drug the hero had to add a further narcotic. When grief became intolerable, the Achaeans took "a banisher of sorrow," which is the meaning of the word *nepenthe*. Apparently, the Homeric heroes employed this drug regularly. Once thought to be opium, it now seems more probable that it was one of those rare alkaloid-yielding plants that give powerful sedation.[10]

The Indian hero, we know, had his *soma*. This was also a rare plant from the Persian Highlands and seems to have become extinct. And from the descriptions in the Vedas it seems that it was, in contrast to *nepenthe*, highly elational. "I have drunk *soma* and become a god" is the classical description of its effect. We also know that *soma* was so inspirational that the god Indra, chief of the Aryan deities, was equated with it, as later Dionysus was identified with wine. But also—and in this way it differed from *nepenthe*—*soma* was highly toxic. Instead of an alteration in consciousness it often produced death in those who took it.

But besides the intoxicants and the anodynes, we can detect a specific method of ordeal and initiation that those who, during the Heroic Age, emerged into the problem of protoindividualism might undergo if they so desired. And it was the specific praxis whereby that particular psychopathic illness of the Heroic phase, hyper-*rajasic* fury (paranoic frenzy), might be cured. As the coconscious phase had its particular ritual for enabling the postulant to rid himself of the trauma of birth (a trauma that, because it produced regressive fear, may well have been the basic psychological cause of the coconscious primal society's failure to evolve), so the Heroic Age, it would seem, had its therapy of antiwrath. Although we shall study this therapy at length in Section III, Chapter 2, we may suggest here that it was the Heroic Age's specific way of restoring, to those who carried on the succession of seership, that freedom from anger, and indeed all sense of separateness, without which extrasensory insight and precognition are impossible.

At any rate, we have seen that *nepenthe* was the drug which, when alcohol would not staunch grief, staved off despair. However,

I - PSYCHOLOGICAL STORY OF SOCIAL HUMANS

a third vegetable drug (moly) is mentioned in the *Odyssey*. It is given to Ulysses by Hermes, who is a pre–Olympian god of the underworld: that is, the subconscious. And as Indra seems to have been identified with soma and Dionysus with the vine, so it is possible that Hermes was similarly identified with the power of moly. Moly was a defender from magic. That is, it made its taker immune to hypnotic illusion and it rendered him invisible to his enemies. This would then appear to be an increase of detachment, which enabled the person to remain free from the power of outer suggestion; the provocations of enemies no longer roused him or entangled him. And because he is inwardly unperturbed, no longer producing (through adrenal excitement) "the odor of anger," he can easily disguise himself and be overlooked, as, for example, [when] Ulysses (whom some authorities believe to be the human manifestation of Hermes) fooled the suitors by escaping their detection.

The reduction of rage and fear by biochemicals will be considered further in the second and third parts of this essay. At this point, in dealing with the hero and his problem of noradrenaline rage, we need only note that psychotherapeutic sedatives and detensioners were used by the heroes themselves. Their *vates* and seers may have used a hydrotherapy, the particulars of which will be discussed in Section III, Chapter 2. However, it is worth noticing that, according to Homer, the supreme seer of the Epic Period is Teiresias who, as mentioned later, is the only one permitted to retain his memory and intelligence after death, who throughout his earthly life retains a hermaphrodite nature, and who is blind from the age of seven years.

To summarize then (and viewing the Heroic Age as the second great psychosomatic phase in humanity's development): after his break away from and destructive revenge on the ancient traditional society in which he had found himself imprisoned, the hero discovered that he could not live merely as an adventurer. For just being free to follow one's impulses meant a life of violence with increasing relapses into suicidal melancholy. He could not live without values. He found that he had to have standards, patterns of prestige, because his nature demanded, peremptorily, that he must be admired, that he must not be shamed. He had to exercise restraint when it was in his power to satisfy, to the full, his passion for revenge or for spoil.[11]

2. The Protoindividual

He still had to respect the rules of human commonalty even though they appeared to be mere negative tabus. It was a terrible offense against heaven to strike a herald, an unarmed arbiter who could and often would interpose between two brawling fighters and order them to desist. Ajax Telamon, the Lesser, after having (at the sack of Troy) burst into Athena's Temple and murdered Philoxenia, who had taken refuge at the altar, was drowned on his way back to his Greek homeland. However, this did not, in the opinion of the brawling world of that day, expiate so monstrous a violation of the unseen moral majesty of Heaven and of the rights of a suppliant who sought that intangible protection. So for centuries the home town of Ajax had to send (and did send, summer after summer) a working band of youths to cultivate the land where Troy had stood. And this obligation was followed right down to the time of the Roman Empire in the reign of the Emperor Augustus.

Definite standards were taught in the epic literature. The sagas had their norms of seemliness. These were not lofty but neither were they mere aspirations. The hero was taught to believe (and did believe) in a world whose invisibility did not render it only an ineffective ideal. On the contrary, the intangibility of the spiritual force gave it power to judge and to strike from an intimate vantage point against which concealment, armor, or circumspection were no defense.

The hero, like the devils of St. James, believed and trembled. The gods had to be reckoned with constantly. And such a concept of deity had so much of an egotist's fearfulness projected onto it that the divine rules were fraught, to the point of confusion, with splenetic tabus. Teiresias, the seer, is supposed to have been struck blind by Athena for no other reason than that he had inadvertently glimpsed the goddess while she was bathing. And, according to legend, Acteon, the hunter, was turned into a stag by Artemis, for the same involuntary offense, and killed by his own hounds. Nevertheless, at the same time the deep preterconscious still projected, from behind the repressive mask of egotism, the profound racial knowledge that all life is basically one, and that it advances through sensitive trust, not through brutal suspicion.

The Homeric epics have been called the Bible of the Greeks. And the phrase is a stimulating half-truth if we consider those parts of the

I - PSYCHOLOGICAL STORY OF SOCIAL HUMANS

Hebrew scriptures that also deal with the same epoch, the Heroic Age. Epics and sagas are the standard-setters, the prestige-pattern-makers of the protoindividualistic society. *The Book of the Wars of Yahweh,* referred to in [Numbers and] much of Genesis (with its picture of pastoralist sheiks maneuvering across the grasslands from wells to springs, seeking water for their flocks), the Book of Judges, Samuel, and I Kings still show, even under the gloss of later editing, the kind of hard-hitting fighter who was "a man after Yahweh's heart." The Sanskrit Mahabharata and Ramayana, even under their glosses, show the same epic standards. The instruction is not by rule and precept. Right behavior is not conveyed by generalizations, still less by legal definition of offenses and penalties. It is conveyed by inspiring illustrative accounts of the fine person in action. Nor did the Epic poets lightly condone the blunders of their heroes. Some authorities have thought that Homer actually came from the race that was conquered by the Achaean Greeks he immortalized. And most readers of the *Iliad* would certainly agree with the insight of Simone Weil: that it is an Epic of Violence. It stands on the brink of despair and is held back from the abyss only by the magic cord of beauty—beauty which often, in a brutal age when pity is dismissed as weakness and truth as a fantasy, still constrains men to consider once more the bright enigma of a world that is entrancing though agonizing. And the Western epic (though it does avoid the final answer of *vanitas vanitatum*), turning from despair, refusing to feel that man is hopelessly at bay, points to the tunnel of tragedy as being the only way on through the rock face of nature's hard indifference.

However, in the East, the epic became allegorized instead of tragic. As the Protoindividualistic, Heroic Epoch passed into the Ascetic, the pattern of prestige changed. It was no longer the man who was absorbed in outer "mighty acts of labor." It became the man who has turned within to do battle with inner conflicts and to achieve conquests by detachment and abandonment. Correspondingly, the epic, with increasing diminishment of disguise, becomes a parable-vehicle for ascetic instruction. The classic example of this change in ideals and education is, of course, the Bhagavad Gita.

But in the West, the problem of dawning self-consciousness found still another statement, though not an answer, in the *Odyssey*.

2. The Protoindividual

The *Iliad* is a summing up. Its counsel is "courage through endurance." But the *Odyssey* opens a new chapter. The protoindividual finds himself inevitably asking, "Is not all morality only a mixture of mistakes compacted into a shrewd device to frighten persons into sacrificing themselves for the sake of the tribe and the timid elders that control it? Could not a truly lively man, a man of many wiles, slip out from under this noose and wander from exploit to exploit through this fantastically entertaining world?" This epic closes neither with noble, tragic death (as the *Iliad* does) nor with the [male] hero living happy-ever-after with his bride (as does the Ramayana). The genius-composer of the *Odyssey* was enough of a realist to know that this is not a magic world. But at the same time, he was sufficiently speculative to realize that we do not know its bounds and that in such a world, therefore, curiosity is, of all the passions, the most staunchless, the most invincible. Ulysses returns to Ithaca to liquidate the suitors, to salute his ancient father, mature wife, and adult son and then, having settled these minute affairs of a past responsibility, to go off on a new exploration. The accident of an incompetently delayed return turned into the opportunity of seeking the outer world for its own sake. If the *Iliad* prophecies the oncoming of tragedy and suspects that the gray morning of asceticism was to follow the Heroic Age's red sunrise, the *Odyssey* foretells that beyond the chill first hours of day (the Ascetic Epoch), there will come the noontide of the Humanic Epoch when man, feeling self-sufficient, will investigate the universe without fear of its wrath or hope of its favor. And further, the story of Ulysses hints that even Humanism will not prove sufficient nor be the final station of the human mind.

For this primal explorer is not content to sail every unknown sea and pass every horizon. Unlike and outreaching the Renaissance mind, he also visits the underworld, the world of the subconscious. And there, with the aid of the spirit of Teiresias, the master seer, he strives to understand his own nature and destiny by attempting to look not merely beyond spatial limits but beyond time. By going in and down (ordeal-initiation), this archetypal, transitional man, who is no longer a hero and yet is still not an ascetic, attempts by a mystery experience to understand completely.

I - PSYCHOLOGICAL STORY OF SOCIAL HUMANS

The seeming irrelevance of the manifold refuses, however, to compose into a totality under his objective curiosity. For he is determined to be the onlooker and he leaves himself out of the picture. So it cannot become a composition of enlightening power but only an unstinted collection of curiosities. Consequently, Ulysses foresees not his assumption but his death, which the unknown author of the *Odyssey* rightly describes as a peaceful killing: a death that comes to him at the unwitting hands of a natural son whom he begot from Circe, the supernatural witch. And, further, it is this Circe who, when he left her, guided him to the underworld where Teiresias shows him his fate.

So from the literature of Heroicism, we can see the standards and education of the protoindividual, the first self-assertive man. Roughly speaking, one third of that instruction is cautionary, minatory. It warns: be careful, be wary, don't let the hot fit, which is a fine starter, take you too far. There is an unknown quantity that is up to something in the world out there, and while you are getting your way, take care that your fishing lines don't foul its extensive nets. Another third of the teaching is admonitory: don't lose face and remember that though you may, for a moment, stun people with your successful violence, the shock at your excess will turn into censure. However, just you may feel your anger to be, you must not act with disregard for the standards of the unangered onlookers. Besides, your own cold fit will condemn you.

And this leads to the third instruction. Your wish is not merely to be uncensured but to be praised, to "live in men's mouths" as the noble man, the majestic pattern of prestige, the man who, because of his courage, munificence, and magnanimity, is honored forever.

The Heroic Age was a necessary phase in the human development: a development that has gone on as a spiral process, an oscillation between outer knowledge and inner comprehension, since the end of the preindividual, primal culture. But this protoindividualistic culture was explosive. It was driven out from the land-locked harborage of the tribal estuary that had become a sandbar-blocked, stagnant lake with no more access to the outer ocean. These huddled squadrons, lifted by line squalls of protest, found themselves to be startled navigators, borne over the bar and out onto the

2. The Protoindividual

high seas. There they found no other port in some island of the blest; only the vast waters welcomed them into a new freedom. And for many this was too much. Unable to manage the gale in their canvas and the waves on their thwarts, they foundered in the storm of passion that was let loose and sank into paranoia. They became incapable of understanding any but their personal demand for expression. But in the main they rode out the storm with the aid of a sea anchor, that long submarine cable and sack that holds in the bucking ship and keeps its prow facing the storm. Such a sea anchor was the modifying morality which, the sagas and epics show us, was being worked out as a means of educating the boastful hero until (when he does not turn into the Ulyssean navigator) he becomes hammered and tempered into the pattern of chivalry, the honorable knight, the guardian of the weak.

However, the knight (the word means "servant") is not and cannot be the full pattern of prestige. He wishes to obey. A man of action, he defers to the one who has the conviction of command. If he wishes to investigate, the soldier does not research into the mind and its motives; he explores nature and its shape. Guardianship preserves; it does not develop, it does not progress. The knight and his descendant, the gentleman, are then maintenance men, and innovation is not natural to them. Therefore, they are collateral cadet lines of the human ascent. They cannot have that individual insight which is the symptom of being possessed by the new and oncoming field of humanity's consciousness.

So the drill-sergeant mind, with its military parade discipline and uniform, is not the nucleus of humankind's next phase. The solid phalanxes of impacted automata that swept away the last relics of the single man-to-man fighting of the Heroic Age are not the formative pattern of the social structure that was to replace Heroism. The successor to the hero (as the unresolved contractive intensity of individualism increases) is not a military type.

But who gives the orders? Who answers the hero's unspoken question, "Where is not merely moral authority for the obedient, but inspiration for the pioneer; not only vision for the explorer, but disciplinary sanction for the original and the creative?" "Who guards the guardian?" asked Roman law. It is a question that cannot be answered without first finding a reply to this riddle: "How can we guard just for the sake of preserving those who are too timid to move and who desire only immobile security? What is the goal for which we act as preservatives? If we are making reservations and protectorates, are these to arrest growth or to promote it? If they are to promote growth, then growth toward what goal? Who has the vision to perceive it clearly and convincingly?"

It was these galling questions that made even the noble hero inadequate. Greater discipline was demanded, but how was it to be achieved and what aim could make it worthwhile? What insight could make the strain of postponement endurable? Man's education had reached a new challenge-level. He was to be taken out of Junior High Heroism as he had previously been taken out of the kindergarten and child grades of the coconscious. He was to pass into the Senior High of a new seriousness and, it must be added, a new self-consciousness and personal concern. He was to enter the Midindividualistic Age, that specific epoch known as the Ascetic, the phase in which man is no longer implicitly, unquestioningly, unconsciously obedient, nor, on the other hand, frankly self-assertive. Now for the first time, man, with a new intensity of self-awareness, will blame himself.

3. The Midindividual
(*Ascetic, self-accusing humans*)

It is clear that about the eighth century B.C., a change was going on in humanity's consciousness. "The rise of conscience" is a datum line in the history of the human psyche, and it is placed at somewhat different dates by students of different cultures. Breasted would put it far earlier than the eighth century B.C. in Egypt. And this may well have been so, because of the unique forcing-and-arresting conditions of the Nile Valley. However, most psychoanthropological students of the Hebraic culture would probably not quarrel with the eighth century B.C. datum line. For the proto-prophets of sexual exclusiveness and social responsibility (Hosea and Amos) appear at this time. Hellenic thought seems to have reached a crisis in this same century. The rise of reflective philosophy in India, indicated by the most thoughtful Upanishads, seems to be about 750 B.C.

Arthur Waley, the sinologist, has said that about 1200 B.C., a change did come over the Chinese ritual, which until then had been mainly magical and compurgative. The emergence of conscience that culminated with Confucius (550–478 B.C.) may well lie between this change in ritual (1200 B.C.) and the rise of the explicit reasonableness and recognition of self-conscious individualism that we find in the Confucian *Analects*.

This sixth to fifth century B.C. period may be regarded as a time during which there was a rapid precipitation of self-awareness, for, as Thomas William Rhys Davids (the Pali authority) and other scholars have pointed out, Confucianism, Buddhism, and Pythagorianism are contemporary. Leading up to these precipitations was a period pregnant with considerable spiritual travail. In India, we know that the Heroic culture of the invading Aryans had, until the eighth century B.C., practiced mainly a luck religion of *do ut des* ("I give in order that you may give"): that is, give the gods (who are simple projections of oneself) what one likes oneself and they will do likewise. Such crude religion has to modify under actual experience. The Hellenic-Aryans (the Achaeans) became tragic while the Indian Aryans became ascetic.

In Egypt and China, we may remark, the ascetic did not appear until centuries after his appearance in India. In their own ways, both Egypt and China succeeded in encysting themselves in the cocoon of their particular, complacent social success. Conscience was limited to social obligation. Neither of them produced its own psychic pressures for neither of them permitted the Heroic phase to go far enough. Nipped in the bud by the counter-development of a semi-militarized priest–king—half general and half magician—the hero could not grow to those intensities of interior conflict that produce tragedy or asceticism.[12] Foreign religions (Indian Buddhism for China and Levantine Christianity for Egypt) were needed to make these self-enclosed lands confront the individual enigma.

In India, with its acute interest in states of consciousness, the hero was under particular stress. First, we see him striving to keep himself with enough aggressive initiative to remain in control of a situation in which climatic enervation, the mirage in the desert, the fecundity of tropical life, and an equally rich jungle of mystic thought made the hard certainties of courage, will, and ambition swim before his eyes. This struggle to hold his supremacy led to *tapas*: those increasingly strenuous exercises whereby at first the hero–king literally attempted to sweat it out. One such common exertion was for the ruler to sit naked under the noonday sun and surrounded by blazing fires.

3. The Midindividual

Such violent efforts may have caused the focus of consciousness to shift. It may also have suggested the procedure of the ordeal by fire (with which this work deals in Section III, Chapter 4).

These grueling treatments of the body could naturally and very easily slip from the wish to become tough into the desire to torture oneself, from the aim of adapting an instrument into the aim of escaping from a trap by prising back its bars. It is difficult to trace the actual rise of asceticism and its intensification into mortification. The mount which at first is to be tamed by being whipped is now to have its will broken. The carnal nature is to be beaten to death. Previous psychological frontiers, like submerged beachlines, leave little trace; spiritual faultings and dislocations can seldom be dated. The word "asceticism" comes from the Greek word *askesis*, which was their term for athletic training. And these first *tapas* or exertions seem to have been just that. But the human psyche was no longer at boastful ease with itself. Self-consciousness, which was at first displayful fun, was modulating, with experience, into its minor key.

In the West, tragedy was interposed between the epic and the manual of self-discipline, the codified rule of the mortificatory order. For the epic is not an art form that was made to express a personal problem, a psychological issue. It is to show a complex of action and to illustrate the mighty deeds of great leaders. The hero is still sure of himself and of the crowd's admiration. Self-assertive man is still the pattern of prestige. True, the *Iliad* crystallizes out around the wrath of Achilles. But the hero's anger is the thread around which action precipitates. And the heroes, even in their rages, are examples of the chief heroic virtue, courage. However, in tragedy we find the hero no longer opposing men, and gods who are mainly but men writ large; he is caught in the toils of nonhuman forces against which arms are helpless. Nature seems to turn on him, and he is attacked below the waterline of his self-conscious courage. A spiritual world is forcing itself on his attention. He is beginning to lose his nerve. He is having to ask for a new defense, another discipline, which the training manuals of the monastic orders will produce.

But, as we have said, tragedy, in the West, created an interlude between the high warrior and the low penitent. An issue that involves the mind-body of man (and must therefore be worked out psychosomatically) is laid out, arranged, and confined in a strictly limited area: the stage. Man's advance toward his next crisis, his progression from heroicism to asceticism, is now postponed by the threefold device of the drama. In the first place, the flood-pressure of the new conflict, the conflict now known to be an inner one, is diverted for a space by being run into the artificial flood channel or sump hole of the theater. The personal issue is now projected onto another person, a hero.

Secondly, it is talked about rather than acted out. Aeschylus, the father-member of the great trinity of Greek tragic art, employs nothing but conversation on the stage. Although he is an innovator in raising monologue to dialogue, words now rule. This strange screen and filter has been put between the onlooker and the deed.

Thirdly, the crisis is projected backward in time. This is the story of a legendary person and the problem need not be regarded as instant. It not only happened long ago but (and this makes it far less immediate) it befell men different from the democratic, equalitarian Greeks. Tragedy, Aristotle saw and said, had to be about heroes, nobles, outstanding men. So the "so sorry for the big guy beaten down" is mixed with a *sotto voce* "serves the arrogant fellow right." When Aeschylus chooses a contemporary figure around which to write a tragedy, it is Xerxes the Great King, a dim image that is impersonally mythical to the small, bright, sharply defining Greek minds. And the Persian is seen (it is significant that the play is not called *Xerxes* but *The Persians*) as a titan force, only half human, who is punished not for attacking the independent Hellenes but for his Luciferian pride, the insane hubris against divine nature shown by his attempt to chain the Hellespont with a bridge of boats.

Another cushion-against-shock was playing with Time by alteration of actual tempo. The dramatic unities insisted that the whole play, with all its acts, should refer only to the incidents of a single day. These rigid rules ran through the entire history of the Greek tragedy. Sophocles, the master second person of the Attic stage, greatly increased the flexibility of the play. Euripides, the third person, humanized even more both story and language. But the close and confining rules were not lifted. The stage is the crucible of art-

3. The Midindividual

convention in which the anarchic passions are to be held and considered, as, through a quartz eyehole, a furnace-minder may watch iron being melted. Hence, every thing, every action and incident that could not be reduced in this receptacle was utterly out of bounds and so, it being impossible to deal with them on the scene, they were called obscene.

So we now see that tragedy is a phase. It cannot last because it is a projection of a crisis, and it is of the nature of a crisis to pass, either into death or birth. Tragedy was necessary because it permitted man (while he was undergoing a rapid alteration of awareness, a contraction of consciousness) to speak out his immediate problem under projected parabolic terms. Using the symbols of a dying pattern of prestige—the hero and his peers, the Great King and the apparently worldwide, time-long majesty that made him superhuman or the Titan Prometheus who defied Zeus—it was possible for the ordinary man to think obliquely of his own problems and not wholly repress the fermenting questions asked by the transitional psyche: "Is the Universe alien from me? What are the limits of human power? Is it possible, if not to be happy, at least to be unafraid?" Tragedy has never been able to answer these questions. All it has been able to do is to give a projection of the conflict through an art form, the play. This device of the dramatist gives some detachment, some ironic temper to an audience and, for a few hours, persuades it that it is looking on at another's suffering—which, as the French cynically say, we always have the power to bear.

But *de te fabula*: the story, although disguised, was about the onlooker himself. And he knew that the catharsis of being purged of pity for another and of fear of a dead hero's predicament was only a palliative.

In the original play, the primal comedy, there had been the real metarsis. It was not catharsis (the purging of the emotions), nor yet anarsis, the raising of the spirit to that level where *patheia* (defeating, demoralizing pain) becomes *agonia* (a wrestling with the antagonist until agony touches ecstasy). In the communal revel of the coconscious society—the saturnalia—the constituents wore animal pelts, and so they were no longer recognizable, either by sight or by smell. And in the spontaneous abandon of the pantomime and masque, there had taken place not merely the loss of personal idiosyncrasy (the sense of separateness) but there was the experience of an identification with all life.

Tragedy, on the contrary, seeks to give numbness by the tourniquet of detachment. It has removed itself from direct touch and is, by becoming a spectator, only being affected by a spectacle. But the tension that produces this attempt at aloofness is temporary because what is being projected is an arc of consciousness. At the start, with the breakdown of Comedy, with man's inability to go on laughing off a growing self-consciousness, there arises the boastful hero, who condignly punishes any attempt to laugh him out of his pompous braggadocio.[13] The hero will not be laughed at. Neither will he permit the beaten-up jester to laugh off *his* punishment. But the hero, largely because he will not acquire the objectivity, proportion, and perspective given by humor, cannot, as we have seen, stand failure. One of his ways of avoiding suicide is to see himself as the tragic figure, sacrificed for people too stupid to recognize him as a social savior.

Hence, there is not much room for tragedy in the process which changes man from hero into ascetic. As a matter of fact, it lasts in its classic form, the Hellenic, for only three generations. This is the century-short span that always lies between the breakdown of tabu and the beginning of objectivity. For when the [male] proto-hero breaks in on the magical matriarchal society, the last phase of the traditional society, he destroys it utterly. He calls all its ways unspeakable, vile, and accursed and he forbids its beastliness ever to be mentioned again. On pain of instant death the former foul practices must be forgotten in absolute silence. The [male] hero's ways: violence instead of craft, blows rather than words, of a father's unbrooked authority, a woman's subservience, and a son's submission: these, the only right ways, must be the only possible ways for a man who is worthy to live.

But, of course, this vain hope of an individualist, that he might revive the unquestioning acceptance with which the preindividual accepts the immemorial tradition, is bound to fail. A tabu, when it is real, is part of an entire system of total awareness and disregard of every possible behavior, save those which fit in with the group's closed interpretation of every experience. The hero, by his emergence

3. The Midindividual

as a destroyer, has made such unquestioning consent impossible. His rule is by martial law and martial law is, at base, no more than an attempt to legalize anarchy: the rule not of the code but of the sword. In consequence, tragedy marks the end of the Heroic Age.

The three phases of heroical man's retreat from belief in his own rightness are delineated by the three masters of the Attic drama. We can watch, in their work, the growth of the critical spirit, its search for detachment, and its desire for objectivity. Their successive dramas show man coming apart from his environment. For tragedy is only possible during that brief time between the traditional aeon, when the tabu cannot be mentioned, and the age of critical self-consciousness. Tragedy emerges as a form of transitional therapy for the short spell of three generations when, intellectually, men feel a new doubt of and even skepticism about the tabu, but when their emotions still register something of the old emotional horror-thrill.

After a century, the emotions catch up with the intellect. For it was the emotional reaction of disgust that was the first step toward the awareness which must turn into concern and end in interest. At the start, Aeschylus had intended to show that pride goes before a fall, and that Nature herself punishes any man, however great, who interferes with her sway. In point of fact, however, Greek minds (when they were told to notice how vengeful Fate could be) began to attend to Natural Law. Would large-scale engineering always arouse Fate to destroy such impiety? So when Sophocles succeeds to the station of philosopher-dramatist, his audiences are shown not a god striking the incestuous Oedipus but the psychotic hero himself putting out his own eyes. And, finally, Euripides leaves the Athens of his humane triumphs and goes to live in the Macedonian north, there to show, in his *Bacchae*, that only by intoxicating frenzy could even women recover their abandon and lose their critical self-consciousness.

Thus, the work of these three dramatists effected, in just under a century[14] the transition of tragedy whereby the Heroic pattern of prestige could be modulated from the early success story and yet not turn into despair, skepticism, or cynicism. Tragedy was an attempt to show that the grand man could and indeed would fail, but that in facing this fact we, the onlookers, need not become life-rejecting or question as to whether life is worthwhile. Failure could be so spectacularly elegant that it could make life actually meaningful. For even the hero himself could live in the hope that men in the future would look back and up to his sublime frustration and appreciate such majestic futility. This is, of course, an attitude of spectatorship, whether of looking on at a dramatic sacrifice or of looking forward to one's own deification. We have already seen a franker diagnosis of the human situation. Homer was more realistic and honest with the speech that he puts in Achilles' mouth, [to quote again], "Better be a poor man's slave than king among the dead."

Tragedy, which begins by being a speculative blueprint of human values in a rapidly changing moral and psychological climate (as self-consciousness becomes concentrated), ends by being drama, an artifice for entertainment. Catharsis turns into elegant estimation and the tears are no longer purgative, postponing the seizure of despair; they are gracious tributes, symptoms of a sophisticated sensibility that wipes its eyes of drops that sacred pity hath engendered.

No longer, now, could these questions be postponed: Is virtue (courage, good sense, the conscious avoidance of fault and trespass) enough to assure a man happiness and a life of worth? Is a man who thinks that his thews and high spirits are enough to win him the good life only a boastful child? Is the world (instead of being a fair field with no favor) but a deceptive sward, concealing a morass? Therefore, Tragedy passed, and with it went the pretense that fine writing can alter hard facts. A skilled description of ruin and despair, with the victim going down to defeat either defiant or submissive, may be enjoyed by some onlookers in a quiet theater seat or readers in a quieter study. But it is no answer to the riddle of life. It cannot explain the unavoidable processes of old age and death that are the experience of every human being. Still less can it speak to the developmental process that we can detect today, now that the vast curve of human history lies extended before our eyes. Looking on at tragedies or writing them may give a temporary and slight catharsis. It does not and cannot permanently alter conduct, character, and consciousness.

The real contribution of the Hellenic genius to the actual education of humanity's evolving consciousness was not made on the stage

3. The Midindividual

and by the drama. It was made at the birthplace of Aeschylus, but not by a playwright, however inspired. Aeschylus was born at Eleusis, the small town a dozen miles from Athens, and it was there, in the Eleusinian mysteries, that the Greek mind blended with the pre-Hellenic, prepatriarchal tradition of preindividual man. This was the tradition of the great Mother and Daughter goddesses: Demeter, the very life of Earth and power of the Moon, and Kore Proserpine, Demeter's undying daughter who ruled the underworld. Hades, the realm of Kore Proserpine, was thought by the first frightened *individuals*, the heroes, to be the Kingdom of the Dead where all things are forgotten and from whence there is no returning. But originally it had symbolized, to *preindividual* man, that hidden base from which all life springs and returns perennially. This basic concept of the underworld was preindividual man's intuitive solution of the mystery of life.

At Eleusis, however, sometime during the rise of protoindividualism, a rite that had been completely intuitive and spontaneous became specific and shaped to the needs of men whose dawning self-consciousness was beginning to make them fear the dark of death. This solution of the main problem of individualism was, however, never put into wide circulation. On the contrary, it was sealed up under the specific spell-name of *mystery*: a word that did not originally mean a puzzle, but meant a voluntary muting, a vow of secrecy, on the part of the initiate not to repeat what had been told him. For what had been revealed to him was the secret that delivered him from the death fear, a fear that is inherent in the ignorance of individualism. Any person could apply for this enlightenment. But it was a private liberation and, while it did remove the fear of death (if we are to trust contemporary reporters), it did not elucidate the riddle of life.

At this stage of further contraction into individualism, what was being sought by the condensing mind of man was an answer to the acute question as to whether life can be lived at all with any certainty of dignity. The hero's crude conviction that only the prison and shackles of the preindividual tradition kept life from being fun, that being free of obligation one would naturally be happy—such a childish misapprehension was amply disproved. The midindividual had appeared. Self-conscious man, who in his early stage had realized that he was distinct from the group and had felt a reactive anger at the group's restraints and exploitations, now, in this third, middle term of the contraction of his consciousness, becomes not only aware of himself but aware also of his helplessness as a lonely creature pitted against an unfriendly Nature. He is also aware that this terrible and alien Nature is not only vastly aloof and indifferent to the individual's fate, but (so it seems to the self-consciously self-blaming midindividual) she can rise, like the snakes round the doomed Laocoon, wrap herself around the small protesting private will, and make the helpless, vainly resisting creature do *her* will.

Here, then, is the base of the Ascetic Epoch, the third stage of humanity's psychological history. Man discovers that he must find a method of disciplining himself. For not only is *outer* nature unpredictable, powerful, dangerous, and uncontrollable, but his *own* nature betrays him. The Universe is unfriendly and man is fallen. His one hope is to escape *this* situation and *this* vehicle. Man becomes life-rejecting and, by denying the body, seeks a state in which, after death, he will be free and bodiless. He now begins to believe that in this present life not only will suffering exceed happiness—there is no armor against fate—but that enjoyment involves one in further suffering, that pleasure is bait that lures and traps the soul into a fresh round of misery. Birth, illness, old age, and death—all these all men must endure and all are suffering.

Asceticism, as athletic training, was inevitable and right when man's psychological evolution, the condensation of his consciousness, reached such a degree of concentration that he became detached from and critical of not only his fellows but from and of himself. Discipline and training were necessary and certainly paid. The organized, planned, and forecast life made the ordered city (with its storing and distribution, its integrated crafts, arts, and administration) able to ride out barren years and cataclysms of weather that were fatal to more feckless communities. While, when it came to war, the drilled phalanx soon showed the free fighting hero that he was as anachronistic on the field of battle (which he thought was his native heath) as he was in the complex of the city streets.

But the mid-self-conscious man could not be content to add self-training to his defenses and, being so armed with surplus resources

3. The Midindividual

and the power to foresee and guard against eventualities, feel that he now held the initiative. This was because the more his foresight permitted him to be forewarned, and so forearmed, not only was he confronted with a wider range of uninsurable risk, but it appeared to be all the more certain that in the actuarial dates against which he provided there must be an increasing number that carried increasing risks. And in the end, there would be one date on which he must lose all that he had.

The midindividual who, because of his self-blame, is already uneasy as to whether he is worth his keep (the guilt sense) and as to whether it is worthwhile keeping on in such an unbalanceable world (the death wish), begins to long for release. Liberation must be not merely from outer molestation but from inner weariness and frustration. The hero felt shame at losing face, at not being outstanding among his fellows whom he could emulate and surpass. The ascetic felt guilty at his lack of anonymity. He began to long to be lost, obliterated. He began to fear that death might only be the gate to another round of such impossibly demanding and conflicting lives as his present one. The dread of reincarnation, of repeating, endlessly, this predicamental experience, of finding himself once again possessed by passions that only created more craving and more guilt—this fear engrossed increasingly the mind of the midindividual. All appetite must be shunned, all possession eschewed, all position abdicated.

But addiction and appetite are two different things. It is untrue to say that all appetites grow with eating. In point of fact, all those appetites that sustain a healthy life are self-terminative. There can be no private salvation from the self which is morbid precisely because it is private, that is, self-centered. The desire for liberation can itself become a fetter if it is for a self to be released into a condition where it will gain self-satisfying ends.

Again, this was clearly understood by the few. We shall see in Section III that the crisis-transition from the coconscious preindividual to the protoindividual had its own therapy whereby that dangerous passage could (and can) be achieved and that, in the event of mishap or miscarriage, it can be remedied. And we shall see that as, in turn, the crisis-transition from the protoindividual to the midindividual also had (and has) its remedial therapy, so too the

I - PSYCHOLOGICAL STORY OF SOCIAL HUMANS

Midindividual Epoch did discover the appropriate praxis for bringing the psyche safely through this stage of development and into the succeeding stage, that of total individualism.

But what we have noted of these first two crises is also true of this third one: the therapy was personal and private. It might deal with pioneers, sporadic advanced types. It might keep them from wholly seceding and even make some of them into seers by giving them not only freedom from adolescent self-blame but also, prophetically, precognitionally, freedom from those two further crises which humankind was yet to reach: (1) the manic-depressive derangement of Humanic man; and (2) involutional melancholy, the final failure of nerve that now threatens twentieth-century man.

However, the greater number, by far, of those who were capable of reflective thought did not find the appropriate method that would give them a state of consciousness that was contemporary. They did not find the technique of that dilation of awareness that would solve the particular psychological problem of the midindividual who was conscious of self-blame for his inadequacy to love the community and who could not deny that community's right to demand loyalty. Although as we shall see in Section III, in India, the source of many such techniques, methods were certainly devised that would make those willing to be trained able to become contemporarily conscious. That is, they would be able not only to understand the stage to which human psychological evolution had reached. They would be able to become themselves trained persons whose psychophysical phase of energy was predominantly adrenaline and no longer the noradrenaline of the previous protoindividual—the self-assertive character (see Section II) who could be self-critical without guilt, without life dread, or despair.

Still, the ascetic failed (just as the Hero had failed before him), although he did have a temporary success. The man who renounced (who disciplined himself, who was uniformed, closely drilled, and always under orders, who was always flouting his self-love) soon became a force in society. Just as the exiled proto-hero, for a while the lone wolf, quickly gathered around him a gang of adventurers, so the proto-ascetic soon found postulants. The monastic order arises. It has a new if temporary inherent strength from its repression. It is explicit, propagandist; and it preaches, continually pointing out two things that its listeners are ready to allow. First, that the boastful hero has proved a failure. He ends personally in a dismal demonstration that the undisciplined are contemptible. Besides, and secondly, even if he ever were admirable as a knight errant, now, in a world of police forces and magistracy, he is out of date, an anachronism.

The ascetic therefore demotes the hero from his position of being the pattern of prestige. He shames both the exhibitionist brawler and also the lazy, sensual man. His discovery of energy generated by repression, his use of propaganda, drill, and uniform are practical discoveries that the new state can employ against its subjects and against its less modern rivals. Diplomacy and coordinated armament are byproducts of this second level of individualism, of a self-consciousness that can be made efficiently loyal by exploiting its sense of guilt. Thus the state can largely depend on its subjects to denounce themselves.

And, just as inevitably, the creation of a monastic autocracy (some of those who began as persons seeking anonymity become autocrats) leads to further questioning in the midindividual mind. Guilt turns into despair and the best seek to escape from life itself. Large numbers were drawn into monasticism by leaders who seemed to have both knowledge and strength; and the dilution of enthusiasm, caused by this influx, led inevitably to the relaxed orders. The ascetic, as the pattern of prestige, is discredited and humanity seeks still another standard (16).

4. The Total Individual
(*Humanic, self-sufficient humans*)

In this chapter, as we consider that contraction of consciousness that has been most intense and has called itself modern humans, we must also contract our purview. Up to this point we have been able to consider the human process as a homogeneous whole. The first step in this process, the coconscious preindividual state of man's consciousness, when he had emerged from animalhood into a creature with a culture, may be said to cover all that there then was of a humankind. Both the number of groups and their possible habitats were very restricted. With the next stage, the Heroic, the increase in area and the restlessness of the personality made for more wandering but *ipso facto* for more communication. The Heroic Age and the feudal companion condition that shares its exhibitionist ideals of honor and dispute broke out at different times in different places. But it was the same movement and caused by the same force: a contraction of consciousness that was provoked by the same outer pressure of an ankylosed priest–kingly tradition.

I - PSYCHOLOGICAL STORY OF SOCIAL HUMANS

All the cultures of the past (save those very few that were protected by complete isolation, as for example, the Aboriginal Australian and Papuan cultures) have arrived, sooner or later, at stage two of man's consciousness: the protoindividualism of self-assertive man. And, in turn, all these Heroic cultures, because they were precipitated by self-conscious, challenging men, had of necessity to challenge themselves. The young heroic prince, born in the warrior caste to rule an army-girt kingdom, becomes the Buddha. The ideal of the ascetic now becomes widespread: as widespread as the ideal of the hero had been.

But Humanic man does not supplant the ascetic so readily, at least not yet. In this phase of sense-of-separateness growth, the West outran the rest of the world, pushing to the utmost the limited knowledge of the outer world given by a criticism and analysis that are confined by the narrow conviction of reason, and neglecting the inner world. Only now are Asia and the rest of the world reaching the psychological crisis brought on by such one-sided physical discovery and striving to keep it from shattering society, which it must do if further *psychological* discovery is not made.

The West is now emerging from that phase and is already learning that economic and scientific advance without equal psychological advance must be disastrous. Asia, which during the Ascetic phase did much to teach Europe about the dimensions of the psyche, must now learn from the West as the Indic and Mongolian peoples go through the Humanic phase and the West emerges from that phase of total individualism. Asia stayed behind, short of the total individualized psyche, because the center of her thinking (India) remained attached to the renunciatory other-worldlyism of the Ascetic phase. This, of course, was due to her absorbed interest in the psyche, in the inner world rather than in the outer. The thought of Western man, resuming the self-assured individualism that asceticism had compelled the hero to abandon, appeared to India to be so preposterously irrational as to be impossible.

On the other hand, China, for an opposite reason but with equal force, rejected the return of the hero now armed not with traditional weapons but with scientific armament. Her concern with society made the independent, irresponsible superindividual appear to be a

4. The Total Individual

monster. The *chung tzu*, though in an essentially urbane way, is as self-effacing as the ascetic. Therefore, when China needed expert answers to the ultimate problems of life and the nature of things, she did not send for the West's technicians. She had already imported what her socially minded masters felt would serve their purpose: Buddhism (40).

In this chapter, therefore, we consider the culminating contraction of consciousness into self-sufficient man as it is illustrated by the West. This is not provincialism. The foreconsciousness of Western man was almost completely insulated from his deeper total consciousness, and this drove him to the search for objectivity. The search for objectivity centered his interest in the outer world and led to his discovery of the scientific technic. This gave him (1) the physical powers that permitted him to threaten all the world and conquer much of it; (2) the economic increases that allowed him to raise his biotic standards; and (3) the physiological information that gave him the ability to get rid of much disease, multiply population, lengthen his life, and increase energy and output. Such apparent victories made it possible for him to believe in progress and an earthly Utopia. Now the West, by its very striving to discover objectivity, has reached psychology and is trying to study the self, which constructs the environment it would modify. While the East, with scientifically armed assault and with scientifically discovered and commended aid, turns to attempt the Humanic phase and to abandon asceticism. In studying the West's experience of the Humanic phase of extreme individualism we are, then, studying not the private story of aberrant occidental man but the first attempt of humankind to be a complete individual. And this is an inevitable step in the evolution of the human consciousness as it strives toward complete understanding.

The ideal of denial and abandonment lasted on as the pattern of prestige in the West until the fifteenth century. True, the last great ascetic enthusiasm, the Franciscan, was rapidly degenerating by the time that Dante had written his *De Monarchia* (1312–1313). This was the book that was to offer the Papacy terms of circumscribed authority, which it promptly rejected, putting the book, when it was published, on the Index of forbidden reading. The Revival of Learning was well on its way but, until Constantinople fell to Mohammed II in 1453, men had not awakened to the fact that they were in a new epoch. As always, and as it is today, human character has already changed for a considerable time before human consciousness becomes aware that this is so.

The ideal of the man who sacrifices himself to save others (into an afterlife from a world that must always be sorrowful) had become, from the Atlantic to the Pacific, the noblest concept for thoughtful, sensitive, responsible men who were capable of that degree of self-consciousness which can blame itself. Though China revered Confucius, she had to allow that the Buddha held the answer for those whose sensitiveness drove them to ask those most searching of questions: "What does life mean? Where does it go? Can this world be enough in itself?" So the two great ideal images that dominated the midindividual consciousness of self-accusing man are both other-worldly. The Eastern figure sits in self-losing salvational contemplation under a tree. The Western figure hangs on a tree in an ecstasy of self-sacrificing, salvational offering. Both call men away from a temporal world of suffering to an eternal world of peace.

But the mind of man alters because his consciousness evolves. The protoindividual, self-assertive man admired the hero, thinking that men could win happiness if only they had the courage to break with the cowardly fears of the ancient group tradition. In turn, the midindividual mind, in its growing self-consciousness, became self-accusing and admired self-denial, submission, and renunciation. But, as once again man's consciousness contracted still more, he no longer felt guilt. This further concentration of awareness gave him a greater degree of detachment, both outer and inner.

Outwardly, he began to question the ascetic authority's right to give him a sense of guilt, and in this respect he recapitulates the heroic protest, but more self-consciously. Unlike the primal tradition, the ascetic order had used argument. For the hypnotic power of the coconscious pattern of culture over its constituents could no longer be exercised. The Heroic Age had served the purpose of destroying the primal magic. And argument, the use of the syllogism, the analysis of words, came to be used more and more both in East and West, whether in Buddhist Taxila or Late Scholastic Paris. This was necessary

4. The Total Individual

in order to prove and convince because direct psychical experience was increasingly lacking. The new Man of the Renaissance, the man of recently intensified self-consciousness, aware of his distinctive and separative individualism, was keen to reason and sharply equipped to argue. The Church had admitted the authority of Aristotle, the inventor of the syllogism. And Aristotle had ruled that there is nothing in the mind that is not first in the senses: a pronouncement favorable to the thinking of modern sensory humans. Consequently, modern humans not only felt it to be natural for them to debate with authority, as an equal, and to have no sense of guilty temerity in daring to question its answers and challenge its conclusions. They also challenged it to test and experiment as to whether its conclusions could stand up under actual examination.

In the West, this revolt, this secession from the ascetic tradition had started. The opening of the way for experimental, empirical science had already begun with the triumph, in the medieval schools, of the Nominalists over the Realists. Words were not things. Species did not exist, they were abstractions. The only reality was a number of separate objects. "Entities must not be multiplied" unless you could show that each name did apply to and describe an actual, definite thing. This, to repeat, was projection. It was man's new acuteness of self-consciousness, his new sense of being a totally separate person, being projected onto the outer world. Nominalism has been the basic philosophy of natural science because it is the self-evident conclusion of the fully self-conscious mind. The semiconscious mind of the mid-individual cannot dismiss species, or other collective nouns, as being unreal. Authority is something more than an average or majority of private opinions, and tradition is not necessarily superstition but often contains inspired intuition. The collective mind is not necessarily a delusion and certain wholes may be apprehended by precritical, preanalytical minds although those same integral wholes become imperceptible to the critical individual intelligence and attention. With the disappearance of this apprehension of fields, of areas in which objects behave coordinately (a behavior only to be understood if the presence of a field is recognized), the total individual becomes incapable of apprehending any relationships between himself and other beings except that of physical contacts.

I - PSYCHOLOGICAL STORY OF SOCIAL HUMANS

Such was Humanic man's outward detachment. And he was able to exercise that outward detachment to such an extreme degree because his inner detachment was equal to it. The tie that still held Heroic man and Ascetic man to the community was their social conscience. And it gave the community its modifying power over the assault of the one and the secession of the other. The hero wished to be outstandingly famous and so feared to be shamed. The ascetic feared being expelled and hoped to be forgiven his guilt. The total individual now saw not merely no reason why he should prefer the pricking of his own finger to the death of any of his fellows who were of no use to him, but no reason why he should feel either shame or guilt. He viewed the oddity of his emotional behavior, whether asocial, antisocial, or absurd, as one more subject for his curiosity, neither to be censured or lauded but to be observed as intriguing entertainment. So Humanic, self-sufficient man, believing in reason alone, can be amused by the extravagances of his own nature, viewing from the citadel of his private intellectual detachment not merely the ridiculous antics of his fellows but the carnivals and carousing carried on in the streets of the self's own town and watched with humor from the battlements of the central keep: the completely self-conscious psyche.

This self-sufficiency meant, at the beginning, a great release of energy. Ascetic man had given his attention to and had spent his repressed drive in striving to expunge his guilt and to escape an afterdeath doom. But that attention was now held by an interest in the outer world, and that energy was now employed in modifying the environment. His efforts were now turned to an attempt to understand not only the human situation but the human physique, not merely the field of vision but the viewer. The very energy of penetration outward was, however, due to and a symptom of a contraction within. The attempt to find and fix objectivity, complete definition, and a final hardness of focus led to the restriction of and final denial of all midterms and indeterminacies. The Renaissance man, because he was aiming at being without shame, guilt, or any irrational, nonphysical tie with his fellows, was also the first man (and, indeed, the first creature) ever to attempt to live without intuitive knowledge and acknowledgment of his preterrational nature.

4. The Total Individual

Humanic man had no specific exercises for contacting and working with his deep emotive being. And toward the traditional exercises of the past, his attitude was skepticism tinged with aestheticism, a contempt for superstition that was kept in check by the antiquarian's appreciation of an object or of a process precisely because it belongs to an extinct culture. His attitude was well stated by Adam Smith, the vastly influential eighteenth-century economist whose *Wealth of Nations* furnished the economy on which humanism was to be based. Smith proposed, as a self-evident policy for humankind, that reason should always be followed and that enthusiasm (the powerful waves of the emotive life) should be dismissed.

Toward the end of the Humanic phase, when man's critically minded enquiry brought him to study not only his economy and his physique but also his psyche, he discovered that, whether it was regrettable or not, reason did not rule man's interior life. It could not alter his conduct, character, and consciousness, while the emotions could and did. Humanic man, in his phase of some fifteen generations (from the mid-fifteenth century to the beginning of the twentieth), went through a cycle that started with keen elation and ended in considerable discouragement. Because his total individualism made him examine critically all the areas of experience, he had, at the start, an unparalleled success in handling what first came to his attention: the outer, molar, inorganic world, the province of astronomy and chemistry. And he made almost as striking advances in understanding his physique.

When, however, in his contracting investigation he reached the psyche, because of his method of approach by detachment and analysis, it presented him with a problem as insoluble as it was distressing. For the psyche, because it is the subject, cannot be understood by making it an object. Nor, because it is not a machine but a field-of-wholeness (as is a work of art), can it be understood by reducing it into its constituent parts. Self-sufficient man, the total individual, therefore became subject to a fluctuation of mood. Instead of the shame–fear that haunted the hero or the guilt–fear that brooded over the ascetic, Humanic man alternated between two states of mind. On looking forward, he considered himself to be a machine that could be made to mesh in perfect gear with the

I - PSYCHOLOGICAL STORY OF SOCIAL HUMANS

environment and so produce a totally satisfying Utopia. On looking back, he regarded himself as an animal that, because of its beasthood, could never be rational nor hope to conceive of the nature of an objective world, a creature whose intelligence only armed it the more lethally to destroy its own species.

Emotionally, then, Humanic man could not be stable. His epoch is brief because he had a psyche that was even more strangulated than that of the ascetic at his most schizophrenic extremes. His personal consciousness was almost completely cut off from his deep, personal preterconsciousness. And the traditional methods of keeping the two in touch, of penetrating through the barrier of the limen (religious procedures such as the Mass), he mainly regarded as being, at best, of antiquarian, romantic interest and, at worst, a superstition that still prevented his release into personal happiness. The critical, analytic method was the only means whereby the hyper-self-conscious, individualistic intellect could conceive of the meaning of understanding and could hope to attain to it by achieving the detachment of complete objectivity. The intensification of this critical, analytic method drove Humanic man, as we have seen, to studies that lay closer and closer to himself, and finally led him to the discovery of his own preterconscious.

Still pursuing objectivity, however, he could not recognize that this preterconscious was part of himself and that it was the complement of his personal, objective consciousness; that it was the link between him and his past, his tradition, and his fellows: between him and all life. He must still look on it as being a power that was alien and hostile to his one means (reason) and his one aim (personal happiness). No wonder, then, that Sigmund Freud, the popularizer and not the discoverer of this sunken continent of consciousness, could only regard it as being the permanent frustrater of reason, good sense, and generous behavior and, therefore, could describe man as being "a base, ungovernable beast." No wonder that H. G. Wells, the popularizer of humanist history and the missionary of man's salvation through physical science, could declare, after the Second World War and the discovery and use of the atom bomb, that the mind was "at the end of its tether." For, of course, to him the mind was the critical, analytic intellect of humanic, individualistic

4. The Total Individual

man. It would have been a better simile to say that the surface mind, like a yacht with canvas crowded to the topsail, had dropped off its balancing keel and so was capsizing.

Nevertheless, even though Blake may be too hopeful when he says, "If the fool would but persevere in his folly he would become wise," we can say that if the mind will but persist in its criticism, penetration, and analysis, it will come upon expansion and integration. Like circumnavigators of the globe, by consistently going away from our point of departure, we find ourselves returned to it. Man, in seeking the absolute detachment of complete objectivity, found the roots of his attachment to the whole. And so he had to admit that, although objectivity was impossible, orientation *was* possible. Orientation, in this context, means the realization that he and the universe cannot be separated, that he and it are two poles between which there is a constant interplay: an interplay that precipitates creation. Therefore, detachment is an impossibility. Man cannot now regard life with a cold curiosity; he must realize that he and life are one.

Neither Freud, who took part in the beginning of the transition from humanic, totally individualistic man to postindividual man, nor Wells, who was concerned with history and saw the transition more than half completed, understood what was going on. Tied to the assumptions of an epoch that was practically ended while they were still alive, they failed to see that the discovery of the preterconscious (together with the subsequent realization that objectivity and detachment were impossibilities) was one more step in psychophysical evolution.

It is an interesting fact that since the seventh century A.D., the changes in Western culture can generally be detected as being crescent by the last quarter of each century, and at half-moon at the century's turn. Greek is rediscovered by Western Europeans about 675. The Revival of Learning takes another decisive step when, about 775, the great Scriptory Schools are founded by the Frankish kings. Each change in the development of style in architecture throughout northern Europe (Romanesque, Lancet, Decorated, Flamboyant, and/or Perpendicular) may be dated at about the seventy-fifth year of each century from 1075 to 1375.

I - PSYCHOLOGICAL STORY OF SOCIAL HUMANS

In our own epoch we can now see, looking backward, that by 1875, the intellectual–emotional climate was beginning to alter. Until then, the chief concerns of man's practical-theoretical thought had been with economics and a biology slanted by economic assumptions. Charles Darwin has left it on record that Malthus' work on population and its pressures had turned his mind to seek an explanation for the evolutionary process and that it had channeled his thought toward finding that explanation in the blind struggle to survive. Karl Marx, impressed by the support that Darwin's theory might be made to give to the class struggle, wrote to Darwin. Naturally, but not rationally, Darwin shunned the possible application. A quarter of a century after the publication of *The Origin of Species*, its popularity was established with the practical reading public, but the growing edge of Western thought was turning from bioeconomics to psychology.

The Modern Age, the age of the four revolutions, had begun with the ecclesiastical revolution. The political revolution came next and was, in turn, superseded by the economic revolution, the revolution that was to overturn industrialism and which, toward the end of the nineteenth century, began to be undermined by the oncoming uprising of the fourth, the psychological revolution. By 1873, J. M. Charcot (at Salpêtrière Hospital in Paris), in his *Lectures on the Diseases of the Nervous System*, had drawn the attention of the educated world to the problem of the preterconscious. As discoverers of profoundly original facts usually do,[15] Charcot missed the true significance of his great find. He maintained until the end of his life that this till then unknown side of the psyche was merely a morbid aberration. For instance, he thought that the hypnotic state was specifically a hysteric characteristic. Nevertheless, as an original researcher, he realized that no narrow exploitation of this strange find should be made. He has been blamed, and with some point, for dismissing the hypnotic state as being essentially one aspect of a morbid condition of hysteria or hystero-epilepsy. But today we can see that Charcot's insight, that the inrush from the preterconscious onto the foreconscious is Leptoid in nature and epileptoid when thwarted, was prophetic.[16] Prophetic also was his foresight when he remarked to one of his pupils, Pierre Janet, about a fellow pupil who

4. The Total Individual

already showed a limiting self-assurance combined with an overmastering gift for systemizing, "that young man will put back psychology sixty years." "That young man" was Sigmund Freud.

By 1882 in London a philosopher of eminence (Henry Sidgwick of Cambridge), a Greek scholar (F. W. H. Myers), and a young man who was to be a British Prime Minister (Arthur Balfour) had decided to risk academic disapproval by founding the London Society for Psychical Research.

By 1884, H. Bernheim, Professor of Medicine at Nancy [University], aided by the work of A. A. Liébeault, published *De la suggestion*, which was a definite treatise on hypnosis. These researchers, reacting against Charcot's physicalism and attempting to consider, empirically, the mind in itself, tried to equate the hypnotic trance with normal sleep. Actually, these two states are mainly polar: for example, muscular tension is at a minimum in sleep and often at a maximum in hypnosis.

During the next and last decade of the century it was clear, from Becquerel's work in fluorine and the work of the Curies in radium, that physics, the science of greatest detachment, was about to enter a new epoch. Classical physics, with its standard of objectivity (the object's mass and position can and must be known), was to be transformed by the field concepts.

As the nineteenth century passed into the twentieth, Max Planck in Berlin, with his concept of quanta (together with J. J. Thomson, his greater pupil Ernest Rutherford at Cambridge, and Niels Bohr in Copenhagen, with their revolutionary notions of the electron and the proton) started concepts that were to lead to the disappearance of what had been the goal of thinking men since the rise of Ionian science twenty-four hundred years before: the goal of absolute objectivity.

Finally, with the Heisenberg principle of indeterminacy (that if the position of a particle can be known, its mass cannot and vice versa) man had reached, as Niels Bohr himself summed it up, "the end of the twenty-four-hundred-year search for objectivity."

Meanwhile, the sciences of life were also in travail. The concept of mutation, based on the evidence that living processes could suddenly leap into new forms, just as the electron did, was as radical as the new physics and was received with violent controversy. Ernst Haeckel, a famous and conservative popularizer of simple Darwinianism, shouted in a biological conference that had reached ecclesiastical conciliar heat, "If this ('Mendelism') is accepted, here we go back to Moses!"

Nevertheless, the process went on. By 1910, there went into biological circulation a term that was more significant, though less convulsant, than mutationism had been. Ecology, as much as any science, marked the end of analysis as being the method of finding the final interpretation of life and so signaled the oncoming shift of consciousness from total individualism to postindividualism. The one science to which the Middle Ages would give money was astrology. And the first clear indication that the Middle Ages were gone for good was when star-study changed from astrology to astronomy. This is the first sign that man's concept of himself and his situation is altering. In the ascetic midindividual stage, he had conceived of himself as being a creature that was struggling guiltily to have his way against the law of an implacable Heaven whose dooms for him could be spelled out in the stars. When astronomy comes in, it is a symptom that man is becoming content to be a self-sufficient creature that can catalogue (*nomos*) the cosmos but cannot and need not comprehend it. The how of the cosmos he may know, and he may find such detached knowledge entertaining. Its why he cannot know and doesn't need to. All the sciences should then have been termed *nomoi*, not *logoi*. And the science that mattered most to Humanic man in his most elational form was economics. (Carlyle called it the gloomy science because in its first phase it was trying to define the status quo.) Economics was the faith that you, the detached creature, are free to carve the environment to shape your personal convenience. Therefore, when from actual observation of how living forms are integrated it was seen that each is in field reaction with all the rest, this was rightly called ecology. And we can see a symptom of a new shift in human attention, a new expansion of awareness.

For the sciences were projections of Humanic man's highly restricted focal length of consciousness. And as that consciousness, in its intensity, contracted on itself, the sciences themselves came

4. The Total Individual

under the analytic scrutiny of the method that had extended them. As a young man, H. G. Wells himself wrote an essay called *The Scepticism of the Instrument*, thus indicating that he was aware of the question raised by epistemology: "How do we know that we can apprehend an objective world?" (Darwin and Freud both recognized this problem.) And as the analytic sciences were found to be partial and highly selective, men began to discover that it was possible to seek for a further method of understanding—what Radhakrishnan, in the nineteen-twenties, had named "integral thought" (see Glossary). At about the same time, the first issues of ecological journals began to appear; the first number of the *American Journal of Ecology* came out in 1922.

Meanwhile, however, such shifts of scientific attention from the critical analytic focus to integral apprehension were not enough to prevent acute psychic distress in Western man (39). His spirit, for a dozen generations, had been on a deprivative diet. The vitamin of meaning, essential for sanity, had been steadily diminished in his food for thought. He had been able to endure this inadequacy of significance, and so to postpone collapse, by three devices.

We must, then, at this point survey these three substitutes to see whether they can any longer prevent the mutation of the mind; or whether we now have to face the fact that another great shift of consciousness is about to take place—is indeed already taking place. And we must ask ourselves how we may best cooperate with the inevitable, how we may integrate ourselves with life's evolution by learning those exercises whereby we may emerge into the new condition.

The three methods whereby modern humans have sought to prevent (and have succeeded in postponing) their psychological collapse are these: (1) utopianism (progress), (2) reactionaryism (counter-progress), and (3) detensionism. Earlier in this chapter we said that humanic rationalistic man was the only creature that had ever attempted to live with no information other than that given by the rational exercise of the senses. This was certainly the hope of the person who felt himself to be the self-sufficient, total individual. Very soon, however, there were many secessionists from such a notion. It is true that since the writing of *The Cloud of Unknowing* (circa 1350) there had been no treatise written in vernacular, and by a mind that was up to date with the psyche of its age, which could serve as a guide for a consciousness that was shifting from the stage of the guilty, mid-individualistic ascetic to an ultraindividualistic, nonguilty state of mind.[17] The succeeding best seller, *The Scale of Perfection*, and the widely popular *Imitation of Christ* are rightly called books of ascetic, not mystical, theology. But almost as soon as Humanic man emerged, an answer to this need for a guidebook was produced by the Counter-Reformation, which threw back the Protestant Revolution and contained and remolded the Renaissance. The Jesuits, who were better disputants and finer scholars than the reformers, better psychologists and better trained than the humanists, used self-consciousness to conquer itself. The core of the Ignatian answer to Humanic man's revolt against asceticism lay in the *Spiritual Exercises* which, although he did not invent them, Ignatius did put into circulation.

For a time, this method proved to be highly efficacious for mastering the emotions of even the most critically minded. In consequence, Ignatius could recruit men of high humanist culture and yet keep them loyal and indeed subservient to an ascetic point of view. For there was a large number of those, even among the intelligentsia, who wistfully wished to feel again the close supporting convictions of the Ages of Faith, if only it were possible. Humanism was still far from certain of its frame of reference and hesitant about framing its own distinctive philosophy. The conservative reformers of the New Learning wished to repair the ascetic tradition, not to reconstruct it; to correct ancient slips of the pen, not to add new information. Galileo has often been cited as being the hero of Renaissance science. But now in his definitive study, Giorgio de Santillana has shown that he was only a very muddled and even petty man who was motivated far more by emotional and indeed irresponsible resentments than by a consistent and practiced philosophy; [he was] an unprepared, vacillatory person who wanted to preach Copernicanism and at the same time to be recognized as an orthodox Catholic.

The ancient ascetic Orders dreaded revolutionary license and anarchy and feared their own nature. The Ignatian *Exercises* gave intellectuals who wished to serve this ancient order a method whereby they might recreate their own belief, whereby they might feed down into their sunken preterconscious those instructions that were in

4. The Total Individual

favor of the past: a thing which the conventional methods of attending Mass and listening to sermons seemed no longer able to do. The success of the system, however, depended on two things. First, the man must desire the point of view of the past, the ascetic position; and second, he must also believe that it is intellectually valid—that is, it is both desirable and true. Heaven is the only desirable goal, a goal that is attained by denying the body and dying to this world. And this desire is, within the frame of reference, unavoidable. For after a few years at most, the soul is faced with an irrevocable situation. If life here has been sufficiently mortificatory then there is the reward of eternal bliss. If life here has been carnally minded, an expression of the appetites, then, as St. Paul says, there is death or, far worse, eternal torment.

Naturally, that being the state of affairs, it was inevitable that men should *wish* to believe in order to be saved. It might not be possible to think with desirous vividness of a heaven the charms of which were unimaginable to the senses. And it was equally impossible to conceive of a Deviser of that Heaven Who, although He was said to be Love, used as His alternative method of extracting obedience and restraint from His creatures the threat of and practice of torturing forever those who, during their brief life here, had failed to satisfy His demands. But fear could do most of the work—a fact that Ignatius well knew and on which he acted. As a very thorough individualist, honestly ignorant of human symbiosis and solidarity, he was convinced that men did best when they were driven. He knew and understood why four fifths of the visions of those authorities which he studied (the mortificatory Saints) had been of Hell and only one fifth of Heaven. And his action was based on their indications together with his own convictions and experiences. His exercises are visualist. Things are to be seen with terrific, mind-etching vividness, and the things that are to be basically branded on the consciousness are the torments of an irremediable, interminable Hell. These two facts, the subject and the method of memorizing it, account both for the immediate success of the *Exercises* and for their subsequent failure. Only an ascetic world, wherein the conflicts of repression had been projected until self-hate became hate of others, could wish to believe such a doctrine. Only a world in which fear for one's own salvation made a man frantic with suspicion and hate against anyone who by his doubt might increase and make indiscriminate God's rage against man could believe such a doctrine to be true.[18]

And as to the method: it could work only with people of such visual power of projection that they could generate eidetic imagery: that is, such visualizers that they literally see before them, as an autonomous vision, what they are imagining. And only a society in which such a type is common could successfully practice this system of autosuggestion. There is reason to suppose, from the work of the brothers Jensch (Dr. Jensch and Professor Jensch of the University of Marburg) that such eidetic imagery is most frequent in children whose parathyroids suffer from a deficiency of lime. And there is a strong probability that this deficiency is the provocative condition that makes the state possible. As dietary conditions improved in Europe, it is then likely that these powerful hallucinatory aids to the ascetic belief faded at the very time that not only the intellectual climate but the emotional atmosphere was changing. The Humanic Epoch, by the beginning of the seventeenth century, had begun to pass from being a request for reform of the ascetic system and an appeal for tolerance to belief that an alternative system might replace the old interpretation of nature and of man. By the close of that century's first third, the last war of religion has come to an end. By the close of the second third, it is possible to detect Humanic man's new aim: humanitarianism. Charles I of England and his Long Parliament that fought and defeated him agreed on at least one point of greater importance than all the issues they disputed: they both abolished torture as a part of judicial procedure.

By the time of the Restoration, the historical student finds references to compassionate conduct as being something not saintly but of common decency. At the very beginning of the eighteenth century, we find (as J. B. Bury [7] points out in his *The Idea of Progress*) the first statements of the belief in the indefinite improvability of man. The great Ignatian system had lost its pristine power; this remarkable psychological method was no longer relevant. For a time it postponed, almost singlehandedly, the humanic process, and headed off the full emergence of the total individual who would know no world but this one, have no technic but reason, and depend

4. The Total Individual

on no providence but his own resources. Now the order that had seemed so irresistible that its opponents feared it more than its own side admired it was itself in trouble. By the time of Ignatius' successor, Laynez (1556–1565), the power of the General, which had been great to begin with, was increased. By the reign of Claude Aquaviva (1581–1615), mistakes had been made that made the still increasing material success embarrassing to many conservatives.[19] As an authority has said, the evil reputation was surpassing the good. When, under the generalship of Vitelleschi, the Order reached the end of its first century—at the completion of those three generations which so often have marked the failure of spectacular success—it had 36 provinces, 800 houses, and 15,000 members. But by 1647, the Pope censured it severely at home, and by 1651 even abroad the retreat was evident. The Society and the Christianity that it taught were driven from Japan, while in Europe it was approaching its eclipse at the hands of the Papacy. And in what were the roots of this decay? If men's actions are consequences of their life process, of their basic consciousness, then the Jesuit movement was fighting a rear action; and having fought that action, the retreat from asceticism to a more prepared humanism could be made.

When, in 1773, the Pope dissolved the Society, it had served its purpose, and when it was re-established in 1814, the human climate had altered. The Humanic Epoch had attained to its humanitarian phase. The psychology behind this remarkable reaction, the reaction to the process of evolving consciousness, seems to have been the subconscious realization that mortificatory asceticism had had its day. The Ignatian *Exercises* had shown those who practiced them that Hell awaited the immoral, especially the sexually loose. But the Jesuits were always generous with salvation. No example of their resentment is more striking and more comprehensible than their attack on the Port Royal Jansenists, who certainly made salvation very hard, and indeed precarious, with their revival of Augustinianism and the issue of predestination. The self-tormenting eremite was suspect in the eyes of the Jesuits who wanted the world to enjoy a cultured urbanity under their sophisticated cosmopolitanism. Although they didn't consciously realize it and so never made it verbally explicit but did render it obviously manifest in their outstanding art, their aim, then, was to revoke and, with the young, prevent the super-individualism of the Humanic phase: not by returning the psyche to adolescent asceticism, or even to boyish heroism, but to panesthetic infantism. Of this, one unmistakable evidence is their most remarkable achievement: the transformation of the classic Renaissance architecture (self-consciously masculine with its rectilinear strength and honest athleticism, wide-shouldered in its trabeated muscularity) into Baroque.

Baroque has rightly been called the architecture of the Counter-Reformation, the style of Jesuitism as shown emphatically in their first church, the Jesu in Rome. It has also been rightly called psychological architecture by its ablest defender, Geoffrey Scott (74), in his *The Architecture of Humanism*. Although Scott skillfully defends this form against the charges of pretension, vulgarity, and dishonesty, it is the brilliant defense of a lawyer who is more concerned to gain an acquittal than to understand the defendant's motives. He does not even use that profound insight of Michelangelo, the founder of Baroque: "He may never understand architecture who has not mastered anatomy."

That statement contains the clue to Baroque and shows it to be the revealing symptom of the Jesuits' unconscious psychological strategy. For the Baroque forms are romantic. But they are not the romantic, fantastic, aspirational extravagance of the Gothic building, such as the Beauvais' arches, which outraged the adolescent engineering of the time, shooting up spires that too often collapsed and crushed in ruin the shrine they were to protect. The Counter-Reformation style produced false domes and sham vistas suggesting avenues and perspectives of horizontal order to bring delusively near a friendly, broody Heaven. But back of these delicious illusions was all the latest engineering skill, even to vast concealed iron chains trussing and corseting the maternal corpulence. In short, as the style of Gothic is ascetic, aspiration–escapism in stone (as the style of Madura, Puri, and all the pure Indian architecture is exuberantly phallic) so the Baroque is infantic. These great curves are projections of both the progenitive Mother and, even more, the baby form, all belly and head. The architecture was the most significant symptom of this daring though unconscious psychological strategy.

4. The Total Individual

The strategy, however, is confirmed with emphasis by the Jesuits' radical modification of the angular, syllogistic argumentation of Thomism in favor of their own construct (Francisco Suárez, 1548–1617), which was far more ingenious, flexible, and indeed modern.

For example, Grotius, the founder of international law, had a high appreciation for Suárez's work. Suárez is preparing for a world where men will have to learn to live together, sin and die with some sort of moral agreement. The prose style is therefore also urbane and florid. This pleader would rather win over by oratorical charm than by the force of clinchingly hard argument. Again, instead of a polemic aimed at confounding opponents, making rivals surrender, and presenting a clear case for the destruction of the obdurate, we have psychological insight, or rather flair, which is directed toward making of its listeners children who are willing to be guided and who need to be given security and rightful pleasures.

But the question, "Who guards the guardian?" has as its complement "Who teaches the teacher?" The Jesuits honestly wished to save man from humanic total individualism by restoring him to infantic innocency. But (1) they had nothing but the outer methods that used symbols and patterns, with which to reduce the contractive pressure of intensifying self-consciousness; their exercises were fear-compellers, not soothers. [And] (2) they had no method for assuaging their own intensifying individualism. Power inflames the desire to dominate; fear precipitates the desire to be secure. Ambition and, next and more pathetic, the love of money made the Church authorities, and indeed the Order itself, anxious and scandalized. Anxiety and shame, however, cannot stop a subconscious passion (repressed fear and a longing for security) from working itself out.

The Counter-Reformation ended in being no more than a counterattack. It had delayed, and perhaps rightly in its aims though often wrongly in its means, the too rapid emergence of total self-consciousness. It had tried to give humankind contemporary psychological exercises as part of a total modern education for the new type, Humanic man. But the exercises were based on fear and they were also imagist.[20]

Humanism, therefore, went on into secular humanitarianism. This, we have seen, was the second means—if not method—whereby modern humans postponed the oncoming total individualism. Even David Hume, [to quote him again], did not believe in his own rationalistic egotism: "There is no reason why I should prefer the pricking of my own finger to the death of a hundred human beings." And the fine society of the second part of the eighteenth century prided itself more on its sensibility than even on its good sense or its reasonableness and rationality. Yet, as noted above, this sensibility was, to the very men who could not help their growing sensitiveness, wholly groundless. They were convinced, in their minds, that their hearts were irrational and mistaken, though these seats of emotion made them act with pity and give rights to the poor. For example, the French Revolution was started by the sensibility of the intelligent well-to-do who were inspired and urged on by Rousseau. But after a reign of terror in which (as in Russia later) nearly all the reformers executed each other or had to fly for their lives, it ended with an autocracy which, in turn, ended with a reaction to the ancient regime. And so France entered on an oscillation of reform (for example, Louis Phillipe, the citizen king) and reaction (the Second Empire) down to the almost autocratic government of today.

In brief, the promise and disappointment of humanism illustrates Humanic man's predicament. Humanitarianism was a symptom that humanism was losing faith in its individualistic rationalism. The appearance of sensibility indicated that good sense had proved to be psychologically inadequate. For individualistic man to feel humane is a frustrant sensation, for it has no reason to guide its gush. Indeed it appears to be utterly irrational, contrary to the truth of things, a flying in the face of the facts, as unnatural as a society for multiplying malarial mosquitoes. Hence, humanitarianism becomes sentimentality, the auto-sensualism of the soul, the enjoyment of feeling for itself, and by oneself. Thus, the cruelest tyrants of the Modern Age have marshaled their forces in the name of sensibility, caring for the mistreated and suffering, championing the underdog. And note the description of this: "For whom one's heart bleeds" (metaphorically), "the flesh of one's opponents shall bleed" (actually and plentifully). The humanitarian pities a creature that has failed. But the creature is a crushed cur which, at heart, he despises. For when he pities without understanding and therefore without any hope that this thing of the gutter could become a colleague, the humanitarian can feel only contempt for this animal that he is going to tame and parasitize. Humanitarianism sends out missionaries who insist on turning natives into their own guilt-ridden, God-fearing, costume-shrouded, inhibited selves.

Thus humanism has ended in a despotism that will employ any outrage, not only on the body but on the mind of those men who, by questioning its methods and enquiring about its ends, dare to show that they have a right to be colleagues and an inability to become slaves.

A suppressed rage was felt by the poor as their lot grew worse. Take as an example (even a fairly favorable area) eighteenth-century England and the driving of the people from the countryside into the cities by the enclosures of the common lands. This indignation was sublimated by Wesley through the catharsis of a conversionism that was not, in basic nature, different from the technique of Ignatius (whom Wesley studied) (18). Rage turned to guilt; and guilt that was balanced, if not quashed, by redemption from Hell to Heaven relieved the social pressure here on earth. In this later case, however, the technique worked only on the uneducated classes: those persons who could upset but not lead society. And it left unaffected that class on which Ignatius had drawn, those who could be patterns of aristocratic prestige and leadership. The conversional procedure was also convulsional. It was not gradual, still less pertinacious. It was an attempt to reduce a dislocation, not to initiate the growth of a new faculty and type. As William James (47) pointed out in his classic study, *The Varieties of Religious Experience*, though it was rapid, it was frequently only temporary. But it did permit time to be gained while the laboring classes educated themselves for gradualist reform and while the growing sensibility of the governing class permitted them to offer themselves and be accepted as leaders of such melioration.[21] The rising standard of life, the spreading distribution of the benefits of large-scale production, the exploitation of non-European areas and peoples, together with humanitarianism at home and some abroad, tended to make utopianism a distraction from the growing contractive pressure in the psyche. Hence, economics dominated Western thought, from the ending of the political revolutionary phase in the Napoleonic fiasco to the rise of the psychological revolutionary phase which, we have already seen, begins to be visible in the last quarter of the last century.

Then when sensibility and revolution, humanitarianism and class war come into manifest opposition, enquiring minds perceived that here must lie a profound psychological conflict, a conflict that was repressed by the religious and disregarded by the secular. People began to doubt the possibility of attaining individual happiness in a highly bureaucratized state, a state that was necessary to give the economic security demanded by the individual who has become self-consciously self-conscious. For it is clear that the individual demands two incompatible things: security and liberty. Because he *is* an individual, he feels insecure and demands protection. But equally because of his individualism, he desires to be free. His state of mind makes him simultaneously an agoraphobiac, fearing to be exposed and alone, and a claustrophobiac, fearing imprisonment and restriction.

Meanwhile, to precipitate the crisis of psychological contraction there came also, and inevitably, the contraction of loyalty. At one time, in the Hellenic Roman Empire and the Chinese Empires, men had known a real veneration for an organized political-cultural power that was coterminous with civilization, and had felt a warm loyalty to their city or district where the range of the senses was the focus of the affections. In Europe, during the nineteenth century, Western man's loyalties became chaotic. Nationalism, which now became the substitute for religion, was not only a secession from civilization and traditional morality. It was also itself hopelessly unstable. Alternately, it desired to expand into a world empire or to shrink to a xenophobic group that would exclude all those who did not find native the local dialect. Men so distressed—their retreat to an earlier state was cut off, the Counter-Reformation had failed, and their hopes in humanitarian sensibility had been defeated—men in such distress hence sought psychological aid.

It was clear that they were under increasing stress and therefore the obvious therapy would be to detension them. At the end of the seventeenth century, when the diet of the well-to-do improved and better coaches and roads meant less of the hard exercise of riding

4. The Total Individual

and walking, men swelled with overfeeding and under-exertion. Blood pressures mounted and apoplectic strokes became about as common for the rich as heart attacks are for the executive of today. Bleeding, which for long was fancied by the physicians as being almost a panacea, certainly relieved vascular high tension temporarily. In much the same way, psychiatry today gives temporary emotional relief and can "cleanse the stuffed bosom of that perilous stuff which weighs upon the heart." And the success of the method seems to be just as fleeting. Digestive trouble cannot be permanently cured by emptying the stomach every time indigestion is felt. The cure will end in death—by starvation. A more apt simile is that of birth. The task of the obstetrician is not to abort, to terminate a pregnancy as soon as the potential mother shows signs of an inconvenience, but to make possible a full delivery without damage or dangerous distress.

So it is with man today as his Humanic phase ends and his hyper-individualist epoch begins to give rise and birth to the next condition of consciousness. He has tried reaction: skilled retreat to an infancy where he will be provided for and guarded. He has also tried humanitarianism—which ends too in the creche state, but of civil instead of ecclesiastical provision and guardianism. This means that the state becomes his guardian and provider, replacing the church. Thirdly, and finally, he has attempted a psychic abortion by means of a therapy of retreat, which could only bring about a miscarriage of the evolutionary process. Dr. William Sheldon once called an old-fashioned psychoanalytic processing "animectomy," an extraction of the soul. It might be more exact to call it defoetation, the constant reduction of passionate experience to pointless pleasure that leaves life, it is true, without urgency but also without aim. We must therefore conclude this historical sketch of man's psychological story by bringing it down to the present day and its fifth epoch.

5. The Postindividual
(*Leptoid humans*)

Up till now we have been dealing with four distinctive epochs of humanity. And not only have these ages been recognized by historians as being successive sections of man's social development; the directive force shaping them can now be seen as being due to changes in human consciousness. First, it is now clear that before historic record, but well-illustrated by superb pictures, there was a culture that was preindividualistic and to some extent coconscious[22] because it was under a comprehensive suggestion by imposed interpretation and rule. And even today there are fragmentary societies which (as in Australia and Papua) still seem to preserve much of the same cohesion and precritical amalgamation of psychological value and economic profit. Secondly, there is the Heroic Age, which helped to destroy the preindividual condition and which is itself only protoindividual; only crudely critical of the old order; childishly ignorant of its own weakness and faults; boastful, displayful, and un-self-conscious in any sense of objective awareness. It did not understand, it simply reacted. Thirdly, this second stage is succeeded by one of self-questioning and criticism that produces a desire for self-improvement, self-discipline, and finally self-reduction. Then, with struggle, this ascetic, midindividualistic condition passes into the fourth stage when individualism attains totality. At first, man's self-consciousness made him criticize only the tradition-bound group. Then it made him criticize himself. And now, in his complete self-confidence, he no longer sees any need either for boast and shame or for guilt and gratitude. He sees himself as neither condemning nor approving, as being the flawless mirror of the world that is as orderly (and so as repetitively aimless) as he is rational and inventively comprehending.

These four phases have therefore given rise to four distinctive types: (1) the nonpersonal group constituent, (2) the hero, (3) the ascetic, and (4) the humanic. And that, until the beginning of this century, seemed to be the culminant end of the story. At last, man had become a critically minded individual who attained complete objectivity. He saw the environment, and it was reality finally perceived with no shadow of illusion on it. He was completely detached from it. It was totally mechanical and he could handle it as he wished. He was self-sufficient.

Of course, as was mentioned at the end of the last chapter,[23] men very quickly discovered that this was wishful thinking. For from both ends came disquieting doubts. Advanced physics denied that objectivity had been attained or could be attained. Depth analysis in psychiatry showed that the findings of psychophysiology had been right. There was no reason to suppose that man could apprehend reality. His senses were biologically confined instruments of apprehension for finding food and a mate, for learning to avoid damaging physical contacts, and for finding those contacts that served his greatest drive—to survive physically. And there was much evidence to show that he had little or no desire to find anything else. What he called reality was a sensory construct that he wished to contact not for the sake of truth but for physical and racial satisfactions. Hence, after these facts had had the necessary generation-of-digestion time, the distress became psychologically acute. That the instrument was inadequate to comprehend an outer world that was really a construct and was made out of unknown data [that was]

5. The Postindividual

handled so as to meet the requirements of projected needs, symbols, and imagery—this alone was upsetting. The inadequacy of reason to control the deep demand-making nature was even more awkward.

The proto-psychoanalyst thought only of reducing conflict, allaying disturbance, and restoring to man his thwarted nature: thus to let him be, at least in erotic expression, an uninhibited animal in the hope that this would detension him. But this was really as mistaken as, and failed even sooner than, the Ignatian effort to restore the climate of dogmatic, persecutory faith and make men otherworldly ascetics. Still, this primary and primitive psychiatry of Freud did serve, as we have seen that the Ignatian system had served, to modulate this new crisis. It would not have been possible for a mechanistically minded medical profession, in spite of its failure to deal with mental trouble, to have accepted psychotherapy unless that therapy was presented as being, at base, not too great a departure from medicine's current assumptions. Freud accepted, with a devout and highly reassuring belief, the axioms of Darwinian evolution that man was a beast that had risen to intelligence by a combination of lucky breaks and ruthlessly cunning exploitations of those opportunities. By agreeing with these postulates, he was able to do something to reduce the pressure on the psyche. At least he saw that rational individualism could be no goal for man with his many-layered consciousness. And so he advocated the search for freedom, even though he thought that that liberty could only be license and atavistic behavior at the cost of the social restraints of a civilized society.

The idea, then, that self-conscious individualism is the end of the evolutionary process and that through this self-consciousness, at last, we attain to objective control of our environment and can direct our destiny, came to be doubted increasingly. And along with that idea, the popular notion of progress also fell into disrepute. Two world wars for establishing peace; an anachronistic economic revolution that spread not among artisans but among peasants and that in the name of human freedom removed the individual's rights, setting up ruthless tyrannies—such major events of this century convinced even the hurrying man in the streets that individualism was defeated and done for. Forecasting essays and utopianist science fiction saw man as a potential termite. Samuel Butler's neglected nineteenth-century *Erewhon*[24] became, to many mid-World-War-I forecasters, a prophecy to be heeded. And there were some psychiatrists who had troubled to inform themselves about modern anthropology and modern evolutionary theory. These men knew, therefore, that such works as Freud's *Totem and Taboo* were out of date because Freud had depended, for his anthropological conclusions, on Sir James Frazer's out-of-date *The Golden Bough*. And these men felt not only that individualism was passing but that it must now be brought to an end.

To cite one example, as late as 1955: The late Douglas M. Kelley, Professor of Criminology (the existence of such a chair is suggestive), who was the psychiatrist chosen for the Nazi trials at Nuremberg, told the Texas Medical Association at Fort Worth that Freudianism, in order to save a child from the psyche scarring of a strict (he meant castigatory) discipline, had let it grow up without self-control. Thus, immature childhood behavior has been carried on into later years by the young who are so left untrained. In adults, infantile conduct is psychopathic and destructive. The noradrenaline energy that projects all the infant's frustrations in rage, and must do so at that level if it is to survive and emerge into self-consciousness, has not given way (at the dawn of self-consciousness) to the adrenaline that turns the child's anger back onto itself. Hence the increase of crime and juvenile delinquency. Kelley had hoped to find a middle ground. He owned that if we use more punishment on the young, we shall only produce more neurotics. That, he held, is the price of the safety of the state which, as the Roman legalist put it, is the supreme law.

Kelley also warned that at present we have no clear line of action, no training rule; we have no way of knowing the exact amount of pain that will produce least neurosis and most obedience. However, he still does not make it clear that while punishment may produce only a servile neurosis in the docile and malleable, it can turn the vital into those "heroically" all too attractive rebels who create gangs, build up "parties," and become dictators. Faced with the problem of the individual and the community, Kelley could only see them and their rights in constant conflict. In short, the socio-historical outlook of this able psychopathologist, whose main study has been the criminal, is still that

5. The Postindividual

of the poetic British educationalist, Mathew Arnold, and his equally eminent contemporary, the eloquent biologist, T. H. Huxley. "Mad man or slave, must man be one?" cried Arnold. "Defy the cosmic process," was Huxley's antiphonal answer.

However, this dilemma, like most of these either/or impaling horns, has proved to have a way between its two deadly choices. "The mind of the Universe can count above two" used to be a cheerful warning of the still open-minded H. G. Wells when people gave way to premature and immature despair over this stalemate of either/or. And we can, with more precision, now trace this middle path.

First of all, ecology has shown us that the relationship between the life of the individual and the field in which he lives is more of a reciprocity than a competition. Secondly, it has been found that much of what was thought to be parasitism is, in fact, commensalism (lives living at and contributing to a common table) and symbiosis (two or more organisms forming a joint organism of the highest value to its constituents). Such facts show that even at animal level there can be a cooperation that does not sacrifice the constituent to the group. Thirdly, we can now see that the idea that man's society, in aiming at efficiency, must turn into a human termitary is a complete misapprehension.

The social insects differ diametrically from man. Termitary, anthill, and beehive all derive their completely specialized workers by atrophy, and in almost every case from atrophied females. Thus, by a reverse process, the insects have built up a society completely instinct-bound and thus incapable of enterprise, invention, or even change.[25]

All this is completely alien from human history and especially from man's present pass. The new concept of human evolution shows that man's structure is that of a creature of unique sensitiveness. Not only does he have a physique that is the reverse of that of the social insects—they have a hard outer husk (exoskeleton); man has an inner skeleton on which sensitive flesh and skin are stretched, a highly impressionable form that he shares with almost all the non-insect forms of life. But in this direction, he goes quite the farthest. Lacking scales, as do nearly all mammals, man disposes also of hair. He is born and remains mainly naked.

I - PSYCHOLOGICAL STORY OF SOCIAL HUMANS

This leads to the new psychophysical concept of the process of man's evolution. Not only is he not a callous creature, a pachyderm, a creature that is insensitive because of the thickness of its hide, but man's particular advance is precisely coordinate with and made possible by his becoming increasingly sensitive. And this sensitiveness is made possible and achieved by the force within him taking an increasing risk in unprotectedness—the risk of prolonging the period of helplessness so as to extend the age of teachability. All mammals are "fetalizings" of the reptilian form. That is, they carry on out into the afterbirth state an unspecialized, uncommitted structure that is abandoned by the reptile at hatching. This is possible because the mammal is specifically the creature which, because it takes care of its young after birth, can give it, in its fetal helplessness, the extrauterine protection without which it must perish. And, in turn but far more strikingly, man is the fetalization of the mammal. Yes, as Louis Bolk pointed out, man is the fetalization, even, of his primate cousin next below him on the ladder of life, the ape. The mammals gave to life the extended possibility of learning and of freedom that a comparatively lengthy and protected infancy can bestow. That power and desire to protect the helpless young and to extend the period of their irresponsible curiosity and learning has been extended even further by man. To man-the-mammal's capacity for the specific stage of infancy has been added man-the-human's endowment of specific childhood, an enormous enlargement of the time and area of education, the stage of paidomorphy.[26]

Such, we now know, is the biological history of man. He is master of the world because he knows more, understands better, and acts more purposively than any other beast. They are all better armed. He has won because he is better informed. And he knows more precisely because he has been cared for more, protected better, given greater freedom, and a longer span of time in which to learn. His group, far from enslaving him and atrophying him, loves him and is proud of his initiative. It encourages his adventures and departures. And it wishes to leave him at large, at least as long as he remains a child—even if at adolescence he is put into harness.

However, although these facts may be allowed (for they cannot be denied in the face of the evidence), they have yet to convince

5. The Postindividual

almost all statesmen and, as we have seen, the influential majority of psychiatrists and sociologists to whom the statesman increasingly defers. They are influenced not by biological history but by the brief individualistic phases of history—written history—the crises of Heroic, Ascetic, and Humanic Epochs when, during each of which, individualism is steadily diminishing suggestibility; during each of which governmental control is becoming increasingly difficult and thus increasingly coercive. Therefore, it is in this partial picture of man (man-the-rebel, man-the-deserter, man-the-cold-cynical-exploiter) that most historians and sociologists have thought there is to be found the realistic analysis of the human being. They have assumed that this is the true description of humanity, given by itself of itself through its catalogue of its actual behavior, its violent acts, and its dishonest boasts. Most of them would still say that man alternates between revolt into anarchy (against an order that has become a tyranny) and a reaction from that anarchy back into the rigid peace of despotism. The totalitarian state or the *liberum veto* of the individual; the loathing of oppression and the horror of chaos—these are the poles between which humankind has oscillated since it became individualized and yet remained incapable of asocial living. And the sophisticated Humanic man has given us a world that is no more secure or noble than the world that was given by the rule of either tyrant or inquisitor.

We have seen, however, that history is not such a pointless and weary shuttle. It is a spiral. In the first age of self-expression (the heroic, protoindividual), the very contraction of the focus of consciousness that made the hero revolt against the preindividual groups leads in turn to criticism not of society but of the self. Still further contraction of consciousness leads again to criticism of the ascetic, self-criticizing society. Now, without the shame–fear of the protoindividual or the guilt–fear of the midindividual, man's totally individualized consciousness can consider, with dispassionate detachment, both its record and its origins. Hence, humanism, the capacity to choose eclectically and combine styles to suit a widely tolerant taste, is followed by humanitarianism, the interest in human beings regardless of the type to which they may belong. So extensive was this enquiry that Humanic man was able, first, to conceive of his animal origin and kinship and, next, recognizing his unique extension up from and beyond any animal condition, he was able to see that *he* was unique. And thirdly, he was able to perceive that the power by which that uniqueness was achieved lay and lies in a continual extension, first of infancy and then of childhood.

We have seen, further, that the final contraction of consciousness, which produced the total individual striving as never before for objectivity, leads to the knowledge of his own temporarily repressed and concealed nonindividual nature.

When man first conceived of himself as being biologically an animal, evolutionary doctrine held that he must have survived by violence and cunning. But now it has switched to the point of view that man survives, is supreme, and advances because he is, by his prolonged infancy and childhood, preserved in his unprecedented sensitiveness and awareness. And so it has been with psychiatry. Psychiatrists, too, began by thinking that the deep, submerged consciousness was merely a subconscious—a residue of frustrated revenges and brooding revolts. In turn, psychiatry today has found that there is also a superconscious of unspent creativity awaiting release. Man's energies, as we shall see in Section II, Chapters 1 and 2, are *pure* energies. That is, they are neutral. Given release they bud; met with repression the bud turns into a thorn.

We can see, then, the vast hope and acute risk with which man today is confronted. We are the first generation of self-conscious humankind to become conscious of the nonself-conscious [Ed. note: meaning, "our transpersonal mind," as Heard later writes]. And we can see that totalistic individualism is finished. The huge cycle that extended from the rise of the protoindividual, out of the preindividualistic group, to the total individual, has now completed that loop of the spiral. We are in the Postindividual Age and world.

What does this mean? First, it means the end of the apparent conflict between the rights of the constituent and the survival of the group. We are symbiots, linked by our common preterconscious. Secondly, it means that we can understand and command creativity through the amalgamation of integral thought (see Glossary) with analytical thought. Thirdly, it means that our interactions with our fellows need no longer be based on violence and competition but on

5. The Postindividual

cooperation. For all fear sterilizes creative thought, and inspiration is possible and only possible when there is mutual understanding and appreciation.

That is not to say, however, that this fifth stage of man is easy. This age has come upon us swiftly, and it is also demanding of us a step greater than the one from the Heroic to the Ascetic, or from the Ascetic to the Humanic. For these steps called only for an increase in individual self-consciousness, an intensification of self-awareness. Our age has to surrender its isolation and experience a vast dilation. For some four thousand years, man has been learning to live increasingly and more powerfully in himself. Now the process must go onto the other tack of the spiral. The huge impersonal nonindividual force that he has sighted, lying back of him and out of which he emerges like a lonely crystallization of the great flux, he now finds mounting up in him from time to time, and momentarily reintegrating him with himself. Suddenness characterizes this experience, and it is revolutionary, mutational. Therefore, the term *Leptoid* (suggested by the Greek word *lepsis*, which means "the leap") has been chosen to describe or at least to distinguish it. [Ed. note: The English translation of the Greek word *lepsis* that most closely approximates Heard's intended meaning of "leap" is "to seize" in the sense of taking hold, i.e., taking hold of the next stage of humankind's evolution.]

Man, in his first age, when his coconscious society lost its capacity to assimilate new data, became imprisoned and buried in the tribal system. He became arrested at a puerile level.[27] In his second stage of protoindividual protest, he became paranoid when utterly frustrated. In his third stage of midindividual self-disgust, his mental danger was schizophrenia. In his fourth stage of total individualism, his mental risk was manic-depressive insanity.

But surely in this, his fifth stage, which man has now reached, the specific symptom of collapse would be that failure of nerve, that sense of being at his tether's end, that melancholy out of which he cries "*vanitas vanitatum*." This has been the indicative terminative disease of earlier societies and civilizations. The West's only attempt at a culture that was coterminous with an administrative civilization, the Hellenic Roman, did sink into such a decline. Its failure of nerve was shown not only in corruption of its administration, increasing inadequacy of its economy and weakness of its political integration, but also in a degeneracy of its crafts, sciences, and arts. Senile paralysis was evident long before the barbarians took over. But with our age, this certainly is not so. The age of Humanic man has passed, and his picture of a world united by persons of good sense and bright reason certainly seems, at best, pathetically premature. But although our confusions are terrific, they are not those of liquidation and decay, but rather of explosion and overabundance. Earlier civilizations were daunted by scarcity; we are embarrassed by surfeit. The anarchy of nationalism and the immorality and inhumanity of fanatic ideologies would seem to be enough to make the creative mind withdraw and abstain. But as a matter of fact, applied research and pure research, experiment, exploration, discovery, and invention have never, in the world's best times of the past or under humanism's most generous patronage, approached the present pitch. The cultures of the past died of a spiritual pernicious anemia. The peril of the present is a risk of death by convulsions. The specific crisis of this fifth epoch of man, postindividual humanity, is caused by the release of power that is too great to be handled by a frame of meaning and application that was devised to be run by, to express, and to deploy far smaller resources.

We can see this in four areas. Economically, we are aware of the problem as we pass from an economy of scarcity, wherein saving was a primary need, to one of plenty when spending power must prevent glut (62). Politically, we are aroused by the fact that speed of communications and range of striking power have made frontiers more absurd than walled cities and have made defense an impossibility. And our emotions, made only more suspicious by this involuntary impaction, still cling to our fatally anachronistic limits, from which foci we would exercise sovran (that is to say, anarchic) power. Religiously, the power of insight into other systems of devotion alien from ours has weakened our assurance of our own rightness. Psychologically, as we discover our other levels of consciousness, the importance that we have attached to our personality grows less. And all these erosions of our convictions are because of our knowledge, and power derived from that knowledge, which continues to advance like a tide, flooding the locks, sluices, and harbors of our old beliefs.

5. The Postindividual

Ours is assuredly a world not of tired melancholy but of almost frantic stimulation—in a word, a Leptoid age. And we are aware of our precarious disbalance: of our persistent and ever-increasing production of power and our inadequacy of purpose; of our critical analytic ability and our creative paucity; of our triumphantly efficient technical education and our ineffective, irrelevant education for values, for meaning, for the training of the will, the lifting of the heart, and the illumination of the mind; of the boredom that haunts our extending leisure and the futility of our recreation. No wonder we have at least one in ten who is in acute mental distress. No wonder that there is hardly one of us out of a thousand who is able to diagnose the situation in contemporary terms, still less who is able to propose an education, a training, a psychophysical praxis whereby we may become adequate to handle our powers; whereby we may be able to release ourselves in creative action and be capable of making those field associations with others that will allow us to explicate the evolutionary pressures that today may otherwise drive us toward racial destruction.

Such then, in the briefest possible terms, would seem to be the outline of man's history as a psychologically driven creature; that is to say, as a unique animal which—because he has (instead of instincts) an unequaled teachability—develops first by a social heredity a coordinate series of developing reactions, which are satisfying, at least economically, to the constituent and the group. When that system has hardened and man has broken out of it, he proceeds to educate himself, first by exploring the outer world and testing the old assumptions by new personal experiences. Next, by questioning himself and testing his own limits. Later he attempts a two-sided exploration, trying to gain a complete objectivity toward the external and the internal worlds, toward the seen universe and toward himself as its seer. This, the humanic education, critical and analytic in its method, leads man to learn that objectivity is impossible because it is a misapprehension of himself and of the universe. Man, therefore, attains a new clarity of vision in regard to his problem of education. Recognizing self-consciously his nonself-conscious, he realizes why till now the individual has been able to gain physical power but not to alter his character and consciousness. Henceforward, he may hope to do even this and so, having become conscious himself of his station and purpose, take part, by his self-education, in the evolutionary process that has produced him.

Section II

THE PERSONAL PSYCHOLOGICAL STORY OF HUMANS

(*The Five Ordeals*)

1. The Ordeal of Birth and Infancy and Its Specific Mental Breakdown (*The trauma of birth*)

In Section I, we have attempted to show that the human story is one of progress, of man's advance; that there is unmistakable evidence that man has risen to his supremacy through his capacity to remain sensitive and so teachable; that he can be developmentally changed because he remains, for so long, an impressionable child; and that this evidence is not canceled out by his historic behavior. Man has advanced by understanding, by his increasing capacity for being taught, and that advance has been in a spiral. When, at the close of the first culture (the Preindividual Epoch), the interpretations and explanations that had once faced and fitted all of the known facts grew too rigid to allow the acceptance of any new data, man was bound to break out, to shatter the suffocating husk of tradition, and explore the outer world. And this reaction, when it became excessive, provoked the complementary counterreaction. Man tried to reimpose order on the new data that he was now confronting.

Chief among these new facts, he discovered himself to be confronting a lawful, powerful, but apparently unfriendly Nature on the outside and strange irrational passions within himself. This new self-conscious knowledge in turn led to a further self-conscious examination of Nature. Finally, this objective-subjective dualism (wherein power increases but self-control decreases) is transcended by insight into the whole problem of the seer and the seen.

Henceforward, man may hope to gain a knowledge of his *total* nature and by doing so achieve a total education. This, as we have said, will mean that evolution is continued consciously by a creature made conscious in order that the process may now be intentionally explicated.

But if this is so, if such a further development is to be possible, then the contemporary individual must now be a creature such as can be capable of this conscious educational-athletic training. For the vast processes of life may miscarry; the greatness of a promise does not guarantee its fulfillment. And even if the process that has brought man so far, and built his endowment so firmly into his nature, is not to be frustrated, it may be postponed. In the past, great insights that seemed about to dawn over all humankind were not accepted at once. The seed that appeared to be due to sprout immediately lay dormant through century-long winters of brutal stupidity. For example, there was the failure of the Hellenic Roman world to understand the mathematics of Archimedes (this was not to be grasped until the nineteenth century) and the centuries-long delay of the Chinese in accepting the Confucian teaching.

But is there any evidence that man today, the present personal self, is a creature who is equal to this opportunity; that he is a being of material that is adequate to be fashioned by the training which is now due and possible? The tempering processes that turn iron into steel cannot turn clay into knives, nor can the best teaching make a mandrill into a mathematician. There must be a substance suitable for the intended shape.

It is the discovery that the individual today is not only prepared for such a training but that without such a training he must go to

1. The Ordeal of Birth

pieces—and indeed *is* going to pieces—that gives such strong confirmation to the psychological interpretation of history. It may be said that all our history is vitiated by selection. Indeed, it is often adduced as being a reason for maintaining that human history shows no pattern or process. Most historians believe that we do not and cannot accurately survey the true human record [because] (1) all that has survived of the past are the fragments that a few exceptional persons chose, for their own reasons, to record; and (2) these fragments are further selected and distorted by our attempts to interpret them, not even in terms of the meaning that they may have held for those who recorded them, but in terms of the particular meaning that we who study them wish to give them (92).

Much the same argument was used against those who, in the mid-nineteenth century, were trying to establish the fact of physical evolution. The record, it was maintained, was so piecemeal that the linkages it suggested could be dismissed as being hopeful leaps. Then the connection between phylogeny and ontogeny was detected. The fact that the individual fetus can be seen to recapitulate the life of the vertebrate phylum—the evolution of the backboned animals—made embryology a vital adjunct of paleontology. The fossil record of the phylum's history (phylogeny) could be confirmed and elucidated by actual physiological study of the individual embryo's development: that is, by ontogeny. Of necessity, however, this dealt only with the physical development. Although, as we shall see later, the child's growth in the womb is not merely recapitulatory; it is prophetic. During the fetal months in the womb, the brain of the embryo is much larger in proportion to the rest of the physique than it ever is after birth. This would seem to indicate that the human brain has yet to reach its full development.

However, what is of immediate and decisive importance, in helping us to decide whether human history is a rapid extension of evolution and whether it shows evidence of evolution and advance by social heredity, is the application of the physiological discovery of the correlation between the life of the race and the growth of the fetus. For this lends psychological insight into human progress.

G. Stanley Hall and Arnold Gesell, Cyril Burt in Britain, and a number of child psychologists in other countries have now made it sufficiently clear that just as our physiological evolution is sketched out in our fetal development, in our growth up to birth, so does the infant, after birth, recapitulate the coconscious, Preindividual Age of humanity (see Introduction). In some thirty months, it relives that whole stage of man's development which, although it lasted some four hundred thousand years, was nevertheless a vast acceleration over the speed of the evolutionary process by which man emerged out of animalhood. This acceleration resulted from social heredity taking the place of physical heredity.

Today, these findings seem to have been largely accepted by child psychologists as being an illuminating insight into child behavior. But unfortunately, owing to the lack of psychologically interpreted history, psychologists in general have not extended this interpretation to the post-infant stages of the individual's life. And, conversely, neither have social historians availed themselves of this master clue for understanding history.

Stanley Hall, Burt, and their fellow discoverers were aware, as are all educated men, that man had gone through a prehistoric phase during which he was neither a group-animal nor a self-conscious individual. These child psychologists, therefore, were able to recognize that this stage of preindividual consciousness was being recapitulated by the infant. As the infant was symbiotic with the mother, so prehistoric man had been symbiotically coconscious with his group. But both the specialty of their study (which was mainly concerned with the vastly important first couple of years) and their unawareness of the growth of protohistoric studies prevented them from seeking in the next stage above infancy—that is, in childhood proper—the child's résumé of the protohistoric (the Heroic Age), which succeeded the prehistoric. Still less could these experts in the growth of the individual child-mind be expected to detect, in the successive stages of personal development, recapitulations of historic man's successive epochs: the Ascetic and the Humanic, the midindividual and the total individual, as did Gesell.

Nevertheless, once their first correlation was made, the succeeding three (and indeed, as we shall see, the fourth) fall into place. The psychological understanding of human history (as being a spiral shift of human consciousness from the coconscious to extreme self-

1. The Ordeal of Birth

consciousness and so on to a self-consciously coconscious condition) can be greatly clarified and made even more convincing by our being able to trace these shifts in the individual life. And we can then see (*a*) how, by a series of crises, the individual emerges into fuller consciousness until he is completely contemporary (that is, he reaches the present Leptoid stage); and (*b*) he is thus ready to be recruited and fashioned into the new type.

The Gesell team (Arnold Gesell, Frances Ilg, and Louise Ames) in 1956 added a new study, *Youth: The Years from Ten to Sixteen* (30), to their first two parent-shaking books, *Infant and Child in the Culture of Today* (31), and *The Child from Five to Ten* (32). This means that the third epoch of the individual's history is now recognized as being a natural growth phase and that sooner or later historians will have to accept this recapitulatory contribution to our understanding of the record of historic and prehistoric man (homo loquens).

In this and the next four chapters, we shall then outline the five stages of birth and infancy, childhood, adolescence, first maturity, and second maturity through which the individual passes; and we shall examine the stresses endured, the damages sustained, the palliatives that are offered, and the levels attained.

That birth is a challenge for a human being has been recognized today. Owing to the exceptional development of the head in man (the mammal with the hypertrophied brain), delivery would, in any case, present difficulties that the smaller-brained mammals escape. And today, certainly, the self-consciousness of the mother greatly increases the trouble. Having foresight, she dreads pain; and her fear provokes the very contractions that cramp and cause the agony of labor as the voluntary muscles try to hold back the action of the involuntary delivery muscles.[28] Further, the woman ... dreads throwing herself, without inhibition, into the indecent abandonment that is necessary for a powerfully effective delivery. Still further, our elevation of the pleasure/pain principle to the position of being the final criterion of worth misleads the mother. The naturalistic theory, that every organism inevitably seeks comfort and shuns disturbance, makes travail appear to be the most morbid of experiences—something to be avoided with anesthetic, something that cannot be transmuted and transcended.

II - PERSONAL PSYCHOLOGICAL STORY OF HUMANS

The child, therefore, experiences a very bad passage, and even when it escapes physical damage it is apparently general for most children to show marks of this distressing experience.[29] Nor does the evidence for this rest solely on psychiatrists' deductions from child behavior and the interpretation of hypnotically raised regression memories of experiences that are probably birth emotions. Isaac Shour of the University of Illinois College of Dentistry reported, in the spring of 1937, the discovery of growth rings in human teeth and that such rings show the incidence of glandular disturbances and other illnesses. Outstanding is the ring called the neonatal ring that marks the stress of birth.[30] Many child psychiatrists are inclined to regard this traumatic shock as being one of the main sources of such psychosomatic complaints as asthma.

The psychological effect of so severe an introduction to the outer world is, to some degree or other, to provoke and sustain a profound subconscious desire to be able to return to a condition previous to this stress and the terror that it has produced. For this terror, as long as it cannot be raised to consciousness, may remain unresolved and so possess an undiminished power to check initiative and to create fear. The child, therefore, strives not to grow but to return to the womb. As Margaret Ribble (71) has pointed out, the frightened infant, instead of breathing, may actually go back to womb lung reflexes, refusing to fill the lung with air and forcing the emptied lung down on the diaphragm. This is the reflex whereby, in the prenatal state, the fetus helped to draw in more oxygenated blood through the umbilical cord, but which now in the postnatal state can only result in suffocation. Dynamic tender loving care; much playing with the infant; the tickling that results in laughter, which increases the sugar in the blood and so feeds the growing brain; the rousing of the baby to react with the exercise, particularly, of its chief member of exploration and understanding, the mouth: all these will bring the child through this crisis. Otherwise it may remain arrested. As Ribble has also pointed out, unless the child is permitted constant sucking-manipulation with its mouth, the growth of the muscles round the head, which are brought into play by the exercise of the jaws, may be defective; brain growth may be [impaired] and, even more easily, too little use of the mouth may

1. The Ordeal of Birth

lead to [impaired] speech. Then, too, when the child reaches the babbling stage and vocalizes for the sheer love of it, this vast range of sounds must be encouraged and allowed to pour, like a melt of metal, into the casts of specific language. If this tide is not taken there may be permanent [developmental delays].

Birth, therefore, is man's first ordeal. And in this generation, we have certainly come to rate highly (indeed, in a way that earlier scientific periods would have thought absurd) the perils and possibilities of this initial test. Yet this high rating has been a faulty one, not because the beginning of life is not of intense importance but because of the overcompensatory emphasis that has been given to the birth experience and has made us tend to believe that this is the *one* significant ordeal; and that if it were properly handled, the rest of the life process would fall into place and flow as an untroubled sequence.

This, however, is not so. For man has to face not one but five ordeals. If we rid the injured child mind of the trauma of birth, we shall do it harm, not good, should our intention be no more than to return it to freedom from conflict. Now that we can correlate our individual development with that of the race, we see that there were some societies that managed to adjust to change of environment and the increasing complexity of their culture without intensifying the quality of their consciousness. Such seems to have been the Indus civilization. In a lesser degree, this has befallen the Australian and Papuan premechanical cultures.

The task, then, of facing the first ordeal is now seen to be doubly difficult. Today the newborn child emerging from the pre-personal, unseparated life of the womb still feels, under the stress of the alien situation, two conflicting drives. One is to stop this differentiation by elaborating a web of dependency ties with the mother (if not to behave so recessionally as to reattempt fetal breathing) and reestablish an external womb situation: the situation of the ankylosed tribe whose inflexible tradition can now have no place for enterprise. The other drive is a protest and defiance that regards any thwarting of its impulses as an outrage: the attitude of the protoindividual hero who regarded the traditional tribe not as a matrix from which to rise but as a prison to be wrecked. Hence, at the beginning of our self-consciousness lies the fissure of man into conservative-reactionary and rebel-revolutionary. Therefore, the task of human education today must start at this base by helping the infant to balance these conflicting drives and to create a comprehending initiative, an enterprise which, by understanding, renders the traditional cohesion into a liquid asset and interprets it as contemporary conservation of wholeness.

The growing infant consciousness has to be led along a knife-edge path. As we have seen, laxness may be as fatal as strictness. Quietude can prove to be as dangerous as overstimulation. But now we know that the child is recapitulating the first human crisis, we can determine the amalgam of encouragement and challenge that it needs to temper its mind and make it capable of agreed initiative, of enterprise blended with communication, of adjustment with originality.

At this stage, when his racial infancy began to pass into the childhood of the race, when the challenge of further intensification of consciousness confronted him, man became divided and began to follow two divergent paths. The reaction of the primary group was to elaborate further and make the social pattern more explicit and more complex. Everyone should have particular parts to play and functions to perform, but no one should extemporize or create a solo air. This led to the heroic revolt in which all orchestration of a comprehensive theme was temporarily lost in a bedlam of soloists, each trying to drown out the rest.

Today we can see that the child need not and must not be faced with the choice of madman or slave. But the middle way is even harder. For it leads to an advance into an ever more consciously reciprocal symbiosis with the parents, with the sibs, with the group. And there is no clearer evidence—that progress through learning by conducive, tempered challenge is the inherent drive in man—than the discovery that, whereas premature exposure to unexplained contradiction can be fatal, conversely the screening and protection from all enigmas and surprises can arrest the child in an infantile state (85). Even dogs, when they are given a completely contained and sheltered early life, do not emerge into full growth with the scarless curiosity of the puppy. On the contrary, they show suspicion, alarm,

1. The Ordeal of Birth

and resentment at every unfamiliar object. Most psychologists have reacted against the careless and unkind handling of young [children] in early life, which leaves scars of fear and resentment. Consequently, most of them have assumed that every organism longs for rest and quiet because its entire behavior is directed toward preserving its stability. But as Thompson and Melzack point out (85), this assumption has proved to be untrue. No creature can live normally or fully if it is not challenged. Without challenge not only will it never grow up, but it will sink to the state of being a febrile alarmist that is capable even of rest only in a completely artificial, nonstimulating environment.

Today, then, the fissure of consciousness that took place historically must be healed in the individual child. He must be shown and directed onto the midpath that combines the enterprise of the hero with the intuitive, traditional wisdom of the tribe. He must leave the womb and exchange the mother love, to which he needed only be receptively passive, for a relationship of an increasing give and take. He can do this, and thus meet the demands of his growing nature, if encouragement is always given with every challenge. For encouragement makes it possible for him to regard failure as being a negative experiment, not frustration: not the closure of an answer but the opening *through* and *of* a new question.

If, however, the birth trauma has been severe, then it would seem that only the regressionally recaptured and relived experience can set him free. Experiments in that direction (by hypnosis and other methods of depth analysis) are, we know, being conducted now.[31] Increasingly, it is being proposed that no person can be considered to be free of deforming subconscious maladjustment who has suffered damage at that depth and not had the damage remedied and canceled by its having been raised to consciousness. No doubt this would prove to be valuably ameliorative.

Nevertheless, we must remember that the undertaking is both more worthwhile and also more difficult than psychoanalysis has, up to the present, conceived. For we are no longer able to think of such treatment as being solely to aid the patient to adjust to and consent to society. He must be prepared to contribute a skilled release to an inherent nature that insists on growing. And this nature insists on growing in a way that not only combines the art of communication with the passion for exploration (and so remedies our social birth trauma that still tries to make us choose between being a rebel-hero or a submissive ascetic) but also, by its growth, leads him as a person toward a new threshold with its new challenge: the offer to become a new type of character.

In the third section of this book we shall see how thorough such a rebirth procedure has been. And in the Epilogue some suggestions will be made as to how such a procedure might be applied today. Meanwhile, one hopeful fact may be noted before we pass on to Chapter 2 of this Section II. Apparently, psychologically speaking, it is never too late to mend. In the physical growth of the fetus in the womb, a failure to advance, a delayed or deviant step in the growth process cannot be remedied. Charles R. Stockard has pointed out that ten minutes' chilling of an embryo results, generally, in an irremediable malformation. This does not seem to be so with psychological growth. It is possible to penetrate down into the depths, thence to regress the consciousness to where the blockage took place and so, reliving the event and making the sunken consciousness loose its paralyzing grip on the evil memory, start the total person anew.

But, we must repeat, that totality of consciousness cannot be won by only one delivery-experience, from the trauma of birth. There are four others. And the procedures whereby this fivefold freedom is won and crowned by the fifth and culminant freedom are more profound and transforming than, at present, even our most extensive psychotherapies envisage.

2. The Ordeal of Childhood and Its Specific Mental Breakdown (*Dementia praecox becoming paranoia*)

We now reach the second stage of the personal psychological story of humanity. The individual has recapitulated humankind's first crisis. For better or for worse, the process has gone through its primary stage. Since growth—the manifestation of the life process—waits for no man, all men must become increasingly implicated or increasingly explicated. Man has not yet lived well but he might have lived worse. He has certainly lived better than any other animal. None of his forms has degenerated into beasthood. And only a small minority of humans have chosen a life wherein tradition is rigid and initiative is practically impossible, such as the Australian Aboriginal people, whose tribal law has swallowed enterprise.

The Heroic Age was wasteful and overexuberant, but it was not valueless in itself. Its epic art forms were unique and of high quality. For in them the hero was constantly asking, with passionate emphasis, this question: "Why is the courage of the heroic will not enough?" Through its expression of energy and initiative, it gave drive to the ages that were to succeed it. The individual, then, as he leaves infancy (mother and child symbiosis) and enters childhood proper, is generally viable, albeit [sometimes] considerably distorted, thwarted, resentful, and unhappy. Though, like the leaning tower of Pisa, he is out of plumb because of poorly laid foundations, the subsidence is not so severe that he cannot, in most cases and by some compensatory if costly adjustment, be prevented from collapsing. Nevertheless, far too often total ruin does take place; and even where it does not, flaws, faultings, and cleavages continue to cause stresses which may, if not at this stage, later provoke disaster. The specific child has won to the station of its age group, to the elevation that permits the growing mind to confront a far wider purview than the strictly mediated environment of the nursery.

But here we need to ask, "How is this done?" The view of most embryologists and paleoanthropologists does not allow any firmly based hope about this further venture of man, once he takes leave of his station as an animal. The common summary that closes any thorough account of the fetus' life in the womb is that at birth we took leave of (or were abandoned by) the marvelous and inherent mastery which, up to that point, had directed and shaped our amazing development. Maybe a few modern pediatricians would allow a small extension of that happy and deft intuitiveness after birth, for that dozen or score of months during which a perfect mother relationship can give the infant an enlargement of the womb's protective response to its growing demands and to which it can instinctively respond and grow. Thereafter, we are humans. We are now creatures who have abandoned intuitive understanding—spontaneous interior knowledge—for vocal communication (that conveys symbolic information) and for tentative exploration of an outer world. From thence on, man's social heredity has carried and will carry him on a warp of tradition into which the painful shuttle of experience will be continually thrusting threads of new knowledge across the web.

In his "Fossil Man and Human Evolution," Loren Eiseley (21), Professor of Anthropology at the University of Pennsylvania, has pointed out—and he is quoting the long-accepted judgment of Leonard Sillman—that "no other species comes into the world with so few fixed reactions for survival, knowing less, inherently, about how to

2. The Ordeal of Childhood

maintain itself" as does man. It is this new brain (denuded of precise, instinctive responses, growing in a curious, mighty spurt during the first few months after birth) that has created man and set him off from his nearest relative.

The factor that was overlooked by Charles Darwin and his critic and co-discoverer of natural selection, A. R. Wallace, was the decisive part played by social heredity in the ascent of man. This second invisible environment replaced man's lost instinctive adjustments. Institutions could take the place of instincts because of the ability of all men to use language—the one great socializing instrument.

Such a viewpoint is hopeful. Speed and intention—and a rapid progress in intelligence—are now considered to be present in the evolutionary process at its growing point, man. But unfortunately this point of view, where it is accepted, is taken to mean that man must expect no help from his nature. Indeed, progress was possible (so runs the argument) solely because man had already been stripped of his instincts. If his prehuman drives remain in him, they will bar his ascent and he must fight them, reduce them, nullify them.

Now it is clear that if the word instinct is used with exactitude—that is, as signifying behavior that is not dependent on the individual's past experience nor his interests but which serves the needs of the species—then it is true that man has no such inbuilt patterns of conduct. But he certainly is subject to innate drives to precipitate action, which distort his judgment and overwhelm his reason and which, combined with his intelligence, can make him the most dangerous of animals. These drives are glandular; and that pair of ductless glands whose hormone secretions most disturb understanding and dislocate society is far away from the brain's controls. These twin glands of conflict, of stress, are the suprarenals that drive the animal to self-forgetful rage: useful for the beast, essential for the carnivore (see below), but fatal to one who must survive by taking thought. True, the brain has grown marvelously in its power of thought and of that worldwide vocalized thought, language. But of what use is this if the emotions (the movers to action) are violent, divisive, anarchic? Then intelligence only sharpens the knife with which humanity cuts its own throat.

II - PERSONAL PSYCHOLOGICAL STORY OF HUMANS

Suppose that evolution has simply provided us with a brain that can think up new schemes for mastering and upsetting the environment; suppose that evolution has given us a speech center that can shape only slogans. And suppose that those slogans were used to make one mass of men (who have no quarrel with others) take up arms and rush to destroy all those who will not submit to their masters. Then, of course, a big brain, because it is a social instrument, is a social disaster; it is society's self-produced destruction. Even if the peace of terror and the fear of annihilation keep humankind on the brink of extinction, at best man must always live in interior conflict, "willing to wound but yet afraid to strike"; fearing to fire but longing to end the intolerable tension; hating his Leviathan state-master but dreading that if the despot were dethroned, he, the little man, might in the scramble for the loot be trampled underfoot by those in the stampeding mob who were tougher than himself.

Surely, it was a mere freak of the tongue that gave him speech. It gave him a premature power: the power of the spell, the intricate snares of the lie with which he could trap those of his fellows who could avoid all other ginns and lures. From pious fraud to election promises, from investment circulars to patent medicines, the word has proved to be the chief weapon of the deceitful seeker after power, and the chief peril of society. At best there must always be in man an increasing interior conflict between what he perceives and what it is wise to say; between what he knows and how this knowledge can be fitted in with the current pattern, the going concern.

Such, certainly, would be our insoluble dilemma if it were true that only man's brain had grown and that his tongue had become his chief means to power. But the full truth is far more hopeful. We have seen that if man's glandular system is still such as can operate only in the conditions of a prehuman world, then all that his reason can do will be to rationalize what his endocrine drives direct; all his unprecedented intelligence will submit to make him only an unprecedentedly beastly animal. But if we examine our endocrine (ductless gland) system, we shall find two pieces of evidence that are as striking as the growth of the human brain, and complement that growth of intelligence with an equal growth in the emotions.

2. The Ordeal of Childhood

The first has to do with the endocrine balance in the present human body. The second, and even more important, deals with the changes that go on in the glands of stress (the suprarenals) during the growth of the present individual. In the first place, it is clear that man's endocrine balance has been modified as much in favor of the reasonable life of sustained cooperative effort toward long-distance goals as his brain has been turned into the path-maker toward those goals and the lens through which he sees them. Compare the endocrine balance of a tiger with that of a man. In the tiger's case, the suprarenals (the energizers for attack) are gross, and the thyroid, the gland of sustained effort, is small. But with man this disbalance is reversed: small suprarenals and big thyroid is man's endocrine setup.

Indeed, glandular research has now led to our being able to find a similar division that distinguishes all the peaceful animals from those who assault and destroy, the carnivores. J. Reusch (the work is reported by W. S. von Euler of Sweden), working on the adrenal glands of African wild animals, found that the aggressive beasts (the lion and others) had a high amount not of adrenaline but of that noradrenaline that (see below) is the quintessence of the rage-creating glandular component, while in the glands of the animals that survived through flight there was found a preponderance of adrenaline. Von Euler had already discovered that this changeover (from a preponderance of adrenaline to a preponderance of noradrenaline) in the secretion of the suprarenal medulla (the core or pith of the gland) could be brought about by stimulating different parts of the hypothalamus, the old brain, the center of the emotional drives. And Nobel-prizeman W. R. Hess of Zurich has mapped two areas in the hypothalamus, one of which, when stimulated in animals, produced rage while the other produced flight. From this glandular evidence, we see that it is the hypothalamus, the seat of the emotions, that triggers the animal organism either to flight or fight. Also, it is clear that even in animals—at least in mammals—there is the possibility of choice, for the two centers that direct attack or escape are present also in them. But animals that live by aggression and those that survive by flight are slanted either to rage or fear by their gland balance in favor of the noradrenaline of fury or the adrenaline of panic.

II - PERSONAL PSYCHOLOGICAL STORY OF HUMANS

This is important. But even more important for our understanding of our human condition and process of development is the further research into this suprarenal balance in man himself. From the work of D. H. Funkenstein (Director of Clinical Psychiatry at Boston Psychopathic Hospital), H. G. Wolff (at New York Hospital), Bernt Hokfelt, and G. B. West, it is now clear (28) that the small child's first reaction to thwarting is rage and that that rage reaction can be correlated with the particular secretion then found in the core—medulla—of the child's suprarenals. This secretion, at that age, has more noradrenaline than adrenaline. In later childhood, and from the influence of its group upon it, the child not only learns to blame itself for mistakes, with the resulting appearance of anxiety, shame, and finally of guilt, but at the same time this older child's gland secretion alters. It is at this age that adrenaline becomes the main secretion in the core of its suprarenals. Further evidence of this important correlation comes from the study of the insane. Those who suffer from paranoia regress to childish behavior. And it is in paranoics that the suprarenals are found to be secreting excessive amount of noradrenaline. Conversely, there is a preponderance of adrenaline in the suprarenal secretions of those patients with acute anxiety and the guilt sense that drives them to the hopeless attitude of the schizophrenic.

Further, the results with (*a*) the mood-changing drugs (for example, Librium) have shown that violent carnivores such as the lynx and the leopard can be reverted to the caress-seeking friendliness of a kitten as long as the drug is active in them; while (*b*) the same results have been achieved by E.S.B., electrical stimulation of specific, pinpointed brain areas.

This is the second piece of evidence that makes us have hope of man because of (and not in spite of) his glandular structure, his basic emotional drives. Here we have evidence to indicate that man is, and has been since he was man, evolving not only intellectually but emotionally. Here we can obtain the physiological data that confirm the meaning of man's past history: that it is a spiral development of consciousness up from the preindividual who is coconscious with his fellows, through the protoindividual of the Heroic Age, on through the midindividualism of the Ascetic Epoch, and up to the total

2. The Ordeal of Childhood

individualism of the Humanic Period. And, on the other hand, these physiological data, just because they are physiological, indicate most clearly the fact that each of us today recapitulates, after birth, man's history since he became the creature with the biggest brain, the needlessly large mind. Our glandular development can now be seen to indicate, in at least three of our five stages (childhood, adolescence, and first maturity), the way in which the life within us urges us to grow emotionally to a psychophysical competence that is equal to our intelligence.

It was mentioned above that even the glands of conflict are now shown to be subject to evolutionary development. The secretion which is at first predominantly noradrenaline, a secretion making for instant, unreflective reaction, attack, protest, does become as we grow up and begin to leave childhood for adolescence, predominantly adrenaline. This adrenaline makes not for fight but for flight. Fear comes in. Fear is, of course, intuitive misgiving, doubt of oneself. The anger that first flashed out against others is now painfully held. It turns against the self, and the longer it is held, the stronger grows the feeling of resentment at one's own foolishness in getting oneself into such a fix. It may be assumed that during these times of stress there grows, in the mind, a capacity to examine its past actions and their proved inadequacy. The gland of sustained effort (the thyroid) may be coming into action. Certainly trapped men, seemingly cut off by their pursuers, have time and again, under such stress, shown inspired ingenuity in effecting an escape.

So to the structure of man another floor is added. On the ground floor of simple protest and defensive attack against another molesting species (even among peaceful animals and clearly among humankind), there has been built a second story, the rapid and increasingly skilled retreat from assault. And this fear is the beginning of wisdom, for it makes the creature judge itself, estimate its deficiencies, and criticize its stupidity and rashness. Then on this second story, man has reared his third: wariness, the foresight of understanding avoidance.

This third addition has negatively been called apprehension and anxiety. But wariness is the better word. *Beware* need not be a command to flee. Rather it means be awake and advance with circumspection. Constant awareness, the constant vigilance that is the price of freedom is no doubt fatiguing. Only a creature that is largely and rightly thyroid-energized (as Hans Selye [77] puts it) can sustain such steady exertion. Further, only a creature that can put implicit trust in its fellows can have those releases from being on watch without which the appetite for constant circumspect investigation sours into that indigestion of the mind and body that we call anxiety or *angst*. Hence the Renaissance man (called here by the wider title, Humanic man), because he was at the apex of individualism, the extreme of self-consciousness, could not sustain his keen awareness as a constantly growing critical curiosity. So he fell into anxiety: that *angst* which, as it has been pointed out, marks and mars all the active countenances rendered by that superartist-genii of the conflicts, Michelangelo.

So important are these glandular discoveries and their confirmation of man's socio-racial evolution and individual growth development that here (where these new endocrine discoveries are in this chapter being mentioned) for the first time we have had to forestall the argument. We must now show how this glandular development provokes (if it does not produce) not only the child's propensity to attack its environment but, as we shall see in the two succeeding chapters, the adolescent's inclination to self-suspicion and the incessant anxiety of first maturity that fluctuates between impudent interference and anxious apprehension.

To return, then, to the ordeal of childhood, we can now see from the evidence of endocrinology that the child (as did the hero whose phase the child is recapitulating) needs to (*a*) be charged with noradrenaline in order to break from the suckling cycle, "full of repose, full of replies" [from Alice Meynell, "I Am the Way," 1921]; (*b*) be weaned from the extension of the womb's condition of dependence, and develop initiative toward new experience; [and] (*c*) be curious about the anomalous, and feel adventurous toward the enigmatic.

Further, in this particular section of our enquiry, and specifically on the psychosomatic action and reaction of mood and function, of physique and state of mind, research in pathology lends additional weight to the evidence that the human being does go through a series

2. The Ordeal of Childhood

of mind-body developments, and that arrest at any one of these levels can be disastrous. We have now known for some time that failure of the individual's emotional life to grow up and out of the childish noradrenaline rage-states of projected fury can and often does culminate in paranoia and its expression, homicidal frenzy. But what we have learned only in the last couple of years is that there is a psychosomatic correlation between cancer and paranoia. The paranoid have been found to have a cancer incidence no less than four times in excess of the cancer incidence among the general population. Also, the cancers start with the paranoid at an earlier age and, in their growth, resist all means of holding them back.

Unfortunately, there is nothing surprising in this grim correlation; indeed, it is only one more confirmation that the paranoid condition is a state of emotional arrest wherein the psyche has become confined at a childish, heroical level. That frame of mind, being one where rage is projected and so never thought about, still less understood by its experient, is, of course, that level of most rudimentary self-consciousness, protoindividualism. At this level, in consequence of this lack of self-awareness, a person is most liable to psychosomatic illness. And if, as MacCurdy (57) in his *War Neuroses* and many psychiatrists since have pointed out, an army conscript, and not an officer, is the person most able unconsciously to give himself incapacitating illness (conversion neurosis), then this would indicate that the protoindividual's desire to kill those who have coerced him turns on himself. He who would be an anarch finds his own cells catching his mood; they attack and anarchize his whole body. Cancer is always swiftest with the young, always deadly with the children; and the paranoid [person] is an arrested child.

Conversely, and confirming this as we shall see in the next chapter, the cancer rate among schizophrenics is much lower than in the average population.[32] Schizophrenia, of course, is the specific mental breakdown peculiar to adolescence, that stage of development in the individual which recapitulates the third stage of development of social man: the ascetic, the midindividual who blames himself.

It was mentioned above and it is, of course, a commonplace that the relation between hormone and mood is reciprocal. Indeed, it is now being proposed by competent researchers that mood may precipitate hormone as hormone can project mood. Certainly every emotional state may be very easily overdone and set up its emotional resonance. What was a good starter, a real source of inspiration, can become simply a bad habit, an addictive behavior pattern, a conditioned reflex. It is clear that at the stage of childhood the individual confronts the issue that the Heroic age, on the whole, failed to face: how is independence to stop short of anarchy and initiative short of irresponsibility? Freedom must not take leave of composition nor must private conviction and personal assurance abandon communication, persuasion, and interpretation of as well as respect for and appreciation of the insights of others.

Again, as they have gotten through infancy, most children get through this second stage after a fashion. They [can be] partly damaged, considerably [disabled], but not sufficiently to turn the growth process predominantly morbid. They are under increasing stress and living less and less to their full capacity. Their happiness diminishes and their spontaneity, welcome, and creativity are growing poorer, but they get along by a series of shifts. Their curiosity has sunken to a conviction that they can debunk everything. This is a very dangerous state and all the more so because it seems to be at worst only subacute. Here is a latent condition which, like firedamp in a mine, a spark will ignite. It is from these partly paranoid, puerile types that dictators recruit their youth gangs. And lately, as is pointed out further on in this chapter, we have been able to detect that there is a delayed psychosomatic cost for this miscarriage of energy when it degenerates into rage.

We have already found the way (see Section II, Chapter 1) whereby the infant may be kept from regressing and can be induced to release its pent-up energies in a joyous friendship and with laughter. By cheerful challenge and entertaining puzzlement, the force, which if balked would become frustrant or destructive, becomes adventurous. Between fear and rage, curiosity is disclosed. The desire to shrink becomes the wariness that is the beginning of awareness, circumspect estimation, detached objectivity. The desire to attack becomes the wish to investigate, to contact; and this is the beginning of interior understanding.

2. The Ordeal of Childhood

But when we come to the education of the post-infantile child, we are far less successful. Most persons, however, are unaware of how greatly the educational situation degenerates after the progress made by a good infancy induction. We are unaware of it because of a fundamental confusion in our own minds as to what the good life is and as to what the procedure and progression of the life process is. Psychotherapy has now made us realize that the child may well become a severe and costly failure unless we give it, for its first two years, that inspiring invitation to generous living. However, such a way of life is not ours today. It is not the climate of our adult world. The child psychologist and trainer is not, as yet, an average person of our life and times. And this teacher-sculptor is molding a substance—the infant mind-body—which is far more eductile than the substance of most adults. The success of the new infant training, which has been in practice for twenty years now, has, therefore, not had the impact that was hoped of it. Indeed, it has in one way made our conflict more acute.

For as our adult society still accepts the idea of struggle and competition as being the way of survival and the procedure of evolution, this outworn aspect of Darwinianism still dominates our mores and education. The present attitude of those who control education is then a compromise. Granted, they would say, that one must not begin to toughen up the infant too rapidly, any more than one should try to teach an embryo to goosestep. Still, as soon as the easy way of early training has brought the young to where they may have practical instruction, the sooner they are taught to be aggressive the better for their success and our security. The infant is, in the main, still considered to be an unprepared, prematurely born creature, representing an unviable type with whom, therefore, one must have patience until this plastic has hardened sufficiently to be hammered into weapon-shape.

However, the new concepts of neoteny, of fetalization and paidomorphy (see Glossary), now acknowledged by evolutionist and child psychologist alike, provide us with a profound insight. For in these concepts, the callous is considered to be the decadent [i.e., in decline], and it is recognized that the capacity to keep tonically sensitive is the mark of evolutionary advance and the indication of man's unparalleled success. But this is yet to be recognized by those who still set the standards of our mores of maturity. Hence, in those cases in which the infant has had an induction to life in accord with really contemporary concepts of the life process and the evolutionary development, this child is even less prepared to confront the stage of childhood, as it is now lived out, than one whose infancy was less encouraging, whose parents were less able or willing to let the psyche open out into generous, unguarded welcome (75).

For just as we know that a child could be born with a too disproportionately advanced head and brain to survive in the present conditions of our contemporary knowledge, so it is evident that advanced infant training that is not accompanied by an equally advanced neoteny training of the other age groups—childhood, adolescence, and first and second maturity—can expose a prematurely opened creature, provided with no defenses, to other groups that are still mainly aggressive. Hence, at this child period when the individual recapitulates the rough and tumble of the heroic bedlam, there is all too great a chance that the tragedy of the epoch of boastful brigandage will be repeated. Nor is the child psychiatrist himself wholly without some share of blame for this confusion. For too many of them have failed to realize the profound implications of the concept of neotenic evolution.

Hence, such experts and specialists failed to see that as essential and basic as was the proper explication of the ordeal of birth, this was but a first step. There were four others to be faced and taken. Only then would a person be complete. To bring an infant through the first phase and then to leave the child unprepared for the second was as frustrant and disastrous as to have exposed it to callousness and callousing from the start. Maybe it would become a beast of prey, but otherwise it was only being prepared to be the prey of the beast.

However, when the childhood ordeal and initiation is not properly provided for and undertaken, the main disaster for the child is, in its most acute and therefore most unmistakable form, dementia praecox. For those psychiatrists who follow the present tradition that labels psychic misfortunes with classic Greek names, this might be called the *Ajax complex*. The child psyche is not attacked by a guilt complex but a shame trauma. Its attempt to show

2. The Ordeal of Childhood

generous love (if it has had a modern infant training, this will be its display initiative) or its attempt to show off its prowess (if it has had the careless, callous, or selfish bringing up) is rejected, snubbed, mocked. Hell hath no fury like a lover scorned. Dementia praecox, essentially the child-age group insanity, is, of course, the extreme state, the full and immediate reaction of the rejected child.

Earl Loomis thinks that it emerges in its full form, as we might expect, in children of high awareness and uncommon hypersensitiveness. If it cannot be cured, this noradrenaline rage will become paranoia and the homicidal maniac results. The actual number of children that so suffer is tragic but not sufficient to constitute in any wise a threat to society. What is far graver, because of its social peril, is the great number of those who carry on, up from a semi-dementia praecox stage, the paranoid cast of mind. This will lead to passionate aggressiveness (see next chapter) if it is not caught up with and eliminated by the time the child has reached the next stage: the pure adrenaline state that makes possible anger-with-the-self instead of anger-with-others. Because of its lack of experience and foresight, uncalculating violence is released in the child; and because it lacks any sense of opportuneness and has little freedom, the violence is often thwarted and the possessed creature is put under restraint. But if the charge is fed back (after maybe only a few exhibitions of that admired role, "I'll beat up anyone who crosses me,") until the man has learned to nurse his wrath, then there will be grave trouble. He may, like Hitler, reach such demonic repression concentration that he learns, through speech and with violent sounds, how to create such a resonance of paranoia in large masses of similarly afflicted men that they, smoldering in their sense of wrong, are willing to have the homicidal experience under his leadership, and he can use them as his instruments of mass murder.

And indeed, for many child psychiatrists this is the whole story. Themselves still nursed in the tragic concept, they are under the limitations of a despair that tries to make itself acceptable by giving those who face up to it a sense of superiority over those who feed on the opium of wishful thinking and self-deceiving optimism. For them, even if they cannot render themselves and their work totally futile by accepting man as being "a base ungovernable beast," the child is completely neutral. There is in the creature no natural drive toward understanding and cooperation. The inherent evolutionary process that has brought it to mammalhood in the womb is regarded as being a series of accidents. These flukes of fortune have resulted in a creature whose high adaptability no doubt made for animal survival. But this adaptability in a group creature whose social cohesion depended on common cries led to complete suggestibility. Any slogan would catch on.

Education, therefore, when it works on the emotions and the will, is nothing but sloganization. Some cries are the auditory rhythms of common pleasure. In this way, we find ourselves feeling good, saying that we are right and asserting that the nature of things means us so to be and so to succeed. Most cries are the vocalizations of fears, warnings, and vetoes; of defiances and excommunications. Man the suggestible is therefore far more likely to become a creature of retractive fear-hate than of enterprising love-curiosity.

History, therefore, has genial spells when events have, for the time being, gone well enough for the main chorus to be cheerful. At such times, most children find themselves subject to a happy family feeling-tone, a social euphoric mood. Children have the highest chance of survival and of reaching adulthood who are born and reared at times of tribal plenty and prosperity, stability and openness. The adults' experience is, however, far more likely to center on a series of grim happenings. Happy living or quick dying, which were the two most likely probabilities for the child, are not the only ones for the adult. There is, for the mature, a third alternative: an unhappy life that endures until it longs for death. Gloom and suspicion form in man's mind; his tone and chant become dismal and forbidding. Finally, the more man becomes conscious of his inevitable fate, the more the carrying wave of all his communication is minor and miserable. On the whole then, man may at best oscillate manic-depressively between elations and despair; or perhaps, what is more likely, succumb to a growing retraction of courage and spread suspicion [that] must end (when he discovers nuclear power) with the opportunity to destroy his entire species.

This view, though unjustifiably pessimistic, is still popular in most scientific circles. It is supported by two natural but faulty reasons. In the first place, the scientist is increasingly a specialist. His actual work has, in consequence, an ever-shortening focus. General significances [and] long-range comprehensive views concern him less and less. He does not, then, feel able or willing to bring within the orbit of his study those peripheral effects which, although they may not be of immediate concern to him, nevertheless do affect his particular subject. Indeed, he believes himself to be obligated to rule out any *general* considerations because he is a *specialist*. Yet his studies and restricted conclusions are used in parallel studies (as anthropology is used by sociology and bionomics by economics) to give them collateral support and general significance. Further, the specialist, because besides being a specialist he is also a community member, must make some generalizations. He is a citizen who has constantly to conform with, develop, or reject the present rulings of tradition and the trends of social heredity.

As Donald Hebb and others have pointed out, perception is largely due to and in terms of social significances, though the researcher may not be aware of this force as a comprehensive field that suggests and modifies his hypotheses.[33] Charles Darwin, we know, was largely influenced, in the general orientation of his thought, by T. R. Malthus' theory of population.

Therefore, in making his generalizations, the scientist, on the whole, tends to come to conclusions not too alien from current expectations. That does not mean that these conclusions have to be palatable to either the conservative or the progressive. A period which assumes, emotionally, that tragedy is the highest form of art and that art is superior to religion; and which believes, intellectually, that increase of means has relieved it from the necessity of a superstitious faith in Providence—such an age's ruling minority is not surprised, indeed it is interested to learn that it is a unique freak without responsibilities toward a creator or obligations toward creatures.

Meanwhile, in regard to his particular branch of study, the researcher inclines to support those first hypotheses around which his own science was precipitated. Hence, in the sciences of life, the old nineteenth-century notions still rule the greater part of scientific opinion: the old notions that life is a blind struggle; that survival lies in the victory of the best competitor (the most cunningly callous) instead of in the victory of those most increasingly aware; and that the life process is an exhausting process rather than a process of creative, emergent evolution. And these notions persist in spite of such radically new and different assumptions as that of neoteny (now present in biology) and that of open systems and their freedom from entropy (now present in physiology and biochemistry). At present, the neotenic concept (the concept of the infant, the growing edge of the life process, as being an emergent type and a unit of increasing awareness that strives—until it is destroyed or discouraged—to manifest and express a still further capacity to understand and cooperate) is hardly built into the philosophy and premises of the child therapists themselves.

We need not, however, give up hope. Indeed, we may expect that as this completely new notion has been in circulation for only some twenty or thirty years, not only the child psychiatrist but psychiatrists in general are about to recognize the decisive relevance of this concept to their work. Then, instead of the more advanced therapists having to be on the defensive and striving to preserve such enclaves and reservations as (*a*) the new therapeutic mental hospital; (*b*) the new child clinic and neo-progressive school; and (*c*) the new psychiatric developmental centers, they can, must, and will issue forth from these special fastnesses. Therein they have accumulated their ammunition of confirmatory data. And with these data, they can challenge the still calloused and callousing patterns of behavior, such as the drill systems of the tough professions: the military police and penal institutions. They can appeal to the paying public to decide as to which system, the old or the new, does produce the human character that is best able creatively to handle itself, its fellows, and the whole human situation.

There is no reason for the new neotenic psychiatry to defend itself, still less to retreat. It must now (and it can) plan its advance. So and so only will we make the world open for life, through cooperating with life's process, neoteny. For neoteny can make life open, safe for itself and with itself only by neotenics, the training of the person so as to know how he may, by refusing to loose the hold on his unspent endowment of fresh response, continue to be creative. And

2. The Ordeal of Childhood

this training must be spread up from the child-age groups until it covers all five stages of the entire human life process.

In concluding this chapter, we must repeat that there is one strong ground for hope and for hope in our own time. As we have seen, owing to the fact that our past still lives in us and that our future is also present in potential, we can, unlike the embryo, relive our past mistakes and release ourselves from our former wrong developments. As we increase our therapeutic processes of deep penetration and, from that depth, regress back to the source of miscarriage, we may hope at any age to untangle the strangling web of the life that has been lived, bring back each of its five cardinal choices, and restore each of them to their original state of freedom from any force or coercion.

And what makes this discovery in the technique of neoteny significant and timely is that this recovery of consciousness is to be made not merely in order to restore the individual to a lost happiness, although this is good—not merely for the individual but for his group. For it removes his debit load on the group's resources and re-establishes him as an asset. But as valuable as that may be, an entire release of the individual psyche holds a far greater promise for society and humankind. For we have seen that the individual, when he is put through this psychic recapitulation, this total recall of consciousness, relives with initiative not only his own personal history but that of the race. And so we may hope, by this new education, to restore directly to the consciousness of the individual (as he passes through each phase of his personal life) the initiative of each corresponding epoch of human history but not the frustration.

R. G. Collingwood, the historian and philosopher, in his repeated attacks on the theories of progress, maintained that they were all false because the only real progress would take place if it were possible to conserve all the insights of the past while advancing into new awareness. This demand can now be met. At last there can be a generation in which the entire richness of the past not only exists as an unconscious endowment of reactions and drives, but is consciously appreciated. The contemporary individual may at last know, by direct interior knowledge, that he is the growing edge of life.

It is clear, then, that this process is no mere therapy for restoring those who have been damaged and returning them to the more or less vicious circle of current affairs. This is a training that everyone must and will wish to undergo. It is a fivefold birth whereby each person explicates and summates evolution. And as this evolution is now consciously pursued, not only is it so accelerated that each generation can advance an aeon but each may emerge into a new and vaster frame of reference.

3. The Ordeal of Adolescence and Its Specific Mental Breakdown (*Schizophrenia*)

We have now seen how two great stages of the individual's development do recapitulate two great ages of humanity's history. These two epochs—the preindividual, coconscious, traditional aeon and its successor, the protoindividual, aggressive, heroical era—make a recapitulating, summarizing appearance in the early years of every person, save in such rare isolated and ankylosed cultures which themselves have hardly, if at all, left the traditional aeon.[34]

We have also seen that each of these epochs (prehistoric and historic) and each of these individual age-stages was and is attended by a crisis. There comes to every person an ordeal that can be made to be a specific test rather than a sudden onrush of spontaneous pressure for which he is unprepared. If this ordeal can be presented to the individual in a way that is adequate to the inherent psychophysical, mental-emotional needs of the growing psyche, then the ordeal results in an initiation. And this initiation is a new birth into a fresh quality of consciousness, for it is a further depth penetration that releases energy levels now repressed. They are repressed because at the historic period of their first emergence they found only partial or frustrant expression and because, since then, we have devised no explicit methods for dealing with these crises in the development of the individual life.

So far, what seems to be the main norm of human history is this: the ordeal has been largely accidental and brought on by outer pressures, which triggered into an explosion inner repressions that have long been accumulating as the standardizing, prestige-giving patterns and instructional interpretations given by society, [and which] grew increasingly inadequate to balance the growth of actual experience. Hence society and the men in it have blindly, and at great cost, psychomutated. Many, perhaps most, have been destroyed by the strain of the disordered, uncomprehended changeover. And those who have survived have only been able to construct—inadvertently and largely by mere reaction, in blind revolt and resentful recoil—a society whose standards must be mainly negative because they are precipitated and energized by protest and almost devoid of comprehension. Further, under this unforeseen and unprepared-for stress, many individuals, though their intense inner vitality prevents their becoming wholly liquidated, nevertheless do become mad.

In the first phase of this mental constriction, they manage to make themselves impervious to the inner/outer process of change-growth. They stabilize at the level of the total conservative. Any change in the tribal pattern is treason.[35] These are the type that produced the first gerontocracies: that iron rule of the arthritic-minded elders, of those old men who can neither live nor die. They are fruit that has dried on the branch, refusing to fall to the ground and preventing new shoots from sprouting. Such elders are killing the last preindividualistic tribes in Australia today.

Later, in the second phase of their madness, monomaniac conviction changes from being broodingly fanatical (and excommunicating all development) to paranoid attack, and the raider–crusader emerges. His mission is no longer to keep his own world and social circle spellbound under the magic of his arresting command but to launch his feudatories out on an annihilating attack.

3. The Ordeal of Adolescence

But on the whole, though at a cost in suffering that must seem appalling to the humanitarian, the process has worked, the progression has explicated, evolution has continued. And it has continued with the prodigious acceleration first made possible by the slow and tentative exchange of physical heredity for the rapid oscillating exchanges of social heredity whereby what begins as question-and-answer sports into criticism and creation, the working equation, and the challenging absurdity. In spite of cruel mistakes and crueler convictions, callous ignorance and frenzied fanaticism, man has come, first, to challenge, criticize, and remold his unconscious tradition, then to test, explore, and manipulate his environment and thirdly, to be aware of, to question, and to gauge himself. Repeatedly, and because man delayed in giving his rising nature adequate release and contemporary expression, there has been such tectonic stress that mutational revolution, not evolution, has seemed to be the unavoidable rule. The violence of the moments of contorted delivery has been so shockingly memorable and the welter of wreckage left from the explosion so obliterative that chroniclers and their moralizing amplifiers, the historians, have felt hardly able to pay tribute to man's capacity to recover or to pay attention to the long-range results.

And yet there is a process and it moves in a discernible direction. For man is not merely the most viable of all creatures, he is also the creature that rapidly and sustainedly gains in consciousness. The process of gaining awareness, though it turns the corners with such violent switches that myriads are flung off at each bend, does survive this vertigo. Humankind does emerge onto another and higher traverse of that tremendous effort—the expression of its inner nature in regard to its comprehension of outer nature. Men's unawareness of their psyche growth has therefore left them unprepared for its sudden delivery pains because the awareness of the psychic pregnancy was repressed. The new births were brought on by forces driven to become increasingly subconscious.

Hence, temporary spastic chaos. But that chaos has not been collapse and death. It has been a birth, however clumsy and damaging. Some inherent power has kept man going and after each convulsion has swung him not merely back onto disciplined acceptance but thrown him up onto a higher level of challenge-exertion and outlook. In Appendix D, we shall enquire as to whether, besides an inherent preterconscious drive, there may also have been present among rare individuals in hidden groups an esoteric practice that was designed to keep alive, consciously, the flame and light of an authentic inspiration. But before reaching that point, we must try to discern how the individual today, in the process of his personal life, confirms by recapitulation the progression of history, illustrates its physical significance, and indicates where and how education can and must cooperate with the explication of the evolutionary process.

In this chapter, we therefore trace in the individual the oncoming of the third great crisis wherein and when the young still have to recapitulate humanity's third great change of consciousness. The infant, we have seen, today has the new child psychiatry to aid him in the birth of his psyche during the first two or two and a half years. He is now cheerfully challenged, laughingly roused to react and explore. But we have also seen that when the child begins to enter his next stage and to recapitulate that further condensation of consciousness that will be his first awareness of separate individualism, our paidogogy is still proving to be inadequate and mainly unhelpful. Whether half a truth is the worst lie, preparedness half done is surely the worst defense, especially when that preparedness has stripped off the defensive armor of growing callouses and wariness but has failed to replace these rigid defenses with the alerted vitality of initiative and understanding. If a sedentary organism discards its shell without gaining agility, it becomes a prey of its foes far more easily than if it had remained shut up in its immobile armor. To prepare infants to be happily responsive in the world of today is not to prepare them for life but for a despairing disappointment. For in the stage of childhood, the next phase into which they must, by their growth process, inevitably move, they will find that generous creativity is considered to be [weak and timid]. And the adolescents, the next group to which they must go after childhood, regard blasé indifference and [for males] a Don Juan "sophistication" as being proof of maturity. Once the skin has been made capable of keeping its resilience, it may lose the power of acquiring a defensive callus and so be able to respond to constant irritation only by producing a malignant sore.

3. The Ordeal of Adolescence

The infant, we have seen, is charged with noradrenaline that remains with it for its first years of tremendous brain expansion, adaptation, and growth. But by the time it reaches the threshold of adolescence, this glandular slant should be beginning to change to adrenaline, or at least to balancing the noradrenaline with spells of adrenaline repentances (28). As Piaget has pointed out in his classic studies of the child, it is not until the age of seven that the child ceases to use the intuitive emotional apprehension of a situation (and/or a relationship) and begins to apply reason and logical analysis.

This is a vitally important sequence of facts; it should make us realize that the change that takes place at the oncoming of this third crisis (the first sign of the dawn of adolescence, which Arnold Gesell and his colleagues place at about the age of ten) is as grave and critical as birth, as testing an ordeal as were the two earlier ones of birth and childhood. The growing psyche has been brought through birth and infancy and protected from collapse-retreat into [developmental disabilities]. Next it is brought through early childhood and dawning adolescence. At this point it is guarded from dementia praecox by letting the noradrenaline energy (which might turn into the poison thorn of homicidal rage if it is balked) bud into a fully developing wish to explore, experiment, construct, and communicate.

How tragic it is, then, that at this point, of all places, contemporary Western society (the confused survivals of Heroism and Asceticism with a smattering of Humanism that still constitute, so largely, the amalgam that we call our social heredity) takes over the adolescent and tries to toughen him up. For it is here, when we try to make him surrender his generosity, that we first suggest to him that he is shameful and guilty. Our schools, with their competitive and aggressive sports, as well as premilitary training, try to turn the adolescent into a series of reflexes that are driven by fear of shame.

The religious bodies whose tradition is ascetic can substitute guilt for shame and so keep up the struggle for the distressed soul of the adolescent. And the humanic notions of the specialized sciences, when they attempt to generalize, can give him the paralyzing anodynes of materialistic skepticism. This condition is, of course, an extremely grave threat to adolescent sanity.

II - PERSONAL PSYCHOLOGICAL STORY OF HUMANS

Why should we be surprised at the high incidence of juvenile delinquency? Such fuel put into any machine would make it corrode or explode. Such a diet fed to any organism would give it convulsions and lead to prostration. Nevertheless, although a basic drive toward growth (in this case the great mammalian movement toward advance through increasing awareness, progress by neoteny) may be periodically thwarted and temporarily distorted, it cannot be brought to a standstill except by destroying the species that carries the basic aptitude of teachability. You can bewilder most of humankind for part of the time and mislead part of humankind most of the time. But you cannot delude and deceive all humankind all the time about its true nature. You can expel nature now and then with bayonets; nevertheless she will return as inevitably as a dammed stream will erode the barrier that has been placed in its path and resume its predestined course.

So it is that when the problem of juvenile delinquency is examined thoroughly, we find grounds for hope. When with our most advanced techniques of detection we study the energy rhythms of delinquents, we turn up evidence that this is a social disease that is attacking a psyche of promise. To quote again Grey Walter (93) (*The Living Brain*, p. 201), 70 percent of [male] youths who, between the ages of ten and seventeen, had given this kind of trouble were found to be giving off the delta waves from their brains when they were tested under electroencephalogram instrumentation.[36] As Walter indicates, these boys were not lone wolves, solitary brigands. On the contrary, they appeared to have failed to grow emotionally. They had remained malleable rather than becoming resilient. Hence (as did the Nazi youth), they became material for gang assimilation. Our society did not give them a modernized heroic group modus and style; and as no man hired them, they sold themselves for nothing.

Of course, the Boy [and Girl] Scout movements did much, and the Big Brother [and Big Sister] therapies have also done a great deal to aid. The problem, however, will remain stubborn until its nucleus can be transmuted by skilled use of the therapies of specific catharsis by which adolescence is given its particular ordeal and initiation.[37]

Then our education will resume its now limited and arrested process of drawing forth the entire man. Having achieved the basic

3. The Ordeal of Adolescence

success of a full and healthy birth and infancy, it will then follow the rightful extrapolation of that first part of man's growth. It will attain to the practice and technique of releasing the paidomorph, the form of psychophysique that is the next step in neotenic development.[38] The child will become heroic but no longer be boastfully afraid of being shamed or attempt to conceal uninformed and mistaken initiative by calling his temporary setback tragic when it calls for reflection.

The stage of proto-adolescence can then be safely entered. For now the secretion from the suprarenal medulla, which has been predominantly noradrenaline, becomes predominantly adrenaline. The energy that was formerly projected out onto the world and onto others (and, if not rightly engaged and entertained, turning into destructive rage) now alters its objective. The adolescent awareness now turns in on itself and corrects the unexamined conviction that outside of itself lay all its tasks, problems, and conquests. It begins to explore, criticize, and attempt to order itself. The task of conquering the conqueror is begun.

Now we are able to recognize how the Ascetic Age inevitably succeeds to the Heroic Age. We also perceive the recapitulating process whereby the individual repeats (and through education may remedy) the psychosocial record of the race: human history. And these two insights permit us to see how a fully informed emotional psychophysical education would give the adolescent age group that contemporary version of strenuous, tempering athleticism (which, of course, is the original meaning of asceticism) whereby this age group may express its inherent need phase, yield its particular service, and integrate with the age groups behind and ahead of it. Then when each individual of the adolescent age group has become fully, completely and neotenically adolescent, he may pass safely into the next phase—the age of first maturity.

And here again, in adolescence (as we also saw in the previous chapter when dealing with the childhood stage) we have biological evidence that the whole physique prompts and cooperates with the psyche in the growth of consciousness. Thus we see that, in each of these stages of psychophysical growth that man goes through, our racial nature is striving to accomplish its further evolution. So great is the glandular drive that the entire bodily structure is mobilized to assist and, if we will not cooperate, penalize and eliminate. A vital force is shaping man—a force far more form-pervading and comprehensive than simply the growth of an enlarged brain that can be taught because the bodily instincts have been reduced.

For remember, as we mentioned in the last chapter, that the paranoid, with his psyche arrested in its simple, projected noradrenaline rage, tends to have cancer four times more frequently than the average person who has made their current adjustment to life. Their cancer attacks them earlier than usual in life and grows rapidly and uncontrollably. And this collapse of the body's controls over its own cells is precisely the psychosomatic hit-back or conversion neurosis that we should expect of one too simple to do other than project its unmanageable charge of energy.

Conversely, we should expect the reverse of this process in the adolescent, ascetic, self-blaming type. And so a study of *The Psychological Variables in Human Cancer* shows the case to be. For whereas the paranoid have a fourfold excess in cancer, the schizoids have only half the incidence common to those who, in our society, are called the sane. Further, the attack period comes at a later age than is normal for the rest of us. And as cancers in later life are nearly always slower growing and often show signs of arrest,[39] there is much greater hope of [inhibiting] them.

Once more, we see how aberrant our departure from life can be and how deadly are the consequences of not using the forces in us for growth into further conditions of psychophysical awareness. Once again, evidence from the field of pathology indicates that the life process is still sustaining a pressure on its growing point: man. Still further, it would indicate that, as that growth process has been the achievement of consciousness, now this consciousness must cooperate with the life process by conscious development of even greater awareness. If it will not and refuses this cooperation, then the human organism will not stabilize or even continue to increase in powerfulness. It will be destroyed by the disruption of its own homeostasis, by the inadequacy of the psyche to control the cell growth to command the cooperative loyalty of myriad coordinate cell lives, lacking which it must rapidly degenerate into corruption.[40] Cancer is

3. The Ordeal of Adolescence

not, in the same sense as other complaints, a disease. It is a resumption, by the cells, of their primal right (eschewed for the sake of a larger life) to reproduce themselves regardless of any greater discipline or purpose. And just because of these two facts, it now seems that cancer may supply convincing negative proof that man can and must continue to evolve.

Not only does the evidence of pathology indicate that adolescent asceticism, with its capacity to blame itself and to judge itself against a universal law, is psychosomatically more healthy (more in accord with the homeostasis of the entire psychophysique) than is the noradrenaline, heroical, child phase. It is even more healthy, in this profound respect, than the stage beyond it, the age group of first maturity. The fact that there is four times more cancer among the paranoid (the arrested child type) than among the ordinary adult population would seem to indicate that the first maturity and second maturity groups are considerably less disbalanced and more sane than those arrested, un-self-aware types whose constant reaction is to blame others. Conversely, the fact that most of us, the so-called sane, composed of the first and second maturity groups, have twice the cancer rate of the schizoid, suggests that the ascetic adolescent's midindividualism, the individualism that blames itself because it cannot live up to a universal law, may be biologically more sane, more balanced in its sense of responsibility than is Humanic man, the total individual who believes in no universal law requiring personal responsibility to it (78). Although second maturity is today subconsciously aware of first maturity's inadequate outlook on the outer world (of its mistaken notion of objectivity) it has as yet put no alternative faith in the place of the Humanic. Hence, while its conscious mind inclines to involutional melancholy, its subconscious, having no faith in a universal law of being, cannot maintain mastery over the cell secession; cannot control the physiological anarchy of cancer.

To return, then, to the adolescent and what must be done to explicate his condition: it is clear that his sense of universal law and the individual's obligation to it is an evolutionary contribution, a growth gain. What must be done today in the new outlook of psychophysical elucidation, eductive education, is to prevent this conviction from leading to self-immolation through the further conviction that it is a law that must execute all who fail to fulfill it.

In the heroic, childhood phase, it is necessary to save the child from becoming caught in the primary oscillation of protoindividualism, the fluctuation between boastfulness and shame that explodes into paranoid rage. Just so, in the succeeding adolescent phase, the training requirement is to prevent the youth, the stripling, from abandoning further growth by degenerating into a fruitless fluctuation between guilt and expiation. He desires now to be trained and to submit, to be drilled and to be habited, to be uniformed. These desires spring from his new self-knowledge as his increasing self-consciousness turns in on itself.

As far as this self-consciousness can be kept as a rightful skepticism of the instrument, a checking up of its actions in comparison with its estimates of its behavior in contrast to its convictions, a desire for an objective and for outer opinion on performance and on views, this is growth and progress. When, however, disappointment at the self's conduct and capacity becomes unbalanced and obsessional, then there is a failure of nerve. The guilt-ridden seek to suffer for suffering's sake. Pain is not merely the cost of becoming tempered and the price necessary to remedy excess and correct trespass. Suffering now is to anaesthetize the sense of sin in and by physical anguish. Such sufferers must then correspondingly seek to find an outer authority, an infallible rule, not to add as a necessary balancing judgment to their own conviction and to strengthen their capacity for informed cooperative, contributory initiative, but to relieve them of all the pain of making choices. Just as they yearn to humiliate the body, for whose appetites they feel disgust, by exposing it to debilitating punishments, so they correspondingly long to sacrifice intelligence, curiosity, and will. Their submission, to satisfy this mortificatory craving, must be to some authority that is just as domineering, presumptuous, and bitterly exclusive as the spirit that unconditionally surrenders is abject, questionless, and without any reservation. Thus they only project the will they long to renounce.

Hence the ascetic—when he arises from a stock that has produced the tragic hero, the suffering servant—becomes the backbone of the persecuting churches and, as the asceticism is persisted in for

3. The Ordeal of Adolescence

its own sake and for life-rejecting, mortificatory purposes, the repression is increased. The appetites are further restricted and strangulated. The primal, undifferentiated appetite that began by being panaesthetic, the basic cutaneously suffused sense of reassurance and of belonging that the infant must have by total uninsulated contact with its mother's body (or be damaged psychologically), is now severely confined and denied to all but infants.

During the heroic, childhood phase, when the ideal behavior is manifested through physical activity and display, this type (which William Sheldon first called the somatotonic and now calls the mesomorph or muscular type) is still largely diffused, sensorily, through muscular development and exertion. Man's attention does not begin to concentrate on specific sexuality as long as struggle and contest are his chief delight and rage is his principal auto-intoxicating emotion. Sexuality per se can be brought to its obsessional pitch and made into the prime cause of guilt only when rationalism begins to ask questions about pleasure and, disregarding panaesthetic sensation, concentrates on the genitalia and the orgasm, neglecting or condemning all the other aesthetic (erogenous) zones; and when heroicism has regarded all tenderness as being weakness, any caress as enervating, and [for males] gentleness as effeminacy.

When, therefore, the muscular violence of heroism and its delighted rage in destruction is over and banished by discipline, the more acute individual, the midindividual, enters a specifically erotic phase of intense sexuality. Inevitably, his sense of guilt seizes hold of this as his main conviction of sin and main offering as expiation. The aim (and goal) of life is made to lie beyond death and the drive to attain that unimaginable condition is found, in the East, through fear of returning to this world, and in the West, through fear of eternal physical suffering in a world to come of eternal torment.

Naturally, that drive today, that schema of the mortificatory mind is fading out. Half a millennium of increasing skepticism extends from the time when this schizoid other-worldlyism was able to hold the mind and conscience of thinking man. That is why the adolescent today does not seek the mortificatory life or even the ascetic way, though he is an ascetic at heart. The educated Protestant churches do not understand the ascetic way, so they cannot, save in dwindling Fundamentalist communions, generate the energy-conviction of ecstatic repression.

Protestantism, although it is becoming aware of the need for a psychiatry, is now mainly a temporary and temporizing mixture of apologetics and good works. Catholicism, too, as we see by the increasing non-enclosure of the modern orders and the increasing hygiene of the ancient ones, is what the Ages of Faith would have called more and more secularized and fatally relaxed. And even so, the number of vocations in proportion to the population is steadily declining. Neither the Second Coming—the end of the material world and of Time—nor hell fire and eternal anguish are stressed any longer. Hence, the adolescent seeking for his rightful phase–expression (*askesis*), has to turn from the ascetic ideal back to the heroic. And instead of serving, with his highest and utmost loyalty, a universal religion that regards this life as an essential phase in spiritual growth, he has to give his devotion to a nation whose standards, values, and goals are at best only heroic.

Still, even in this national religion he is looking and must look for an absolute. His attitude toward the State cannot be the same as that of the humanic gentleman. The eighteenth-century Man of Reason, with a civil loyalty well on this side of idolatry, and as a free, uncoerced partner, was able to support the State. This he did just as much by constructive criticism of the nation's executives and veto against their interference with private rights as by his willing defense of his nation against those who might trespass on *its* legitimate rights. Today, in consequence, there has arisen the frantic, fanatic, racist nationalism that has twice imperiled civilization in this half-century and whose example has seriously corrupted and intimidated the freedom of citizens in those democracies which still do not consider the title shameful.

Clearly, however, this atavistic heroicism of nationalism is such a psychological anachronism that it cannot last. Twice (three times, if the Japanese militarists' lunatic and paranoid attack is considered a separate manifestation of this madness) having seized the initiative after deliberate preparation, these racists have nevertheless suffered a disastrous defeat, even when confronted by a divided and uninstructed civilization. Because it stems back behind asceticism to heroicism, this frenzy of nationalism is paranoid.

3. The Ordeal of Adolescence

The real danger today lies, therefore, in some religion or ideology that would really satisfy the ascetic drive of the adolescent by claiming inevitability, universality, and supremacy over racial morality. The churches cannot provide this because they are divided, and what the ascetic adolescent is seeking is an absolute authority. The nation, the total state, has tried to claim this total authority, but it has failed. No person of even sufficient mental competence to keep modern machinery going can for long prevent his critical intelligence from challenging and corroding the completely unsubstantiated superstition of race, and the equally insane notion that a sovereign government or people can be above the general principles of humanity.

In the Communist ideology, the three requirements of the ascetic type are answered, albeit falsely: (1) utter anonymity for the subject, (2) historic inevitability of the process (the fulfillment of man's story and the finality of his striving), and (3) world universality. Here, and again, we see the pressures being attempted which in the great Ascetic Age produced (1) the man who accuses himself, denounces his own actions, and informs on others: "the right-acting man"; (2) the examiner of conscience and the spiritual judge, the ideal; and (3) the one revelation, absolute and final, the code to which utter submission must be made in the name of *Quod semper, quod ubique, quod omnibus*. And today, Russia and China are split.

The heroic and pseudo-heroic, when they crack, become paranoid. The ascetic, when he goes to pieces, becomes schizoid. And here we have two correlations that lend further support to the hypothesis that the adolescent is recapitulating the Ascetic Epoch. The first is the fact that the noradrenaline child, representing ontogenically the Heroic Age, if it goes mad will tend in its specific madness, dementia praecox, to the madness of the hero, paranoia. The second is the fact that the adolescent, in turn, when he goes mad will tend mainly to the specific ascetic madness, the schizophrenia that seems to be a split of the mind brought about by the pressure on it of a code that is conceived to be one, infallible and all-embracing, but which, nevertheless, the individual finds he cannot keep.[41] Here is guilt madness, while in the earlier heroic phase there is the madness brought on by intolerable shame.

The educational, remedial, and developmental method for dealing with this adolescent stress (which, if it becomes extreme, can end in collapse) is through showing the adolescent how he may further develop his paidomorphic trends. For man today is a creature that is rapidly evolving through growth of awareness, and this awareness can and must now be deliberately expanded and drawn out by the construction of a social heredity that favors and explicates neoteny. Man needs the encouragement to accept that type of dedication which most often appears in adolescence. He often feels that to accept that role would be both pretentious and unsophisticated. The urge has been so misrepresented and exploited that now it is debunked. And the need that the adolescent feels for athleticism must be met by a psychophysical training that avoids the blind alley of specialized competitiveness. The need that the adolescent feels for discipline must also be met. Today, our education of the almost mature youth, the upper teenager, is at best an amalgam of scientific skepticism; the uninformed and straining discipline of heavy intellectual, informational, and technical instruction (for example, engineers, physicians and surgeons, lawyers, managers); plus a faint flavor of sophisticated culture. This means that courses in literature are given engineers to remedy the fact that they have become so specialized in the study of stress in materials that they are totally ignorant of how nervous stress in themselves and their fellows has rendered communication almost impossible.[42]

As we have seen, the concept of the gentleman that at one time tried to substitute for the hero and the ascetic is, with the passing of Humanic man, no longer relevant. For the gentleman's temporary ascendency as a pattern of prestige depended on a type of consciousness that no longer exists. We shall go into that a little more fully in the next chapter when considering the next age group, that of first maturity, and its specific standards and risks. For it is that age group, and not the adolescent, which recapitulates the Humanic Epoch.

Meanwhile, to finish with the adolescent phase, it is clear that only through neotenic education, which teaches insight into one's self by humor, can the keen self-criticism of adolescence be kept from producing a schizoid condition. The tempering tensile strength to produce this dynamically balanced endurance will be achieved by

3. The Ordeal of Adolescence

that reconciliation of toughness with tenderness whereby these states of the psyche are seen as being complementary and not as being mutually exclusive antitheses.

William James, who did so much to reconcile apparent opposites, nevertheless on this important issue made one of his few great and tragic mistakes. The world is not divided into the tough who can act because they cannot feel and the tender who, because they feel, cannot act. For as the child becomes the preadolescent, the plasticity that it still retains from the healthy responsiveness of the infant must be gradually replaced by the elasticity of the adolescent. Psychophysical elasticity, in contrast to plasticity, is the capacity to react with the combining reply which brings its own contribution to the blend of informational opinion. The tenderness, which at the start is a delicacy of impressionability, does, as it thereby develops, become capable of that tensile strength without which there is no retentiveness; otherwise each new impression obliterates the one before. Retentiveness requires that the new be blended with the old. This is a demand for a resilience that accommodates fresh data by composing the present findings in the basic conception. Significant form is preserved while it is constantly enlarged. This is the principle of all growth. Toughness, seen in this way, is polar to callousness, for the callous is the rigid. Toughness is tenderness grown to a full equality of response to stimuli; for, to take its dictionary definition, it is strong but not brittle, yielding to force without breaking, capable of resisting great strain without coming apart.

To sum up then: in this third athletic-ascetic phase, the personal psychological story of every person calls for an immediate new advance. We have begun a modern psychophysical diagnosis and therapeutic education of the first two phases, infancy and childhood. But as yet we have done nothing significant toward a similar psychophysical diagnosis and education for Phase 4, first maturity, and Phase 5, second maturity. And we shall do nothing as long as we do not provide Phase 3, adolescence, with a new training, a fresh therapeutic education. Further, as we have said before, as long as adolescence remains uninterpreted and unexplicated, the successes of the new training in the first and second phases of infancy and childhood remain anomalous. That is to say, they are successes that

II - PERSONAL PSYCHOLOGICAL STORY OF HUMANS

temporarily alleviate the conditions of infancy and childhood but do not affect the overall mores of society (which are those of arrest), still less those of the State (which are coercive). But once we win over the adolescent phase and make it resilient, not callous, once we can give it its rightful place as the third step of a sane series of natural development that is begun with infancy, then we have a majority of the five phases of the individual's life now constructively slanted and in favor of a developmental and creative psychophysical training. That is why the new therapy for adolescence must be carried out now; that is why, if it is carried out, it can prove to be decisive.

Meanwhile, there is reason to hope that this new step (which will shift the balance of society from denial to affirmation, the authority of the community from veto to inspiration) is being taken. As we have just mentioned, diagnosis has made its next advance. With the psychophysical chart of the individual's life brought up to the span of the third octave (from the age of ten to seventeen), we now have the map of organism behavior in our hands. We have a skilled estimate of the quality and release rate of that phase of human beings which, when it was the high tide mark of man's urgency, the great middle phase of individualism, the Ascetic Epoch, produced the superb desperations of Fakirism, the Thebaid, and the Dervish. It produced the rocket aspirations of Beauvais and the equally unstable agilities of later Scholasticism. And still, even after that magnificent failure and the reaction back to the horizontal perspectives and level horizons of the Humanic phase, it appears in the lives of each one of us. A potent spirit from our past, it rises and complains that it was wrongfully dethroned and submerged; it calls on us to re-express its misstated need or otherwise it will, with its fanaticism, make nonsense of our reason and our science and shambles of our steel-wrought cities and teeming populations.

When the domesticated reindeer herds of the Finns have grazed contentedly and obediently for months, they will one day begin to sniff the arctic air. The owner-herders must perforce follow their stock for the annual sojourn in the far north. Man is a migrant of eternity. The culture that does not provide for these rhythms of infinitude will be wrecked by the force which, had it been expressed, should have given replenishment.

4. The Ordeal of First Maturity and Its Specific Mental Breakdown (*Manic depression*)

If the principle of recapitulation that we have posited is valid, then it should carry through all the age groups. If the newborn infant, the child, and the adolescent recapitulate the social history of humankind (the top section of human evolution since humans became psychosocial), then when the individual develops on past adolescence into their first maturity, we should find such persons recapitulating that stage when humankind first tried out the concept of personal self-sufficiency; when they alternated between the optimism that came out of the certainty that they could now attain Utopia and the pessimism that arose out of the feeling that they were only an animal.

And of this we do find sufficient evidence. First, if we follow Bernard Hart's[43] classic estimate of madness as being such a magnification of the normal web of life that tolerable eccentricity becomes insane aberration and departure from the viable pattern, then in each epoch and age group we should find a characteristic madness. The type of mental collapse should give us a clue to the total character of that epoch and group. Of this we have found evidence in (1) the trauma of birth of the newborn; (2) the dementia praecox (ending in paranoia) of the child that is heavily charged with a noradrenaline that is not rightly channeled; and (3) the schizophrenia of the adolescent who is collapsing under a sense of guilt, longing for an overall authority whose incessant total demand he feels he cannot meet.

These forms of madness do appear in other age groups, but when they do it is because the person's emotional life has not advanced beyond the level where that specific insanity is endemic; his emotional age does not correspond with his biological age. Hence, when he breaks down, he produces the insanity that belongs to his emotional age. Thus, dementia praecox is the disease of a child mind that is showing off, and schizophrenia is the illness of an adolescent mind that blames itself. Yet today the main impact of these specific miseries appears in the age groups of the child and the adolescent. Similarly, we find that the fourth great mental disaster, the manic-depressive madness, makes its principal invasion into the area of first maturity.

As the late Louis Cholden remarked, the manic-depressive form of insanity might well be regarded as being a temporary effort to escape from the schizoid state. As the sense of a universal law that can be neither denied nor fulfilled becomes intolerable, the psyche hopes to avoid this agony by making its own self-consciousness so acute that it may become wholly independent of the law. The changeover of the Ascetic movement into the Humanic is the outward symptom of man's consciousness striving, by further contraction, to escape the sense of guilt. But basically, this only aggravates the condition, for guilt itself is a symptom of growing self-consciousness, just as, before ascetic guilt, the primal self-consciousness of the hero was manifested in his sense of shame. Shame, guilt, and skepticism are three successive symptoms of an intensifying sense of separation. The Age of Humanic man, therefore, is a transitional and comparatively brief epoch. The total individual either regresses back to authority and expiation or goes on into that melancholy of second maturity that only the Leptoid state can eliminate.

4. The Ordeal of First Maturity

The problem of assigning actual years to these age groups is a difficult one, at least in all but the two earliest. We can say that most individuals have completed their psychophysical birth by the time they have reached the age of two and a half years. By then their emotional life has taken on its contours. And although a severe neurosis may still be inflicted, a good start during the first thirty months probably means that the danger of a psychosis springing from traumatic pre–self-conscious experiences is past. We can say, too, that the specific age of childhood, between infancy and adolescence, ranges from the age of two and a half or three years up to ten or eleven.

But adolescence is far harder to fix in terms of specific years. As we have seen, Gesell has provided a map of adolescence that follows the modern accepted span of ten to seventeen. However, in our rapidly growing neotenic extension of consciousness, this may omit those who, though they are not average, are most specifically representative of our present age-group distribution. Undoubtedly, a number of individuals remain arrested at adolescence and, indeed, many at childhood level. But though many may still be growing emotionally, the rate of growth may be slower than at other times. For example, it has lately been discovered that many men who have been given life sentences for murder can safely be released after the age of forty. They had been homicidal because the noradrenaline of infancy (the hormone of aggression needed at that age) had lasted on into adolescence and early adulthood. Some mistake in their early handling had prevented them from adequately using the noradrenaline for the effort to live, grow, and expand, and then, its purpose achieved, from being able to develop the adrenaline necessary for social growth.[44] However, after having continued to function (but atavistically, that is, murderously), the noradrenaline did at last diminish. When at length the social level of adolescence and first maturity was reached, the individual was under the endocrine control of pure adrenaline and at fifty the person had the contrite amenability of the adolescent and the required responsibility of the mature.

Further, this whole problem of age grouping and assigning year-spans to each group is made far more complex by the fact that there is much real [developmental delay] among present-day groups. Not only are there many individuals who are [developmentally delayed], but the whole issue of neoteny makes it doubly difficult to say whether an individual's delay in becoming mature is due to a morbid arrest (such as the above example of a person's emotional life still being in acute noradrenaline conflict) or to a paidomorphic retention of an early uncommitted openness and flexibility that may appear to be irresponsibility. Under the Kentish Saxon law of "gavelkind," a male was considered to be mature at fifteen; the Australian Aboriginal is said to attain maturity at twelve, and an ape is mature at three.

We must expect our present-day youth to take longer and longer to grow up. If, as J. B. S. Haldane has said, urged on by the neotenic drive, man is heading for a growth retentiveness that will permit him to postpone committing and uniting his thought to speech until he is five, and that will allow him to learn until he is forty, then human beings will still be adolescent at thirty when, at present, almost half our life expectancy is over. It may not, then, be inaccurate to advance the year span of the three later age groups of adolescence, first maturity, and second maturity and so find, as some modern authorities believe, that from the twenties even on to forty there may now be an incidence of schizophrenia: that is, the retention of an adolescent-ascetic self-blaming frame of mind. And the succeeding phase of first maturity (the Humanic stage) may not come into action until between forty and sixty. Certainly there are psychiatric authorities who hold that the specific manic-depressive state of mind is mainly endemic in that score of years of the fifth and sixth decades.

The ordeal of first maturity, as it is recapitulating the Humanic phase, will then consist of two stress factors. In the first place, as we have seen, it will be subject to the conflict between the relief of independence and the distress of isolation. The man is now responsible. He may and must make choices. As an adolescent, he might and often did break down into schizophrenia because he was faced with one all-embracing, all-exacting law that he must acknowledge and revere but could not obey. The very humility that made him accept it made him confess his inadequacy to fulfill it. As a completely self-conscious individual, his breakdown risk lay in the opposite direction. He was now in danger because he now saw himself as a person who could seek no final authority to give him the true

4. The Ordeal of First Maturity

and complete law. But at the same time, he saw that he must, out of many findings, numerous opinions, manifold dogmas, and even conflicting hypotheses, decide for himself as to which were the better ones and as to how, from these possible advices, he could best guide his own life. Such a state of mind is the seedbed soil of manic-depressive insanity. And it is made more acute by this frame of mind having been accompanied by the complementary stress of critical education which it has, itself, largely brought forth. The Humanic phase, as we have seen, was the epoch which, in the West (its real home), produced the new learning. Tradition and reason itself, in its form of Scholasticism, were put on trial. Tradition was demoted from its office of supreme judge. Reason was ordered to take on experimentation as its vicar or suffragan. Dogma and argument could stand only if supported by experiment.

Therefore, not only does the individual—who, out of adolescence, enters first maturity—have to undergo the ordeal of finding himself in the position of having to reject the hope of one utterly trustworthy authority and of having to choose among experts, specialists, and a variety of devotedly closed minds. He has to face the even more distressing fact that his is no longer the simple will of the hero who knows that the past was futile and wrong and that the present is here for the strong-willed to take. He realizes that certainty may never be possible for anyone, least of all for himself. Skepticism offers the only possibility of knowledge; and skepticism will not work unless it leaves the skeptic free to find that if the facts show that no answer is obtainable, nothing can be done.

The first maturity of the fully self-conscious individual, therefore, is very different from the assured defiances of the protoconscious heroic individual, the noradrenaline child. He realizes that he must reject authority. Moreover, he sees that even he himself is not adequate to be an unbiased authority for his own conduct, since he has neither sufficient information about the outer conditions nor sufficient understanding of and control over his own inner states. Nevertheless, he knows that by experiment he must and can do much to produce powerful, predictable, and profitable results in the outer world, among and with his fellows and on and in his own physique. Conscious, experimental education therefore becomes his concern.

II - PERSONAL PSYCHOLOGICAL STORY OF HUMANS

It is this aspect of the humanic first maturity—its growing belief in experimentally established instruction—that ushers in man's next phase, crisis, and ordeal. For the isolationism of complete self-consciousness, which produces this skepticism of first maturity, leads such a type of mind to jettison every belief and practice that cannot quickly and obviously be shown to be experimentally accurate. It even leads to the rejection, without experiment, of every practice for which a mistaken explanation has been given (for example, the efficacy of prayer or the anomaly of extrasensory perception). Hence, man disregards his preterconscious and refuses to give attention to any data that are anomalous within his confined category or sensory judgment. This naturally produces an increase of repression, misgiving, and fear. Thus, those threshold pressures are generated in the psyche that make the total individual, the man of first maturity, aware that he is something more and other than an individual.

Still further, as we have seen and will note again later on, as the process of evolution works through the extension of paidomorphism, the person who is coming into first maturity will naturally (but inexplicably to those who do not grasp the neotenic process of evolution) dislike being called on to accept maintenance responsibility. As was mentioned earlier, J. B. S. Haldane (as well as N. J. Berrill) has pointed out that even now biologists can foresee the time when men will not become adult until they are thirty or thirty-five. It is not an escapism that makes the young adult object to being called up to administer codes that he questions and that also cause the young scholar to doubt the current belief in the increase of means as being a criterion of progress. Intuitively he feels, through the evolutionary urge within him, that he must have more time, room, and freedom to grow; that man's future lies in an upward growth in quality of consciousness and not in a crude extrapolating, horizontal advance in gear and economics.

For first maturity, the fourth stage of the individual, represents, tallies with, and is the parallel of the fourth stage of the human social heredity. Today, however, we are in the fifth stage, the Leptoid Age of the postindividual; although that stage has not yet been recognized; still less has it achieved a pattern of prestige. And so, as our society still regards itself as being Humanic, individuals in first

4. The Ordeal of First Maturity

maturity are still regarded as being the age group of executive authority, the focal range of power. Therefore, our society, precisely because it is itself predominantly manic depressive in its outlook,[45] welcomes the manic-depressive man.

Hence, the overly energetic young man of today can escape into action. He can project his conflict on others in that confusion of misunderstandings and thinly disguised ill-will called politics, and in espousing that patriotism which, because of its element of paranoid heroicism, Doctor Johnson in a moment of understandable exasperation called "the last refuge of a scoundrel."

Although the reckoning with reality is thus postponed, with the aid of frequent transferences of mental conflict into such psychosomatic diseases as ulcers and coronary seizures,[46] nevertheless the individual does meet, in second maturity, the disregarded Sphinx returning with accumulated vengeance. Not only this, but he finds that society itself, now becoming increasingly either Leptoid or melancholy, with corrosive satire debunks the impudent opportunist and seeks for his superseder, the truly mature and contemporary person.

It is clear, then, that the evolutionary process of our consciousness calls for a new step in education. As each of us individually passes through first maturity, we need to learn from the experience of Humanic man from the stress he had to endure in becoming a total individual. It was a two-sided stress and projected itself, alternately, as a challenging skepticism of the tradition (the tradition that the ascetic had tried to resuscitate and make into the all-comprehensive, infallible authority of veto and repression), and then as a challenging skepticism of himself. The education that begins as being critical and analytic at last arrives at the self, at which point integral constructions and creative methods are required, not the reductional technics of skepticism. And this involves a re-examination of the tradition. At this time, too, when this re-examination has become requisite, we discover that the tradition has already been found to be, in origins and at base, not repressive and ascetic, but expressive of the total mind-body consciousness plus the individual group-consciousness as a psychosomatic whole, that is, the life religion.

Originally, the tradition was the extreme growing edge of evolution, its most highly accelerated part. Mind and body were being developed together by neoteny, by (biologically speaking) the rapid extension of infancy and, next, the even more rapid intercalation and extension of the specifically human phase of childhood, paidomorphy.

The fourth ordeal in the individual's life process, the ordeal of first maturity, is then the first life phase wherein specific critical teaching becomes part of the test whereby the individual is driven to make three specific growth discoveries about himself: (1) He has to reject all the tradition that does not conform with his experience and experimentation. (2) Feeling himself to be an individual who is purely physical, he confines his critical faculty of evaluation only to data that come to him through the "five senses." (3) This confinement-isolation in turn leads to a skepticism of his physiological instrument as being an adequate apparatus for apprehending the continuum, and to an even greater skepticism of its ability to understand or to control itself. And so those in first maturity discover intuitively, and by the negative process, that the concept of total individualism is a misapprehension.

The critical analytic method of education must be supplemented. For under this ordeal of growth, some try to retract and return, to get rid of their total individualism by retreating to the ascetic totalitarian authoritarianism, whether it be of a church or a commissary—ecclesiastic, communistic, or fascistic. To some degree, today this must mean a schizoid state. Many become manic depressive, while others, avoiding withdrawal, nevertheless hang on with no keen pleasure in the present or hope of the future. So they are transferred, by the inevitability of the biological process, into second maturity. Physically, they are carried on but, being psychologically uneducated and unequipped to cooperate with the process, they are bewildered and it is compulsive. As old age comes on, what should be second maturity is in danger of becoming involutional melancholy; the fear of death becomes the basic phobia, unbalanced by any compensatory desire, let alone significance. The life declines from being even the pretense of a rear action into a rout. Every observer now realizes that without an adult education of the emotions, first maturity only sows the seeds of a harvest of futility which, in second maturity, must be reaped as a suicidal despair; for the increase in the incidence of suicide follows the increase of age.

5. The Ordeal of Second Maturity and Its Specific Mental Breakdown (*Involutional melancholy*)

We have now reached the at-present final state of the individual. We have come to old age, the phase that Aldred Scott Warthin, in his *Old Age, the Major Involution*, has called the period of involution. These are the terminal years when the organism begins to shed and diminish its structure and the mind must become either senile or detached. And in considering this fifth ordeal of humankind's, which today has given rise to the new science of geriatrics, we must recognize a vital fact that may give significant help to gerontology.

Up to this point, we have seen that the recapitulatory relationship between the life process of the individual and the five stages of man's social heredity is discernible in the postbirth stages of psychophysical development (just as it was in the uterine prebirth physical stages). In this fact we have an invaluable clue to interpreting and elucidating each age group.

As we have also seen, (1) the insights that anthropology has given us into the preindividualized mind of cave man, and those cultures that until now have preserved much of his outlook, have aided us in understanding the state of consciousness that individual infancy still recapitulates. (2) Protohistory, in turn, with its elucidation of the Heroic Age, permits us to understand the child's exhibitionist urges. (3) Religious history, with its central theme of ascetic other-worldlyism and the sense of sin and guilt, allows us to orient the adolescent's self-blame and longing for discipline. (4) Sociocultural history (especially the history of experimental technology, scientific method, and critical apparatus) and in particular, modern history of Western Renaissance man (with its specific pattern of prestige—the critically minded, power-loving individualist) has given us the clue to the major drives of the individual's first maturity, the tableland years between the climb of adolescence and the decline of second maturity and old age.

But at this point (and it is this which makes the problem of old age uniquely difficult) our guiderail ends, our psychophylogeny gives out. We have no pattern of prestige up to which the age may live. It is true that in the past, from the Stone Age cultures of Papua to the exquisite aestheticism of China, there have been societies that had a place for and gave authority to the aged. But, under this retractive influence, such societies always became arrested. For better or for worse, the old have had to be dismounted (just as they have been) if man's development was to continue.

The problem of second maturity is as severe and acute as it is precisely because there is no traditional pattern with which to meet and into which to fit the old. Later on, we shall see that it is just this lack of a pattern of prestige that is today holding up neotenic evolution in the younger groups.

Meanwhile, as we saw in Section I, Chapter 5, it is clear that our epoch has yet to find itself a name. We have begun to realize that it is post-Renaissance, post-Humanic, postindividual. We begin to suspect that its character will be of that specific cast given by the experience and realization that it is the first generation of self-conscious men to find themselves conscious of their nonself-conscious. Also, among those who have accustomed themselves to such an estimate of the present human constitution, there is a feeling that this change has been brought about through a mutationally swift

5. The Ordeal of Second Maturity

alteration in awareness: not merely a shift in values and compositional capacity, but an enlargement of consciousness. As yet, though, no pattern for post-Renaissance man has emerged; there is no design in which it is possible to imagine the stature and orientation, the place and profile of the postindividual person.

However, we can clearly recognize that the units, the members, the raw stuffs for such a new integration and new age class, which can have its specific vision and value, have emerged. We now have a fifth estate, a new extension of the life process, a new category of the biological process. Nor is it made up of stragglers and worn-outs, or of those stubborn, dried-up integuments that did, in the past, cause those social arrests called gerontocracies. It is, in its way—which is more wary but not one whit less minatory—as rebellious and as mutinous as is adolescence. The adolescent, if frustrated in his deep desire for service, sacrifice, and discipline, will literally gang up on us, just as the Hitler youth yahoos did. Similarly, the sullen and reactionary old (who are jealous of the young, bitter at lost opportunity, and fearful of an immediate future) will seek revenge by retaliatory punishments, repression of liberty and exploration, and the persecuting suspicion that corrupts all free government. The ancient gerontocracies respected and incarnated tradition. This new class of the old, unless they are given vision, can only respect themselves, as did Stalin. The damage that, today, the rebellious young can do to the community is great. It is smaller, though, than that harm that can and must be wrought by the growing mass of a new class of elders who have a greater sense of political power and a deeper selfishness because they have a more profound, far better-founded hopelessness and fear toward a tomorrow that holds for them no promise: only negation.

Hence, since we find that each of the growth phases of the individual is marked by a particular type of breakdown at the time when the person should pass into the next phase and fails to do so (that is, womb-retreat trauma, dementia praecox, schizophrenia, manic depression), it is not surprising that, later on, second maturity is marked by its specific mental risk and all too frequent culmination, involutional melancholy. And this mind disease, which is peculiar to the aged, is doubly significant. First, because of its stubborn resistance to therapy and, secondly, because of its clear association with and relevance to the fact mentioned above, that the advanced elders of today have no traditional, inherited pattern of living, while all the other age groups have. This great category of the healthy grandparents is such a latecomer, so unprecedented among social phenomena that it has, as yet, no libretto, no part written for it in the play of life and human process. As the old of today, like the newly rich, do not know what to live for or how to use this new endowment, these unparalleled years of freedom, and as the community with its traditional, standard fourfold code that ends short of this newly added section knows no more than the newcomers do, everyone is at a loss and painfully embarrassed.

Further complications are added by the very success of our economic system. For instance, vast amounts of our surplus wealth have gone into medical research and the development of new medical and surgical techniques that prolong the life span.[47] As a result, there are more persons above the age of sixty still living than at any other time in man's history. But at the same time, our successful economic system also means that fewer workers are required. And the old are not wanted as producers. Naturally, the required cut in the labor force comes first in the upper age brackets. The oldster's tempo is not suitable for turning things out. However, they can still serve as consumers: as an army, not of hands but of mouths, for getting things out of the way and preventing the ship of prosperity from being swamped by the following wave of glut. Nonetheless, the more alive the old are, the more alive they are to this situation. They do not want to be banished to pensioneerdom, that reservation fenced round with the eyes of their guardians who are vigilant lest these prisoners should try to break back and flood into the labor stream, who are watchful with hope that death will evaporate these useless and dangerous snowdrifts of time.

So pathetic has this situation become, so futile the pension-and-get-rid-of-them method, that some firms let them seep back into their business circulation, as kindly drivers will risk a skid and even a collision to avoid running over a blind dog that is crossing the street. In the past, the only pattern for the old was that of the man who had had so much experience that he could be referred to in every crisis. For life was repetition and he had seen all of it.

5. The Ordeal of Second Maturity

Today, of course, life is not repetition. Even encyclopedias now become out of date in a decade. Nor are the oldsters sound bases for mummification. The elders of today are more alive than ever before and in a new extension of life. And this new aliveness is even more disquieting to our conventions than their mere survival and their wish to be in circulation. They don't want to be treated as dignified, immobile, antique statuary that is set in the background, against the hedges of formal gardens and at the end of blind alleys. Nor do they wish to be considered as busts of the ancients that are ranged on the top of library bookshelves. They don't feel that they are in arrested animation, or laid out on the cooling board and awaiting the embalmer's hand. Just as King Saul on Mount Gilboa, after his army's defeat and while he was still unwounded, felt that "it repented him that his life was still whole within him" and committed suicide, so, as we said at the end of the last chapter, the suicide rate steadily climbs and increases in the higher age group. And the old, we must repeat, are themselves as ignorant about their condition as are all their juniors. They feel their unprecedented aliveness but they cannot, any more than can the other age groups, explain it or know what to do about it. They are without any pattern of behavior, without any particular prestige-giving standard of conduct.

Therefore, feeling their life still whole within them, they can only do one of two things. In a last echo of manic-depressive alternation, they may fluctuate between a nervous elation and a chilling despair. Or they may, with finality, turn in on themselves and, burying the mind because the body will not die, sink into the specific madness of the aged, involutional melancholy.

And it is a significant fact that not only is melancholy endemic to old age, but it is, of all the psychoses, the most stubbornly resistant to all treatment. New medicaments are all highly promising aids in the treatment of other mental diseases. Yet psychiatrists are all too aware that these drugs, shock treatment, carbon dioxide plus oxygen, or the [milder] therapies can do little to shift this final dark cloud of the spirit. Why?

The answer to both these questions—why is the psychiatrist helpless before this despair and why does it attack the old most heavily?—is the same. The other mental collapses can be challenged as being irrational. The rage and suspicion of paranoia (which rises from the person's being balked), the schizophrenic's conviction of inadequacy and guilt and his withdrawal (arising from a too perfectionist desire to fulfill a too little understood law), and the manic-depressive extremes of the man in first maturity who recoils into premature depression because his undisciplined temerity has led him into overplaying his hand: these complaints are all subject to challenge by reason, and to reinterpretation by good sense. First win the attention of the patient. This is what the new tranquillizing drugs do; while shock treatment does temporarily jolt him out of his obsessional attention to his private plight and out of his personal conviction that his problem is an insoluble one. Recover for one who is mentally ill his capacity to listen to another's evaluation of the situation, and he can be shown that his view was wrong, that the sensible view of sane men is accurate.

But this is not so with melancholy when it comes to the aged. Even if it strikes in the younger age groups, it is not really to be answered by modern psychiatry, though its challenge may be deflected and postponed. The protoindividual can be given the euphoria of exercise, the anodyne of the healthy appetites. The midindividual can find respite in romantic attachment to a person or cause. And the total individual can take to the amassing of means, the exercise of power, and the intoxicant of recognitional praise. But even when these are available—and generally they are to be had only in strictly limited amounts—they are, by their very nature, only temporizing palliatives. Sooner or later, and inevitably with old age, their power to distract sinks to the vanishing point. In the present picture of the life process that still gives scale, map, and chart to public opinion and professional psychiatry, there is no place for age. Still less is there a place for a new extension of age.

The Freudian position, which because it was first is still the most popular with a profession that felt its chief enemy to be asceticism, still regards detensioning of sexual pressure as the one sound therapy. The socially amalgamated therapies of Harry Stack Sullivan and Erich Fromm mix biological release with the promise of a juster society and the concept of man as a being whose sanity must be social as well as personal.

5. The Ordeal of Second Maturity

The Jungian position is more helpful. For it admits that the history of man consists of more than biological and social records. There is also a psychological record, which is discernible in the study of the archetypal images. And this teaching permits man to make some peace not only with his racial inheritance, his appetites, and his socio-economic heredity, but also with humanity's standards of value and significance. But even the best psychiatries aim at little more than adjustment; most of the men who practice them are still looking backward. Very few if any of them foresee psychological evolution as being the future of the race; so we are still waiting for them to make any real contribution to the problem of geriatrics. Have any of them successfully challenged melancholy (in any of the age groups)? Have they been able to deal with it when it forecloses on those who have bought it off, when it triumphs as involutional despair?

But is there anything really to be said to the old—this new and latest class that nature has permitted? For they are the embarrassing and accidental resultant of new realistic, specialized medical and surgical skills that have been irresponsibly worked out and, so far, are being employed by a sentimentality that is equally irresponsible and unthinking-out of the consequences of its emotional pity. Similarly, and at the other end of the line of life, infant hygiene has permitted the results of unrestrained and unplanned-for breeding to survive beyond our means of subsistence. If a headlong increase in population is all that has been brought about, if we have simply disregarded earlier checks and balances of society and Nature and have admitted, without foresight, a flood of lives for which our scale of life has no place, use, or purpose, then there is nothing to say to the old.

But in the schema we have set out in this thesis, and which can now be detected in our actual history, it is clear that the sequence is still incomplete if it stops short of this fifth stage of second maturity. Very few thinking persons today are willing to go along with our proposal that man, since he has been man, has gone through the first four great psychophysical epochs and that each person recapitulates these four stages in their own life. However, even if we do allow that this is true, and in spite of the studies of such men as Peter Drucker,[48]

II - PERSONAL PSYCHOLOGICAL STORY OF HUMANS

Roderick Seidenberg (76), [and] Friedrich August von Hayek (90), which show that the age of Humanic, total-individual man is over, we still seem to be unprepared to recognize the implications. The emergence of second maturity, of the large class of healthy grandparents, can be understood and be availed of only if we see that this fifth phase is inevitable; that it is the essential requirement for the [functioning] of a fifth category of humankind, the fifth age of man as a race and as a person. Involutional melancholy is caused by the fact that, although this fifth rank and estate of man has been recruited today, nevertheless it has to wait about for its equipment, office, and accouterments. For though we knew that Humanic man was no longer the growing edge of the life process, we were not able to think out what the new type would be and, therefore, what its specific contribution, standard, and behavior should be.

So involutional melancholy will remain to consume and challenge us until we learn how to burn it out of the system. We must recognize it as being a symptom of unreleased, damped-down forces, just as flame-suffocating fumes are indicative of fuel that is only turning into gases below ignition point. We can answer the riddle it poses when we can see it for what it is, for what all the mental illnesses have shown themselves to be: symptoms of balked disposition, or energies that have not been given their appropriate expression.[49]

We have said earlier that these new elders shock the old-fashioned pension planner by their failure to enjoy their pensioned freedom, or even remain sane, when they are "put out to grass," when they are taken from the shafts of social traffic and left to browse, doze, swell, and run to seed. Not only this, but they scandalize their concerned juniors even more by their refusal (or inability) to behave as the drained aged used to behave; to carry on, at best, either as fossilized tables of the law or in a chrysalis of comfort and so "shut up in measureless content," rewombed, and readied for the tomb. The new and latest age group wishes inevitably to live, but neither they nor their juniors know how that may be done.

Hence, as there is no part written for them and they must play something, they can only go back and attempt to replay old stock parts. They not only long to be recalled to power, they wish to resume

5. The Ordeal of Second Maturity

or continue (with their still valid potency) personal relationships. This is a theme that has often been dealt with by authors in the last few years. It is both pathetic and exasperating. But it will remain as incurable as it is inexplicable until we put our knowledge of the point at which humankind today has arrived (the age of post-Humanic, postindividual, regeneralized, whole-conscioused man) together with the personnel [that will populate] the new age category with which the evolutionary process has now provided us. For if the principle of neoteny (the increased capacity to comprehend the experience of living through an ever new, youthful, fresh, childlike approach) is the aim of life, and the process of paidomorphy is the means whereby neoteny is made possible, then we should find neoteny actually working precisely where the newest step is being taken by the life-process today: in second maturity.

The main tragedy of this vital and new old-age group is that, because it feels that its growth is not over and that it is not at its *Nunc Dimittis*, it imagines that it must return to a repetition of those activities which belonged to its first phases and now belong to those who are in those first phases. The present mind of the man in second maturity can conceive of only two alternatives: death or repetition, elimination or recurrence. The third alternative is, of course, the way between the horns of the dilemma—the spiral that, on a higher level, re-dilates and emerges to a recovery of unspecialized function. In addition to the *rajas* of activity and the *tamas* of resigned inertia, there is the *sattva* of understanding composition (see Glossary).

What, in actual terms, does or can that mean? Are we not compelled by such a suggestion to fall back on Nicodemus' protest against the statement, "You must be born again"? "How can a man go back into his mother's womb?" he asked. He cannot, but he can and must recapture the freedom of the young. The first step to understanding how this process can and does work, if we will understand it and cooperate with it, is to be able to conceive of the life process of every individual as being a spiral, just as the life process of the race is a spiral. The neotenic process works out from a high degree of unspecialization to an apex curve point of specialization and, that achieved, back once more to unspecialization, generalized expression. To put this in the simplest terms, the newborn child of today is the least specialized of all creatures—more potential and less actual, more of promise and less fulfilled. It is an uncommitted, fetal creature. Yet, as we have seen, even now it is not able to be born as completely unenclosed as the fetus is in the sixth month.[50] But after the prolonged infancy that belongs to it as a mammal (another extension of uncommittedness that is its birthright as a primate), followed by the particular and uniquely human stage of childhood (a third enlargement of freedom and opportunity for spontaneous learning and experiment, curiosity), the individual does begin to specialize.

In adolescence, the diffused generalized interest-affection begins to focus. Particular interests begin to canalize the mind's radiation of curiosity. Just as the small child in the second year of infancy, having spontaneously vocalized and experimented (just for the sake of expression) with the whole gamut of all sounds ever used in any speech, now begins to confine itself to those speech sounds (its mother tongue) that produce results and permit communication, so it is later in the mental-emotional life of the adolescent. The youth begins to specialize his intellectual pursuits. Similarly, and at the same time, his emotional life also turns from being a tide into a stream, and begins to carve out its bed. First, instead of a generalized companionship, particular persons become a concern. Intensity, with its complement exclusiveness, begins to appear. And next, a particular person begins to epitomize satisfaction, the fulfillment of demand, the absorption of devotion, the embodiment of ideal, the inspiration and purpose of all endeavor.

However, we know that this is not a final stage. Only in the romantic fairytale that dates from the last phase of the Heroic Age ... does the formula of "and they lived happily ever after" terminate the plot. The focal intensity of reproductive passion, passing from suppliance to dominance, passes on again to companionship, division of concerns, and an awareness of other and alternative associations. The late Ralph Linton, the anthropologist, and many other students of the social sciences have pointed out that because our civilization has accelerated community and social interrelatedness, the requirements of education and hygiene have restricted the familial phase to an ever-fewer number of years. As our years of life expectancy have

5. The Ordeal of Second Maturity

increased, as the ages of maturity are extended, the years of the marital-parental phase that used to cover all the first maturity have contracted. At the present pace, it may well happen that as the child, for its right emotional and physical growth, requires some parent to be devoted to it for the first three or four years (and a devoted foster parent is better than even a dutiful but vocationless begetter or childbearer), the home phase may be confined to those who have the inborn gift of [child-rearing]. Being "in love," it has always been known, does not last in its exclusive and others-eclipsing phase. And jealousy, the oxide of a mono-devotion in the corrosive atmosphere of a possessive-exclusive society, eats away the inherent strength of a truly loving relationship that is by its nature nonpossessive. Mothers snatch and fasten; fathers elide and elude. These painful symptoms are simply negative proofs that the personal life process is a spiral, not a straight line.

It is natural and also social that, at his present stage of development and with his extended life span, man should find, beyond the marital phase, a period far longer than was the premarital and in which he must make at least as distinctive patterns of value-bearing behavior as the period of parenthood (marital period) had permitted.

This is, of course, only to say that second maturity is neither a rest-house annex nor an extension to "real living," nor is it a paddock in which to cool off before being led into the dark stables of death. In its own right, second maturity is a creative epoch of life. Indeed, it is an epoch of such unique potentialities that, because it is not an echo or an encore of the achievement of any other and earlier phase, we have found it hard to believe in and to develop. For in this stage of second maturity, because it is evolution's latest gift to man, he is given, in still larger measure than it is given to any other epoch or any other age group, life's greatest gift to man: the liberty to *choose*, freedom of choice. Throughout the history of all mammals and particularly throughout the history of the primates, we can see that gift of choice, that power of selection, being increased. Natural selection's culminating test is selection of the best by giving all promising candidates themselves the capacity to select. Choice and the way it is used, to gain or lose liberty, is the supreme criterion of character, the swiftest and most searching method of picking the creative type who believes in a meaning that he, the chooser, must explicate and exemplify.

This flexibility of choice is possible only if the person is left inherently free. That is, as we say descriptively but still with an uncomprehending bewilderment, if the person is left at a loose end. In order that the mammals should have the first inkling of freedom, the close-stitched selvedge of instinct (the web tucked neatly in upon itself) had to be partially unraveled. A further fraying made the minds of the great apes capable of curiosity and anxiety.[51] The curiosity with which we come into this world can endure years of disapproval by timid oldsters and punishment by security enforcers before it is wholly cauterized. Now, with old age and at the upper end, Nature restores freedom of choice and permits, once again, that rightful irresponsibility to enquire and explore regardless of consequences. Being relieved of the armor of authority and the enforcement instruments of command, those in second maturity are once more at liberty to enquire rather than to order, and to question rather than reply.

A promising sign of this is that several original minds, having held high administrative office and then been honorably retired, have expressed delight not only at the release from executive detail but at the deliverance into a liberty in which they are free to think aloud and to say what they notice. For as private persons, in a State that still declares that it guarantees freedom, they need no longer fear that what they say will be taken as being more than the opinion, the *obiter dictum* of an individual insight. This, of course, is a very simple but quite hopeful example of the spontaneous and indeed almost unconscious de-crystalizing development of the mind of second maturity into its rightful and unique liberty.

To go back to an earlier, cruder simile, which was used to illustrate this latest phase of life: after completing first maturity, after the administrative phase has followed the parental-familial phase into the past, after retirement from office, the tracks of social life end; the known and well-trodden paths of typical behaviors, the sequences of character-parts run out and are finished. This is dismaying to the routineer and authoritarian. But, once show this new class of the old that they *are* a class and that they can find a

5. The Ordeal of Second Maturity

specific cooperative consciousness, that they are not only the latest class, the growing edge of life, but that they are therefore free, as no other class is, to write in their own unique and original part, to lay out the new pattern of creative liberty—and at least a large number will desire to live up to this stimulating offer. So being able comprehensively to consider the historical life process and the individual life process, they will see, first, how they can regard themselves as being the latest though not necessarily the last step in that process. Secondly, they will see that as they are the latest achievement of the life process, a creature of choice and initiative, they may and must now consciously cooperate with it by specific conscious development—that is, self-education.

The basis for that education is first a clear realization as to the aim and purpose of that education. What kind of person are we hoping to produce? (1) Clearly such an education must aim at a further development of the whole person, the entire psychophysique, for the full release of that being's still hardly realized potentialities. (2) That release-development can be, and can only be, by further deliverance from those specialized commitments, those individualized characterizations and stations (of profession and office) which reach their apex in history with Humanic man, the total individual, and which reach their climax in the personal life history at the last stage of first maturity: retirement age. (3) And that further deliverance is only possible if the principle of neoteny and its process paidomorphy are willingly and comprehendingly applied by the latest age group, the unstereotyped personality, those in second maturity whom the State and the community must leave free to pioneer because no social pattern, today or in the past, has had a place for this new and advanced variety of vitality. The question of Nicodemus can be answered, not esoterically but socially and biologically. Those that are most mature need no longer harden up, callus, crack, flake away, and die, identified with their husk. They need no longer attempt to repeat their past phases of adolescence and first maturity. They can regeneralize. And what in actual fact that will mean, how they may perform this metamorphosis, we shall see later.

For before we consider this next evolutionary step, we must answer the practical question of what possible use to society and to the life process such a regeneralized type could be. Its function is clear when, for a moment, we reconsider what the evolutionary process has now become. The first factor, we must stress again, is the process of heredity as it actually works with man, the growing edge of life. Once a creature was evolved who advanced no longer by physical hereditary modifications, but by the exchange of vocal information—by speech—then social heredity had begun. And, through the exchange of new findings and the collecting of these findings into traditions of skill and behaviors, not only was social heredity a growth far more rapid and purposive than any physical hereditary improvements. The very growth of these gainful skills, uniting behaviors and defense powers, permitted the infant to be born increasingly in an unprotected state of body and therefore of unprecedented responsiveness to teaching.[52] Later, the steady extension of these protective resources and capacities permitted the infant's sensitiveness to new stimuli, and its welcome toward original experiences, to be further extended until true childhood emerged.

This was the period between the symbiosis of the infant-with-the-mother and the allotted service of the adult (and in our society, to some extent, the adolescent) to the tribe—the stage when the child is free to move on its own but not yet called on to use its main activities for the community's needs.

Meanwhile, *pari passu*, a third factor was added to and accelerated human evolution. The growing tradition-by-speech permitted first the infant and then the child (who were the recipients of the tradition) to grow in receptivity. And under this reciprocal growth of finder and receiver, of widening knowledge in play with enlarging capacity to understand, there arose the beginnings of understanding for its own sake. This was the start of comprehension that welcomes new data as contributions to an enlarging frame of general understanding, a view of Nature as a whole. Here lies the source of the mythos. Here we see the first faint dawn of *religio*, that total interpretation of experience in one embracing meaning, the weaving, into a totally significant whole, of the entirety of events. This task of keeping the social heredity always sufficiently flexible, of having always a sufficiency of wonder, curiosity, and a delight in composing new things into the picture of the whole—this gift must always have

5. The Ordeal of Second Maturity

been of the highest social and survival value. For the tribe that needed least to reject new discoveries, because they could find a place for the anomaly in the *nomos* (the law of things as they are), was the tribe that must advance ahead of all others and become their teacher. For example, there was the triumph over the dread of giant wild beasts through the concept of totemism (53). And it is now thought that knowledge of the wonderfully improved technique in making flint implements by "pressure flaking" (it was called the Solutrean and was one of the final phases of the Old Stone Age) was spread, most probably, by the handing on of a new idea that was commended by its inherent superiority, and not by conquest as had been assumed.[53]

And such a gift would, of necessity, tend to shine most brightly in those minds that, most neotenically, could retain the child's gift of pure curiosity. Hence, there would be a natural selection in favor of those who could thus remain young, who could fend off the arthritis of fear by the constant suppling activity of curious interest. So the seer-shaman type would tend to be selected. This is a type that (a) specifically and developmentally carries on the social heredity and instructs the open-minded young in the comprehensive meaning of the circle and cycle of events; and (b) he selects from those young such as show neotenic capacity for this compositional curiosity, this search for the new that will enrich the tradition. We can now clearly recognize this seer type in history and prehistory's preservers, the pre-urban and even pre-agricultural societies. Social heredity and physical heredity, the way of the God-possessed and inspired, and the way of the property-possessed and gear-involved, soon become distinct though complementary, a reciprocal relationship of contemplatives and actives. And further, it is discovered that the seers must remain paidomorphic for another important reason. Seership, the extrasensory power to foretell, has been persistently and highly prized by tribes whose rudimentary economy could hardly afford to retain members whose only function was a fancy one and whom natural selection would punish with extinction for a very moderate number of mistakes. In view of this fact, we are now less inclined to disregard evidence for the faculty and more inclined to research and to find confirmatory data.

II - PERSONAL PSYCHOLOGICAL STORY OF HUMANS

This gift was always supposed to be correlated with youth and to be commonest and brightest in prepuberty. During the ascetic phase, this traditional opinion was construed to mean that erotic feeling destroyed this capacity for apprehension and, further, that violent mortifications could release the gift. It is now well understood by researchers that there are various assaults on the psychophysique (such as intense strain, great anguish, the acute but quickly depleting stimuli of the relatively large sheathed nerve fibers that carry keen stinging pain, fasting, sleeplessness, rapid breathing, and any tormenting denial), which may jar the normally fixed focus of ordinary biologically valuable consciousness and give glints of another frame of reference. Under such stress, and especially when it has been damaged and wounded to the extent that it assimilates such toxins as its broken-down protein and infection byproducts, the body will give rise to apprehensions, all of which are not always illusory.

This subject must be dealt with more fully in Section III. However, it is raised at this point because of the misinterpretation made by asceticism of the pre-Ascetic, traditional finding: that the capacity to shift the focus of consciousness from its fixation on that focus which is of immediate biological importance to a wider range (for instance, the range that permits a certain degree of precognition) is a capacity, a state of mind much more easily fallen into by the young than by the mature. The fixation of attention on the biological construct of experience [and] the concentration on the utilitarian view of things and persons contracts as first maturity reaches its height. This is necessary, for it is correlated and synchronized with and may be provoked by that concentration of the emotional life which, in the beginning of maturity, fixates it on one person for reproductive purposes. As Freud noted, and plenty of other observers before him, eroticism that had been diffuse in childhood becomes concentrated on the genitalia in adulthood. Freud, in one of his case-history examples of how the sensation is thus restricted, tells of a man who regularly had congress with his wife while the midday dinner was being heated. The procedure had become so routine, so conditioned that the man would often ask his wife, after they had eaten, whether or not they had copulated before the meal.

5. The Ordeal of Second Maturity

We can then see that the high incidence of extrasensory perception in prepuberty must be because of the paidomorphic openness and freedom from biological fixation at that time of life and not because of a lack of erotic feeling.

We shall deal with the further and fuller implications of this distinction in the Epilogue. Meanwhile, we shall conclude this chapter by pointing out, and as a summary of the argument so far, that second maturity is a return from the reproductive focus of first maturity, which had been narrowed in two ways: first, in its marital concentration and, secondly, in its administrative concentration. Second maturity is a return to a regeneralized outlook emotionally and intellectually, a resumption of generalized response. Hence, it can be the state in which it would be natural for the capacity of seership to be attained, to re-emerge. And, with that capacity, to regain a generalized affection, good will, and anxiety-free concern and vision into the nature of time that would explicate death by uniting the mind with eternal life.

This may seem to be a surprising solution to suggest in answer to the problem of geriatrics and the riddle posed by the emergence of a new class that is without any recognized social part to play, or any present standard of prestige to fulfill. But such a denouement may appear to be less improbable when we recall the three main elements of our present situation. The first is the unprecedented speed of our advance, a speed that is not only greater than that of any change process before, but that accelerates with arithmetical progression. The second is a convergence of pressures. Our social heredity has reached the psychological revolution, and the total individual has discovered that he is more than an individual. An increasing number of individuals, those who are in second maturity, find themselves to be a new class, a fifth estate, for which there is no place in the former classification of humankind. The very intensification and triumph of individualism, it is clear, culminates in first maturity, the age group out of which they, the postindividuals, have emerged. Thirdly, this sense of not being wanted has provoked a specific and serious mental disease, involutional melancholy. Because there is no place for them, this new category of humankind, these latest of the mature, instead of dying off, become an additional burden by turning into mental patients, whom we are not callous enough to kill nor understanding enough to cure.

Something, then, must be done. Further, something certainly could now be done if we could find, for this new contingent, a real place and purpose. But what must be done must be done quickly. It, too, must be mutational. It must forestall degenerative collapse, involuntary elimination, [and] despairing decay. This is why I have called the postindividual Leptoid man. Schizophrenia has been fought with electric current and other relief agents—clumsily at first, but now with an increasing aptness that opens the blocked way so that the force of encouragement may be thrown into the beleaguered citadel of the spirit. Even so, the second attack of massive despair, the later melancholy now can and must be tackled by a surge treatment. The particular methods whereby this therapy might be applied are outlined in Section III, Chapter 5, and in further detail in the Epilogue. Here we need only say that after those who are in second maturity have been intellectually assured of their position, their condition, and their promised contribution—after this informational education—then they would be prepared to submit themselves to the psychophysical therapy whereby (1) the two aspects of their consciousness can be combined; (2) their thinking can be made integral (which is the modern concept of seership); and (3) their explication made voluntary, intentional, expert, and desired.

Section III

THE DEVELOPMENT OF INITIATIONS OR PSYCHOPHYSICAL RELIGIOUS EXERCISES

(*The Five Mysteries*)

Introduction

In Section I, we have traced, in outline, humanity's history as a psychological five-act drama of development. We have seen the evolution of its consciousness following a spiral path. For first, man becomes increasingly self-conscious and so attempts to educate himself in skills, to modify the tradition in the direction of efficiency and to control and alter the environment in favor of his individual desires and needs. And then he discovers his own preterconscious and realizes that he must educate himself so as to modify his self-consciousness and be able to cooperate with his setting.

This is man's five-phase psychological sequel to his embryonic recapitulation of his evolution from the first vertebrate into man—the specific and unique development of the one creature that has not only modified his environment but has vastly extended it, and has done so by the preteranimal, invisible instrument of speech, the intangible grapple of ideas.

III - INITIATIONS/PSYCHOPHYSICAL RELIGIOUS EXERCISES

In Section II, we find this theory is both confirmed by evolution and made immediately apposite by the fact that the recapitulation and extension of phylogeny (in the five stages of humankind's social heredity) can be recognized as being ontogenically evident in the developmental growth of the individual. The psychophysical unit, the person, the constituent of the group, the representative of the race also goes through the five stages through which the race has traveled. As in the womb and before birth he recapitulated the vertebrate record, the development of the backbone-aligned creature, so after birth the person runs through the story of humankind. In consequence, today the race and man, the person and society, have each reached the same crisis of consciousness. Humankind and the individual are both at the ends of their tethers if individualism and its rational use of the five senses (or the twenty-two channels of apprehension) to master an objective, aimless, unconscious outer world is the goal of evolution and the senses are the one means for survival.

However, we have also seen that this is not the only possible prospect. Man, today, may hope to understand his total nature and, through that means of understanding, he may educate himself. Through his preterindividualistic consciousness, he may reconcile his individualism with society and also with his environment. But that education, though it be conscious and informational, must be total to be efficacious in this task. It must be a psychophysical developmental therapy, a mind-body hygiene.

For that reason, and to confirm the fact of our psychological evolution whereby instinct was turned into tradition and tradition into education, we must and can trace a third thread in the human process. Besides the obvious story of humankind and its recapitulatory résumé in each individual's life story, there is another sequence, an esoteric series that follows the five stages and epochs of human history. And this third aspect of humanity's story has made it possible for the violent social mutations of humankind, which we have called catastrophic revolutions, to lead to an evolution of consciousness.

This has been obscure until late. Now, however, anthropology and historical psychology (especially the Jungian *Eranos* investigations) have laid bare sufficient parts of this neglected record. Its significance becomes evident when we perceive that in this sequence,

Section III - Introduction

also, there is a fivefold development. And these five stages of the process do correspond, as a therapeutic reply, to the five developmental crises of historical humankind and to those five developmental crises of the individual, each of which, when not corrected, shows its complete destructiveness in a specific form of madness.

Further consideration of the data and investigation of the process certainly suggest that it was, and indeed is, due to these remedial psychophysical processes that man's development, though it has been spastic and convulsive, has not proved to be catastrophic or fatally disastrous. It is true that time and again large areas, entire branches of man's social heredity have collapsed in confusion under noncompensated stresses and disbalanced growth. But always, after a delay, there has been not merely a resumption of growth and an increase of power, but an increase of comprehension as well; not merely of capacity but of vision too.

In Section I, it was suggested that all five of the "mysteries" of ordeal and initiation may not have existed since the dawn of man's culture and the beginnings of his religious rites. Indeed, if each "mystery" is a therapeutic reply to a particular contractive crisis in man's development, the contrary might be argued. It might be maintained that as only today has humankind produced the fully [populated] fifth class, the class of those in second maturity, the veterine with their peril of involutional melancholy and their specific therapy of electric surge treatment,[54] the fifth ordeal and initiation would not emerge until now. But this is certainly not so. For the ordeals and the initiations of the mystery sequence are fivefold and, as we shall see in Chapter 5 of this Section III, which deals with this final initiation, this fifth mystery called aether, or the finer fire, is electric surge treatment.

The truth in this obscure matter would seem to be that whereas humankind has advanced, roughly speaking, in three divisions: (1) spiritual pioneers, early developers, exceptionally early seers and sensitives; (2) the main body of average people; and (3) laggards, then, throughout history, we should expect an advance column of experimenters and explorers to be at least one stage ahead of the main body. The entire sequence of the fivefold mysteries may then have been worked out by a spiritual elite. By the time of the rise of Asceticism, these pioneers may have reached what is here called the

III - INITIATIONS/PSYCHOPHYSICAL RELIGIOUS EXERCISES

initiation of transformation: that fifth initiation of which those in second maturity stand in need.[55]

However that may be, there can be no doubt that humankind does develop in the above-mentioned divisions. And there can be no doubt that in the past, when the average person was thinking only of cathartic asceticism as being the highest life (and the laggards were still playing anachronistically at being heroes and producing militarism), the most advanced were considering those stimulations that are intenser than mortification and more informative than critical analytical knowledge.

Today this entire fivefold series is needed as an explicit therapy. For today we have not only the entire fivefold series of humankind at last present, with each of the divisions fully [populated], but also we have reached the fifth stage of human history, the postindividual phase that has brought us to a self-conscious knowledge of our non-self-conscious. What was esoteric and intuitive can now be exoteric and explicit. What had been a traditional ritual may now become an experimentally verified science.

Until now, this complete knowledge and praxis were confined to the few leaders, a sparse and generally hidden number of seers. Their inspiration and guidance had to be fed cryptically, if not clandestinely, to those leaders (administrators, judges, kings, generals) who were obviously in control. And these advisory powers were exercised chiefly as an inhibiting power over violence, a conservational minatory force rather than a message of initiative and creativity.

Now, however, this secret of a complete and elucidating education, of a process that can alter conduct, character, and consciousness, can be employed openly for the birth-delivery not only of each present stage of humankind, but of the stage in the epoch that lies ahead of the postindividual person, for the conscious forwarding of the evolutionary process.

[Ed. note: Reviewer Robert R. Kirsch correctly notes that this "final portion of the work ... bears the signs of haste ... as though a brilliant seminar is ending because time is running out." Heard's at-times lilting prose turns much more oblique and discursive. To better aid in identifying the key elements in this Section III, please see the Tables.]

1. The Initiation of Rebirth
(*Earth*)

We now know that the five mysteries, certainly since the Ascetic Epoch, were developed to produce successive states of increasing release and awareness. The basic mystery is rightly called that of earth; the second is that of water; the third that of air; the fourth that of fire; and the fifth that of aether (that is, electricity).

Correlating these both with the five epochs of humankind and the five recapitulating phases of the individual's life, we see that the first initiation is to remedy the trauma of birth. This trauma has its two aspects: one social and historical; the other personal and immediate. We find its socio-historical aspect in the fissure, the faulting that occurred when our prehistoric coconscious social growth (which was advancing too slowly) was broken by the eruption of our proto-self-conscious, heroic revolt. Its personal aspect lies in the fact this event has to be recalled in order that it may be gone through again, recapitulated intentionally, accepted consciously. This process of psychic regression is now a commonplace of psychotherapy.[56]

III - INITIATIONS/PSYCHOPHYSICAL RELIGIOUS EXERCISES

However, only now can its full significance and value begin to be appreciated. We had to understand that each individual is recapitulating human history; that his frustrations are its tragedies still calling for explication in a contemporary interpretation, in a third act of metacomedy (see Glossary) which can now be written to follow that second act that seemed so futile, so unresolvable, so final that it was called tragic. With that understanding, this third act can now be conceived. It can be more majestic than the second act of tragedy and more hilarious than the first act of comedy, more significant than any personal drama.

In this chapter, then, we must deal with the primal ordeal of birth and its initiatory therapeutic process whereby, getting down to base, to earth, a firm rebuilt foundation is made for the four other and successive re-elevations of the human psyche. Racially, anthropologically, we now have clear evidence of this rite and its therapeutic value. The trauma of birth echoes and indeed recapitulates the racial crisis that occurred when animal intuition and anxietyless immediacy began to be interfered with by the cross light of reason and the tension of expectancy and apprehension. And this deep stress point and faulting require remedy.

As studies of the Arunta and other Australian Aboriginal tribes have shown, those who would be the wizard tribal leaders must undergo this earth rebirth. The cave is the womb and the tomb. As we know, it bore a similar duality in the consciousness of Paleolithic man. From its opening, one emerged to do battle with the tundra beasts. Into its depths one penetrated and sank, there to die to human identity and become merged with the life forces, to become one with the common basic life power, the universal soul out of which beasts and men (men pelt-garbed as beasts and beasts anthropomorphically souled as men) loomed and mingled in mystic communion in the wavering dimness (53).

From thence onward, we can recognize the cave burial, the yawning dark mouth that leads down into a sightless world, as being *mors janua vitae* (the death gate of life), the strait between the inland sea of life and the outer ocean of death. Even when man no longer was compelled to seek shelter on the cave's lip and in the cavern's forecourt, still he brought home his dead to be reborn in those

1. The Initiation of Rebirth

fecund, transforming depths. The proto-patriarch of the Hebrew people, Abram, purchases the cave of Machpelah in which to bury Sara, his wife. The later editor of the account has to rationalize this rite by making the father of the Hebrews say, "that I may bury my dead out of my sight." By then, man's concept of his soul had become so personalized and body-identified that the crumbling of the corpse meant the evaporation of the spirit. Therefore, as this materialistic concept gained ground, flesh became the awkward, embarrassing and, in the end, foul element; while spirit was the sweet, elusive, evanescent spectrum. Thus death became a penalty of ultimate degradation, and the faint spirit itself remained only a wraith, a ghost, a last echo of the sigh of ultimate despair, the last groan of irremediable defeat.

As Henri Frankfort has pointed out, the Egyptian civilization held so firmly to the reality of the spirit, and to the reality of the body as its wholesome expression, that the dead were supposed not to haunt the night but to sleep comfortably in their tomb house, rising with the sun and, while others had to work, spending their day carelessly, seated like a gay plumaged bird in the leafy branches of a tree. Because the dead were living a so much fuller and more relaxed life than those still in the first hard working stage of human existence, the yet-working living used to come to the tomb's door for their picnics, there to enjoy a foretaste of liberation from hard labor and in the company of those who had arrived at that cheerful station. Thus the Nile culture was able to resist the despair that comes in with the Ascetic phase until, in the third century A.D., the epidemic of mortificatory eremitism found its fastnesses in the Libyan Desert.[57]

Egyptian civilization very early formed around the powerfully binding mythos of death and resurrection, of the tomb being also the womb, of burial and procreation being parts of one act. The rite of Isis and Osiris, at Abydos, is known to be very early because of the fact that this brother-and-sister marital couple were moon deities, not sun gods. Therefore, they date from the lunar monthly calendar that precedes the solar annual chronology. They are also earth (chthonic) deities, not day-sky gods; and they belong to the phase of human consciousness when the dark is the time not only of fecundation but is also recognized as being the time of psychic vision to

III - INITIATIONS/PSYCHOPHYSICAL RELIGIOUS EXERCISES

which day vision is only detailed foreground, present-time supplementation. The myth describes how, when Set the enemy has slain Osiris and scattered his limbs over the land, Isis reassembles his body and, having buried her recomposed brother, is fertilized by him while he lies mummified and subsequently bears their child Horus, the Sun God, who incarnates as the reigning Pharaoh. Indeed, so quickly, powerfully, and comprehensively did this cosmological-political conception grip the mind of the Egyptians that, though there were feudal periods when Heroicism did appear, it never destroyed the basic social heredity founded on the pattern of death and resurrection and the idea that the tomb was also the womb.

Nor should we so state the reciprocal polarity of the two apparent extremes of this conception, as though death were the master theme (as though tragedy were the bedrock fact with redemption being an afterthought, a desperate contrivance whereby, at frightful cost, victory is snatched out of defeat) with the issue lost here, and the remnant, though annihilated in this life, by heroic sacrifice rescued from the stricken field and translated, Valkyrie-wise, to a nonhuman heaven. For even in our own Anglo-Saxon tongue, the word *Hella* in no wise referred to a place of retribution or even a realm of the lost, any more than, as we noted earlier, was the Hellenic Hades other than the underworld. *Hella* was simply the hidden place, the dark area. And the dark, as we have seen and shall see again further on, is the prerequisite of seership.

As we have noted earlier, in the Eleusinian mystery, Persephone, who was the wife of Pluto (King of Hades), was supposed to have risen again from her married state in the underworld to rejoin her mother Demeter. When considering this most famous of the classical mysteries (see *The Mysteries*, especially "The Eleusinian Mysteries"), W. F. Otto (65) points out that Persephone cannot be thought of as being the seedling that dies in the earth to give rise to the new plant. The appropriate image, Otto goes on to say, would be one of fertilization or impregnation, not of death.

The midindividualist ascetic thinks of birth as committing the soul to death. And the two other phases of individualism, the Heroic and Humanic, think of death as being the final frustration, the annihilation of consciousness. The coconscious know that death, voluntary and

1. The Initiation of Rebirth

understood, is right rebirth. It is a second birth that explains, explicates, and elevates the first birth, which had been an involuntary, psychophysically distorted birth, a miscarriage.

In short, the first of the mysteries, that of earth, consisted in a burial, either in a cave or an artificial cave: a dug grave. The individual was given back to Mother Earth, restored to his seminal state in her fruitful womb, and then, with the mistaken husk of his calloused selfhood shed, he was reborn rightly. Therefore, in the power of endless life, he lived forever, free of wrong time and of mistaken identity. He was deathless, for henceforth every change would be no destruction or defeat but a further and voluntarily undertaken expansion and growth.

To experience this earth mystery of voluntary death and resurrection was, we know clearly, present as a requisite of the Egyptian Pharaoh's right to reign. After a certain number of years on the throne, he who was the incarnation of Ra, the Sun, nevertheless shed his golden insignia, was wrapped in the grave clothes, placed in the sarcophagus, and buried. There is no reason to suppose that, at the beginning of the Pharaohonic sacramental rulership, this was a mere pageant—at best a miracle play to recall a past magical event; at worst a cynical method whereby an aged ruler, by pretense, claimed to have restored his sexual virility, lacking which he would be killed by his subjects. As Frankfort points out, there is no evidence that the Egyptians sacrificed their king when his reproductive potency disappeared. On the other hand, there is plenty of evidence of the intense group suggestibility of every person in an early traditional society. There is also evidence from India (from early dates down to the present time) that by hypnotic suggestion, and sometimes by autosuggestion, catalepsy is induced; that in this state the subject is buried with mouth bound, body ceremented, nostrils and ears plugged with wax; that he can remain so, in suspended animation, for as long as thirty days; and that when he is resuscitated it is claimed (he maintains it and his behavior would certainly suggest it) that his consciousness has been changed and that the sensory ego has disappeared or has been vastly modified.

Let us grant then (1) that there have been some persons in the past who retained, to a large extent, an earlier quality of consciousness: a

III - INITIATIONS/PSYCHOPHYSICAL RELIGIOUS EXERCISES

preindividualistic psyche that had not become divided by a threshold into a personalized foreconscious and a preterconscious, and that such persons used the earth mystery of burial and resurrection to cleanse the mirror of consciousness from the oxide of personal and immediate concern. Let us grant further (2) that ancient societies (even cultures as explicit and complex as the Egyptian) employed this method to restore to the priest–king his sense of universal identity, which old age was corrupting and contracting into body identification. Then it is possible to see the primal place that the earth mystery and its ordeal and initiation have held in man's history and so holds in his preterconscious today.

We can see that it has been an essential psychosocial therapy in man's developing culture. For as individualistic consciousness increased, birth, in consequence and as it does among all individualized peoples, becomes a dreaded and sinister event.[58] And the mother catches the contagion of panic. She contracts (literally trying to shrink from the delivery process) and the child, inevitably having a bad passage, carries the trauma of birth in its subconscious. The person who would be freed of this birth–death fear had, therefore, to undergo a regression, repassing through the process and so, Persephone-like, rise again from the cave womb–tomb to become an immortal one who knows that birth and death are two names for a single process.

We can see also that the individual today, if he is to be emotionally educated [and] psychophysically taught, must have the repressed memory of his misbirth raised to contemporary consciousness and relived constructively. There is great hope that this can now be done and that a generation can now be reared that will be basically sane because it is freed of this earliest, most deforming and unnerving fear.

Even forty years ago, this hope might have seemed far-fetched and vain. "Those who can do can't know, and those who can know can't do" seemed to be the modern form of the well-known Taoist dilemma, "Those who know don't say, and those who say don't know." As C. Kerényi (49) has put it in his "The Mysteries of the Kabeiroi," "arreton" (ineffability) "is the more exact word for 'mystical.'" For there are no words to describe the mystical experience:

1. The Initiation of Rebirth

none are needed, although sounds can be and are used in the third mystery, the initiation of air and inspiration. Not only this, but wordy explanations and the disputes into which they degenerate render the creative process impossible. The state of mind is literally unspeakable; for speech is a calling across to someone else who cannot otherwise understand—while the mystical experience, at the very start, is the sense of that chasm being closed; a sense of being taken back and restored to the original symbiosis with the mother who is Earth; a sense that a primal unity has been re-established. As Kerényi says, even Plutarch, the devout practitioner of the Eleusinian mysteries in the tolerantly appreciative, syncretic climate of the Hellenic Roman Peace, lived when "atmosphere had changed to object" (*ibid., supra*); when what had been an unquestioned field of timeless experience had to be objectified in a relic and a rite.

But the very fact of the outrageous stresses to which Western youths were exposed while the psychological revolution was dawning and the postindividual type was emerging (the First World War of 1914–18) led to an acceleration of advance in psychiatry, owing to the outbreak of war neurosis. This led to the discovery that men broke along a line of previous fissure; and this, in turn, led to the tracing of these fissures back to infantile traumas, the primal and most profound of which was that of birth.[59]

Nor did these discoveries end simply in diagnosis; they led to remedial therapy. For it was then that the therapy of regression began (see above). This sprang from work with apparent paralysis, blindness, deafness, and other psychosomatic disabilities. [Three observations were] soon noted. (1) These disabilities occurred almost entirely among conscripts and/or simple, unthinking buck privates. They were very rare in the officer class (57). A higher sense of responsibility made this subconscious mechanism of autosuggestion–escape almost impossible. The officer, when his nerve broke after long strain of intensified anxiety, could only commit suicide.[60] (2) By using the electric detector on the conductivity of the skin, it was possible to show the patient that he could and did see, hear, and feel, although his unconscious deep controls could prevent his showing visual, auditory, or sensory reaction. This method, very moderate in its usefulness, afterwards became vulgarized as the lie

III - INITIATIONS/PSYCHOPHYSICAL RELIGIOUS EXERCISES

detector and has now become refined as the polygraph examination. (3) Hypnosis then showed that the deep consciousness that had caused the inhibition could be spoken to and, in some cases, could be persuaded to revoke the escapist device.

During the Second World War, these techniques were advanced and improved. For example, pentothal sodium and other drugs were used to put the patient into a suggestible sleep. He was then regressed to the moment of the traumatic shock when he would have a convulsive horror shock as the fear block was raised to consciousness, after which the psychosomatic inability (paralysis or the like) was removed. However, it was soon realized that just to strip off this defense was of even less use and more damaging than tearing off the scab from an unhealed wound—reinfection is very likely to follow. The deep area of weakness had to be strengthened, or collapse must be repeated whenever the patient was exposed to fresh stress.

Here, then, we find psychiatry today. The map it now has of the mind shows that misintegration of early experience, shock and faulting when the character is coalescing, must mean a basic flaw and weakness that makes the subject liable to collapse under strain. Therefore, psychotherapy now stands faced by the fact that all further advance in power education, in mastery of the environment (technical equipment and the like), all intellectual instruction, all executive and administrative skill (indeed, all understanding of the management of men) may prove to be worse than useless[61] as long as the emotional life is untrained and the psychic life is still subject to and motivated by infantile fears, resentments, panics, and rages.

The psychological revolution is about to move out of its first phase of theory and experimental private therapy into the mass fields of corporate action and sociopolitical ruling. As the child psychologist, the criminologist, and the psychiatrist find their work interlocking and their conclusions converging, the demand for preventive measures made by these three experts should prove to be irresistible. For their three fields, put together, cover education, law, and mental health: a vast area, in which the consequences of disregarding expert advice are demonstrably disastrous.

The argument is greatly strengthened when we realize that prevention is not merely the avoidance of felony and insanity, of

1. The Initiation of Rebirth

neurosis, psychosis, and criminal psychopathy. It is not merely the damming back of floodwaters into reservoirs less demonstrably inefficient and harmful than are prisons or even mental hospitals. Nor is it merely the detensioning and release of balked energies into comparatively harmless channels of expression. Prevention can now be considered to be focused deflection, the carrying of forces that are otherwise destructive not down to the entropic ocean of desirelessness but through the turbine dynamos of enlightened control to a new level of creative energy. In brief, the real hope of adequate prevention lies in a far higher value-developmental creation. At length a truly progressive education is possible because at last a true progress is possible—a progress through a psychophysical training that can purposively release the emotions, and so be the conscious deployment of the evolutionary drive.

Nor need the consequences of this revolution be slow in becoming apparent. We are not compelled to await the arising of a new generation that is freed from the trauma of birth, that has been brought into the world by mothers who have been taught how to bear a child without damaging it. For, although physical misgrowth in the womb is largely irremediable, it seems that if the right method is used, psychic misgrowth can always be corrected. This means that the first initiation, the rebirth through regression to the mistaken birth, and the reprogression from the recovered birth memory and its misapprehension to a true understanding of birth and a voluntary acceptance of the psychophysical beginning, can be reinitiated, that is, gone into again.

It is now necessary, therefore, to see how this may be done and what actual step in this process psychiatric and psychophysical research already suggest. We have already seen that a rebirth by burial has been used throughout history, at least to the rise of the Ascetic Epoch and, in Egypt, down to the end of the Pharaohonic priest-kingship; while in India this rite has lasted on among some sects to the present day. We have also seen that our psychiatry, now that our own culture is in the psychological revolution that ushers in the Postindividualistic Epoch, sees the importance of and applies the method of regression while the subject is under either hypnosis or a dissociative drug, or both.

III - INITIATIONS/PSYCHOPHYSICAL RELIGIOUS EXERCISES

This new therapy, however, is not as yet general; still less is it part of the emotional education that is the necessary complement of intellectual education. It is employed almost solely for those who have indicated serious psychic maladjustment pointing to some traumatic birth experience. Nor does the method as now employed seem to avail itself, as yet, of the indications given by study of the past employment of this primal mystery of earth and sepulture redelivery. Again, neither are we yet incorporating, in regressional therapy, such research findings as have now been made as to the effects of what has been called "limited environment," the re-creation of a womb situation. Whether it is the method used in the royal Egyptian Sed Festival procedure, or the one today practiced for entombment by the Hatha Yogin in a suspended animation that has been brought on by self-induced catalepsy, either by autosuggestion or heterosuggestion, the traditional method would seem to aim at insensibility brought on by breath control. The tongue is swallowed, blocking the throat, and the heart's action slows down to the point that, although a minimal supply of blood is kept in the brain, a heartbeat cannot be detected except with the aid of X-ray, which shows not an actual beat but a slight movement in the valves of the heart (96).

We should note here that our psychiatry, reacting from the failure of chemicalized medicine to "minister to a mind diseased" and "pluck from the memory a rooted sorrow," has tended to neglect the physiological side of the psychiatric problem. It is true that a number of sedational drugs have all had much initial promise.[62] However, the Menningers and others believe that these can only assist at most some 10 percent of those requiring instant aid. The concept of using a therapy which would go beyond both drug and doctrine is still unfamiliar. Psychoanalysis has grown in expression and communication techniques from speech (words) through drawing and now on to psychodrama. From the other side, [by the use] of simple massage there has been emerging the tentative procedures whereby the subject, with his attention confined to his physique, is communicated with and released by tactile rhythms.

If, however, as the correlation among the fivefold stages of man's developing social heredity, his individual recapitulation of

1. The Initiation of Rebirth

that process, and the initiation series suggests, we are today at an age and crisis when our psychophysical history, our individual psychophysical development, and our psychophysical research all indicate that we must consciously cooperate with and elucidate this process, then we should be able to outline the procedure and method of a modernized mystery.

As the first mystery is that of earth (burial and resurrection), we shall conclude this chapter with a tentative sketch of the procedure in a modern version of this initiation. The first and prefatory step, naturally, must consist in explanation to the subject. As we have seen, regression has been of great interest to therapists, and thanks to the success of Morey Bernstein's (4) *The Search for Bridey Murphy* (a case based on regression under hypnosis), it was for a time a popularized notion. The trauma of birth is also a familiar concept to anyone who is acquainted with psychotherapy. And as we have mentioned earlier, dental evidence of the severity of this shock is now available. There can be little doubt, then, of the fear block, of the repressed distress, resentment, and panic that, from this birth level and throughout their lives, is distorting the basic emotional reactions of all but a very few. Once this has been explained, and the need and method of release has been shown to the person, the researches of Donald Hebb (of McGill University, Montreal) and John C. Lilly (formerly of the National Institute of Mental Health, Bethesda, Maryland) become highly relevant. Their work with the limited environment has indicated the profound modifications of feeling tone, of body image, and indeed of ratiocination, that are brought about when a person is so comfortably confined that no major stimuli or familiar contact is experienced.

Stretched out on his back, with his hands in large, roomy containers, his body resting in great softness, the only light coming through a filtering visor, sound reduced to a minimum by the soundproof sarcophagus in which the couch was enclosed, the person was rewombed. After a few minutes, the effect was most striking. Active athletes seemed to suffer the most. The sensation of isolation rapidly became distressing, and when the mind began to function in an unfamiliar manner, the distress became acute. The new type of imagery was at first alarming and finally terrifying."[63]

III - INITIATIONS/PSYCHOPHYSICAL RELIGIOUS EXERCISES

It is clear that if this encapsulation were undertaken by an instructed and prepared subject, the results could be quite otherwise. The instruction, the reasons for the treatment, we have considered above: the therapy is to bring about a regression to the moment of the trauma, a re-remembering and a reprogression. The preparation should include presuggestion, to see how far the subject is easily suggestible. If there is a resistance to hypnosis, light suggestibility and an introduction to the preterindividual conditions of consciousness may be aided by 25 micrograms of LSD. Then it is best that the subject make a tape recording of his own voice, which should be quiet, relaxed, and assured. In this recording, he should tell himself that he is now going to be regressed to his birth experience; and he should then instruct himself to look on at this event with interest and without any alarm, to watch as both spectator and actor. He should further instruct himself that, should he at any point become aware that the delivery he is re-enacting is changing from a vigorous struggle to frustrant panic, he will correct the story; that he will witness and experience the delivery as something in which he can retake the initiative and as something which he can perform with a dynamic realization of its purpose and outcome.

This experience is much more than the mere witnessing of a crisis from the past, much more than the reliving of distress which releases repressed fear and ends subconscious conflict. Considerably more than a mere return to normalcy can be effected, and by this method will be achieved. The fully accomplished rebirth releases a vast fund of energy that permits further evolution. The consciousness that both looks on and also releases, untying the knot of tangled birth and delivering the soul, is more than the personal consciousness, far more than the individualistic aspect of the psyche. The relived birth, in that presence and through its invoked power, means the first step toward bringing forth the total consciousness, the complete person who is the aim of evolution.

When this tape has been made by the subject, he goes into his confinement. However, to the conditions of limited environment, as described above, are added two further aids to dynamic recovery. The first is the means, which is now known, whereby respiration may be suspended and yet lung aeration be maintained.[64] Yes, a

1. The Initiation of Rebirth

consciousness remains, which is not only clear but is possessed of a steadiness, a lack of distractions and minor fluctuations, that is otherwise unknown and probably unknowable.

For any full regression, the advantages of this are clearly great. For in the first place, how is an adult, [with] respiratory, alternating consciousness, really to recapture the fetal prerespiratory consciousness if the body-mind is still being disturbed by the wave of inhalation-exhalation?[65] The attempts to achieve the necessary stillness, through an encoffined limited environment, are largely frustrated by this steady, fluctuating internal disturbance. Secondly, how can the subject attain the detached, reconstructive interest of the onlooking, remolding self (the consciousness of the scanner of Wilder Penfield, the organizer of Spiemann, the causal self of the [Vedic] Vedānta-sāra) if he is still a respiring creature whose respiratory rate automatically accelerates with any alarm and whose alarm is reciprocally aggravated by the respiratory increase? Further, the heart action (which combines with every alarm to accelerate and further distress the emotions) is itself cut down by one third when respiratory breathing is exchanged for still-lung aeration. The state of mind now achieved is one of a serenity that is utterly unfamiliar to the present-day, high-pressured person-of-action. Nevertheless, it has proved to be delightful. Especially noticeable is the cessation of those small restless movements of the hands and feet, which most of us continually make with as little purpose as a cat twitches the tip of its tail. Perhaps even more remarkable is the total disappearance of any wish to smoke. The two package per diem semi-addict no longer fidgets for a [cigarette]. For hours, the hands are still, the body position easily maintained without any movement. The mind, even of the most active person, appears to pass into an effortless contemplation which is peaceful, somehow significant, and strangely satisfying to those who are at odds with themselves.

It is obvious that such a state is a powerful adjuvant to that of the limited environment. For, in the space of a few heartbeats, it changes the forbiddingness of isolation into a welcome vacation. Further, it is not a state of vacancy but of creativity. It creates that frame of mind which the Stoics called *ataraxia*, the God's-eye view that permits one to be constantly interested and highly concerned

III - INITIATIONS/PSYCHOPHYSICAL RELIGIOUS EXERCISES

but incapable of anxiety or the lower sympathy of distress or, still less, of heartbreak.

And now something more can be added. While the entombed, expired subject lies motionless in body and with steady, unwavering mind, and after his own prerecorded voice has spoken its instructions and encouragements to his totally attentive ear, the other senses can be brought into cooperative play. Set at the speed that will give the precise flicker that is needed to rouse the encephalogrammic delta wave, the stroboscope can stir again the nerve energy which was present in the infant's brain at birth.[66] And certain subsonic vibrations (which can be felt as well as heard) do produce a sense of awe. In the unprepared, this sound wave generally causes dismay, as do mescaline and lysergic acid; while in a person who is prepared for it, it induces a vast sense of wonder. The olfactory sense, with its direct access to the very base of the brain, should also be employed. With a corrective use of the indoles (the chemicals both strongly stimulating to the olfactory center and also associated with chemicals that shift consciousness, for example, lysergic acid), those odors which are considered to be repulsive may be adjusted to be evulsive, leading to an exultation and transmutation of revulsion. (For instance, the first violent scents of the mother's ammonia, made harsh by her panic and her blood, may have led to pathological disgusts and aversions.[67])

So, in modern psychophysical and psychochemical terms, the birth process can be not merely relived and rendered innocuous, like a lanced abscess, but it can be relived in terms of a process that transcends the personal, private individual and renders him reborn, enabled then to go on to further stages of new growth. Now possessed of a true and full birth, he is prepared and equipped to grow.

It is certainly a gain that the patient has now attained freedom from the dead hand of a misunderstood, dreaded, and repressed past. However, it is considerably more that he is now possessed of the free use of the energies that were locked down within him in the effort to hold back his primal fear. Still, this is not enough: far from it. We cannot rid a man of wary fears, set him free with new energies, and not let him know where he is going under this released steam, and how he is to handle his new powers in the fuller categories of enlarged living. This would only be to make the psychological

1. The Initiation of Rebirth

revolution a dreary repetition of the three preceding ones: the ecclesiastic, the political, and the economic. This would only end in another weary round of the tyrannies of sects, of parties, and of ideological fanaticisms, only this time armed with an apter violence and subtler weapons with which to subject the soul.

It is a fact (and it has awakened much comment in psychoanalytic circles) that although tens of thousands have undergone successful analyses during the last forty years, these large numbers of freed individuals have not affected society; still less have they become even a leaven that is slowly altering it. Further, in the last generation, even larger numbers of children (many now adults) have been brought up with a careful avoidance of those harsh and violent methods that caused traumas. And these undamaged recruits have proved to be no more efficacious socially than their restored and recovered elders have been.

However, in the light of the facts that we have been considering, this is not surprising and should have been expected. Successful analysis may release and clear up damage done to the psyche in the portentous first forty months. It can, however, make little impression on the physical shock of the actual birth when this delivery has been from a mother who was contracted in panic. To cure that, a far deeper, more actualized re-experience is required. Talking about it and so merely recalling it is not enough. And even when the birth trauma is raised and its repressed complex is released, this is only one fourth of the full and necessary recovery. A successful analysis may teach a man not to be frightened of his deep emotional life, but if this release of the infantile fears is not followed up with a release from his childish, heroical rages, then his shrinking has only been exchanged for aggression and assault. Too many of the well analyzed have turned from being timid retreatants into callous-conscienced persons who feel free of any compunction about enjoying themselves, if not at the expense of others, at least with a disregard of public benefit. The community gains little, if it gains at all, when, in exchange for members who are fearful, it is given persons who consider loyalty to be a crippling inhibition.

Therefore, the very success of the ordeal and initiation of the first mystery applied to modern, postindividual man would demand

III - INITIATIONS/PSYCHOPHYSICAL RELIGIOUS EXERCISES

that we render and apply the other four mysteries in equally modern terms. Then with these four explicated, we should be able, at last, to produce that complete person who alone is adequate to life's demand and the situation's challenge. In the next chapter, therefore, we shall deal with the next step: the reintroduction to the specific child crisis and the reinterpretation of the heroic ideal.

2. The Initiation of Catharsis
(*Water*)

The initiation of rebirth leaves the individual not only free but recharged; not only with his adhesions removed, his inhibitions loosened, but with a new zest for the larger living that is now made possible. For it has brought the psyche out of its historical and individual infancy. The actual historical process, when man was born out of the coconscious aeonic life of the tribe into the protoindividualism of the Heroic Epoch, was a miscarriage. Or rather, it was a kind of auto-cesareanism whereby the child tore itself out of the mother-matrix that wished to deny it birth. He was delivered through his spasm of hatred, revolt, and revulsion against the tradition that he spurned as being suffocating and foul. And this scar-trauma in our tradition still remains in our mind. In our conscious mind, it is our repression and deliberate ignorance of the pre-Heroic phase. And so we have interpreted history, until today, in terms of exclusive individualism, physical force, competition, and violence. In our unconscious mind it can be seen in the destructive or tragic character that typifies our images and patterns of prestige.

III - INITIATIONS/PSYCHOPHYSICAL RELIGIOUS EXERCISES

Hence, every infancy (the first psychological history-recapitulating phase) has also been damaged: first, by a bad parturition inflicted by a panic-stricken mother, and then by the inflammation of the child's race memories, generally by the passions of the parents. We are born into national hatreds. This scar tissue (of the bad birth of the child's social heredity and of the child's own psychophysical bad birth) can, we have seen, be removed by the ordeal and initiation. It can be taken away by the test and going in which, when it penetrates in, down, and back, replays the misrendered birth drama.

Man then has new liquid assets with which to start again. He can now have a proper respect for the primal aeon of coconscious conscience and consent, for the social heredity as a growth process, and also a proper evaluation of his psychosomatic freedom to forward that growth. He can advance—but whither? He has recovered his infantile plasticity and has at his disposal the potentiality of generalized response and awareness. He can have the panaesthetic alertness if he will, and if he knows how to employ it.

But, as we mentioned at the close of the last chapter, this is only one quarter of the human task today. Indeed it is only one fifth of the regrowth and on-growth that man must achieve if he is, by complete initiation, to win a complete initiative toward the human situation and complete cooperation with the life process. Those who have achieved this first freedom will only face defeat if they are taken no further. If with their sensitiveness they are left to confront others who have themselves failed to grow, in blind defensiveness these newly free may even produce thorns instead of buds, stings instead of egg ducts, weapons of destruction instead of tools of production.

So if the first liberation is to be worthwhile, and this correction of miscarriage itself not miscarry, it must be the first of a series. And however remarkable be the gain, if it is to be harvested it must be looked upon as being only a beginning. Certainly the mysteries, as we have now been able to uncover them, are a fivefold series; although in various epochs men have been content with two: for example, the Eleusinian and Samothracian initiations of the Greeks[68] and, in more modern times, the conversion and second blessing of the Methodist praxis. Still, there seems never to have been a time

2. The Initiation of Catharsis

since the Heroic Epoch, and for the peoples that have gone through that protoindividual stage, when less than two was considered adequate.[69] For although the first initiation was an essential initial step, it called for a further advance. All it could do was to deliver the subject from the consequences of a wrong emergence; from the consequences of an involuntary, panic-stricken, resentful expulsion out of a condition where, though things had become restrictive, no other life is conceivable. The end of a golden age is imprisonment in fetters of gold. Every question has its closing answer, and life is locked in inflexible replies. A state of suffocating security is the fetus' condition during the last month in the womb. Oxygen shortage and intolerable congestion, consequences of its successful growth, have turned the sheltered paradise into a trap.

Then the infant, with its birth struggle over, able to breathe its fill and be suckled amply, begins again to adjust and settle down to the all-found-for-you Utopia of the mother-matrix external womb. Against this indolence, as we have seen, the healthy child has to struggle with its noradrenaline charge. And, historically, the later hero struck out destructively against the blandishments of the mother-deity city cultures.

The second initiation, therefore, is to correct and reconstruct this not unnatural but mistaken reaction. The first initiation teaches the psyche how to be born into distinctiveness, from unison to harmony. The second initiation is to teach the psyche how to correct the excessive reaction, [which] the race and the individual made and still make, against a too long retention at the level of possessive motherhood: whether this be in a religious cult or in a nursery climate.

And as this second stage is a correction of a personal excess, a protoindividualistic, destructive revolt, this initiation has in its procedure something more active and, indeed, more penitential than the first one. The returning to earth, as a symbol of return to the womb, demands only a gentle resignation, a reteaching of the initiate so that he may consent to have performed for him a rightful, peaceable birth to take the place of the spastic, violent expulsion that had so wounded his soul and overwrought his body. But the second initiation differs from the first in demanding more of the person. For it is dealing with a new state, a state in which there must be choice

III - INITIATIONS/PSYCHOPHYSICAL RELIGIOUS EXERCISES

and a new act: one of revolt. An individual, however rudimentary, has struck out for himself and has raged against restriction. This second process of redemptive deliverance, therefore, requires more than that the postulant should go within himself and be relieved by reliving a repressed nightmare. What is now necessary is an act of repentance for a mistaken act of the will, a definite surrender of willfulness. The individual must emerge and he must have the noradrenaline charge to do so. But that charge must be *rajas*, the Sanskrit word for force that is controlled by discipline, not rage, the blind reaction of destructiveness.

It is clear, then, why the second mystery after that of earth is that of water. But as we now preserve it in a traditional, atrophied form, consisting of the sprinkling of a few drops or at most a quick dip, it is naturally difficult to recognize why such a gently dampening procedure should have been considered adequate to quench the flame of anger or to smooth the contortions of rage. However, a study of the research evidence can leave us in no doubt that in the water initiation there was once a power to reduce fury: a power that was as demonstrably strong as the power of a physician to reduce a dislocation.

First, there is archaeological evidence to consider. For example, the most striking features of the great twin cities of the Indus civilization (Mohenjo-Daro and Harappa) are its huge baptistries. This would seem to indicate that a tremendous importance was attached to the water initiation by this civilization, which retained longer than any other culture, and raised to a higher level, a premilitary, nonphysically coercive, hypnocratic way of life.[70]

Secondly, the philological evidence indicates that the actual process was no idle swimming pool exercise or elegantly appointed ceremony such as we see, for example, in the [waning] form of the Sed festival in Egypt. Nor was it the empty pageantry of the Venetian Doge wedding the sea with a ring that he cast into it, or Queen Victoria having her son and heir sprinkled by her Archbishop with a little flask of water from the Jordan. Baptism, by the time the word took its present Greek form, did mean to dip. But in its ruder root it meant something much more strenuous. In Old Norse, the language of the tribes that went northwest while their fellow tribes went southeast

2. The Initiation of Catharsis

into Greece, the word that the Greeks turned into *baptein* is *kafa*, to dive and, more, to swim under water. Further, this word for strenuous effort and risk is linked with the minatory verb *kvefja*, to suffocate.

Thirdly, anthropology throws a confirmatory light on this sequence of dive, swim under water, suffocate. In his thorough study of shamanism, Shirokogoroff points out that the man or woman becomes aware of his or her vocation to become a shaman between the ages of fifteen and twenty-one through experiencing spells of excitement and trembling. However, although this may convince the individual personally, it falls far short of persuading the other members of the tribe that the person will be of psychic use to them.

As a first test, not merely of his sincerity but of his stamina, he is told to go out (or is driven out) into the Siberian forest to live alone and as best he may. After he feels adequate to face the tribe's further testing and "because he has won some spirit-mastery," he has to recite, accurately, a list of the spirit names. Then, however, come the real ordeals of water and of fire. The fire we will leave until, in Chapter 4 of this Section III, we come to consider this particular aspect of a possible recharging: the initiation of illumination. Certainly, the water test is sufficiently severe; indeed, it is a kill or cure, a dissolution or a transformation.

The postulant is taken to a frozen river. Here he has to dive through one ice hole, swim under water and emerge through another hole in the ice which is a considerable distance away. This he may be called on to do as many as nine times. It is not a surprise to learn that some drown. One would certainly not be surprised to learn that most seminaries were closed for want of ordinands if such tests were used to discover whether our candidates for the ministry or priesthood had the conviction and stamina to face such ordeals. And, just as certainly, one cannot regard these shaman cultures as being composed of credulous creatures ready to accept anyone who is odd enough, or sufficiently impudent, to claim supranormal powers.

The initiation by water, we can then say, has always been the great method of bringing the protoindividual to a coordinant balance of mind wherein his individualism, his personalized consciousness, may be able to work with his generalized nonpersonal consciousness.

III - INITIATIONS/PSYCHOPHYSICAL RELIGIOUS EXERCISES

The force that would otherwise express itself as violence culminating in homicidal rage is thus turned back and given release through the desperate struggle to survive drowning. If the subject can struggle through, this ordeal is intense enough for the personality to be dilated until it discovers its superpersonality. The ordeal by water, then, even when it proved to be fatal, might prove to be socially valuable. For those who were strong enough to undertake it would be types of such energy that if they did not attain to knowledge of their superconsciousness, they would become ruthless power types.[71] Here, then, would be a socio-natural selection removing those who were powerful enough to mutate psychologically and who, if they failed to do so, would become public enemies.

So, in the stage of consciousness in which he might otherwise fall into heroics, defiance, denunciation, and destruction, the individual can become the seer, the eyes of his community. He can give to his fellow beings that open vision without which there is chaos and sanctionless activity; without which, as the writer of the Hebrew Book of Judges says in describing a period of heroic chaos, "Every man did what was right in his own eyes" (Judg. 21:25).

We now know what is being aimed at in the training of all seers, of the shaman, of the *rishi* (to use the Sanskrit name for him), who can either prevent or reorder the anarchy of a Heroic Age. It is to make it possible for both sides of the mind, the conscious and the preterconscious, to work at once.

Two steps are necessary for this. The first, being considered in this chapter, is the reduction of the passionate egotism of the protoindividual who, if left unharnessed, becomes the stallion that kicks the chariot to pieces. The next step, which we shall consider more and more in the three following chapters, is the increasing of the power to balance the energies of intuitive, whole, total understanding-insight against the polar energies of specific, particular, immediate communication and instruction. This will then make it possible to answer the practical questions: What do we do now? What is the next step to be taken from here? What is the future of humankind at present?

We have now considered, most briefly, the outward purgation, the catharsis. (1) There is the removal of social support, of sustenance

2. The Initiation of Catharsis

from the world of the ordinary warm human atmosphere. There is the banishment into the wild: into an exercise ground, a natural gymnasium where the postulant, denuded and sundered from humankind, wrestles with unseen forces, hoping that they will give him the nonhuman power and insignia-stigmata of being able to defy his nature's basic need for a modicum of warmth and a minimum of breath. (2) The ice-capped water is again a womb; but it is not a quiet tomb where, closely held in suspended animation, the psychophysique may intuitively understand prebirth and birth and come forth reborn, refreshed, and re-energized. The postulant is now choosing consciously to abandon a private willfulness: the conscious willfulness of the child, of the protoindividual who, through its self-awareness, is far more set in its separateness than the embryo can be. This stage, then, requires definite renunciation, specific retraction of an already emerged and committed egotism. Swimming under the ice is the immense effort of an ego which knows that if it cannot transmute, and transmit into active skilled effort the superhuman powers it has attempted to release and league in its own interest, then it must suffocate, drown, die. If the "spirits" refuse to aid, refuse to recognize that this creature is willing to be their instrument and vehicle, then it must perish, having gone out past human safety but fallen short of superhuman power.

So the rebirth, the initiation through water is now a stage more active than the first rebirth of earth. And although the postulant desires to slough off the mistaken proto-personality of the hero and the angry child, he must not retreat or hope that just by surrender and leaving himself to be rehandled and remolded he will be brought back to an effortless innocency "full of repose, full of replies." He suffers, voluntarily, to the edge of death in order that he himself may become the troubled oracle who struggles to convey the ineffable universal, in temporal terms, to aid the action—or at least to limit the mistakes—of those who are involved in temporary contriving.

Yet, as the full rite of initiation by water shows by its very name, catharsis, an outward cleansing is not enough. By itself, an outer exposure to and drenching by water, however overwhelming, still is only external and only one half of the purgation. For man is a creature of two surfaces, external and internal. And, as all

III - INITIATIONS/PSYCHOPHYSICAL RELIGIOUS EXERCISES

teachers have pointed out, he can be defiled more deeply, more lethally if less perceptibly, by inner foulness than by outer stain. Hence, in the Yoga practices of India, the internal purging by water is even more essential than outer cleansing. Nor is this purgation merely a matter of physical hygiene. The Yoga methods never take mind and body apart; no therapy that really works ever does. Millennia before Freud, the Yogi therapists of India realized that grasping, retention, avarice, and self-defensiveness are reflected by visceral clutching. Hypertonic sphincters are symptoms of (and, in turn, provocative of) a psyche that is determined to hold its ground and not to give or to yield. Embryology confirms this intimacy by showing that the viscera and the genitalia spring from a common area of the fetal protostructure. The tradition retains this intuitive knowledge by maintaining that the bowels are the center of compassion and that the hard, shut heart goes with a costive fear and refusal to eliminate and release. The deep lavage, the colonic irrigation, has been known ever since the second mystery was found to be the next step in the deliverance of man. It has been used ever since the catharsis of water was discovered to be the method of restoring to the individual his binary nature, to be the remedy for his wrongfully asserted protoindividual ego of revolt, through purging him of his defiant destructiveness, his secessionist assault, through liquidating his congested, impacted recoil and restoring him not to the stagnant pool of conformity but to the current of an out-flowing life.

Therefore, and as we did at the close of the last chapter, we must now ask "How, today, could we apply such a therapy?" If such, then, is the mystery tradition in its second phase and we could, through this water ritual, correct the mistaken Heroic phase; if we would permit the enraged child now buried in our repressed subconscious (just above the birth-wounded infant) to release its pent-up energy—what, in modern terms, would be that procedure? As we did in the first mystery, we first need right knowledge. The postulant must be intellectually informed and convinced that he is part of the living process (phylogenic and ontogenic, racial and personal) which, willy nilly, must grow. Further, this process, once self-consciousness has emerged, must be understood and then an active, conscious

2. The Initiation of Catharsis

cooperation with it must be undertaken. Otherwise the process is bound to be largely frustrated by ignorant and inhibitory fears of the individualistic foremind seeking a false homeostasis by arresting all development. Even before the emergence of the protoindividual, we have seen that the traditional, preindividualistic society had reached the point where, more and more, fear of growth had rendered the social heredity as fatally rigid, though no longer as competent, racially, as animal instinct. With the rise of individualism, increasingly the foremind must be informed if it is to remove its veto on any modification of its instrument and matrix. In the first mystery, because it deals (through regression) with reduction of the psyche to a preindividualistic, preargumentative condition, the verbal procedure need be no more than affirmational.

In the second mystery, we have to work with a personality that has its case and is prepared to assert its wrongs and to claim its rights. The subject, therefore, has not merely to submit; he has to put out skilled effort to heal or reduce his own dislocation by relocating himself. All psychoses and neuroses are, to some degree, basic atavisms, anachronisms, inabilities of personalities (in varying degrees) to live contemporary lives: a willful determination to take refuge in some emotional state that crystallizes out of the past.

After this instruction, this explanation of the process and this giving to the subject his bearings, we can go on to the procedure itself, the outward conditions in which the therapy can be performed. We can now see that these conditions must be a further development of that definably limited environment that was the frame of the reenacted birth process. The research that led to immobilization of body and retraction and dilation of mind, in the burial, close-contact process, has led to experiments with immersing the body in a tank of water.[72] With the tank water at a neutral temperature, the subject was equipped with a mask and a breathing tube (snorkel) and his naked body completely submerged. He was anchored to the back of the tank by a light harness. Even with these simple conditions, the alteration of consciousness has been reported as being striking, and for the unprepared, alarming. The change from solid contact to fluid apparently modifies the sense of the frontiers of the self even more remarkably than does the burial experience.

III - INITIATIONS/PSYCHOPHYSICAL RELIGIOUS EXERCISES

The condition, however, seems to be too passive to act as the best medium for the emergence of the protoindividual, noradrenaline-charged level of consciousness. The possibility of rhythmic effort in a liquid medium would seem to be the condition that would give best results. It may be that immersion in a deep, dimly lit tank of tepid water and the use of some form of aqualung would allow such extension.[73]

There would be a distinct risk, however, in using the aqualung. For even those who are stimulated by the cold have, when they have descended beyond a certain depth, experienced a dissociation from biological consciousness. This was accompanied by either elation or an indifference that made them neglect their respiration. In some cases it would seem that divers have actually removed their mouthpiece and so were drowned. However, these states seem to have been experienced only at very considerable depths, of one hundred feet or more. And such depths seem to be unnecessary for the experience of liquid suffusion of the frontier-signifying and self-defining internal and external surfaces. The reduction of congestion, the loss of self-contained alertness, the loosening of unconscious defenses and resistances—these psychophysical undoings and releases seem to be of the nature of a nondebilitating catharsis that is free of self-pity. And in comparison with this, the non-psychophysical catharsis of drama is little more than a literary simile. Tragedy, at least Greek tragedy—Destiny playing with the self-ignorance of humans—could, as we have seen, undoubtedly give a cautionary release. For it was a religious rite, with the audience taking a visual and auditory part in the self-induced sufferings of a hero whose individualistic pride led to an infatuation that ended in death or mutilation. Deep pity could be stirred in the person watching his sufferings and commiserating with him. Deep fear could be released through the realization that the worst had been witnessed.

But not only was such catharsis really faint; it was not actually felt. It was, we must repeat, also adulterated. There were present the two alloys of the surrogate situation and projection. So there was self-pity masked as sympathy, and there was that repressed and secret elation [which] pities in order to patronize, the *schadenfreude* that covertly rejoices that the proud and noble are brought low.

2. The Initiation of Catharsis

The actual procedure of the water initiation would, then, involve first an immersion, naked and in a tank of circulating water kept at body temperature, and wherein the body would be irrigated exteriorly and interiorly. The eyes could see, through a glass visor, the water-suffused and wavering light that should probably also have rhythmic light patterns given it by the use of a stroboscope. The ear should be vibrated by sound rhythms of a comparable frequency sent through the water, which is a better sound-carrying medium than air. In this medium and state, the postulant should first be floated. But after ten minutes, the water in the tank would be made to begin a pulsing, vortex movement. And against this whirlpool, he would have to struggle until exhausted. At this point, he should achieve a further loss of self; he should emerge into an enlarged state of consciousness.

The ordeal by water, the initiation by catharsis, is then the psychophysical therapy whereby the noradrenaline, paranoid child rage, the dementia praecox which in a spasm of contractive revulsion is homicidal, is reduced. At the same time, the energy of the protoindividual stage of consciousness, which caused the tragedy of the Heroic Age, is rerouted into productive channels. This leads, without convulsion, revolution, or reaction and by evolutionary development, on to the next stage of the pure adrenaloid, self-blaming type.

The next chapter deals with the release of that type, through its specific initiation of air. It will be indicated how there can be an *askesis* without self-hatred and how self-criticism, by being made to be creative, will not provoke the despair arising from a sense of irremediable guilt.

3. The Initiation of Inspiration
(*Air*)

In this chapter we consider the third mystery, the third process of ordeal and initiation through which the earliest psychophysiological therapists worked out a technique that would remedy humankind's third mistake of excess. Excess of conservatism had led traditional coconscious society to lose way, to cease to continue coordinating new data in an expanding, flexible frame of reference. In turn, the excess of protest generated by this repression had led to destruction and pointless violence (the Heroic Age). And this social chaos had, in turn again, led to just as intemperate a reaction, from projected anger to self-anger, from revengeful shame to expiatory guilt.

But these psychic pioneers, these torch bearers of the race, had themselves gone on ahead. They were the first to practice on themselves the rebirth therapy when they had found that the traditional coconscious tribe was strangulating itself and suffocating the new life to which it should be giving rise. Again, as forerunners they had devised the initiation of the second mystery whereby, through catharsis, passionate protest might be prevented from turning into infatuated rage. And then, after having practiced their method of delivery on those who were struggling to emerge from an arthritic tradition and those who were seeking a way out from their own imprisoning rage, they devised a process that made it possible for self-criticism not to fall into the abyss of guilt, self-detestation, and despair, but with clear sight to balance itself on the brink.

Therefore, these therapists, these midwives of the soul, were prepared to salvage those who were caught in that convulsion of contraction, that schizophrenic revolt of self-revulsion, which appears in history as the great mortificatory movement, the flight from life. And because they were prepared by their own pioneer experience, they were no reactionaries. They had learned to understand the three reactions of blind clinging to tradition, the blind defiance and rejection of it, and the blind desire to rage against and destroy the raging self. They had learned to understand that, blind as these three reactions were, still they were not death throes or vain, convulsive efforts to return to an ease that only existed, even in the womb, in the early fetal months. This was a natural insight: first, you mustn't lose intuitive coconscious understanding, you must conserve contact with the preterconscious; secondly, you must have freedom of expression; and thirdly you must attain that disciplined skill [which] combines energy with empathy and enterprise with comprehension. In short, these spastic movements were mishandled parturition contractions, as the spirit of man sought a delivery that would permit him to be born whole, with his every endowment, faculty, and member preserved, developed, and expressed into a fuller stage of being.

And therefore, understanding all of this, the mystery therapists knew that the Ascetic movement was not a reaction to primal, coconscious tradition. They saw, on the contrary, that it was a further development of individuality, a further conscious knowledge of the separate self and a wish to master it. And they realized that the earlier mystery methods of rebirth–burial and catharsis–immersion could not be used as the specific therapy for the midindividual, the adrenaline, self-blaming person who is in peril of schizophrenic collapse.

The ascetic must go through the rebirth–burial and water-catharsis. But he specifically stands in need of a third release, an

3. The Initiation of Inspiration

inspiration that he must be given or the other two are for him in vain, not speaking to his actual, immediate, and urgently critical condition. The ascetic type, therefore, after having been delivered from birth trauma and catharized from pathological rage, must have his particular treatment. As earth–burial permits the righted rebirth of the psyche into a cooperative empathic society, and as water-catharsis is the means of reduction for the strangulated, anger-distended ego and the way of turning the duellist into the pioneer companion, so the psychiatry of air causes the ascetic to correct his drive to mortification and life rejection.

And the ordeal phase, the first stage in this mystery process, has its specific test. The raising and removing of the first fear block, by the first mystery ordeal, was and is achieved by reliving through the birthdread of death by confinement. In most births, the heart is in danger of stopping as the umbilical cord is jammed by the pressure of the mother's muscles, cramping in panic and refusing to open the womb channel. Hence, in all the mystery procedures that we can trace in some detail (for example, the Eleusinian), we find this repeated pressure. At Eleusis we can still see and go through the narrow, dark birth passage through which the postulant had to work his body or be thrust.

The raising and removal of the second fear block by the ordeal preliminary of the second mystery initiation was through the fear of drowning and, simultaneously, the fear of being washed out and away, of being drained of all substance and of being purged of any power.

The ordeal of the third mystery, that of air, is less physical but certainly not less terrifying. For air in its psychophysical aspect is a mixture of gases: by volume, 78 percent nitrogen, 21 percent oxygen, 0.94 percent argon, 0.04 percent carbon dioxide, 0.001 percent hydrogen, 0.002 percent helium, neon, krypton and xenon, with variable amounts of water vapor.[74] This mixture is brought into the lungs and there mixed by them with the blood. This gas-loaded blood then delivers its charge to the brain. So fueled, the brain is then able to select and construct, from its twenty-two channels of sensory apprehension, that comprehension of experience [which] is necessary for biological survival. And as we all know, in this generation of

III - INITIATIONS/PSYCHOPHYSICAL RELIGIOUS EXERCISES

anesthetics, analgesics, anodynes, sedatives, and stimulants, a slight modification of the brain's diet will cause it to experience a change of impressions. The biologically necessary view or construct of the environment, mistakenly called reality, will alter. Not only is this alarming to those who assume that any possible construct other than that of the biologically useful one must, *ipso facto*, be insane. It can be highly dangerous. And not merely because it may well be illusory, [but] because the impressions may not answer to any reality or may not be an accurate interpretation of any external experience, [it] may be sheer delirium.

There is another risk and one that can be even more perilous. Some range of experience, some new awareness of a condition or conditions usually unapprehended and in some way out there, may have come upon the soul. The experience itself may be valid; it may be more potent and portentous than any event transmitted to the mind from that range of data (or sensa) of which the mind, when in a waking state, generally is biologically aware. But whereas the body-mind has more or less learned to make the responses that are necessary to keep its body-mindedness adequately tending to its business of physical survival, the mind by itself has no such learned reactions to another range of experiences and events. Hence, the delusions and fanatic convictions of the enthusiast who (without instruction and after his first fear [which] confirms for him that the experience is wholly external and imperative) translates his "revelation" in terms of his own prejudices. He is certain that God has spoken to him, giving him an authoritative revelation or a sentence of eternal doom. It is an important fact, therefore, to note at this point that work with the insane has always shown that no madness is more grave and has an uglier prognosis than the disturbance that begins with the patient hearing voices. One would think that visual hallucinations would be more serious. It seems, however, that the hypnotic and suggestive power of the ear bears more on the will than does vision.

The air mystery does not ignore this danger but faces it, and by treating it as an ordeal can make it of necessary profit to those who under guidance endure this trial. The sense of being lost, the wandering in one's mind is usually associated with the delirious states of

3. The Initiation of Inspiration

high fever and of mental decay. But this wandering (and we know this from Apuleius, Plutarch, and the others who went through the Isis initiation as it was practiced in the Hellenic Roman Peace during the first two centuries A.D.) was an essential part of the ordeal that preceded the initiation of true inspiration.[75] And that a shrewd mind could utterly lose its bearings, that a reasonable intelligence could wander—lost, without rhyme or reason, memory or intention; pestered and bewildered by false voices, threatening and insane words, absurd and outrageous terms and sounds—this was an experience that reduced personal pride. This grave disturbance, which had to be endured in the dark where the ear can give no proper sense of distance or direction, undermined the self-confidence of common sense, the assurance that the ego is master of itself and its situation if only it keeps its head, believes in its own competence, and knows that the senses give it contact with reliable reality. Then the spirit becomes aware that it is not the ego; that, as Heraclitus said, "The senses are bad witnesses" and that the soul must realize its communion with others. And it must be saved by putting its confidence in these others who not only do not want it to be a subservient slave, but who wish to deliver it through this third birth. They wish to bring the struggling soul into the new life of true inspiration where, as an intelligent, critically minded being, it may yet know its deep non-self and the powers of revelation and communication that belong to this group-spanning consciousness.

As we have said above, we can trace this third ordeal and initiation through the references that have survived from the classical and preclassical mysteries, from Greece, Egypt, and the Levant. Indeed, we know, for instance, how sound in darkness was used in Paleolithic times (and by the surviving Stone Age Australian Aboriginal tribes today), through the use of the bull roarer. This is an orificed stone fastened to the end of a leash. And when it is whirled in the air it produces a whirring, throbbing siren ululation, with resonance, in a cave. And when we come down to Eleusis, we find that the appearance of Persephone, the sudden flash of vision, took place when the postulant, after being through a long period of darkness that was filled with minatory whisperings and sinister echoes, suddenly heard the note (probably of a particular pitch) of a massive bronze

III - INITIATIONS/PSYCHOPHYSICAL RELIGIOUS EXERCISES

gong being struck. The pulsating rhythms of such gongs play a critical part in Chinese and Japanese ancestral (and now Buddhist) ritual. This gong was also sounded when a Spartan King, at the moment of his death (still identified with his body by the Lacedaemon obsession with physical violence), must be shaken out of his body. At Eleusis, when that shock airwave burst on his anxiety-strained eardrum, the postulant knew that he was confronted by the goddess who was both Queen of the Dead, sovran in the realm to which he and all humankind were irrevocably bound, and also whom he must now take as a bride. Even though the Hellenic mind had no naturalist's knowledge of those families of creatures wherein the male is consumed by the female as he fertilizes her (he is her impregnator and her nourishment), it is no wonder that in the Greek language the word *telos* is used for both marriage and death.

So much for illustration of the air mystery, with air used as the vehicle of sound waves to affect the mind through the eardrum. The Greeks also employed air mixed with carbon dioxide as a pulmonary method of altering consciousness. The Sybil of Apollo at Delphi was first put into trance (dissociated and sometimes extrasociated consciousness) by being made to breathe the carbon dioxide fumes that came up through a cleft in the Delphi temple floor; and then, when that gave out, by having her head held over a hot copper bowl in which laurel leaves were being scorched.

But the full and late development of the mystery of air is seen most clearly in India where it is still present today in the yogic practices of the Sanskrit and pre-Sanskrit tradition. There, it has not been the main aim to use sound either to shock the eardrum or to give hypnotic suggestion in the dark. Sound—the airwave—is used, but almost entirely in an interior way. The use of the syllable OM (pronounced AUM and giving, as the instructors in its use say, the whole rhythm and gamut of sound from open mouth to closed mouth, from alpha to omega) is to vibrate not only the eardrum but also the thyroid and, some believe, the skull bones sufficiently to tremor the pituitary and the pineal. The main use of air by the Yogin has to do, however, with the control and extreme modification of respiration. This discipline is to teach the postulant how to alter consciousness by control of breath.

3. The Initiation of Inspiration

The normal rate and depth of respiration give the brain, through the oxygenated blood, the gas fuel that makes it possible for the mind to make that biological construction of the environment, and of its own physique, which is necessary for it to operate in the everyday world. By shifting that normal rhythm of breathing, this common-sense construction is dissolved. The Yogin is then free to seek for or devise another construction. The rapid breathing exercises, by intense acceleration of the respiration rate, produce hyperoxygenation of the lung and so permit considerable pauses without need of respiration.[76] In Chapter 1 of this Section III, we have seen the importance of these rest pauses for keeping the mind one-pointed and free of distractions; and we also saw the value attached to respiration cessation by the Yogic traditions.

It is also worth noting here that that unique mixture (unique in the modern world) of an intellectual genius and a psychic sensitive, Emanuel Swedenborg, left it on record that "my breathing was such that I could respire inwardly for some time without aid of external air and so converse with spirits." He goes on to remark that "this tacit breath" he first experienced as a child in prayer and "lately, when thinking deeply."[77]

However, other students of respiration have pointed out that rapid and/or deep breathing may and, indeed, should increase the carbon dioxide in the blood. [Ed. note: Heard's assertion that "rapid and/or deep breathing ... should increase the carbon dioxide in the blood" is inaccurate. According to experts, the exact opposite occurs.] And this would lead not to clarity of consciousness but to visionary experience: delusions rather than inspirations, fantasies instead of insights. As we shall see in a moment when, in the second part of this chapter, we are discussing modern therapies and research that employ and explore varied respiration mixtures, apparently the preparation, intention, and attention of the subject is a primary factor in deciding whether the experience will be dissipatory and delusional or concentrative, constructive, and truly explorational.

We must also remember the particular purpose for which the postulant, in this air ordeal and by means of altered respiration and held breath, was seeking inspiration. The purpose of this was to save the man when, in his midindividual stage, he falls into self-hatred

III - INITIATIONS/PSYCHOPHYSICAL RELIGIOUS EXERCISES

(pure adrenaline) and when, seeking for an infallible authority and a completely repressive discipline to which he may become slave and victim, "like a corpse in the hands of his Director,"[78] he becomes schizoid. Having asked for law that is inflexible and without exception he finds that he cannot keep it when it is given to him. Like a completely closed suit of armor with no chink, it encloses, defends, and supports him, but it also suffocates him. The all-embracing, all-confining iron law kills with its clauses that shut down every avenue of growth and deny every expansion of living or lifting of the heart.

First, then, the mystery of air, of respiration, was a therapy to restore the adolescent mind, the midindividual personality, from that self-hatred that seeks an outer law for the sake of security and to destroy its self-will, only to find itself invaded by guilt because that law condemns it for not abiding by the rigid principles which alone can save. As Paul of Tarsus says, the letter kills but the spirit makes alive, and the spirit is, at root, the pneuma, the breath that inspires and exhilarates. The basic therapy was, then, to remove guilt and prevent schizophrenia by showing the postulant that he was not totally depraved, that in him there was the living breath, but that, owing to his individualism, he had lost inspiration and was subject to illusion. He must, therefore, open himself to the cleansing breath. Then his biologically confined consciousness (which was, at least in the beginning, racial good sense and the desire for racial survival, and which is now only a selfish, cowardly concern for personal escape) will be raised to the knowledge and insight of the true preterconsciousness.

There is a further significance in this the third initiation, the air mystery. As we have seen, the age group and epoch that this third mystery was developed to serve is the midindividual, the adolescent. And, as noted in Section II, Chapter 3, it is at this age that the individual (just as it was at this epoch that man did so) becomes specifically sexual, particularly and almost exclusively aesthetically and sensorily aware of the genitals as being the source of pleasure and release. This concentration and consequent loss of the panaesthetic euphoria led to frustration and next to the sense of guilt. The air exercises, by concentrating on the lungs, first raise the sensory awareness from the viscera and the genitalia. Secondly, they give respiratory euphoria and thirdly, by expanding the rib cage and

3. The Initiation of Inspiration

convexing the sternum, they increase the pectoral area and awake the thoracic nerve centers.[79] Hence, there is both a tonic restriction in the abdominal musculature and also a complimentary tonic dilation of the upper chest and neck. It is possible that by such exercises, and the carriage that they induce, the thyroid is stimulated.[80] And there is some evidence that the thymus—the mid-chest ductless gland that prevents premature sexuality and in average cases atrophies after puberty—may be brought into action. This would help restore the paidomorphic panaesthetic sensorium, which, in turn, would restore the generalized euphoria and prevent a disbalanced sexuality, concentrated on the genitals. And as they are a neotenic zone of dilated sensibility, the breasts, when they become the center of the body's alertness, aid in removing that shrinking, self-centered attitude that is the pose of the self-accusing and which, as attitude increases mood, aggravates the abject state of mind.[81]

~~~~~~~~~~~

Having finished this brief account of the traditional air mystery, we can now turn to the subject of the second section of this chapter: What might this ordeal initiation of the third mystery be if it were performed under present conditions and with today's psychophysical knowledge? As in Chapters 1 and 2 of this Section III, we saw what practical steps are being taken, and could further be taken to apply the psychophysical releases and developments that the ordeals and initiations of earth-rebirth and water-catharsis suggest. Now, in concluding this third chapter on the ordeal and initiation of air, we must see what steps are being taken in modern therapy to explore respiratory methods.

As we have seen, this the third mystery has never, like the earth burial and rebirth mystery, become lost. Nor has it, like the water-catharsis, become diminished and atrophied into traditional baptism. Through the East Indian interest in yoga, the mystery of air has had constant exoteric, explicit practice. And although yoga, especially in its Hatha and Tantra forms, uses other psychophysical exercises along with breathing (especially that of raising Kundalini and other techniques for activating the ductless glands and increasing the electric charge on the brain), still the changing of consciousness mainly by respiratory control has been the principal yogic technique.

III - INITIATIONS/PSYCHOPHYSICAL RELIGIOUS EXERCISES

Nor was the West without evidence that in between the final expiration of death and normal respiration there did exist many other states of consciousness, many conditions resembling sleep but, on examination, [were] found to be radically different. There was hypnotic sleep, discovered by Franz Mesmer (1733-1815), in which normal attention could be so altered that severe pain, such as caused by amputation, was unnoticed. However it was not a sleep of relaxation, as is normal sleep, but of high muscular and nervous tonicity.[82] But normal attention was altered; it became so absolute that in hypnotic sleep the subject was rendered completely oblivious to the most intense agony. And unfortunately for pure research, it was this physical anaesthesia, and not any change of consciousness, that alone concerned the doctors who were using hypnosis.

Meanwhile, Humphry Davy, the chemist, experimenting with "the airs—gases other than the mixture we call ordinary air—discovered nitrous oxide. Chloroform and aether followed. Research into hypnosis, had hypnosis been the only anaesthetic, might have been pursued by medicine and so come to be a detached study, a pure research. But it was fanatically attacked by that ugliest and most dangerous, because it is the most dishonest, alliance of superstitious conservatives (who think that suffering is good in itself provided that they are not in its grip) and materialistic specialists who believed that the mind was a vapor given off by the brain. Very few troubled to enquire further into this enigma of consciousness, although the medical profession was constantly being reminded, with every major operation, of how much consciousness was altered by changing the gas that was given to the lung. They were only concerned with rendering the body insensible. Their one interest was to make the patient temporarily as dead as possible. And his frequent accounts, on his return, of the experiences he had when breathing these gases were regarded as being tantamount to the ravings of a lunatic.

Now, however, research in hypnosis is being pursued, although lack of an adequate hypothesis of the structure and range of consciousness delays our being able to coordinate all the data. Further, even in the West, breathing exercises, at least in moderate forms, have gained considerable attention during this century. And it is an attention that owes not a little to the West's interest in operatic

3. The Initiation of Inspiration

singing, the need to study breath control. And still further, in the last couple of decades, psychotherapy has become specifically interested in respirational treatment.[83]

After a number of experiments, a mixture of 30 percent oxygen and 70 percent carbon dioxide was found to be the gas blend most suited to bring on a shift of consciousness. After five breaths, most subjects—and I am included among them—experience a sense somewhat similar to the first couple of breaths of nitrous oxide. After ten breaths, and with the eyes closed, vivid, iridescent rainbowlike effects are seen and these rapidly become decorated with moving jewellike prisms and other crystalline forms. Those who have practiced in training themselves to do so can retain consciousness of the outer world (biological consciousness) even up to twenty breaths, but this is rare. Most persons pass out between ten and fifteen respirations. Also, there is generally distress, partly because of the strangeness of the breathing mixture to which the lung and, indeed, the throat are not accustomed, partly because of the inconvenience of the nasal-oral mask on the face, and partly, no doubt, because of the traumatic, subconscious birth-respiratory memory. The system is used by L. J. Meduna and other psychiatrists to raise repressed memories and fear blocks that are due to past psychic damage. It became very popular for a couple of years. Lately, however, many psychiatrists have turned against it. There is a feeling that it not only adds to the distress of the patient but that it does not—or very seldom does it—permit him to raise his repressed fears. Also, it may release such fears too spastically. As the patient is out of normal consciousness at the time, the shock of recollecting a deep traumatic experience, under these conditions of loneliness and nightmare fear, may be too severe. The rapidity of the process does cut costs of long conscious analysis, but the price may still be too high.

This work, however, is only in its initial stages. The effect of previous informational instruction, given to the subject by the psychiatrist, is very great. Also, the attitude of the psychiatrist toward the subject appears increasingly to be of importance, and all the more so if both of them are not conscious of the tie. This, of course, is in keeping with the mystery process, when the postulant is rendered wholly dependent on his trainer and hierophant, one

III - INITIATIONS/PSYCHOPHYSICAL RELIGIOUS EXERCISES

who has already been sent through the tensions of liberation and so attained to enlightenment.[84]

As, then, respiratory methods of psychotherapy are clearly part of the air mystery, and as the air ordeal and initiation are specifically for dealing with the midindividual—the person in training, the adolescent, athletic, ascetic mind whose specific mental peril is schizophrenia—it seems reasonable to suggest, in the light of these facts, two proposals for obtaining better results.

The first is definitive: that is to say, we should stress the respiratory method particularly with that specific age group, or emotional-mental category, which has already, by regression to the limited environment (burial and rebirth), been freed of the trauma of parturition, and which, by the catharsis of water, has been released from the paranoid, heroic, projected rages of the small child's emotional reaction. For the guilt sense of the midindividual has back of it the primal, panaesthetic dilation of infancy, which, when it reached childhood and was rejected, became rage. That rage has now become guilt and is largely, though not wholly, composed of the sense of sin. The original, primal desire for general cocharging has now, in mid-self-consciousness, shrunken to a confined sexuality.

For, as we have seen, in the heroic person and the child, as in the coconscious man and the infant, sexuality is not dominant or ripe. It is the ascetic, the midindividual with his sense both of separateness and yet of obligation (that semi-independence that seems to be banishment and exile rather than liberation and enterprise) who is specifically sexual. That this guilt cannot be dealt with by vetoing the act and repressing the emotions, all now agree. But absolution cannot give peace of mind. For absolution, which is bought at the price of promising never to repeat the act, cannot provide certainty that the act will not be repeated and so rekindle guilt. Nor can the mere recollection of the deed cure the guilt, even though the person may be temporarily salved by being told that it is rationally trivial. For the guilt springs from a profound disappointment with the self, a profound feeling that specific sex—the genitally centered orgasm—is so far from being the promised whole that it seems a bitter, shameful travesty.

3. The Initiation of Inspiration

Here we must repeat that in spite of the value of Freud's insight into the great unrecognized part that the trauma of birth—psychic damage sustained in the first thirty months—inflicts on the psyche, his belief that the infant is a polymorphic pervert was a grave mistake. If accuracy is to be maintained, there must be a distinction between specific sexuality (which, as the productive rhythm, is only specific when it centers in the genitalia and culminates in the orgasm) and eroticism. The body has a number of erogenous zones, and this condition of suffused libido and dilational euphoria does not need to center down in the genitals and culminate in the orgasm. As Ivan Bloch (6) pointed out fifty years ago, specific sexuality is the confining and restricting of a generalized tickling and tonic sensation that is primarily and generally suffused. The child, therefore, should not be called a polymorphic pervert, for it cannot yet achieve sexuality. It should be called a panaesthetic transit as long as it is in symbiotic relationship with its mother (or mother surrogate) (84), and a panaesthetic exvert as it explores and activates its various hyperaesthetic areas.

Therefore, we come to the second recommendation: besides raising the memories of adolescent ascetic-erotic failure, the therapist must also interpret them. He must be able to explain, not explain away, the guilt–disappointment by showing the postulant (1) what the life process is and what it is aiming at; (2) where actually, in that embryo growth, the midindividual finds himself to be; and (3) how he may cooperate with that process and recover this lost wholeness by neotenic fulfillment.

This the therapist does first by rational discussion, showing the intelligent critical surface mind that this explanation indicates the meaning of the life process, the sequence of evolution, and the particular position in this sequence that the patient himself occupies. Next, when the patient is under the respiratory treatment, and so transferred from biological consciousness, he will be witnessing and experiencing his adolescent shames and disgraces. And in this state, which we know is also a state of high suggestibility, he can and should be given the inspiration that will grant him the assurance and energy to handle his separateness, not only without guilt, but in the clear belief that, after he has gone through the reproductive phase

III - INITIATIONS/PSYCHOPHYSICAL RELIGIOUS EXERCISES

(the marital phase of first maturity), on the higher level of the spiral he will be able to recover the panaesthetic condition that is the psychophysical aspect of neotenic development.

Such then, in bare outline, seems to be the ordeal and initiation of the air mystery. This treatment, then, of breathing gas mixtures close to but other than air we may regard as the specific therapy for the ascetic, self-accusing man of schizoid tendency.[85] By breathing this mixture, he is transferred to a state of consciousness other than the biological, wherein with the aid of hypnotic suggestion not only are his repressed emotions raised but they are reinterpreted and reconstructed, not dismissed. And the midindividual may now go on, untrammeled, into his next two stages of psychophysical growth, that of total individualism and that of postindividualism. In the chapter that follows, therefore, we consider the stage into which those who have been healed by the air mystery must then pass and how its specific ordeal and initiation may be undergone.

4. The Initiation of Illumination
(*Fire*)

We now have to deal with the fourth therapy. For if the first therapy, by regression, cleared the basic infancy level of consciousness and made it possible, through the second therapy of catharsis by water, to deal with the paranoid frustrations of childhood so that in turn the third therapy of auditory explanation and encouragement can be worked for those who are going through (or are still held by) the adolescent, self-accusing phase, then we are now ready for the fourth therapy. And it is essential; for not only have the other three led up to it, but for us today this fourth stage is more critical, more apposite than the earlier ones. Each of them serves a specific purpose, for each can, when it is achieved, refer the freed person to an appropriate and, for the time being, fulfilling pattern of behavior. The child of today can have, as their specific standard, a contemporary rendering of the heroic behavior that thrills them—for example, the interplanetary explorer, the astronaut who will soon travel to our close satellites.

The adolescent, in turn, can have as their ideal the selfless, anonymous member of a research team on an assignment full of

III - INITIATIONS/PSYCHOPHYSICAL RELIGIOUS EXERCISES

unknown risks (for example, X-ray and nuclear study) and with the laurels going to the Lab and to no one person.

The person in first maturity, however, is our contemporary type, the modern executive. He it is who has to decide what adventures are to be planned and assigned, who has to order the advance and to pick the pioneers. And it is this key person whose problem is second only to that of second maturity, who is of first concern to most of the concerned today. For immediate power is now in the hands of first maturity. And he has no authority above him; second maturity is not producing social vision but only self-commiseration. The man in first maturity, the most acute example of the intensifying triad of the individual, is now cruelly torn.

Always, from the time that the Chinese achieved the great Confucian pattern of culture, the conflict between the family and the State has torn the heart of the administrator. Today this manager is key man in a secular State made up of routineers, engineers, and managers, but which lacks seers (41). So he must be his own guide, for his social and psychological experts tend to tell him that conscience is, at best, a tradition that is largely out of date, and, at worst, a conglomerate of wholly misguiding tabus. Nevertheless, he who is most acutely an individual is the person who has all the principal controls of the community in his hands. He has to double the parts of lookout-man and administrator. And his pattern of behavior is based on the humanic concept of a humankind that is completely self-seeking because it is completely individualized into separate physiques that can have direct knowledge of only their own private pain and pleasure, inferring but faintly the feelings of others. Such a race of ingenious animals, each able to see and to seek his own advantage, must be kept in combination with each other by appealing to their separate interests. Such, of course, is modern democratized Machiavellianism, the latest edition of Hobbes' *Leviathan*.

No wonder, then, that the more intelligent and contemporary are those in first maturity and the more they strive to have principle and achieve statesmanship, to avoid opportunism and the mere playing of power politics, the more they find themselves under the strain that has brought this age group into the main killing range of coronary heart disease. There must be found one preventive therapy

4. The Initiation of Illumination

that is aimed specifically at relieving their tension. Nor is the search hopeless. But it presents difficulties that are greater than the earlier therapies. And, as we have seen, even these preliminary treatments are anything but easy to apply.

One of the main obstacles in the way of this fourth therapy is the acute self-consciousness of the subject. The patient who is at an extremity of individualism puts up the most intense intellectual and emotional resistance to any therapy. He looks on himself, for better or for worse, as being the type picked by natural selection to have the highest survival rate. For does he not out-climb all the rest? Though he reaches the top only to fall stricken. Considering himself to be a master at managing others, he scorns (and fears above all) being managed himself. Well masked to look what others like, he is naturally full of well-hidden misgiving should anyone suggest prizing off his visor. The skin is always most raw under the scab and the callus. He is inexperienced in viewing his character, for he finds it best not to know his motives too precisely, and to believe in the pretenses and defenses he makes for his actual conduct. Hence, he suffers mainly from conversion psychosis, the transference of subconscious conflict out into physical functioning. And so he often dies from heart rupture or brain artery lesion before he knows he is ill; long before he could have been brought to any mind-body knowledge, let alone any mind-body renovation. He may believe that psychotherapy can do something for the young. For instance, it may help to solve the problem of juvenile delinquency. But for the mature, in their armor of success, what release is possible, feasible? A recreation tour, a discreet or at least clandestine love affair, a fairly heavy sedation in which alcohol is still the main ingredient—these are the only let-ups from the strain.

And still the strain is growing. There is a steady increase in the hours of unavoidable vigilance and decisiveness, management, adroit adjustment, and subtle maneuver. The psychosomatic disease incidence mounts. Mature man is running himself wrongly and, in his extensive study, *The Stress of Life*, Hans Selye (77) has gone far to show just how wrongly.[86] Man today is driving himself (naturally enough, once we allow the humanic premise as to what man is) in a way that must lead to breakdown. Kicking himself along with the suprarenals,

III - INITIATIONS/PSYCHOPHYSICAL RELIGIOUS EXERCISES

the glands of combat as they have been called, modern humans fight off depression with aggression.[87] The thyroid, the gland of sustained effort, is neglected. And lately it has been discovered that not only may a too active suprarenal system provoke heart disease, but that a too lethargic thyroid may make the body fail to deal with the cholesterol that sludges the arteries and, in the end, will cause blockage.

Meanwhile, for those mature who are too self-awarely intelligent to misinterpret a warning from the psyche by transmuting it and projecting it into a psychosomatic disease such as a coronary or rupture of an artery in the brain, there awaits the mental disease of the manic depressive. He is the one whose life has to be run on a megalomaniac, self-believing elation that is paid for by catastrophic bouts with suicidal despair.

Yet the resistance of the total individual, the Humanic man who believes that he is mounted in the saddle of life with the reins in his hands and with a generation of mastery ahead of him, remains highly formidable. In all that he can affirm, he is a positivist. It is only in the world that he perceives through his senses that results can be achieved. Negatively, he denies any other possibility for the future. He regards himself as being the apex of growth. Up to this point, the vague impractical generosities of the [child] and the superstitious self-blaming of the adolescent had to be outgrown and brought to the keen cutting edge and fine penetrating point of a skeptical individualism. This is the culmination of consciousness. This is man's final comprehension, his final and completely competent grasp of circumstances. After attaining to this stage, there remains only the problem of making one's mastery more automatic until at length the younger generations, coming up into maturity, push the elderly into retirement.

Hence, at this point any therapy can only be restorative, not developmental. For with the age group of the first mature, every sign of change must be evidence not of yet another stage of growth, but of decline and decay. The psychophysiological therapist or counsellor is dismissed as a quack if he suggests that just as adolescence led to this maturity, so this maturity itself is a preliminary stage for a further, even more mature condition. The whole notion is utterly alien from the assumed psychology and physiology of today. We may

4. The Initiation of Illumination

propose that old age need not be and should not be decay and yet, at the same time, affirm that the hope does not lie in rejuvenation. We may point out that the foreconscious, critical mind of the individual, with its concomitant self-consciousness, with its awareness of separation and its desire for objectivity, has, by its growth and intensification throughout written history, given necessary power. But at the same time, we must insist that individualism, having now done its work and made its mistakes, must, when men have completed the spiral curve, develop beyond individuality, objectivity, and self-consciousness. However, such propositions seem to be pure paradox—metaphysics brought back, masked and made up as some Newer Thought nostrum.

Yes, it is difficult to persuade the man in control that he must grow. Such a suggestion to the young mature (with his maintenance physicians honestly grooming him to avoid any further development, they, as much as he, believe that first maturity is the end of growth) raises in him the resistances of both greed and fear. For even if he did believe that there was another stage ahead of him and that he ought to grow into it, he would resist any call to leave his enjoyments. It is hard enough to make the too happy child put away its toys or the too successful athlete stop his games. Still and all, they have the pressure and command of society to call them up to further trainings for further development. But who can call the leaders of society and order them to undergo a still further training for a still further development? See how impossible it has been, in spite of medical advice, to get the central power executives, the chief politicians and the chief judges to allow a ruling that, at certain advanced ages of say sixty or sixty-five, a general check-up should be made of their involutionary processes[88] and that this estimate be available to the electorate who has to decide on their capability to stand the strain of office. Greed, therefore, makes men cling to power, which is the chief lure of the total individual.[89] Then the fear of what lies beyond makes even those for whom the exercise of power has become a wretched fatigue, and executive work a task to be shirked, [a] dread to resign, to vacate a seat however stormy, and to step down into the dark.[90]

But if acute self-consciousness can, at best, hardly conceive of a state of mind beyond individualism and if, therefore, the young

III - INITIATIONS/PSYCHOPHYSICAL RELIGIOUS EXERCISES

mature, at the height of self-consciousness, can seize power (for society thinks that those in first maturity are at the peak of human possibility, and the Western World, being ignorant of the seer, knows no category of social value above the manager), then there is little hope of getting the total individual even to consider further growth.

Nor does the task appear to be any less improbable when we consider the specific technique which is, in the mystery tradition, employed at this fourth stage (at the crisis when those in first maturity must pass into second maturity) in order to bring about the new quality of consciousness. As mentioned above, today's regression therapy for curing birth trauma and the techniques of restricted environment actually re-establish the ordeal and initiation of second birth (rebirth) by burial (rewombing) and resurrection. Also, today's water-catharsis treatment can deal with rage states, eruptive or repressed, and deliver patients from the mistaken child reactions that prevent emotional maturity. While thirdly, the hypnotic techniques, yoga breathing, and such respiratory psychotherapeutic treatments as the use of carbon dioxide are the ordeal initiation of air, practiced in modern form. All these means can be and are being accepted; for although they are sometimes shocking, psychically, they are safe; any physiological risk is nonexistent [Ed. Note: See Disclaimer in Publisher's Note]. In these first three, only solids, liquids, and gases (all at comfortable temperatures and at familiar pressures) are being used. The customary innocuous tangibles (for even a gas can be felt) are being employed. But, further, the ends for which they are employed can be approved by the therapeutic authorities: that is, removal of the trauma of birth, of the possible repressed paranoia of childhood and of the schizophrenia of adolescence. So, in turn, the adult leader can approve such therapies for, through their use with the young, he may hope to be given more dependable future members of the society he rules—members who are returned to normalcy once more accepting the reality that he controls. But not only will he reject any therapy that is aimed at altering *him*. He will be able to dismiss the traditional technique of the fire initiation as being absurd, utterly impossible, and to be vetoed as clearly dangerous: indeed, highly damaging if not lethal.

And what is even the most openminded researcher to make of the fourth mystery? True, the others have established their value.

4. The Initiation of Illumination

But how can this one? Fire is a destroyer, not a stimulant. The ordeal by fire, practiced under Anglo-Saxon legal procedure as a method of establishing innocency, has always been regarded as being the survival of a cruel use of credulous belief in magical superstition in order to assure a conviction. Here there was no hint of giving the defendant any recharging, any initiation, any resistance. The innocent person, it is callously assumed, will be able to receive protection against the fire from God, Who thus indicates the person's innocence and so vindicates his case. This is akin to, indeed it is worse than, the utter injustice of flinging into water a bound woman who has been accused of witchcraft, and assuming that if she sank she was innocent and that if she floated she was guilty.

It would seem, then, that the association that we have now traced among (1) the psychophysical phylogeny of man—his history since he was homo loquens [and] homo *fax factor* (i.e., the torch maker); (2) the psychophysical ontogeny of man (the life stages in which the individual, from birth to maturity, recapitulates human history); and (3) the successive particular insanity risks that threaten each of these successive developments, here breaks down.

The preindividual, coconscious infant, the protoindividual of childhood, the midindividual of adolescence—each of these, we have found, can be brought past its particular danger (of the trauma of birth, dementia praecox becoming paranoia, and schizophrenia) by (1) a regression to birth and reliving of the experience; by (2) the catharsis of unreflective rage and its transmutation into tears and fearful awe; and by (3) psychophysical inspiration through pulmonary salience that helps to restore the panaesthetic sensory awareness and so lifts the body-mind out of its despairing disgust. These three technique-therapies specifically meet the struggling person at his successive personal and ancestral crises and bring him through and into a new age.

But when we reach the age of total individualism, the period of office and power, that cresting moment when energy is not yet past its apex and skill is close to its climax, then we have no answer to the problem of its particular process of ordeal-initiation. The issue of first maturity seems to be insoluble. For although second maturity exists today, it is, as we have seen, without power, purpose, or plan.

III - INITIATIONS/PSYCHOPHYSICAL RELIGIOUS EXERCISES

It is the stepping-down stage, the declension that is sedated so as to break the fall into the grave, the dietary training to teach the unwanted that, though go they must, we spare them the time to take two bites at the bitter apple of death rather than make them bolt it at one gulp.

In the face of such fact, then, the mysteries' offer of a fire therapy as being the technique that is apposite to and for those in first maturity (the age group which, of all the age groups, is the most critical, the most powerful, the most assured, and the most individualistic, and so the least conscious of its preterconscious and its psychosomatic linkage) seems worse than mistaken. It discredits all the others. The other therapies might work for the other classes. This one is absurdly out of the question.

And it is true that only a few of the scholars who have studied them have been able to view the mysteries as being anything but ankylosed and romanticized fertility rites. Even fewer have been able to regard them as having a possible or real therapeutic value, at least to cultures in which such rites were indigenous. But even of these rare researchers, most have fought shy of the fire mystery. And as very few of them distinguish between the air-fire and the aetheric-fire, the air-fire is usually considered to be the final mystery. Further, their way of dealing with it has been to regard it as being a mystery not of fire but of light, the visionary byproduct of fire. The final rite (for example, at Eleusis) was a matter of seeing; it was purely psychological, not physiological. "They see something," said Aristotle, "they did not learn but were moved." Up to this point, our few informants all agree, the postulant was in the dark: masked, blindfolded, groping, stumbling, ear-straining to catch echoes and cudgel his bewildered brains over enigmatic, threatening sounds. Then, when this stage drew to a close, there was the encouragement of inspirational affirmations. But all the while not a thing was seen, no authority appeared. The whole experience might be a delirious dream, a private nightmare. And the ear is one of the worst guides, the most rumor-creating of the senses. Seeing is believing.

So suddenly—and of this there can be no doubt—the postulant, after all these strivings, wanderings, blunderings and recoils, instantaneously saw. What it was we cannot be sure. That it was dazzling

4. The Initiation of Illumination

light we know from Apuleius. "The sun shining at midnight" is his well-known phrase. Surely the postulant was both startled and relieved, both shocked and delighted.

This was, therefore, called *Epopteia*.[91] The Homeric hymn says, "Happy is he who has seen it." It was vision-producing ecstasy. The *epopt* is the postulant now, in a flash, made a seer. As we have seen in Chapter 3 of this Section III, here at this moment and climax of the process, a bronze gong sounded. Speech and auditory instruction, listening and trying to make sense of paradox—all of this was ended. Now, with a crash the veil of darkness was rent and the postulant, instantly initiate, saw.

And then? If he were going through the rite for the first time,[92] then when the light broke, he saw Demeter, the Earth Mother of the dark mysteries of fecundation and birth travail. If he were there for the second time (generally several years after the first time), he saw the Great Mother's even more terrible daughter, the Bringer of Death, Persephone of the even deeper dark—a dark not of the womb and the earth but of the tomb and the realm of the dead.

So fire must be considered to be simply light, and the clear vision to be that given by light. So and so only can the critically minded total individual accept such psychotherapeutic symbolism. For does it mean more; need it involve more than believing (a belief very welcome to the individual) that in the end a man must, if he is to be a leader, take leave of secondhand authority, go beyond being a dutiful listener, see for himself, and have his own vision?

And if it is maintained that this insight is more than seeing one's way through argument to understanding, more than the self-satisfied, self-congratulatory "Eureka!" when one has made the solitaire card game come out or adroitly fitted the clinching piece in the jigsaw puzzle, even then the modern individualistic master can be persuaded to undergo a little mind training that pays off highly. He can honestly and respectably accept the phrase, a flash of inspiration. All executives who employ expert managers have now heard of integral, creative thought—the complement and indeed the crown of analytic, critical thinking. After wrestling with a problem, you put your mind into a suspension, into a kind of blind, uneasy incubation. You wait in the dark and suddenly the light breaks; the answer

III - INITIATIONS/PSYCHOPHYSICAL RELIGIOUS EXERCISES

shines, daylight clear, before you. So Tesla worked; he was the seer and creator-inventor of original machines that were worth millions.[93] And so, from Descartes down to Henri Poincaré and the supermathematicians and physicists of today, the breakers-through into new realms of understanding and power have made their spectacular advances (38). Thus, illumination (as indeed the word has now come mainly to mean) would simply stand for a particularly bright moment of understanding.

Today, of course, with the new attention that is being given to the processes of insight,[94] we know that we have to learn how to dilate the mind, increase its span and grasp. The process is quite difficult for the critically minded person of strong convictions and quick decisive action. For it lies in knowing how to stop arguing and analyzing and to await in alert passivity. And he finds it bafflingly difficult to keep the mind so open. But it pays to learn it, for it makes for a further step toward efficiency. However, that means, as a matter of fact and inevitably, a further step toward making the man of executive power, who is in the upper rank of first maturity, more definitely and inescapably what he has been and what he now (if he continues in outward growth only) should and must cease to be.

But might not this revolution in the technique of the Humanic man in first maturity, while bribing him to use it in the name of efficiency, lure him into self-knowledge and self-growth? This certainly seems to be what, in actual fact, is now happening. Methods employed to increase profits (or, at most, to advance insights into the outer world) may tend to advance a true progress toward enlarging consciousness.

Just look at the advance during the last ten years in the new sector of restorative medicament, which may be called that of the psychiatric wonder drugs. They are certainly proving to be as promising as—and, indeed, more promising than—the magic molds, the many bacteriophages and antibiotics. Beginning with the barbiturates that finally yielded the sedative Seconal and, on the other hand, such tonics as Dexedrine and the tension-reducers such as Tolserol, a new advance is now under way with still finer aids: for example, the drug distributed under the names Miltown and Equanil. However, all these lead up to work now being done with vegetable

4. The Initiation of Illumination

extracts which, it has become clear, lead to far more extensive, profound, and releasing effects on consciousness. Further, we now see that this process can be considered to be part of the tradition's method of giving illumination. And, from the present practical, empirical standpoint of psychophysiological research, it is the part that gave to the mystery its efficacy.

Obviously, then, at this point we must ask: Did the traditional practitioners of the mysteries, and especially the self-conscious Greeks, have any physical aids that they used in changing the focal length of consciousness? Did they employ any means other than darkness and confinement (claustrophobia) and a complete sense of wandering and being lost (agoraphobia) followed by the sudden auditory and visual shock that imprinted, in an impacted association, an image of majestic terror and a feeling of assured discovery and insight?

Undoubtedly they did. From the early times when the Indo-European tribes were up on the Iranian plateau, they had found the *soma* plant. However, and although the Veda saying runs "I have drunk *soma* and become a god," it was apparently highly toxic and death, it would seem, often resulted from drinking it. The plant became extinct, but later Herodotus reports that the Scythians (on the plains region north of the Black Sea) used sweat houses and, probably, *Cannabis indica* (Indian hemp) as aids to their shamans in achieving ecstatic states. We know that at Eleusis the drinking, by the postulant, of a special potion made of a number of herbs was part of the rite of initiation. And Plutarch mentions the *leucophyllus* as being the plant principle in the draught given to those about to be initiated into the Mysteries of Hecate (Demeter). This potion, however, was employed to act as a truth drug, purging the candidate of his sins by driving him to make a full confession, not merely of his past deeds but also of any guilty intentions. It was a preliminary catharsis—a frenzy, it would seem, of fear and remorse and, therefore, not a direct aid to illumination. Still, we must allow that this mixed potion may have aided the critically minded Greek to become capable of recovering integral feeling-thought.

Certainly the work now being done on the psychedelics, those chemicals which render the mind able to see and hear with the attention and insight of the artist and apprehend with the

III - INITIATIONS/PSYCHOPHYSICAL RELIGIOUS EXERCISES

comprehension of supreme intuition, has shown that, under the influence of this ... medicament, minds of the highest critical intelligence do have experiences of an intensity, assurance, and completeness that leave on the consciousness a lasting impression of dynamic significance and coordinant initiative. Nor do these chemicals seem to be confined either to mescaline, which was first discovered in the peyote button cactus and is now made synthetically from gallic acid, or the lysergic acid which is derived from ergot of rye. The mushroom cult, it appears, was widely distributed from the Levant to China and was later known to the Norsemen of the Icelandic culture.[95]

Then there is the Yage snuff, which is employed from Cuba to Patagonia. When taken in small amounts, it also seems to give (as do mescaline and lysergic acid) a sense of communion and "at-peacefulness" with one's fellows, while in larger amounts it gives the similar sense of an equal communion with all of Nature. Indeed, as anthropology abandons its preliminary attitude of patronage toward all cultures other than that of its own Humanic phase, it is being found that there are cultures, now widespread throughout the Old and New World, which employ the aid of some psychedelic medicine to assist the mind in viewing the world with unpossessive, unexploiting charity and delight. Still (and this seems to be the important point in this enquiry), research in the therapeutic use of the psychedelics seems to indicate with increasing clarity that the value of these medicines lies in the fact that they provide two preliminary aids to attention.

In the first place, they remove distractions—those incessant animal-alertings that the human mind involuntarily makes to any irrelevant stimuli, outer or inner.[96] It has been known to all trainers-in-attention (for example, spiritual directors and psychiatrists) that these dissipating interferences only intensify when the surface will is employed to banish them. Four decades ago, Charles Baudouin of Lausanne well named it the Law of Reversed Effort. The psychedelics smooth away such irrelevances, and attention attains to that wholeness of focus which is as flawless as that of a person under deep hypnosis. But there is this profound difference—the hypnotized person attends totally to the instruction of the hypnotist, while

4. The Initiation of Illumination

the person who is freed from distraction by a psychedelic is perfectly free to attend to whatever area of interest on which he may choose to concentrate. He can range, at will and with equal totality of attention, over the whole phenomenal field, over everything across which his vision passes.

This brings us to the character of the second contribution that the psychedelics make to that attentiveness which is the essential preliminary to preter-analytic, meta-critical insight. Not only are the distractions removed. But, and this is more important for it is a further step toward insight, the observational construct (the way we have of instantly seeing the world around as being a series of separate objects, an assumption that is useful enough for exploiting our environment) is corrected. For though this observational construct is convenient and, indeed, necessary to us if we are to prise loose bits of the continuum and consume or store such fragments for personal use, it is not, in point of fact, an accurate picture of what is out there. What is actually out there is an unbroken series of events in a variously accented panorama. The artist, with native realism, has always seen the Nature around us as being a design that is made, as Constable said, "by light falling on light." And this is where art and science differ. For art is always composition while science is always bent on analysis. As Adelbert Ames Jr. and H. Cantril of Princeton have shown, this modern, scientific, humanic way of instantly fractionating the total presentation *is* perception, but it is a perception that is so largely influenced and distorted by instantaneous assumption (that is, construction-interpretation in terms of use and convenience) that it is constantly misleading the perceiver when he would comprehend.[97]

With the corrective aid of the psychedelics, the mind is presented with a world that is commanding in its unbroken coherence, arresting in its flawless intensity of color and form, startling in its immanent aliveness. But it must be repeated that these aids are and can only be preliminary. Spectacles can only assist defective vision; they cannot give sight to the blind. They cannot make the world appear friendlier to one whose myopia is a psychosomatic symptom of a neurotic wish to shun and disregard strangers. The psychedelics can correct our utilitarian deformation of what is around us. But, as

III - INITIATIONS/PSYCHOPHYSICAL RELIGIOUS EXERCISES

tens of thousands of experiments with thousands of subjects have shown, though everyone has the same intensifying of experience, though to many it is one of amazement, to a considerable number it is one of dismay, alarm, distress. While to a few minds, well trained in modern philosophy and at the acme of critical defensiveness and denial of wholeness, the removal of the imposed barriers can be resisted and the arbitrary distinctions and abstractions still regarded as continuing. What the subject makes of the experience is what he brings to it. All that the psychedelic biochemistry can do is to remove the barriers to attention and permit the observer to consider the scene without the assumptions regarding it that are currently made by Humanic man.

We may say, then, that although it would now appear that when he has become self-consciously critical and individualistically analytic toward his surroundings, man has often employed psychedelic medicine to cleanse this oxide of utilitarian assumption off the presented scene, these aids are only preliminary. At best, they can only assist the onlooker to have an experience that will be constructive or daunting according to whether his cast of mind is open and curious or defensively assured.

We are back, then, at the point where we started when we were attempting to explain away the fire mystery of ordeal and initiation as being nothing more than illumination; nothing more than a new-found conviction that somehow life is more than (and can be enjoyed as more than) personal success, economic mastery, and the psychophysical capacity to enjoy life for those in first maturity and a sedated calm for those in second maturity who are undergoing a painless elimination.

True, our present psychophysical diet may neatly taper us out of life without dismay to ourselves or embarrassment to those who wait, needing the room we occupy. But not only is this no true solution to the problem, the riddle of second maturity. It is simply a slow, sentimentally rendered, inefficient way of getting rid of the unwanted whom (were we frank and rightly urgent) we would, with true kindness to all concerned, euthanatize as soon as they fail to be effectively productive or enjoyable to themselves. The method itself, it becomes increasingly clear, cannot work unless it is accurately

4. The Initiation of Illumination

and fully as psychological as it is physiological. For not only do these mental wonder-drugs do no more than bring the subject to the threshold of a new experience. Even if we are to bring him thus far and render him able to regard and profit by this new presentation, numerous experiments are beginning to show that the subject, the postulant, must be prepared, accompanied, and led by those who have already advanced along that path. They must know (from their own experience), and they must tell him why he is being so processed. Illumination, if this is all that the fourth mystery can yield, must at least be used honestly. It cannot be based on a pretense, a device the real purpose of which is to get the old out of the way.

It is clear, then, that the psychedelic aids, when given by devoted and experienced guides, can prepare those in first maturity for their next beginning, their next entering in.[98] Having, in the phase of first maturity, become completely *self*-conscious, they can, with this new help, penetrate down through the layers of their being and recover their knowledge of the *whole* consciousness that works in them. But it is equally clear that this is only a preparation.

We return, then, with additional assurance that we are right in pressing further our enquiry into the real nature of the mystery of fire—this mystery for which the first mature, when they have completed their phase, must be prepared and which can give the second mature a personal and social significance. We cannot, in honesty, any longer say that information or even inspiration, insight, or illumination is the final answer to this riddle, the truthful interpretation of this fourth mystery.

Formerly the other three mysteries were dismissed as being as nonsensically impossible as this one. They were play-acting: first by men who couldn't distinguish between fantasy and fact, pretense and reality; and secondly, by actors, pretenders, and frauds.[99]

But we have found that each of these three successive, traditional therapies do fit in as an apt remedial measure for each of the successive miscarriages of development that man, as a race, had suffered and that the vast majority of men repeat as individuals. First, there was the failure of the primitive coconscious society (and its constituent, the preindividual) to permit psychological growth and

III - INITIATIONS/PSYCHOPHYSICAL RELIGIOUS EXERCISES

to keep alive and flexible a tradition that was able to comprehend a widening circuit of events. Secondly, there was the failure of the Heroic society, and the protoindividual consciousness, to be protesting (critical of others) without becoming paranoic, to be independent and yet not to be anarchic. And thirdly, there was the failure of the Ascetic society, and the midindividual, to be self-critical without a sense of guilt and to be disciplined without becoming mortificatory.

Each of these three excesses was in turn sufficiently corrected for man's psychosocial evolution to continue. Man did not stay arrested; still less did he collapse into a feral condition. His consciousness continued to intensify. Some degree of initiation was given him: not enough to resolve his conflicts but enough to prevent them from reducing him to chaos, and enough to permit him to continue making discoveries. And this degree of disciplined understanding, this extent of resiliency of mores, was due to a minimum of leavening being given to the congeries of humankind. At each of the three crises there were rare, unnoticed but catalytically influential individuals who were able to undergo, fully and successively, the appropriate mysteries: the earth mystery to free the coconscious, the water mystery to make liquid the assets of heroicism that were in danger of paranoic spasticism, and the air mystery to give a capacity for true inspiration.[100]

The correction of each excessive deviation was, however, only sufficient to permit recovery from mistake and the most painful progress. Anyone who studies history cannot but allow this. It is true that man not only survived; he also advanced to a keener definition of his problem and a more intensive and extensive study of his situation, mistakes, and predicaments. Yet what he was actually doing was this: he was carrying forward his unresolved conflicts in a growing suspense account that was increasingly forced below the level of conscious awareness. And this repressed suspense account, *pari passu* with the growth of his new focus of self-consciousness, was becoming a new and corresponding area, the subconscious. The suppressed conflicts with compound interest increased his liabilities. As we can see, the ordeal and initiation of each mystery did permit him to go on, but only into an increased condition of psychophysical

4. The Initiation of Illumination

stress, an increased sense of separateness, an intensification of self-consciousness and so of individualism. Each ordeal is a more severe strain and centers in on a more immediately urgent area of awareness. Earth is mainly muscular and cutaneous release; water is muscular and visceral stimulation and unbinding; and air is respiratory transference. Yet none of them reduces the conflict and leaves man at last balanced and whole, one with his whole self, his community, and life.

Hence, a still more strenuous experience and stimulant is demanded. "Nothing fails like success" is too simple an epigram to interpret the problem and process. We might better say that a partial success, a particular answer, because it lets the one who makes the answer get by, always adds to the depth of the total enigma. The complete self-consciousness of the Humanic phase is, as we have said, completely cut off from the total consciousness, from those layers of integral awareness that have been forced down and out (along with unresolved conflicts) and so have become the subconscious. Among other disadvantages of unawareness, this results in the fully self-conscious mind being able to treat its body as only a machine. It cannot purposely affect, cooperate with, and aid its body through intuitive use of emotion, frame of mind, and attitude. So individualistic man, regarding his physique as a chemical still, tries to keep himself in good health (energetic euphoria) by the use of drugs, diet, and excisional surgery.

And hence, our immediate situation (the predicament of Humanic man today) compels us to hypothecate some further procedure, some fourth process of development. For three reasons, a specific treatment is required for the present dominant type, the totally self-conscious man, the person of first maturity. (1) Cut off from his own deep, intuitional mind, he must suffer increasingly from a subconscious anxiety. (2) Cut off from interior knowledge of his own body and function rhythms, he must be increasingly attacked by psychosomatic illness. (3) Cut off, psychologically, from the society whose granulation into separate cells he acutely expresses and coercively commands, he must create an international anarchy.

Up until now, a tiny minority of men has been able to correct these three excesses by undergoing the three ordeal-initiations of

III - INITIATIONS/PSYCHOPHYSICAL RELIGIOUS EXERCISES

burial for rebirth, of catharsis for reducing pride, and of inspiration as an absolution for banishing guilt. And this small group has, in each age, kept the main line of man from straying too far from the road of growth.[101] And today we find that as the individual, in his personal growth, ontogenizes the phylogenic growth of psychosocial man (man the creature of conversation around a fire), each of us recapitulates these three stages. And all of us (or at least nearly all of us) need a corrective process that is specifically designed to remedy our ill-performed developments at birth, in childhood, and in adolescence.

Finally, when we trace these psychophysical therapies that were esoterically named mysteries, we find that they were not completed with the third one. That this could not be so we can see clearly. For up to the third mystery, the entire triad together can only release and reinduct (1) a social pattern that has reached the Ascetic phase of midindividuality (midconsciousness); and (2) an individual who has reached and is arrested in a misdeveloping adolescence, and whose self-knowledge turns into a guilt that makes him despair of progress and long for a schizoid imprisonment, a submissionist escape. Neither the individual nor the social pattern that the third mystery can achieve is complete or contemporary. If left there, the individual would remain (as so many do today) only half-mature, one who must seek a peremptory leader imposing a dogma. And so the society would also be an arrested medieval form: pre-experimental, precritical.

The fourth ordeal and initiation is then called for by the phylogeny and also the ontogeny of man—as an individual necessity but equally so as a social essential. Personally and socially we cannot be sane and cease from mutual destruction (let alone develop) if we cannot solve the problem of the total individual, the age group now in control. Just to set free the other three more preliminary age groups is to do one of two things. It is to give more flexible material for his delirious aims to the total individual of the power class, the man of frustrant, unexplicated violence who is still caught in his destructive self-ignorance.

Or it is to cause such an internal conflict between the master and those who cannot or will not obey him that (because he has the whip

4. The Initiation of Illumination

hand of concentrated violence) he will destroy his challengers and himself. They might serve him; they may defy him. But they cannot supplant him, for they are not in the age group that can take power.

Enough, then, has been said to show that this fourth ordeal and initiation is required, that the creators of the mysteries understood this, and that, whether it was for a tiny minority or an influential elite, they did try to provide such a psychophysical therapy. But although all of this can be made unavoidably clear, the great difficulty remains. Earth, water, and air can be used as contact materials for psychophysical therapy. But nearly everyone will still maintain that fire cannot be so used. To them we must state the challenge as we truthfully must and can, as a clear question: "Is there any evidence that man can go through flames given off by blazing logs and the temperatures emitted by a bed of brightly glowing charcoal and not even be burned, but actually be refreshed?"

First, however, we must ask whether back of the ordeal by fire there was a method which, at one level of culture and for one type of consciousness, did act as a test of the acquisition and possession of extraordinary and protective resistances and controls? To refer again to Shirokogoroff's thorough study of shamanism in Siberia: in addition to the severe water ordeal (previously referred to in Chapter 2 of this Section III), the shaman also had to show his resistance to fire. After he had gone through the preparatory self-training, undertaken when he went to live in solitude in the forests, the candidate had to walk on heaps of hot coals and, immediately afterward, show that his feet had not been burned.

But the fire walk is not confined to one culture. Nor is it practiced only by those unusual persons who have an odd and rare psychophysical balance; [or] adolescents who between the ages of fifteen and twenty-one have shown symptoms of a possible vocation; [or those] who, further, have been able to endure severe isolation and who have also cultivated some form of extreme autosuggestion which utter solitude favors. Even now the fire walk is practiced in India, in Japan, and in the Pacific Islands; it is a part of the procedure in the rituals of certain Buddhist, Brahmanistic, and Islamic sects.

As Ruth Benedict (3) points out in her now well-known *Patterns of Culture*, page 176, in British Columbia the ecstatic worshiper dances

III - INITIATIONS/PSYCHOPHYSICAL RELIGIOUS EXERCISES

with glowing coals held in his hands and at moments puts them in his mouth. Olfert Dapper (17) reports the same practice in South Africa, in *Description de l'Afrique*. Lane (52) (*An Account of the Manners and Customs of the Modern Egyptians*, page 467, f.) witnessed Islam Sufis doing the same. J. G. Warneck (94) (*Die Religion der Batak*) studied the identical fire rite in Sumatra, and Adolf Bastian (1) (*Die Voelker des Oestlichen Asien*) describes it in Siam.

In 1956, there appeared two careful reports on the fire walk as it is still practiced in Europe.[102] One of these reporters, Martin Ebon, is editor of the quarterly review of psychical research called *Tomorrow*. The other is Admiral Angelo Tanagras, a student of long-standing and high reputation in psychical research. Both of these researchers, Ebon in 1956 and Tanagras on May 21, 1940 (the feast of St. Constantine in whose honor, and of his mother St. Helena, the rite is performed), witnessed the fire walking: Admiral Tanagras at the village of Mavrolefki; Mr. Ebon at the village of Agia Eleni (St. Helena). These two villages and the nearby country (it is a district in the Macedonian mountains some forty miles from Salonika) are populated by a sect of Paulicians, a Christian heresy, which has always preserved firewalking as a mystery rite. The two observers note that the rite has about it no fraudulence. In both cases, careful examination was made of the dancers' feet after they came off from dancing in the glowing beds of charcoal. The feet were not calloused nor were they inflamed; still less were they blistered or burned.

In the ceremony that Mr. Ebon witnessed, two men and three women took part. Each went over the glowing charcoal not less than five times; one of them went over it fifteen times. The dance in the fire continued for some twenty minutes; the dancers were barefoot. Previous to the actual firewalk a service of chanting began at about 5:15 p.m. From 6:30 until past 7:00, the pyre was kept blazing. Then about 7:15, the pyre was spread into a floor of embers, and the dancers, carrying icons and the scarf covers of the icons, now executed their dance (which they had been performing for two hours already) on the live charcoal.

Admiral Tanagras notes also that, besides the quietly ecstatic dancing to the sober rhythm of the music, the dancers take deep respirations while they perform. This is so striking that, for this reason,

4. The Initiation of Illumination

they are called *anastenarias* (or *nestinars* for short) which, in Greek, means "sighers." Before this rite in the evening, there has been a Mass, general dancing, and the sacrifice of a bull. Admiral Tanagras also notes that, on the occasion which he observed, when the pyre was level enough to be danced on, the coals were nearly a foot thick over an area of some twenty-five square feet. In this case, the dancers were three women who bore the icons.

Admiral Tanagras believes that this rite is a survival from the classical Greek worship of Dionysus. This certainly seems probable, for the worshipers of Dionysus did so perform: a fact to which Euripides bears witness in his play *The Bacchae*. Also, in the present-day rite, a bull (which is the beast sacred to Dionysus) is sacrificed, not the lamb sacred to Christ. And, [because] the dancing of the Maenads was a chief feature of the Dionysia, the preliminary ecstatic dance and the fact that the fire dance is not undertaken until ecstasy has been attained, is an additional confirmation of the Admiral's theory. Even more, we know that the musical instruments still used today (the lyre, the flute, and the drum) are the orchestra that was employed by the worshipers of the ecstatic god to raise themselves to *ecstasis*.

A number of careful studies have shown (*a*) that there is no fraud in the rite. The heat of the fire is enough to ignite a piece of paper thrown into it. The initiate goes through real flames and walks on live, red-hot charcoal. These studies have also shown that (*b*) calluses on the soles of the feet are not the explanation of the protection from burning; (*c*) that there is a careful, pre-ritual method of preparation; and (*d*) that the rite is intended to heighten health, strengthen vitality, and restore damaged body tissue.

Also, as we have seen, the anthropological literature dealing with this subject is not small. *The Journal of the Society for Psychical Research* contains several full and careful accounts by qualified observers. Particularly remarkable are two cases. One is the account of a fire walk as it was conducted by an Islamic initiate. This account was written by a British banking official who took part in the procession when those in attendance at the ceremony were permitted to walk the length of the fire trench, treading on the burning logs and the live charcoal. The other case was from the Pacific Islands. There the ... observer did not

III - INITIATIONS/PSYCHOPHYSICAL RELIGIOUS EXERCISES

himself walk in and along the fire trench, but he tested the temperature by throwing pellets of paper onto the glowing embers and clocking the length of time it took the pellets to break into flame. A couple of seconds and they were fully ignited. The bona fides of both of these observers, and their competence to judge the experience objectively, do not appear to be in doubt.

However, I would like to add to this evidence two cases, witnessed by two authors, both of whom are known to me personally. The first is an account, given to me in a letter, by Joseph Campbell (11, 12). He is author of the important anthropological studies, *The Hero with a Thousand Faces* and *The Masks of God*. He is the editor of Heinrich Zimmer's outstanding *Philosophies of India*, co-worker with Dr. Zimmer, and also editor of the volume titled *Papers from the Eranos Yearbooks*. Campbell had lately completed a year of anthropological travel and study in Asia, and his experience with the fire walk occurred in Japan. The following quotes I make, with his permission, from an account that he wrote for me at my request.

The ceremony took place in an area behind a small Shingon temple in Kyoto. The Buddhist sect that practices this fire therapy is called "Yamabushi." In a roped-off space of this back lot of the temple, a large square pyre had been built. Outside the ropes and on three sides, a congregation sat, and there was an altar covered with flowers and fruit. Over fifty Yamabushi priests were in attendance, chanting as they circumambulated the altar. Next, three principal priests recited prayers in front of the pyre, after which the pyre was ignited from two sides. One of the principal officiating priests now seated himself on the ground before the pyre, pointing two wands at the pile from which smoke was now pouring. The smoke swirled out, as though the pyre were the center of some vortex, forming a cloud that drove sideways following a circular path twice around the burning pyre "nearly smothering all of us each time it came our way." Then, with the increasing conflagration, the smoke gave way to flame and the whole pyre was one blaze. Nearby, some bundles of wooden votive tablets had been stacked, and these were now fed to the fire. Then, with long rakes, the mass of blazing wood was formed into a trench some fifteen feet in length. The bigger logs, ablaze but not yet broken up by the fire, were arranged crosswise in the trench,

4. The Initiation of Illumination

above the bed of flame made by the pieces that had broken down into small brands and bright charcoal. So a kind of cattle-guard or corduroy walk was made, through which grate or grill the flames rose.

The priest with the wands, who had sat before the fire while it was being lit and brought to full conflagration, had now moved and sat at one end of the trench with an assistant seated at the other. They stayed sitting like this for a few moments, after which all was ready for the therapy. The first to walk the length of the trench was one of the chief priests. By then a considerable portion of the lay congregation had been brought near and lined up. Old people, the middle-aged, and youngsters—between seventy-five and one hundred persons went along the trench. Dr. Campbell himself went in his turn. He reports, "I deliberately stepped on some nice fat flames, smelled the hair burning on my legs but found the flames were cool. When I put on my socks again I found that my right ankle, which had been swollen and sore from a strain acquired at Ankor Vat some weeks before, had gone down to normal and no longer hurt. The next day I walked some nine or ten miles and the ankle was still OK. The skin of my feet had not been damaged in the least—not even reddened by the flames. ..." Dr. Campbell adds, "The Yamabushi priests are particularly celebrated for their handling of fire."

The second account is given by Mr. George Sandwith, a Fellow of the Royal Geographic Society, who also carried out an extensive anthropological travel-study tour, more especially in Polynesia. His experience of the fire initiation was at Suva, the rite being performed by an East Indian priest who was the officiant of the Maha Devi Temple there. The deity worshiped in this temple, so her priest said, was the goddess who gave fertility as well as the goddess who could protect from burning. She could be called (indifferently, for all the names meant the same thing) Devi, Kali, or Mariamman. These titles only indicate a manifestation of the Divine Power that is available to everyone of any race or creed who believes sufficiently to undergo the essential preparations. Fear and guilt must go, driven out by love for the Divinity who was here called the Universal Mother.

It is worth noting that here we have the same image of the terrible and also benign All Mother that appeared in the therapy at

III - INITIATIONS/PSYCHOPHYSICAL RELIGIOUS EXERCISES

Eleusis as Mother Demeter and Daughter Persephone. And this is not all. For Demeter (who is also the dreadful Hecate, the moon-power of the dark and night side of life) appears in what is perhaps the earliest myths regarding the beginning of the Eleusinian mysteries as the All Mother Goddess who can give mortals immortality through bathing them in fire. She roamed the earth in disguise, so the myth runs, seeking her daughter. She comes to Eleusis, and the local royal couple take her into their house as a nurse. Every night the goddess puts their child to bathe in the glowing ashes of the fire, until the Queen discovers this and rushes in. The goddess then reveals herself and tells the mother that she has prevented her son from being made immortal [i.e., the son was denied immortality because his mother abruptly interrupted Demeter's ritual].[103]

One of the particularly interesting observations made by Sandwith, in his study of the rite at this Tonga temple, is in regard to the methods of stepping up the tonicity or resistance of the postulants.[104] The first method is water purification. The postulants bathe in a pool. Next, an object of concentration is made. It is called a *khalasam*, and it is a kind of monstrance made of a water-filled pot crowned with a peeled and pierced coconut held in place by a skewer which, like a dowel, goes down into the pot. The postulants stood circled around this object, concentrating. Suddenly they shouted. A young man sat down, cross-legged, before the priest. The priest took up six bamboo skewers, three of which he pressed through the boy's cheeks until they were completely penetrated. Then, in the same way, the boy's arms and pectorals were pierced and the skewers left in place, transfixing the muscles. The postulant did not wince and no blood appeared.[105] At this point, attendants went around laying their hands on the foreheads of the other postulants. This roused some of the group to dancing and singing, while some fell to the ground, foaming. (Clearly, a Leptoid seizure had been precipitated.) One became violent and had to be held. Cold water was then thrown over all of them. After that, each one was able, with quiet elation, to be pierced and have his muscles transfixed as had the first boy. They gathered in a circle, and drum rhythms were begun. The priest, putting the *khalasam* on his head like a crest, called loudly on the goddess. Chanting, he led the procession carrying a long whip in his

4. The Initiation of Illumination

hand. At intervals, one of the followers would come abreast of him, hold out an arm which the priest would lash furiously. No blood ever appeared nor did any weal arise. Instead, the postulant laughed and asked for further stimulation.

The procession took two-and-one-half hours, and all the time, in the midday heat, the pierced performers kept up their vigorous dance. Behind the Devi temple, forty tons of firewood had been burning for fourteen hours and was reduced to a pyramid of glowing charcoal. Poles fifteen feet long were used to rake the heap into a trench. Police, doctors, and members of the governor's family were present in addition to a large group of onlookers. The fire was hot enough to make the sweat pour from the bodies of the men raking the trench. The priest went to the edge of the trench, stopped, prayed, and then walked slowly along the live charcoal. As soon as he was near the further end, the postulants were allowed to follow. They all walked the length of the trench twice and then returned, unscathed, to the Temple. The fire was certainly of considerable heat for, when the initiates had gone, some Europeans, certain that it was merely autosuggestion, tried to walk the trench in their boots. But they were burned as the leather soles peeled off rapidly in the high temperature.

This case has been noted at some length because it indicates that not only can fire be endured and not only, when it can be stood, is it a high stimulant, but that it is a culminant therapy that can be taken only by those who have stepped up to this intensity. True, in this case and even more so in the Kyoto Yamabushi case of Campbell, the officiants can and do exert, vicariously, some kind of stimulation control and suggestive hypnotic power on behalf of those whom they conduct. Nevertheless, we see that there is a degree of preparedness and that this points to the fact that the fire mystery has always been the fourth: an accumulant and a culminant experience for those who would complete their psychophysical education; their psychosomatic, developmental therapy.[106]

The earth burial, water catharsis, and air respiration are indicated now, by research therapy, to be apposite when by regression and reprogression they deal with the trauma of birth, the revolt of protoindividualism, and the despair of midindividualism. So is it

III - INITIATIONS/PSYCHOPHYSICAL RELIGIOUS EXERCISES

possible to suggest, then, that total individualism, with its threat of manic-depressive collapse, might yield to radiation therapy? Infra-red, heat ray treatment is highly stimulating, curative, and restful. The intensity of the radiation can, step by step, be increased. ... Work with hypnosis shows that resistance to heat damage can certainly be heightened to levels that would be considered impossible were the body-mind at what is now its customary slackness of coordination. Certainly here is a line of research that we cannot neglect. For racially and individually, phylogenetically and ontogenically, we have reached a state when acute individualism of the power-desiring and power-holding type will ruin us. And it will frustrate both the evolutionary and growth processes unless, to the other three therapies, we can add this fourth one.

5. The Initiation of Transformation (*Electricity*)

In Section I, we traced a record of the psychological development of social man. And we saw, at the close of that section, that man today is no longer in the Humanic Epoch. He has passed out of that phase during which he considered himself to be a complete being, a finished product, the fully rational, objective, individual self. We are in a postindividualistic period. For we are now aware of the fact that we can no longer regard personal self-consciousness as being a final irreducible state, a condition that cannot be analyzed further. We see that we are, and must know ourselves to be, parts of a field, nodes in a web of patterning forces, synapses in a whole of intercommunicating ranges of consciousness.

This post–Humanic Epoch was clearly detectable by the beginning of the twentieth century. And indeed, symptoms of the oncoming change, we can now see, were increasingly evident during the last two decades of the nineteenth century. Therefore, it is now apparent that humankind has reached another phase in its history beyond any that it has so far known, an epoch of a state of mind that lies above and beyond individuality.

III - INITIATIONS/PSYCHOPHYSICAL RELIGIOUS EXERCISES

This is hard to realize. For up until now we have extrapolated. That is to say that up until this generation we have naturally assumed that individuality has always been the characteristic of human consciousness. It is true that studies of the great Paleolithic cave art galleries did compel us to realize that in our prehistoric ancestors there was a quality of awareness, a type of consciousness, essentially different from that of the three historic phases of individualism. Still, to most individuals, even that gave no insight into the evolution of their own consciousness. It seemed to indicate only that primitive man was still largely possessed by an animal consciousness and that his art was akin to the spontaneous musicianship of a bird or the architectural skill of a bee. The millennial and score-millennial creep of craft development in the Prehistoric, Paleolithic Epochs seemed to be proof that, although they were in their way as ingenious as birds or insects, the capacities and awareness of these men could [not yet] be called human. Naturally, then, man has felt that he was right in being critical and analytical; he was right in shunning integral states of mind. For the only true and valid humanity (the only possible progress) that could emerge would be insofar as man gained in intensification of self-consciousness and definiteness of individuality.

The notion, then, that the path of progress might be a spiral, instead of going straight on in simple extrapolation, has been very hard to accept. But it is also difficult to see how individualism could be intensified further or, if it could be, what would be gained. Certainly, our present perils that are due to lack of awareness of others would be mortally increased. Even so, a new concept of consciousness, the ideal of another quality of consciousness, is clearly inconceivable to nearly everyone. We can now detect other levels of consciousness in ourselves, outside of our self-consciousness, and many of them show greater insight and power than that self-consciousness. Yet we still cling to the ego as being the ultimate unit, the only possible final value.

And there are two further symptoms to indicate that we are at the end of individuality, that it is not the final term. In the first place, we have enough evidence that man in his first maturity, the shrewd power type that is now the main manager and executive sector, is no

5. The Initiation of Transformation

longer sufficient to handle the human situation. The rational critical intelligence, shrewd and decisive in its own realm of the sensory world, today sets up, in the psychophysical world, conflicts it cannot understand. As long as materialism was held, by the Western World, to be the ultimate explanation of reality, the practical individualist, with his mechanist faith, could not be withstood. Today, however, resistance is growing against his blind faith in a purely physical view of life. As yet, men have little to put in its place, but the power type's conviction no longer gives him control over them. His high-handed action, his drastic surgery on the body politic is like that of the pre-aseptic surgeons. "Operation successful; patient succumbed" is now the verdict on much coercive social planning.

The very fact that communication now has to become a science shows that the mere announcing of orders and directives is a woefully inefficient way of getting things done. The resistances to and stoppages of the flow of idea-exchange are found to be due to pararational, subconscious hostilities. These hostilities are provoked, without his being aware of it, by the rationalist, power-type efficiency manager through his absence of insight, his basic belief that he has fought his way up in strenuous competition with the rest. Hence, he is incapable of cooperation. Meanwhile, not only does this deep-seated attitude block the efficiency of his team, it exacts a heavy price from the man himself. His repressed hostility creates in him a psychosomatic bad conscience which, more than the excessive pace at which he lives, provokes such psychosomatic diseases as cardiac, respiratory, and arthritic trouble. In short, the total individual, the humanic type, the man of first maturity is no longer adequate. A new person must be produced.

In the second place, we have already seen (in Section I, Chapter 5, and Section II, Chapter 5) that just as in the history of the race the Postindividual Epoch succeeded to the total-individualistic, Humanic Epoch, so in this century a new age group has appeared that is above and beyond the first maturity age group. At last, instead of semi-solitary survivors from a generation, the vast part of which has perished, we have a large new class of oldsters. And they are in no wise senile, unless they wish to be. They are in the new category of late, post-familial second maturity, the veterine type. But they are

III - INITIATIONS/PSYCHOPHYSICAL RELIGIOUS EXERCISES

utterly untaught, their education is completely neglected, their part is unwritten, their pattern of behavior unprovided, their contribution unknown.

All the age groups today need a specific emotional training. Evolution will continue only if we, understanding its drive and direction, provide those exercises whereby we may express its urges. The child must still strive to be heroic, the adolescent to be anonymous, those in first maturity to be critically wise and personally responsible. Enterprise, discipline, conscientious supervisorship—these three successive standards of conduct exist and only need to be adjusted to the present situation. But the new class of those in second maturity not only has no class solidarity, it has no standards, it has no role.

We have, then, a threat, a hope, and a demand in this new human category, this latest age group that has been produced by what seems to be a series of accidents in hygiene (the prolongation of life through medical advance: surgery, diet, and drugs), but which clearly might be the particular class needed to be the new racial epoch-making type, the postindividual type. The threat is now unmistakable, for geriatrics draws attention to an acute danger. We need not repeat those serious views, expressed by experts in the grave problem of old age, which were referred to in Section I, Chapter 5, and Section II, Chapter 5. These experts agree that they can warn but that they can do little else. Solutions to the problem remain stubbornly unobtainable. And they evade us for the double reason that society can honestly see no raison d'être for the senile and that the old can just as honestly see no reason why they should hold back from senility as long as they are unwanted, as long as they are not provided with some specific purpose to fulfill.

The hope, of course, is that the history of man, the force of the species' drive, the urge of evolution—the aim of life—all point to the production of this new class. No one knows the upper limit of a human being's life expectation. At present there are stocks in our species that can be traced back even to Hellenic Roman times and whose natural viability extends to one hundred and more years. So we should be prepared for a large new age group of the hearty aged, those in second maturity, as we continue to put a check on the accidents of wear and tear.

5. The Initiation of Transformation

Further, not only is humankind today postindividualistic in psychophysical development, with the present population producing and carrying this new and growing original class that demands a new category for it to fulfill. But the great traditional therapies, which when esoteric have been called mysteries, are not merely four but five.

The four mysteries, as we have seen, do cover the four categories: the four epochs of the race and the four age groups of the individual. Until today, save for comparatively rare cases, humankind was contained within these four great stages of the traditional psychotherapy. But there must be and there is a fifth mystery.

It was, no doubt, confined to the most advanced.[107] Very few would go beyond the fourth mystery. For until today the only thing that lay beyond was the rare situation of the lonely seer who can look back on life from the station of one who is already above the battle and left without contemporaries. Already he is aloof from action, already dead to and departed from the drives that involve the younger age groups.

But today, the fifth mystery is the fifth freedom for the new fifth age group of man. By regression and reprogression, the four former cramps and adhesions can be released and broken. So there is achieved (*a*) a voluntary birth instead of the actual birth trauma and protest; (*b*) a voluntary childhood of energy and enterprise without rage; (*c*) a voluntary adolescence of discipline and self-criticism without guilt; and (*d*) a voluntary maturity of ambitionless responsibility that voluntarily accepts office for the general good (Plato's wise ruler), instead of arrogant, elational authoritarianism alternating with loss of nerve.

The fifth voluntary acceptance of the fifth phase is, of course, voluntary relinquishment of all specific personal status, of all executive authority. All that is retained is an advisory influence; but even so, no specific rulings would be given. This person is consulted only because he can give the inspiration of true seership; he can give a true picture of the process as a whole, in which frame of reference all the executive functions must operate or they must in the end miscarry. Yet his influence is all the more authoritative precisely because he exercises no personal coercion. He must be obeyed because, instead of his having to enforce his rulings, the nature of

III - INITIATIONS/PSYCHOPHYSICAL RELIGIOUS EXERCISES

things carries out the enforcement. The authority of those who really know the laws of life and nature is self-sanctioning. No pilot who wishes to live thinks of disregarding a warning from the weather tower. Patients who wish to recover know that the diagnosis and prognosis of the great physician must not be flouted. Those who are aloof can see further than those who are involved in action. Foresight is an increasing need as the immediate issue grows in complexity.

Therefore, the fifth ordeal initiation is the elimination, the explication whereby the person (who from birth to first maturity has been intensifying in individuality and self-consciousness) now re-expands, re-dilates, becomes regeneralized and finally, completely released, can pass liberated from all the ties of appetite, possession, and recognition into a state of consciousness in which he no longer requires particularity, locality, or a specious present. This sequence is shown in the Sanskrit phases of life. The child phase is succeeded by the period of the dutiful youth (Brahmachari), after which he becomes the householder, the Grihastha, the man of first maturity. In turn, that focus,[108] that concentration on social and racial obligations being over, the [husband] and wife, following the way of the fathers, begin their education for second maturity, for rising out of the "cycle of births and deaths," and aim to go on to the nonreturning way of the gods. Then, having learned this path out and up, the solitary life begins. As a forest seer or *rishi*, having nothing but wisdom, homeless and begging for his food, the gymnosophist, the wise man utterly denuded, the man who has cast all the husks is ready for voluntary death and complete volatilization. This Indian view of life is even more realistic and eliminatory than that of the Chinese.[109]

But how can either of these traditional answers to what Buddhism calls the fourth dislocation be made apposite today? The old need help, and society must find it for them on the double utilitarian demand made by sound economics and by psychosocial hygiene. We have seen that their increasing power of consumption (not merely of ordinary consumers' goods but of those skilled medical services that should go to keep producers in cheerful action) is a grave and increasing strain on civilization.

On the other hand, we are expending our finest therapies just to keep alive those who are now made unnaturally to endure. We are

5. The Initiation of Transformation

extending the consuming uselessness of those who are holding on not to be an inspiration but who are clinging on out of fear, and so spreading depression. This exhibition, from the psychosocial point of view, is the worst kind of pattern of prestige to give all the age groups below second maturity.

The [child] can be a hero, the adolescent can become the disciplined, obedient member of their team, the person of first maturity can be a critically minded administrator, but what lies ahead for the old? This head contingent, which can neither go on nor clear out, is a miserable snarl that is jamming the traffic on the bridge of life instead of leading it forward to the other shore.

Is it possible to shed any light on this problem that would be neither wishful thinking nor brutal realism? Must either the community or the individual be sacrificed? If the prestige patterns of our race present no specific, socially valuable ideal for the postindividual, this fifth category of humankind, and if the four age groups of today can offer no place for the old (for in second maturity we are producing no type that serves a specific social function; that has energy, vision, and enterprise; that knows its purpose, its contribution, and its direction), then what are we honestly to say?

However, two possibilities remain to be examined. In addition to the life of the race and the life of the individual, we have seen that there is another pair of sequences that indicate the course of human development. (1) There are the specific breakdowns that each epoch and each age group has suffered when it failed to achieve the stage of development next above it. And (2) there are the specific therapies (mysteries) that were devised to remedy these breakdowns and permit the resumption of human development.

We have seen that the particular insanity of second maturity is involutional melancholy. This breakdown is of particular interest, for in the first place it is rational. Melancholia at any age, it is admitted by all psychiatrists, is the hardest to handle of all the mental complaints, and the psychoanalyst shuns it. It is one of the prime provocants of that baffling and stubborn addiction, alcoholism, which, therefore, analysts also shun. For the melancholic is asking the basic question that always arises when the life of irrelevant appetite fails: "To what end?" Such is the question that drives all the

III - INITIATIONS/PSYCHOPHYSICAL RELIGIOUS EXERCISES

ascetic movements to attack the unreflective, boastful heroic. Even the intensely vital Jew reaches that wall across the easy, unreflective way of life when Koheleth, speaking for Wisdom, gives as the final verdict, *vanitas vanitatum, omnia vanitas*.

For the melancholic does not have illusions. He is not the paranoic, thinking that if he could slay his persecutors he would be happy. Nor is he the schizophrenic, drawing away from a challenge he feels he cannot answer. He is not manic, in a phase of groundless optimism, nor depressive because his dream has proved to be baseless. He questions those who conform and who claim to make it possible to persuade those who cannot conform to come back, to re-adjust, to face up to reality and to accept conformity as sanity. He asks them, "Do you believe that life has any meaning? Can you say, even, that our senses let us contact reality? Do you think that man is capable of rational action, that he possesses free will and that society is run intentionally, let alone nobly? What are your own arguments for establishing that the world, as we perceive it, is not a tale told by an idiot with sadistic tastes?"

The materialistic analyst has no answers to these questions. The vast majority of psychiatrists accept, via Freud or some other channel, the nineteenth-century notion that evolution is a result of chaotic randomness. Naturally, the man who has, with critical intelligence, asked these basic questions and, through his responsible sensitiveness, [has] been depressed by finding that most psychiatrists believe that there is no answer but the worst, ceases to discuss and withdraws into himself.[110]

Melancholia, if it is to be looked on as a disease, should then be regarded as being a psycho-deprivative complaint. Our society is deranged because, although it is intelligent, it cannot give an intelligent reason for living, or at least for living well. No society has lasted that did not have a psychotherapy. As we have mentioned before (Part I, Chapter 4), the Humanic society is the only one that has attempted to live on the deprivative mental diet of a rationalism that was ignorant of the preterconsciousness. So we must regard melancholia not as being a disease per se, but rather as being an acute condition of thwarted appetite, such as thirst pains, hunger pangs, or the vitamin deficiency of the alcoholic whose diet, in consequence of

5. The Initiation of Transformation

his heavy drinking, is a deprivative one that brings on delirium tremens as well as bodily breakdown.

By sound psychosocial prognosis we might have expected, then, that in a still humanically oriented society, a new age group, those in second maturity, would slip out of gear. Finding that they were not needed by society and that society is convinced that life ends in inexplicable futility, such a group as those who are in second maturity must regard their melancholy as being all too rational. Howard Fabing, out of his great experience, has said that the will to live depends mainly on the capacity for interest, the conviction that life is worth living. There is dismal proof that the collapse of old age is not the fault of the body. It bears us into these advanced years with patient efficiency. It is not the worn-out weakness of a brain that is finished [which] is the main cause of second maturity's failure. And, as John Pfeiffer (66) has pointed out in his *The Human Brain*, there is no evidence that the brains of the second maturity group are in any way inferior to those who are still in first maturity. The body grows less capable of muscular exertion, but the mind appears to be just as able to learn if it can see any reason why it should.

Second maturity's defeat, the collapse of the veterine, is a problem of the intelligence, a failure of the understanding. It is a lack of purpose, the absence of any creative function by which the old can find that they have a rational right to go on living. It is the lack of an insight, an experience that can convince them that their advanced sector of life's great line demands of them a unique service, leadership, and message.

We can no longer shirk this problem. For besides the dark cloud of despair that now settles in a spreading eclipse over increasing numbers of the old, we can also see the widening pit above which that cloud hovers. The latest figures show that today the rate of suicide increases in each decade of life. The incidence of suicide among the old is five times what it is among the young.

The rate of suicide is lowest among those who accept, with implicit obedience, the orders of the authoritarian religions. Orthodox Jews have the lowest number, then Roman Catholics, next Protestants, and after them secularists.

III - INITIATIONS/PSYCHOPHYSICAL RELIGIOUS EXERCISES

The ancient religions do not argue; they order and threaten. But today the educated must have their questions answered and their fears honestly faced and truthfully removed. Possibly we could continue to make men, who are filled with the futility of life, hang on to their bodies for fear of worse misery should they let go. But fear cannot drive out fear. We might prevent suicide from spreading among the obedient and the ignorant. But if we cannot convince them that they are needed, that they matter, we cannot prevent them from going out of their minds. And we must recall William Sargant's (73) grim warning (see his *The Battle for the Mind*) that a frequent cause of suicide today is precisely the fear of going mad—the supreme fear of having to go on living in a tangible nightmare where every value and joy has turned to dust.

The specific mental disease of second maturity appears, then, to be as significant a symptom of a failure to develop rightly as the madnesses of the other age groups have now shown themselves to be. Mental disease—all insanity that is specifically psychological[111]—is a state of mind, a failure of nerve, a failure to find the way onto a higher level of comprehension and more adequate response.

Having seen the direction in which this fifth insanity points, we can now see how the traditional therapy dealt with this demand for the next stage of higher sanity and wholeness. We have already mentioned in this chapter that, above and beyond the ordeal and initiation required to bring a man through first maturity, there seems to have been a fifth mystery. It was rare, because few lived to need it; and it was esoteric because the experience turned the individual into the lonely seer, who was often blind and always much aloof from life. The Greeks seem to have known of it, but mainly, one judges, by hearsay. So their description has in it not merely mythic confusion but meteorological misapprehension. The Hellenic cosmogeny tended to be ranged round the atmospheric levels of the snow mountain that they knew best, Olympus. The Greeks recognized that there were two levels. There was the basic level where trees could still grow and animals could live. But above that was rock and snow; the air was rarer; you panted and were chilled to the bone as well. Here, therefore, dwelt the nonhuman gods. The gas that we mortals breathe is a thick, vaporous stuff (*aer*), but the breath of the

5. The Initiation of Transformation

gods is *aether*; and there in that thin, fine medium everything is clear, keen, and cold.

But what has this to do with fire? Dazzling light is there, but though the mountaintop is nearer the Sun himself, the cold is greater than below. Zeus (Diós) the shining one ruled there. And everyone who has climbed mountains knows that besides those fine days when the peaks can be seen rising in the clear, hard blue, often the summits can wrap themselves not only in mist but in thunder cloud. Zeus is just as much the thunderer and the slayer-by-lightning as he is the Light of Heaven. Further, anyone who is on a mountain during a thunderstorm is in considerable danger of being struck by lightning. And even if he is not struck, he will feel electric shocks of various intensities, for the whole rock is charged. He will see the glow and hear the hiss of St. Elmo's Fire, the static electricity being given off by his own body, and when he steps off the rock of the mountain peak onto earth, he will feel a very distinct electric jar. The Greeks knew, as did the Sanskrit Aryans about their sacred peak Mount Kailas, that there are two fires: that of the flame, from the sun's heat and the volcano's fire (the heat of molecular activity), and also that of the lightning flash.

What, then, would be the fifth therapy? Only of late have we been able to be sure. The final initiation, the one that alone can cure melancholy, enlarge consciousness, and release the psyche into its final explicatedness is electricity. This is clear from the growth of electric shock therapy during this century. It is significant that as we have moved out of the Humanic Epoch and, at the same time and for the first time have produced, but provided with no role to play, the fully [populated] class of second maturity and their specific mental disease, involutional melancholy, we have also introduced the strangest of all the therapies, a degree of electrocution. The steps whereby this came about are also instructive.

In the 1930s, it began to be recognized that epilepsy was, for all practical purposes, the state that was polar to melancholy. Freud wrote an essay on how epileptic seizure could be postponed by emotionally moving the subjects so deeply, by pathos, that they would break into tears and the fit would not take place. Electric shock treatment became so popular a way of dealing with withdrawn and

III - INITIATIONS/PSYCHOPHYSICAL RELIGIOUS EXERCISES

gloomy states as to be almost routine. And it was soon recognized that this was a way of bringing about a controlled epilepsy. It was also recognized that, although this treatment permitted the patient to resume his customary and normal life, the effect might fade; the tormenting questions might return and the shock would have to be repeated. In some cases, the shocks became a routine part of such subjects' lives. There were also cases where this routine treatment produced, in the end, the same result as did persistent epileptic seizure: the brain itself was injured by the shock and the subject died insane.

Here, then, we have a temporary cure for melancholy, but with two distinct disadvantages. (1) It can be physically damaging if repeated. (2) Psychologically (and this is the reason for its repetition if the patient suffers a relapse), it does nothing to answer the questions that caused the melancholy; it simply disregards them. It is regressive but not reprogressive.

However, before going on to consider how this method has been further developed as a palliative therapy and individual relief (and also noting parallel lines of pure research in electric shock that suggest further progress), we should see what can be learned from the traditional esoteric mysteries, insofar as they may throw some light on this fifth stage of life and its specific ordeal and initiation. The Sanskrit psychophysical researchers, we now can recognize, not only had become aware of the ductless glands by detecting the fields of energy around them (called *chakras* or wheels). But they realized that this series of glands, from the interstitial in the genitals, through the suprarenals, past the thymus,[112] on past the thyroid to the pituitary and culminating in the pineal, is a sequence coordinated with and branching out from the spinal cord.

Now we know that central to all yogic exercises is the raising of Kundalini. And if breathing exercises (especially in the intense form of the breath retentions of Hatha yoga, the yoga that is mainly the physiological rather than psychological method of changing consciousness) are the primary technique in the yogas, then we may say that the raising of Kundalini is the final goal of such disciplines. Kundalini is no longer an unfamiliar term now that anthropological investigation and psychophysical research have been able to

5. The Initiation of Transformation

exchange their findings. Kundalini, literally the coiled serpent, is that stored nexus of electric energy which, according to the Sanskrit theory, lies congested at the base of the spine and especially around the perineum. This may be raised by such specific exercises as (1) breathing rhythms, (2) breathing rhythms with other physical contractions, (3) glandular pressures, or (4) physical contractions and tensions by themselves. Others hold that constant mental concentration accompanied by strict sexual continence will make this surge of energy take place of itself. The customary and traditional theory is that this energy, when it is triggered and released, runs up the spinal cord and flashes into the brain, making it superactive but also unconscious of the sensory world. But Vasant G. Rele (70), known for his *The Mysterious Kundalini*, and some others trained in Western physiology, who themselves are also trained in this yogic technique, hold that the current does not run up through the spinal cord. They believe that the impulse, the energy, and the effect on body and mind, are due to the vagus nerve[113] and its automatic functioning being altered and brought, to some degree, under conscious control.

Whichever theory may be true, there seems to be no reasonable doubt as to the following facts, for they are backed by a great deal of evidence from a large number of qualified observers. By specific exercises, the yogin can bring on a surge of energy that rises up from the perineum area into the brain. With the aid of this surge, the yogin can put himself into suspended animation, catalepsy—and, what is more, he knows how to bring himself back from this state of arrested vitality. The yogin claims that this condition not only permits him to remain without breathing, anaesthetized, unaware of the physical world, but it also permits him to enter other levels of consciousness that are not restricted to biological time, and to enjoy a state of health that is unknown to us who are running on more sluggish rhythms. He can endure stresses under which we would break and succumb. With all these certified data, the psychophysiologist today is less inclined to cavil. The psychic claims still await rationalization in an acceptable frame of reference.

But we can now understand how the physical modifications that the yogin manifests could be explained in terms of biological energies that modern physiologists are already prepared to recognize.

III - INITIATIONS/PSYCHOPHYSICAL RELIGIOUS EXERCISES

The electrical field of the body is at present well gauged and mapped. All nerve impulses are electrical, the spine does channel these charges to the brain, and the brain does handle these surges. Further, if and when these waves become breakers, the brain is swamped. The rhythmic energy, which should drive the dynamos of purposive action, has become an inundation. The brain, like a flooded irrigation system, its sluices gorged by too high a tide, is lost to sight under tumbling waters and all control is lost. This, as we have seen, is what takes place in an epileptic seizure.

Therefore, the yogin's claim, that he can at will both induce and also control and feed into his brain the full leptic energy so that it will not stun him but, instead, will give a superdrive to his consciousness, does not seem improbable today. And an epileptic seizure is what takes place when the organism gives itself its own self-generated shock treatment. Haunted by the futility of remaining confined to our present sense-limited knowledge, to such weak and jejune emotional experiences as the senses as we use them can give (and especially such as the panaesthetic current can give when restricted to sexual–genital sensation), the mental-emotional life seeks an enlarged, dilated experience. This is specifically so when the reproductive cycle is over or unrequired, then it is that the consciousness longs for the larger frame of awareness and the enlarged power of response.

But epilepsy—because it *is* epilepsy and not prolepsy; because it comes as a leap upon, an attack, a tidal wave from outside the victim's awareness; because it is not a surge that is induced by a prepared consciousness that can then ride this wave, as the surf-rider breasts the breaker, is still a disease. Often, as Penfield and other researchers have demonstrated, the fit is brought on by a purely physical blockage. A callus or scar tissue has formed on the brain as the result of some past skull injury. This callus bars the flow of electric energy over the brain and, the energy blocked, the rhythm thwarted, the convulsion follows. The channels of the brain having bars in them, the blocked current no longer surges but bursts through.

But, just as a blocked streambed may be flooded by a moderate rainfall, so a clear streambed, adequate for an average rainstorm,

5. The Initiation of Transformation

may be wrecked by a cloud burst. Should the spinal cord send an exceptional charge to the normal brain that is accustomed to only average disturbance, and so unprepared for such a shock, then *pro term* the normal man would go into a state of seizure. And this condition we now know can be provoked in persons otherwise never subject to fits.

Metrazol is a chemical that makes the nerve channels more sensitive. Give a person who has never had a seizure of any sort fifty milligrams of Metrazol (orally) and then let him look at a flickering light—a stroboscope—and he will begin to twitch. But give the average, normal person a dose of less than fifty milligrams and he will show no abnormality; none of the healthy reactions will be disturbed. On this basis, a very valuable scale has been worked out. At the top of this scale is the fifty-milligram dose required to disturb the normal person. At the other end is a dosage of from zero to ten milligrams, which is the amount, together with the stroboscope, that will bring on a seizure in the epileptic. At zero, there is the person who is a victim of the grand mal, whose fit may come on at any time and who can be put into a state of seizure by looking at the stroboscope. Then from zero to ten there are those who suffer from the petit mal, those who, when seized by it, do not fall to the ground and foam, those whose seizures may be brought on by stress, fatigue, or a dosage of up to ten milligrams of Metrazol and the stroboscope.

However, the illuminating fact that has unexpectedly emerged from these researches has nothing to do with the damaged and weak who cannot handle these tides that are brought on by the Metrazol-induced heightening of their nerve channels. It has to do with the healthy and the strong who can handle them and do. The French psychophysicians who conducted these researches studied a number of ace test pilots. These pilots, of course, were men who had been picked for their job only after going through the most strenuous and most thorough laboratory and field tests. They were selected because they had been proved to be men of the finest and most advanced control and initiative. Their reflexes and their power of making decisions were equally swift and sure. Yet on the Metrazol scale test, they came out as being at twenty-five! It took only twenty-five milligrams of Metrazol to disturb their normal reactions:

III - INITIATIONS/PSYCHOPHYSICAL RELIGIOUS EXERCISES

twenty-five milligrams less than the average, normal person and only fifteen milligrams more than the epileptic. Their nerve sensitivity was double that of the person who was found to be normal.

In short, persons who acquire adaptability to strange experiences and quickly learn how to react originally are not normal. The routineers who can never be excited are no use on the speeding edge of modern advance. Our need today is the person who has been given a high charge and been taught and learned how to handle it. At the same time, if he is to serve in the present crisis, he must be no daredevil. That is why, since originality of mind and daringness of speculation are today more needed than sheer physical courage and unquestioning élan, this problem of lepsis is one for old age. For as Grey Walter (93) has shown in *The Living Brain*, when the system is facing a severe challenge, the brain produces the special delta wave, sign of the mobilization of organized defenses. It is present when brain areas are being attacked by growths or are deformed by scars. Yet it is also always present in the first year of life. The electroencephalograms taken from the fetal brain as it presses against the mother's abdomen show this wave, and sometimes even the full wave and spike that is characteristic of epilepsy. We can see then that this lepsis[114] (this superpulse of electric energy on the brain) is not itself a disease but a spur to a new leap out into a larger frame of reference. It attended our birth out of the womb. It comes again to summon us to a second birth.

Also, we must not disregard the high association between genius and epilepsy. This, too, makes it difficult to avoid looking at the Leptoid condition as being a progressive state of mind, a condition of the nervous system that is culminant and, therefore, can be the next step in evolution. It is a newly stepped-up pressure that is seeking for a new and adequate vehicle of expression, a new energy that destroys if it is not allowed expression but, given that expression, builds up new faculties, a new character, and a new quality of consciousness.

It is clear, then, why I have given the name Leptoid to this latest age group of humanity that stands in need of a treatment that can deliberately rouse and canalize this energy. For the controlled surge is the therapy answer to this age group's specific mental distress and disease: involutional melancholy. The electric shock treatment is

5. The Initiation of Transformation

now being increasingly modified to the point where (with the weaker and more prolonged current that is being used and the antecedent sedation and anaesthesia that have been added) it may now be called surge treatment rather than shock.

Further, it is now being realized (*a*) that though one surge may give temporary remission, repeated surges are required to lift the patient to a level where the counter down-flow and riptide of depression will not suck him back into the abyss. And (*b*) it is rapidly becoming evident that all that the surge can do, as it is now administered and understood, is to throw the victim out of the sea and onto the beach. Once there, he must be secured, made fast, and raised above high tide and storm danger, by persuading him to take hold of life and its larger interests and by giving him such rational encouragement as he and his counsellor can believe to be valid. Even when modified, as it has been, into surge therapy, shock treatment, as Dr. Karl Menninger of Topeka has said, can aid only some 10 percent of the mentally sick. The remainder must have a far more comprehensive therapy. We may hope that when this therapy is fully worked out it will incorporate the surge as part of an entire "pro-lepsis," in other words, a leap forward.

And as has happened with so many therapies, we can see how this modified treatment also may and indeed must be shifted from being a last resort (or even a curative method once melancholy has set in) into being not merely preventive but developmental, as all truly preventive methods must be when they are intended for a growing creature. If second maturity is a new class that is waiting for a new experiential discipline, then we may look to electric shock treatment for the therapy that will take the energy that will otherwise sink, thwarted, into the frustration of despair, and transmute it into a new quality of experience, a new superpersonal, postindividual consciousness.

Have we any further insights as to how this may be done? We have seen that electric shock (or what we may now call electric surge treatment) was not a product of pure research. It grew up out of the simplest empiric attempts at palliative and relief measures for dealing with those insane who had sunk into incommunicability. Yet it has brought into clear light the polar relationship between melancholy

III - INITIATIONS/PSYCHOPHYSICAL RELIGIOUS EXERCISES

and the Leptoid condition, and between the Leptoid condition and electric surge treatments. Meanwhile, and converging with this practical research, a series of studies have been made that, from another aspect of restorative therapy and from pure research, may give us some insight into how a fifth developmental therapy may be devised. These studies may give us some idea as to the nature of a fifth ordeal and initiation, which would give those in second maturity a specific quality of consciousness, a specific social position, and a specific service to the community.

After an accidental electric shock, the victim, although not mortally injured, generally dies of a respiratory failure. The breathing reflex has been thrown out and is not spontaneously resumed. This, again, is due to fibrillation of the heart: the muscle fibers twitch but no beat is produced and, after a short time, all cardiac activity ceases. Therefore, death by electric shock was presumed to be practically instantaneous. But twenty-seven years ago, Stefan Jellinek, giving shock to monkeys under anaesthetic, obtained cardiograph records which showed that although the heart did stop beating and begin to twitch, frequently it resumed its beat again. The lower animals certainly succumb to weaker shocks. But—and this is highly significant when we consider vitality and a large central nervous system together with the effect of electric stimulation on them—the larger the creature's brain the greater is its tolerance.

Jellinek (48) (who was professor of electropathology at the University of Vienna) has pointed out, in his *Dying, Apparent Death and Resuscitation*, that there are on record cases of men being struck by four hundred volts of direct current, being certified as dead by a physician, and yet after persistent artificial respiration being brought back to life. In fact it now seems clear that electrocution is anything but instantaneous: a thought that should be disquieting to those who retain capital punishment by electric shock on the ground that the criminal does not have to endure a lingering death. As long ago as 1934 at the International Life Saving Congress at Copenhagen, experts gave it as their judgment that a victim of electrocution may remain alive for at least an hour. Some of them even judged that death might not take place for as long as three or four hours. I know, myself, of a man who tripped, fell on a live cable and, as the current

5. The Initiation of Transformation

could not be shut off immediately, was subjected to strong shocks for some moments. Although he lay as one dead, he recovered and later reported that he had been conscious but incapable of movement or speech, and that as long as the current was flowing through him, he felt a strange heat. In short, as Jellinek points out, the victim is in suspended animation and is in no wise dead. He gives as proof the evidence of autopsies. They indicate that victims of electrocution frequently have not died instantaneously but slowly and by asphyxiation.

And in a lecture in London which I attended, Jellinek established the fact that even the burns produced by electricity (and their subsequent healing) are different from the burns and their healing produced by hot gases and ordinary molecular activity. Electric shock, then, is neither a physical blow, though it feels like one, nor a burn by flame though the aftereffect looks like it. The discovery of such a strange distinction between the effects of an electric shock and such an apparently similar damage (cell destruction by flame, bone fracture by a blow) led Jellinek to investigate further. He arrived at striking and (I believe) illuminating results, especially in the specific line of enquiry being dealt with in this chapter. When he had observed the odd fact that the more highly developed nervous system had a greater resistance to damage by electric shock (certainly a startlingly unexpected correlation—indeed, the very opposite of what might be expected), Jellinek began an extraordinary experiment. Considering the fact that the more highly developed the brain (though it be more elaborate), the better did it withstand shock, Jellinek felt himself driven to assume that a psychological factor must be involved here. Somehow mentality and not mechanism must make this difference, which was so completely contrary to what might be expected. Like all good researchers, he decided to experiment on himself. Although he knew that forty volts of direct current could sometimes be fatal, he felt that this was a very low level for a healthy man. For he also knew that far higher voltages are frequently taken without damage. Wishing, then, to detect the danger threshold, he started with one hundred and ten volts taken through the hand, and found that it was possible gradually to build up his resistance to the point where he could sustain four hundred

III - INITIATIONS/PSYCHOPHYSICAL RELIGIOUS EXERCISES

and forty volts direct current without any damage. This is certainly a lethal dose for most human beings.

Realizing now that the mental factor was involved and that it must lie in the training, in teaching the subject to prepare himself for the shock, he instructed a number of electricians in how to train themselves. None of them met with bad effects. Finally, a meteorologist friend of Jellinek's, caught in a thunderstorm on a Swiss peak, used the method. Having braced himself against the possibility of being struck, he was hit three times by lightning. But although his clothes were torn and his skin broken, because he was prepared he was neither stunned nor did he suffer anything but the surface abrasions.

Electric shock can then be vastly modified simply by knowing that it is coming and by having learned how to prepare for increasing voltages. But what is the factor that makes this possible? Jellinek consulted a fellow Viennese physician, Sigmund Freud. Freud agreed that this was a factor of the psyche, and made the interesting comment that in preparing for the blow one is preparing oneself against fear, and that thus psychic resources can be and are summoned, which do hold up or transmute the violent shudder. He added that it was not possible to avoid the conclusion that electricity and the field called the psyche were somehow aspects of the same thing.

We have now seen that electricity can be taken as a tonic, a tonic of consciousness. And just as a person can be prepared for the fire ordeal so that the experience becomes not destructive but stimulating, so electricity (which is the breath of the brain, the warmer of the intelligence) can be given in gradually increased charges and become, as it were, a transfusion of superenergy. But how may this be still further developed? Could this energy be used as a real re-energizer? Jellinek's work does suggest an extension of this research, an extension that would link up with the *aether* ordeal and initiation and supply a cross reference to those tribes which, in their development of the fifth mystery, use the severe shock given by the electric eel. However, we must remember that this fifth mystery was—as is our still rudimentary electric shock treatment—an attempt to produce a death of the old anxiety, fear, and foreboding and to start the person off with the *tabula rasa* or fresh rhythm of a new emotional attitude

5. The Initiation of Transformation

and outlook. Somehow, the old record, the old matrix and stereotype has become hopelessly corrupt, corroded, and defaced. If it is possible, as it now is, to take the sounds from a worn record and re-record them on a new disk or tape, then it should be possible to raise the electrical field of consciousness off the old disk, the old tape of the brain and, after resting the mind and cleansing the brain, resettle the consciousness on a refreshed matrix. We cannot even put it beyond the bounds of possibility that this field need not dissipate on being separated from the brain but could be induced to continue in a state that could be contacted, at least for a while.

This, of course, sounds like science fiction, but some additional evidence that Jellinek gives certainly seems to point in some such direction. The important fact is that these further results were obtained with animals, as indeed they could only have been. But that a creature so low in the mental scale that it can be completely stunned and probably killed by a sixty-volt electrical charge should show the following amazing reaction makes the report all the more significant. The phenomenon was quite unexpected.

For humane reasons, hogs in a Vienna slaughterhouse were electrocuted before they were hung up, head down, their throats cut, and their bodies drained completely of blood. The bloodless carcasses were then thrown into tanks of water that had been heated to one hundred and seventy degrees Fahrenheit. As they sank into the scalding water, the animals first shuddered violently, then righted themselves and, for some seven seconds, proceeded to swim. As Jellinek says, this coordinated swimming was quite other than the spasms of animals just killed. Further, it was quite different from the usual reaction of hogs that had had no electric shock before their throats were cut and their bodies drained of blood. Must we not suggest, then, that in the case of the electrocuted hogs, the electric field on the brain, instead of being dissipated by the electric shock, had been congested onto the brain and the creature was not dead but in the suspended motor animation of shock resulting from too much stimulant? Therefore, when the blood was removed this did not produce death. For the immediate function of blood, circulating in the brain, is to carry to the brain its food, which, together with glucose, is oxygen. And, in turn, the oxygen is the medium through which the brain keeps its electric field running. So to remove the blood, and so remove the oxygen, need not mean death. For if (in spite of the fact that the normal essential sequence of steps for producing it have been removed) the electricity could itself be kept present on the brain, then the creature without blood or breath would be alive. And the shock of the scalding water would activate its sensory and motor centers, make it struggle for its life, strike out, and swim. But the electric field of consciousness, so crudely retained on the brain, would not, of course, endure, save for a few moments in such a damaged vehicle. However, the fact that for some seven seconds it remained present and could cause coordinate lifesaving effort shows that such a strange noncorporeal survival is a possibility.

If, then, we compare the data of this experiment with the diagnosis of the human psychophysique that is given by the Vedāntasāra, of the Sanskrit tradition, we may find a significant correlate. Here it is recognized that in addition to the gross body or circuit—the biochemical physique—there is the subtle body or circuit that we now know as the electric field of the body. Can it be that electric shock, and especially when employed as electric surge, can produce in those prepared for it the rising of Kundalini, the raising of consciousness until it can first be kept at this superphysical level and then later, and at will, be raised and detached to function in its own right and independence?

How then, from these indications, might we hope to see the fifth mystery devised today? How could it be constructed in a modern form that would give ordeal and initiation to those who need and desire to be raised to complete postindividual consciousness? What can we suggest as a contemporary technique, one which would serve the immediate and double demand of our age? First, we need a developmental therapy for this new age group, those in second maturity, simply for their own sake. But we also need this therapy because it is from this group (when it has developed its postindividual consciousness) that we could obtain that pattern of prestige, that specific function and service [which] humanity now requires.

Naturally, such proposals can only be tentative suggestions, extrapolations from our present convergent lines of knowledge. But if we summarize these findings, (1) we see that the most advanced

5. The Initiation of Transformation

types are and must be highly strung, highly charged. The stolid cannot help the advance of life any further. They are maintenance men, not pioneers, creators. (2) We see that this great natural charge must be given expression; channels of constructive release must be found for it, or it will either break the system by its pent-up pressure or, if it is finally crushed, the person must sink into melancholia. (3) We see, further, that owing to the kinship between vitality and electricity, between the psyche and the biological field and charge, it is through rightly directed electric stimulation that the balked energy can be lifted in a way that will raise the psyche from its melancholy and sense of futility at having exhausted all earlier experiences, from its weariness of the physiological round, and yet avoid throwing it headlong out of all coordination into convulsion. It is true enough that without knowledge of it as a growth process, life is a knife edge between boredom (security) and catastrophe, between lethargy and frenzy. And man, when he is ignorant of his true purpose, must and can only oscillate between the two.

But, as Shirokogoroff has pointed out, even the shaman culture had discovered that, whereas it is necessary to raise the normal biologically diffused (and indeed dissipated) consciousness to total attention (the one-pointedness of the Sanskrit disciplines), that intensity must be tempered so that it can be sustained without collapse. As we mentioned earlier, Shirokogoroff shows that not only must the shaman not take refuge in the hysterical detensioning of tears or laughter,[115] but, as he is raised to the Leptoid level, neither must he o'erleap himself and crash on the other side in the epileptic seizure. In short, the shock must be made a surge treatment. And this surge must be so adroitly and gradually fed into the system that, as Jellinek says, the subject may learn to cooperate with the charge, blend it with his own charge and so, balanced on the crest, not be thrown but raised.

We may now propose the following procedure: first, the subject must be informed. The person in second maturity (and those in the earlier age groups if they are prepared by already having gone through the preceding therapies) must first of all learn intellectually about the process and why it is required. Every individual will come to the age when he will require such therapy. Otherwise the futility

III - INITIATIONS/PSYCHOPHYSICAL RELIGIOUS EXERCISES

of the life process will lead to some form of melancholia, which is either acknowledged or repressed. Every responsible person of today must arrive at this conclusion: that the new age group, second maturity, with the aid of this fifth therapy can make their true social contribution. And that without this development, their lives are as useless a miscarriage of life's purpose and the community's needs as is a stillbirth.

After this instruction, and having acquired the intellectual insight and conviction that it can give him, the subject will undergo the specific training. The aim is, by the administering of a series of gradually increased electric impulses, surges, to make it possible for the subject to experience an elation that can be held clearly in uninterrupted consciousness. The person must not be stunned or in any wise shocked but must be lifted into an increasingly intensified quality of awareness and sense of vital interest.

For a considerable time it has been known that the nervous system can be trained, right down to its deepest reflexes (for example, the Pavlovian techniques). It is possible for the conscious will to be taught how to obtain complete control over reactions caused by physical disturbance: reactions which, if the person is not trained, have always resulted in his being completely incapacitated and which, in consequence and if he is in an unprotected situation, often lead to his damage and possibly his death.

As far back as 1933 (and read before the annual meeting at Leicester of the British Association for the Advancement of Science), MacCurdy reported, in a paper, that he had devised a successful method for training air pilots to be able completely to disregard the vertigo caused by large disturbances of their semicircular canals. The derangement of these, the controllers of our sense of balance, will in any ordinary person cause him to be unable to stand and, even when lying down, to feel helplessly unbalanced. So deep and primitive are these centers that it was taken for granted that they could not consciously be controlled, and that if they were behaving abnormally, not even the visual, rational evidence that the floor was neither tilting nor slanted could help the person to disregard the delusory feeling. Nevertheless, MacCurdy discovered that after three months' training, practically any pilot could acquire this unsuspected

5. The Initiation of Transformation

mastery. We may therefore assume that the ninety-day term (which has generally been the span of time found necessary for the acquisition of a skill, a language, or any other psychophysical achievement) is the period best suited for this preliminary training.

Two further suggestions would seem to be proposed by the Tantric teachings:

(1) If the electric physiological current, which this therapy re-enforces and combines with the ordinary electric current, is flowing up the spine and its main residue is at the base of the spine, then the place where the external current should be sent into the body and onto the central nervous system should not be through the temples and into the forebrain (the customary practice). It should be fed in at the base of the spine (or the perineum) and so conducted up into the brain stem. Indeed, as a preliminary this surge should first be mediated through the body's main muscle and cushion of the spinal nerve base: the gluteus maximus.

(2) If the physiologically generated electric current is in every practical sense the same as that generated by coil and magnet dynamo and stored in batteries, then surely, as some Tantric practices suggest, it would be wise (at least as an initial practice and preliminary treatment), to pass the current first through another person who was more prepared by training (and actual experience) and from him let it pass to the postulant beginner. Indeed, it has been suggested by some practitioners that it is possible for a linked circle gradually to step up its own joint charges so that, finally, without the auxiliary contribution of battery or dynamo, they can give a postulant sufficient current for him, cooperating with it, to experience the dilation of consciousness.

In closing this chapter, which ends our enquiry into the mysteries' fivefold sequence of intensified therapies of ordeal and initiation, a word should be said as to the twofold purpose of this culminant therapy. The aim is not merely to remove the phobia of death, which is the chief misery and mortification of the large and growing class of second maturity. It is not merely to remove a social nuisance, a biological scandal, and the worst possible example (for the younger age groups) of the meaning of life, the triumph of biology, and the achievement of civilization. It is to attain a development that is as useful to society as it is necessary for the individual. The usefulness for society is to produce a type, a social class, an age group that has reached the position where integral and analytic thought are combined. At this point, the mind, made accustomed to postindividual consciousness, can function with conscious control of the extrasensory apprehension. And this is possible because the individual consciousness and the preterconscious are in touch. In consequence, a far larger specious present is comprehensible, a more extensive time-binding (Korzybski's phrase) is possible. And yet these insights can be conveyed down to our sensory-bound society for its use, or at least to warn it.

The needed usefulness for the individual is twofold. This is an experience in which there can be first a frequent and then a constant awareness of life that is necessary for the percipient at that level; that is, it is an experience in which the field of consciousness is always at high pitch and kept at the highest level of the psychophysical frontier. Secondly, when this has become regular and easy, the consciousness, its center of gravity already above the physical nexus and fulcrum, will have achieved its physical experience and service. Then by a voluntary act it can lift itself free to function as a field that is no longer dependent on an entropic structure, on an organism that is subject to decay.

Photographs and Manuscript Drafts

From left: artist Vera Stravinsky
and her husband, composer Igor Stravinsky,
with Gerald Heard, ca. 1961, Hollywood, California.
(Credit: Jay Michael Barrie)

THE FIVE AGES OF HUMANITY

From left: Time, Inc. founder Henry Luce with Gerald Heard in the library at the Luce's Sugar Hill estate in Ridgefield, Connecticut, summer 1962, slightly lightened from the original. Clare Boothe Luce's right hand, with cigarette, can be seen. This scene is fully captured when viewing the photograph on the opposite page.
(Credit: Jay Michael Barrie)

Photographs and Manuscript Drafts

From left: Gerald Heard with writer, congressperson, and U.S. Ambassador Clare Boothe Luce in the library at the Luce's Sugar Hill estate in Ridgefield, Connecticut, summer 1962. This scene represents a continuation of the photograph on the opposite page.
(Credit: Jay Michael Barrie)

From left: Gerald Heard with novelist and Eastern religion writer Nancy Wilson Ross, 1962, at the Old Westbury, Long Island, New York estate where Ross lived with her husband, Stanley P. Young.
(Credit: Jay Michael Barrie)

THE FIVE AGES OF MAN.

by Gerald Heard.

The new insight into the rythms in Nature, is now bringing back the old idea of cycles. For the study of cycles began with the idea of historical rythms. Men first suspected there might be great laws of rythm running through all of life and all matter, because they thought they could see such cycles in human history.

The Greek thinkers may have been the first to see this. Having so lately emerged from their Heroic Age they perceived in the Epics, their heroic ancestors left for them, clear traces of a pre-Heroic society which their own founding rulers had destroyed/ The Etruscans, whose society at its most energetic bears striking likeness to the early Greek City State culture, had apparently also made the same discovery. For we know that they had a concept of historical sequence. They spoke of there being a rythm of social man. They called it "The Great Year" -- a series of great "seasons" through which human societies proceeded. Starting from a Spring that arose from a Winter of discontent, this Spring of promise was succeeded by a glorious Summer of achievement, inevitably followed by an Autumn of too great abundance, to be ended by the return of Winter's desolation.

Even before the Greeks, men had looked down the corridors of Time. The Egyptians, taking the opportunity offered by living in a land which was a natural museum (with a built-in dehydration system) preserved the records of an unparalelled succession of dynasties. However, their reason for so doing (see Henri Frankfort's ANCIENT EGYPTIAN RELIGION) was not to learn about history, to gauge where its time-stream had carried them and so discover from the process whither they might go. On the contrary, their aim was to prove by the overwhelming evidence of unvarying persistence that, though the individual might pass away, the character, the role, the function, the drama, the performance, the entire social tradition was constant, unvarying, perpetual; as unchanging as granite, as enduring as basalt.

The Brahmanic Indian (descendant of the Aryan invaders), with victory-achieved status established, also reflected on the life of the race. But

Above: Facsimile of an early draft page (page 1) of *The Five Ages of Man* [*Humanity*], retouched from the original to remove blemishes. Copyright 2024 The Barrie Family Trust.
(It is likely that this manuscript was typed by an individual other than Gerald Heard.)

-2-

emerging later than the hieratic Egyptian, and so being more individualized, Brahmanic thought (with the rise of the movement of introspection that was to culminate in Buddhism) could not see beyond what seemed a perpetual (and perpetually unhappy) conflict between the critical understanding of the self-conscious individual and the unconscious life-drive which, with the bait of shortlived animal pleasure, snared the body to serve the reproductive process, then discarded its duped tool and left the mind to struggle in the closed trap.

Past views of the meaning of life, the significance of human history, have, then, existed. But either they described, as did the Egyptian schema, a process that never changes, yet in which man may be taught how to encyst himself; or, as the Etruscan Hellenic saw it, a Great Year in which the giant Tree of Life goes through its four great seasons, and the leaves of which, when they appear, had best try see themselves as an inevitable part of the Tree's inscrutable growth -- that is, each give himself, as does the arboreal leaf, to its few days in the Sun and then fall, letting its essence be withdrawn back into the Tree's true self; or the view of the Brahman Indian, becoming Buddhistic, who regarded the life force as only a blind wheel revolving ceaselessly in the void and going no where, only causing pain to that fine film on its outermost rim which has become capable of pain and which has only one advantage and power -- through its consciousness that indicates it is in pain, to gain the power to sever its contact with the wheel and so become free of pain, because free of feeling.

However, soon after modern, self-conscious, Renaissance man arose, between five and six hundred years ago, he began (having mapped his circumstances) to scrutinize his past, and realized that here was a field which he might and should interpret. Attempts at a philosophy of history were resumed. Between the Ancients (whereby was first meant the Romans and Greeks) and himself he placed the Medieval; and between the Medieval and the Ancients the Dark Age.. When the Roman Societas lay wrecked, barbarism (peoples in a crude Heroic culture) spread over the ruins, and the interior life and the preservation of

Above: Facsimile of an early draft page (page 2) of *The Five Ages of Man* [*Humanity*], retouched from the original to remove blemishes. Copyright 2024 The Barrie Family Trust.

EPILOGUE
The Psychophysical Future of Humanity
(*Evolution resumed*)

The aim of this study has been to see whether it would be possible to discover any method (or methods) whereby humans might educate their emotions. All who reflect on our present predicament agree that this is our supreme need today. Further, enquiry now shows that it is possible to change not only conduct but character and indeed consciousness; that though the deep emotional life is not altered by reason and argument—or at least it is altered only slightly and slowly—the basic forces of a man's nature can be and are molded and channeled by psychophysical experiences and exercises.

Again, investigation shows us that the advances of humanity and its recovery from periodic reactions of frustration and collapses into disorder have been due to successive discoveries made in this area of emotional training. The majority of humankind has repeatedly—to be exact, five times—failed to keep its emotional responses abreast of its growing mental powers, and so each time has come to temporary ruin. Nevertheless, there has always been a series of inexplicable recoveries. Now, however, with modern psychological and anthropological insight, it is possible to detect the cause and reason for such restorations. Today, we can trace throughout history a series of five such procedures whereby a small but decisive minority of humankind was able, at each crisis of human development, to devise a discipline (*a*) through which the new balanced order could emerge and (*b*) so that the gains and powers of humanity's outer achievement should be salvaged and extended. At each of these crises, because of humankind's indolent unpreparedness, because of its inability to cooperate with the growth of its consciousness and keep its emotional capacity equal to its intellectual power, there was a temporary submergence of civilization, an international anarchy. But, each time, the gains of the past were carried forward to future generations by the esoteric praxis and organization of the seminal few, an elite of the spirit.

Finally, enquiry along these lines has shown that not only has man's progress followed an oscillatory spiral as he alternates between the exploration of his environment (and the expansion of his power over it) and investigation of his subjective being (and an attempt to achieve peace with it), but that that spiral has accelerated greatly in the speed of its ascent. In consequence, man, by following a process of detached investigation, has in this generation (and for the first time) become a self-conscious creature that is conscious of its nonself-conscious. This fact, which has been the core of the psychological revolution, the mutation in thought that ended the Humanic, total-individualistic person, the alteration in consciousness that has produced the Leptoid person, this discovery by humans of their whole self, made it possible to recognize the actual force operating in human evolution.

As long as individualism was intensifying and man was able to define himself only by making his personality entirely separate (by regarding the ego as the one real unit of consciousness), he could only regard the life process as being one of competition and a blind struggle for separate survival. But once man could recognize himself as being part of a field, as being a nexus in a larger whole, then

Epilogue

economy turned into ecology, and cooperation (symbiosis and commensalism) took the place of competition as the directive activity of increasing consciousness. In turn, this discovery of the symbiotic field led to a further insight into the process as it culminates in man.

Louis Bolk's principle of fetalization (that the young and flexible, the uncommitted and open-minded inherit the earth) led to Cope's "law of the survival of the unspecialized." As the mammal is the fetalization of the reptile and retains some of the generalized features the reptile lost when it specialized out from the amphibian; as the primates neotenically retain fetal freedoms that the rest of the mammals have lost; as man remains an infant longer than the ape and, to his infancy, adds another span of uncommitted freedom, his specific childhood—so this principle of paidomorphy is now seen to be the power of human evolution and the capacity and promise of its further advance. Applied to specific human history, this insight makes comprehensible the vast acceleration of the growth of consciousness since the rise of man. For as man has no instincts, he holds together and advances through social heredity. Hence, the human advance has been and must always be through the reciprocity of the two parallel lines of man's physical heredity and his social heredity. The social heredity is the die that stamps its pattern of developing behavior on the matrix of the human brain. While the physical parents beget, bear, and rear increasingly impressionable, teachable young, the begetters of the social heredity have to keep themselves young and open so that they may creatively accept new data and incorporate the new evidence into those new comprehensive conceptions that can feed the fresh, open minds of each generation.

There must, then, be achieved a seer type. This type, we can now see, was obscurely recognized in the shaman, the witch doctor, and the prophet. But theirs was an esoteric dark art, mainly wrought by dangerous stresses and self-violence, and in the interests of the past and the old. Conservation became conservatism. The mysteries were a subterranean stream sunken so deep that we cannot even tell whether there was an unbroken succession of psychophysical knowledge and practice containing and composing new knowledge of means and power and, step by step, compensating for the automatic behavior of the outer world. (See Appendix D.)

Today that knowledge and practice must be neotenic. It must work toward a balanced progress, an enlarging vision. It must never deny but affirm, never arrest but release. The intuitive artist, afraid of losing his conviction if he altered or even explained any detail of the tradition, can now become an explicit, forward-looking scientist. And now this consciously understood method can and must (because of the fact of neoteny) be in the hands not of conservative and reactionary elders but controlled by those who best retain the faith, hope, and cooperative trustfulness of the undamaged young.

In concluding this enquiry, I shall attempt to indicate what these contemporarily unspecialized persons would be; how they could be preserved and retained; how they could be kept open and trained to be the carriers of the immediate social heredity, the producers of comprehension, the feeders of understanding. But first we must glance, in a final résumé, at the exoteric methods of emotional education and character training that have been used in the past, tracing them in outline down to the present day.

We have seen that no society has ever been so complacent as to imagine that its young could acquire adequate psychological equipment either through contagion-suggestion (simply by living with its elder kin) or through being left to learn by themselves. We know now that in the cave life of the coconscious there was pictorial instruction and organized ritual exercise.[116] With the rise of the hypnocratic urban organization,[117] the ritual instruction was obviously elaborated. Even at the time of the heroic explosion, the young were still instructed not only in martial exercises and conduct worthy of a man-at-arms, a hero, but also there were inculcated those precautions necessary to keep pride from going too far. Naturally, the Ascetic Age gave persistent warnings, and [it] engraved inhibitions on the growing mind. For by then, man's increasing self-consciousness had made him increasingly frightened of his repressed emotional nature. When the ascetic ideal could no longer serve as the master pattern of prestige and the total individual emerged, there was an attempt to get rid of fear, to form character, and direct emotion by an appeal to reason and by a demonstration of its personal advantages.

However, we have seen that this appeal and argument were, naturally, quite incapable of dealing with the preterrational mind;

especially was this so as the critical mind had now thrust this aspect of consciousness down to become a vast rebellious subconscious. Hence, the Ignatian attempt at psychological education. Unfortunately, as this was a revival of the ascetic frame of mind, it had to be based on fear. And it was aimed at defending the past, not at explicating and inspiring the present—still less at welcoming the future. The Jesuit exercises were the great attempt of the sixteenth century to balance, by psychological training, the physical and critical advances of the Humanic person.

In the mid-seventeenth century, the English-speaking Protestant world was momentarily affected by another religious genius, George Fox. Fox happened on the fact that a silent meeting of devotees, who were compacted by a common experience and the common peril of being outlawed, could generate a force. The Quakers, as long as they quaked,[118] did generate a current. When this procedure led to seizures, however, they repudiated it and disclaimed any connection with the Holy Rollers and other paroxysmic ecstatics who were practicing it. Therefore, this uncharted power, unchanneled and suspect, had largely left the Quakers by the middle of the eighteenth century when they had become wealthy, socially concerned, and interested in education. They did not become ascetics or rationalists. They were neither guilt-stricken nor materialistic. ... They were exceptionally balanced. They were aware of the need of cultivating a deep interior life. But by the seventeen hundreds, the movement had come to resemble Judaism in some respects. It acquired new members still, but its hard core was the birthright membership. And for some generations, it practiced the excommunicatory persecution of driving out those members who married outside the society. They claimed, with complacency, that they were a peculiar people and were content to be a social enclave, wearing archaic dress, using archaic speech.

By the middle of the eighteenth century (the rococo phase of the Humanic person's sensibility), the new attempt at altering conduct, character, and consciousness springs from the missionary zeal of an Oxford lecturer in Greek. John Wesley carried on the Ignatian tradition: the ascetic fear-therapy. He studied Ignatius Loyola and worked out a system. About this system, Sargant, a well-known

London psychotherapist who was brought up in Methodist traditions, points out: first of all, it brings on a panic-crisis that destroys any self-security, and then offers vicarious deliverance, the relief of an unexpected, undeserved salvation. This violent repentance (or rather *metanoia*, change of consciousness) (1) not infrequently fades, sometimes completely.[119] (2) It works, in the far greater number of cases, with simple, [less] educated people whose critical faculties are undeveloped and whose emotional and passional life is strong.

Wesley, therefore, had his great success with the poor and dispossessed; he failed with the educated.[120] He was opposed not only by the skeptics but also by the quieter pietists and mystics[121] who mistrusted and shunned the fear emphasis and undesirable theology of eternal damnation. Wesleyanism, as had Jesuitism and Quakerism, turned increasingly to organization and educationalism. The follow-up methods that characterized the new order (or company), the new sect, the new church, were necessary to shape the softened-up character of the convert and give it lasting form. But Jesuits, Quakers, and Wesleyans alike all took to critical education, scholarship, natural science, and ultimately to big business. The psychophysical evolution of man was arrested, deflected. The opportunity that Quakerism and Wesleyanism might have had to make a contribution to the emotional education of man and to the progress of consciousness was lost.

After Wesley (and his successful prevention of the French political revolution spreading into England, a key country), there is no advance in psychological education. The milder mystics, such as William Law who tried to make a nonfear-motivated psychiatry out of Jacob Boehme's hell-warmed visions, never worked out an empirical method. Subconsciously, they feared ecstasy, apprehending that it might become erotic. They had, then, no driving force equal to the Ignatian–Wesleyan fear of hell. Swedenborg's revisitings of Boehme's limbos made a mélange of psychical research and evangelical piety in which hell was retained as a very powerful forced draught. The consequences of this strange insight have been the rise of a small church based on these revelations. However, this religion, because of Swedenborg's own notions of hell, has not been able to free itself from fear-pressuring undertaken to avoid unpleasant after-death consequences. Therefore, it makes no contribution to a modern education of the emotions.

During the nineteenth century, evangelical revivals repeated, but always less memorably, Wesley's attack. From Charles Simeon (of the Church of England, who reintroduced the Wesleyan method) through William Booth (the founder of the Salvation Army) on to the varieties of Southern States conversionism and American missions to Britain (from Moody to Graham), fear-generated repression worked with decreasing performance. Psychoanalysis, though it was not prepared to consider the emotional development of the "base, ungovernable beast," was ready and able to debunk the old energy-generating or energy-compressive terrors and so hamstring the nightmare. The patient was to be detensioned; and the detensioned will seldom if ever explode into conversion. In the Southern States, Southern Methodism still works with considerable method, not only to bring on salvation from hell but also the "second blessing," the experience of Pentecostal outpouring, possession by the Paraclete. The pressures are high and in many ways generate intensities that produce the paraleptic condition at which the shaman and the witch doctor aim: the parallelogram of the two forces, the epileptic tension and hysterical expression. But again, the generators of such paroxysmal power do not know what to do with it.[122]

Meanwhile, these methods are marking time and, it must be owned, losing ground, for they are, at base, ascetic, fearing the body and ignorant of evolution. And since these churches are defenseless against scientific education, since they cannot handle insanity, and since they fail to answer either psychiatry's criticism or its offer of an alternative therapy, another education of the emotions has arisen.

We have noted earlier that psychiatry itself is as helpless against that extensive complaint, alcoholism (and the powerful neurosis of which alcoholism is the symptom) as is Evangelicanism or any of the other ascetic disciplines. Each can gain only an occasional success; none really makes any recognizable headway against the disease. It was the extent and intensity of this addiction that gave rise to the first of those peculiar and specific methods which have been the particular contemporary contribution to emotional education in the last couple of decades. In studying them, I came to the conclusion that they are best described as *ad hoc* churches. For as an *ad hoc* hypothesis in science is an arrangement of a particular group of data so as to give a provisional explanation of the interrelationships of such incidents, and as an *ad hoc* committee is one charged to enquire into and report on a single, specific issue, so it is with the *ad hoc* church. It is an association of persons concerned with one challenging threat and peril. They are not, and in their condition cannot be, concerned with collateral dangers or ultimate goals, any more than a drowning man is able to be interested in the sunstroke casualties on the beach, water contamination problems, or bylaws of shore behavior.

When we consider our heavy reliance on alcohol, it is only natural that the first *ad hoc* church, the now worldwide Alcoholics Anonymous, was for alcoholics. But although it was a method for addicts, a method that has effected more cures than any other system (whether by drugs, by therapy, or straight religion), it could not work for a group that seems so much the same: the takers of habit-forming drugs, the narcotic addicts. A second organization (or better, a salvage system run by those who have suffered from the same attack) had to be founded and put into action for drug addicts. A third one of such self-help associations had, again, to come together when, beside alcoholics and drug addicts, the insane had to undertake getting themselves sane. Psychotics Anonymous now lives and grows alongside the elder AA (Alcoholics Anonymous) and the younger AA (Addicts Anonymous), which is sometimes called NA (Narcotics Anonymous). There are, to my knowledge, at least fifteen other leagues of sufferers joined to meet and take disaster with the strength of that unlimited liability that is given by actual experience, both of the full weight of the attack and the full strength of united resistance.[123]

We have, then, the interesting phenomenon of a general associative method of psychophysical salvage (not only from addiction but from many sorts, maybe all sorts, of emotional peril and defeat) which is, we must recognize, at the same time always specific. In short, the same procedure is employed, but each specific sufferer can only be helped by this procedure if the specific helper has been through the same specific defeat.

Epilogue

Before we can hope to propose why this unexpected limitation should appear (and all limitations, being definitions, guide us to understanding the method and its way of working), we must first note the procedure, study the steps. Alcoholics Anonymous has twelve. From these, it becomes clear that what we are viewing in this ladder of deliverance is the traditional mystery discipline. There is the ordeal, there is the guide who has been through it before (the hierophant), and there is initiation (the rebirth, interior understanding, illumination) that not only explains but empowers.

But the procedure is *ad hoc*. That means that it is curative and restorative. These two practical limitations mean that the *ad hoc* church comes into action only when the ordeal is already half over. For the disaster of addiction, breakdown, or despair had to drive the victim to the edge of destruction, to the point where he or she was ready to seek any possible aid. No *ad hoc* church seeks to act as a general guide for unaddictional characters who desire to grow. These associations rightly stick to what they know. Further, they have found that they must wait until the drowning person calls; and, still, most of those who are drowning drown before they call.

So the *ad hoc* churches cannot prevent. Their function is cure, salvage of the sinking, not teaching people how to swim or how to sail without capsizing. Nor can they do other than restore. Knowing their job, knowing that they are life-savers who have learned how to make the shore, each one of these rescuers who has won freedom from a suffocating addiction, fear, or collapse aims at retrieving and relanding one who had ceased to swim. The task is to return the victim to the shore circulation and see him back safely high and dry. For the *ad hoc* churches, being *ad hoc* and directing their efforts toward immediate salvage, can have no comprehensive philosophy.[124]

They cannot load themselves with a theory as to life's overall meaning. They cannot answer the basic questions of where we are, whence we came, and whither we are going. They cannot, therefore, give rules as to how we should live, as to how we may grow, as to how we should be prepared and developed, as to how we should educate ourselves. They are not dealing with humanity and its problem and destiny, but with anomalous persons and their predicaments and disasters. The concern is personal and primarily private. When, then, the victim is rescued, his future is with similar victims. He keeps [the ability] to make the shore while having often to be swimming in the ocean (that is, he retains his sober life of responsible sanity though often being with the irresponsible and the immoral) by keeping his moral muscles in trim through the constant practice of life-saving, of rescuing others. To change the simile: a firefighting team cannot spend its time insisting on rebuilding people's houses with fireproof materials. Once a fire has started, the job of the team and its equipment is to put it out. They have no right, even, to go round soaking people's drapes to lower fire risk.

The *ad hoc* church, therefore, has to let disaster have the first move.[125] For these rescue squads have to depend on the threat of imminent destruction to generate the necessary intensity of demand for retraining. That the peril has to be acute is shown by a fact often observed by AAs of longstanding and with distinguished records of salvage service. Now that AA is widely known, many persons join who, though they are drinking far too much and are aware that the habit is getting out of hand, are not within a short distance of complete disaster—death or loss of their minds by alcoholic poisoning. They are gravely concerned but not yet desperate. Their motivation is preventive rather than salvational. So their ordeal is not yet sufficiently severe to produce a mutation of consciousness, a real *metanoia*. Hence, there is not an initiation. A bad habit has been arrested; they return to their past norm but they do not develop further. A number of these persons, after some years, finding life too dull, resume their drinking.

Thus, since the starting ordeal has to be a specific disaster, in order to salvage the victim, the specific device or method of overcoming that particular disaster is then needed. Give all children a full vitamin and protein diet, and rickets disappears, tuberculosis incidences sink, and many other diseases shrink toward vanishing point. But fail in this preventive dietary hygiene, and then all kinds of special surgical and medical skills must be called in to deal with the many and varied pathological conditions, with the particular diseases that have arisen as a result of the deficient diet.

We see, then, why each *ad hoc* church is confined to one particular type of patient. In spite of the fact that once the patient calls

Epilogue

[and] he is given the same restorative treatment, each patient can only call out of some specific hole or pocket of the abyss. The method is that of the mysteries, but with these two definitionary limitations. The patient must ask, and to ask he must have fallen into acute disaster. His ordeal cannot be prepared for, balanced, tempered. Already, he has been through an infancy and childhood which has, in nearly every case, left damage in his subconscious. And this damage, because it has not been remedied, may well be the deep root of his alcoholism, drug addiction, or nervous breakdown. It hits him as a line squall hits an unwarned yachtsman. He capsizes. The chances of salvage are at best slim.

To use still another but more helpful simile, this is curiously like the first stages of modern medicine when preventive medicine was dawning. When the pandemic of smallpox hit Europe as the seventeenth century was ending, when it was said that no woman dare call her child her own until it had been stricken, no prevention was known. Then at the close of the eighteenth century, Edward Jenner discovered that a cowpox serum used as a prophylactic, a vaccination, gave immunity with very small risk. General preventive medicine is still seeking for a panacea miracle drug that would so raise general resistance that every disease would be held at bay. And it seems increasingly likely, as psychosomatic medicine advances, that this elixir will be found only when the psychophysiology of man is well understood—so well understood that the psychophysique can be brought to such coordinated, comprehensive functioning that the entire person will have become so alive that every attack will only rouse the organism to greater resistance and initiative.

The *ad hoc* churches must continue their unique services and their specific salvages. But the very particularity of their success points up the need for the extension and enlargement of their process. The first step, of course, is to decide to forestall attack and not wait to be overrun before striking back. This requires an overall strategy. And this preparedness cannot be merely defensive, a plan of prevention. It must be a process of initiative and development. We are now prepared to be told that we must make such comprehensive preparation if we are ever to gain the initiative in the struggle wherein the *ad hoc* churches put up not only gallant defensives but remarkable rear actions and counterattacks. For those who know because they have been there—the ex-alcoholic, the ex-addict, and ex-psychotic—all recognize that the specific breakdown is the final phase of a reaction, of an imbalance, of a growth process that was never properly fulfilled.

The craving for alcohol, narcotics, and/or the relapse into psychosis is an escape from a situation that has become acutely stressful but out of which no one has offered the patient any way. They must conform and they cannot. As Earl Loomis has pointed out in regard to the dementia-praecox children (see further above), they are often of high intelligence but are also intensely sensitive. They are therefore too frequently stung to passionately resentful reactions by slights, disregards, and roughnesses that do not actually madden children of average toughness and resilience. In short, as almost all experts in the addiction psychopathies now agree, we are, in these destructive categories, dealing with men and women whose sensitiveness would not let them endure our incoherent and pointless way of living. Their addiction is an anodyne adopted to staunch a purposeless pain: the exasperating futility of aimless living.

Once the situation is so diagnosed and understood, the next step toward prevention is evident: education. And, as the addicts and psychotics are different from the rest of us only in the extremity of their reaction, since we all must be to some extent frustrant in a society that cannot say in modern terms and rational language where it is going and why it so conducts itself, this education in understanding must be available to us all. We must act on some such hypothesis of history and some such picture of the individual's growth as I have proposed in this thesis. As we have seen, the psychophysical development today cannot be begun unless it has as its premises a rational, empirical instruction. Man must be shown whence he has come, where he is, and whither he may go. He must realize that his present stress (which reaches breaking point with the addicts and psychotics) is due to a force that cannot find fulfillment unless he provides it with that process of expression; a force which, if he will not give it a procedure of development, must destroy him. To attempt the readjustment of an individual to a society which itself is out of gear because it does not know where it is going (and when that individual has become deranged for that very reason) is like trying to cure a consumptive, who has fled a slum, by putting him back in the infected air with the pious hope that he will learn to build up resistance and adjust to reality.

Having arrived at this intellectual agreement, then, we can see, as the inevitable third step, how we may act to implement our knowledge. It is clear that every child, and, in turn, every adolescent, every person entering first maturity, and every person becoming veterine must have his specific ordeal and initiation. By these means, by psychophysical training, and specific raising of initiative, we may and can and must do for the emotional life of man, for his psyche, what preventive medicine, development diet, and exercise-hygiene have done for the physique. Then, and then only, will our mental health equal our physical health; then will our age of revolutions and reactions be over and our evolution be resumed through man's intentional cooperation with the force within him.

Therefore, this essay can now conclude with a hypothesis of social development through psychophysical education. Such an education, by following and explicating the principles of evolution that are now understood, may enable man to achieve a new progress and to develop the potentialities in himself which, until now, have been thwarted. The idea of progress has been written off by the microscopic historians who believe that a tapestry can be understood by chemical analysis of its threads. The design of the future has been left to embittered satirists, such as we now know Orwell to have been. With a dislike and ignorance of the human animal equal to Swift's (but without the excuse of Swift's dementia), they project their hatred on "the damned race," as Frederick of Prussia named it, under the disguise of righteous protest. But as John Pfeiffer has pointed out, these "Base Late Worlds," these dismal perspectives of degeneracy, are purely perverse fiction. The opposite of all this satire is first the rational expectation and then the reasonable extension of our present knowledge of human evolution.

As Weston La Barre (51) has stressed, the more we study the infancy of apes and men, the more unmistakable and outstanding does Louis Bolk's principle of fetalization appear to be. And as John Pfeiffer has pointed out, man's nature and the society that human nature constructs is utterly unlike the ant and its hill, the termite and its termitary, or the bee and its hive. These insect prisons are all precipitated by creatures that have atrophied until they have become automatized by instinct.[126] Human society springs from a creature still so generalized that he is inexhaustibly inventive because he is insatiably curious. Edward Drinker Cope's "law of the survival of the unspecialized" works through life. But it reaches its overwhelming vindication in man, the incomparable creature. J. B. S. Haldane the biologist, we must repeat, points out that this neotenic capacity has paid man so prodigiously that the man we are in process of becoming will remain free of the commitment of speech; will still be vocalizing with unrestricted variety of sound responses and auditory experiments, until he is in his sixth year. See also *Man's Emerging Mind*, page 290, by N. J. Berrill (5).

And so it will be with man's learning; it will extend into his fifth decade. Not only are some of the nerve centers that served us with lightning-flash reflexes and powerful passionate drives showing signs of atrophy. But other areas, the ones that learn most easily and quickly, where curiosity reigns and wonder inspires, the ones that are the foundation sites of freedom, invention, and creation, seem to be growing. As John Pfeiffer points out, it certainly looks as though the very life in our bodies is making us ever more easy to inform and to persuade, ever harder to deceive and to coerce. And as La Barre has remarked in his *The Human Animal*, man has no innate pugnacity. The one innate characteristic he has is teachability.

That, however, puts a unique responsibility upon the teaching and the teachers. For without psychophysical teaching of the most thorough sort, this birth of a new type of consciousness will not be achieved. We have to make clear to ourselves both the goal that we can now see and the means that we now know are the way to that goal. That goal is the increasing capacity to retain and to express the vast potentiality that is in the brain of the embryo and which, we must always remind ourselves, has not yet been able to be born at the height of its fetal promise. Just as the gorilla fetus, when it approaches birth, loses roundness of skull as the brain is compressed by the jaw muscles and muscle-keel that run across the skull-dome, so to a much less degree (but still to a serious amount) the proportionately vast brain case of the human embryo has to be reduced before birth.

To permit such a child to be born and grow, this creature (see above for the negative side of this, the collapse into dementia praecox) must have an environment of dynamic stimulation, generated by the tonic loving delight of a parental field that believes in the child's tremendous promise and that keeps it in an optimum, unwavering atmosphere of cheerful expectation. There is no sentimentality or soothing repose in such an environment. It is one of constant courageous wager and tempering challenge. Indeed, in the future it may well come to be that this stimulation will be started while the child is still in the womb. If, as we have seen, its leaps are really evulsive (plus shudders—spastic exultations as it prepares to throw off a now cramping security for an energizing risk), soon it may be possible to send back into it a responding rhythm.

It has been found that on the human brain there are, as it were, very fine recording tapes. And those areas that record sound can hear music when all that is being transmitted to them are the electric impulses used to carry musical sounds and record them on magnetized tape. No sound wave travels; it is only an electric impulse. Considering the effect that deep sounds and parasonic vibrations have on the brain,[127] certainly the possibility of such a method of both soothing and bracing the central nervous system of the embryo for its oncoming challenge should not be neglected.[128]

When the child is born, then, it is clear that it should feel, taste, smell, hear, and see only such sensa as reassure and stimulate. It should have only those contacts to which it will respond with delight (such as caressing and tickling); tastes that attract and intrigue; scents, sounds, and lights that rouse and fascinate. We now know that the mood of the mother or foster-mother (according to whether it is friendly, anxious, sullen, or angry) affects the infant: bitterly, if the mood is negative; stimulatingly, if it is positive. And, a little later, the parental group together with all others in contact with the child (which has yet to acquire its protective filters) can profoundly help or hinder its growth. Their mood, involuntarily expressed by their scent and sound even when they are at a distance from the infant, can make it prematurely harden and close or can help it to keep supple and open its consciousness. This is all the more impressive because these involuntary influences are involuntarily accepted by the defenseless infant.[129]

After this preliminary treatment of welcome, given to all children, then it would be possible to estimate inborn aptitude, revealed at this point because the child has expanded freely in such an atmosphere. We must remember that because the progress of man now depends on two unique, reciprocal human factors, two complimentary types must be prepared that are as interdependent as the two sexes have been throughout bisexual evolution. Man, since he now advances by social heredity, requires two representatives to forward that heredity. The first is the type that composes. Every generation, every decade, every year, those who value a true and living morality should bring the ruling mores up to date, should be continually adding new and fuller knowledge as to how we could behave more effectively. This seer-coordinator is constantly taking new data and using them to construct a wider frame and range of reference from which to deduce an ever more significant and creative way of feeling, thinking, and acting.

However, these inspiring conceptions, together with the behavior patterns and processes whereby they are performed and actualized, have to find a perfectly responsive matrix: a subject, a recipient, who can absorb and practice what is given. This double gift seems to be what evolution has bestowed on man. On the one hand, he is the most suggestible, the most teachable of all creatures. On the other, he is the most original, the most constructive. The teacher-seer must then be picked; and to that selection and training we shall turn in concluding.

~~~~~~~~~~~

Prophets have always spoken in vain if there were lacking those who can hear, apply, and produce the superfine material adequate to take the impress, who are adequate to express in actual form the new vision. Nothing has caused more discouragement, disingenuous casuistry and, in the end, hypocritical cynicism than those hyperbolic ideals that spring mainly from the guilt complex and life-rejecting revulsion of the ascetic. By what may only be called the "whitemail" of shaming people into a "potlatch" competition in surrender, they have made countless numbers attempt to live a life described as that of perfection without proof of results, without process of specific instruction, or without first getting rid of their subconscious traumas and repressions.

The chronicle of Salimbene, a Franciscan who was born in 1221 (five years before the death of St. Francis) and who spent his life as a Friar, shows how rapidly success and degeneracy came upon the great Friars movement. It set as an ideal a life of ecstatic detachment that was to be lived out in the actual world.[130] However, not only must the lofty ideal be worked out in contemporary terms. Two preliminary factors must be clear and proved: (1) the steps by which it may be attained, and (2) the manner in which material capable of being worked into that shape may be produced.

What in Sanskrit is called "The Way of the Fathers" is to produce and rear children under those optimum conditions we have just mentioned, so that they may be more flawlessly responsive, flexible, open, and aware than any other creatures before them. This is the basic receptive aspect of neotenic evolution. It is the essential premise and ground without which vision cannot be actualized but must remain only a heartbreaking ideal. We must repeat, this is the matrix that can take and retain the full impress of instruction.

Once, however, such receptivity exists, then it is equally necessary that there shall be not only a message and an instruction but an exemplar and trainer who is penetrating and comprehending enough to fill the full stretch and capacity of such suppleness. In the Sanskrit tradition, the seer, the teacher, the trainer, is said to go "The Way of the Gods." The fathers produce ever more open, teachable, inspirable children. The trainer produces an ever apter, wider, more inspiring doctrine: one that is wholly realistic because it is wholly apposite. This picture, of a parenthood that is able to produce ever finer psychophysical stuff and, reciprocally, a teacherhood that is able to bring forth ever more stimulating training techniques and character ideals, meanings of life, and goals of consciousness, is, of course, the development and culmination of the neotenic conception of evolution reaching its apex in man, the paidomorph.

We see now that the particular characteristic of man is this: he is the social creature which, of all the social creatures, has succeeded in building a highly functionalized and indeed specialized social structure without destroying the adaptability and curiosity of the individual constituent. All the social insects that have raised the most elaborate social structures have done so at the price of all initiative and by the complete subordination of the individual unit to the consequently rigid group pattern. Their worker type is an atrophied form, generally a female. Humankind has a vastly complex set of inventive societies and an expanding, unfinished concept of civilization. These may be dangerously diversive, but certainly they are not arrested. Their very confusions and anarchies are evidence of their inherent vitality-of-variety; and their story, as we have seen, has been one of convulsive advance, spastic progress.

From the start, then, man's process has been through neoteny; and as his history has gone on, its progress has been through increasing paidomorphy. Through retaining increasingly, and to ever later ages, the child's curiosity and desire for adventure, the result has been societies that are increasingly inventive, constructive, and enterprising. There have had to be, and there have been, plenty of reactions. Life leafs off the husks that lose flexibility, and as they stiffen, inevitably they try to throttle the force which, since they will not expand, breaks them and casts them off. The new living shoot, as it thrusts off the old husk, can itself be deformed by the dead rind that it struggles to discard. The task of civilization (and its instrument, education) is by insight and foresight (by developmental therapy) so to supple the whole process that the old, instead of clinging on and deforming the new, will explicate their own elimination. The violent, oscillatory process of revolution and reaction, of martyr–prophet and counterreform–conventionalist, must and can be made to cease its spastic alternation. Then progress-with-conservation can take over.

The society that can be foreseen (the civilization that, with such knowledge as we now have, may be extrapolated) would then be a restoration, or rather an explication, of the primal trinity: father, mother, and child. Wordsworth's phrase, "The child is father to the man," was much more true than he understood. In Taoist tradition, the same basic idea is expressed. Lao Tzu, the traditional founder, is called the young old one, the ancient boy. Complementing the parents who produce the flawless supereducatable young, there has, of

Epilogue

necessity, to be the advanced neotene. For he is the one who can take the perfect material and feed into it that complete diet of charging stimulant, tonic encouragement, and open inspiration whereby it becomes a completely contemporary creature of constant growth. This image of the divine foster-parent, the godparent, has been present in man's archetypal consciousness since the basic social heredity ritual was put together at Abydos in Egypt. This was a rite of *religio*, of total meaning and comprehension which, as Egyptian civilization grew, was able to contain and compose all the vigorous gear of a highly elaborate and developing nation for two thousand years.[131] For the story of Demeter (visiting Eleusis in disguise, becoming nurse to the son of King Celeus and Queen Metaneira, [and] almost succeeding in making the young prince immortal) must certainly derive from the far earlier account of Isis. She, too, wanders the earth in disguise, seeking a lost loved one and doing a precisely similar (and similarly misunderstood and spoiled) service for alien mortals who befriended her.[132]

To sum up then: first, we must have a parenthood capable of begetting and rearing a child that can be born and be viable with the extreme neotenic promise shown by the fetus; a creature of unprecedented uncommittedness, unspecialization, and receptivity, of intense openness, sensitiveness, and responsiveness. Next, we must and can produce from this very type a trainer, an educator who can instruct and inspire this child not merely to adapt to and serve the present, but to advance into and create the future. Here again, from the very limitedness of the complete social insect societies' reaction to grave challenge, we can gain a hint as to how, with our knowledge, we may react in our present crisis: not to preserve the defenses of a threatened pattern but to rise to a new level of initiative and progress. The most deadly peril that can confront the beehive is when the Queen, through some accident, has failed to lay royal grubs, or the grubs have died in their cells. This supreme danger rouses the worker-tenders of the grubs to a rare reaction. A few common grubs, which under ordinary feeding would emerge as workers, are fed the royal jelly and transmute into queens.

The most deadly peril that confronts humankind today is lack of contemporary seers; for lacking these we have nothing but a tradition of fossilized ideals, irrelevant disciplines, and vestigial praxes. We could now know how to take the at-last full-born child and, out of those who show the highest neotenic development, to raise and rear a creature that will be a complete, viable paidomorph.

It is clear that such a being could, if given the whole range of even our present psychophysical knowledge (endocrine stimulation, dietary supplementation, body-mind exercises, profound suggestion) attain to the capacity to use the entire resources of the body-mind, both lobes of the brain, all and wholly the endocrine system, and every aspect of consciousness. Such a creature would retain its perfect generalization to full growth and never lose it. The wide compass of association, the complete freedom from prejudice, that would go with such a range of comprehension, would render this paidomorph not only able to see and forecast correlations and conjunctions that must appear abstract or prophetic to our limited minds. But with the authority of superknowledge would go the persuasiveness of one who understands and empathizes with those he can instruct.

Human evolution must be so regarded. The present data of fetalization, paidomorphy, and neoteny do not permit us to see the process of man in any other terms. The risk, of course, is terrific. But it always has been, if a higher station is to be won. And, up to the present, the risk has been taken and the new station attained. Besides, we have seen that even among the apparently completely rigid social constructional finalities of the social insects, even in the beehive when the peril is sufficiently acute, the challenge sufficiently desperate to be beyond the flawless repetition of the instinctive pattern to fulfill or to solve, daring invention (for example, the use of the royal jelly) saves the system that is otherwise doomed.

However, the possibility that we will accept this new way and undertake this new experiment will turn on our having some concept of our goal. For we are creatures who act with originality only when we can have some hypothesis, some vision of whither we are going, of how that end will fulfill and not make futile our past strivings and earlier experiments. So, first, can we visualize how such a reciprocal process of development would fulfill man's past attempts

Epilogue

to live the binary life (social and individual) of biological survival (persistence) and also permit him to go further by an ever-larger actualization of an ideal?

From the earliest ages, from the cave rituals, there seems to have been a leader–magician. In the Heroic Age there was not merely the hero type but also, keeping him in bounds, the *vates* and heralds who set forth the limits and molds in which exuberance must be shaped. Even more strikingly, in the Ascetic Epoch there are the two lives: (1) that of the contemplative who surveys and envisions, and the clerk through whose canon law the scale of values, the scheme of life, the plan of creation and salvation that has been envisioned by the seer can be applied; and (2) that of the lay folk who supply the means, secure the foundation, and implement the findings of the clerical side of life. Humanic man alone (because he was cut off from knowledge of the paraconscious by his total individualism and its entire dependence on his individualized senses) neglected the binocular vision, the inner and outer sight, the integral-plus-analytic thought that until then man had never wholly ceased in some wise to attempt and never anywhere utterly disregarded. Because he is a creature that can exist, not to say advance, only with and through a social heredity, man must require, and increasingly require, the seer who can weave a web of purpose out of those ties and linkages of energy and data that would otherwise be only destructive and baffling. This is a new belief, but its roots are to be found in man's tradition. And this long sustained, often frustrated hope for a meaning that would coordinate all means, for a purpose that would embrace and order all powers, for an understanding that could interpret, give significance to, and derive value from all experience, today has a greater possibility of fulfillment (as well as peremptory demand that it be fulfilled) than ever before.

We must have a type to reassemble and reissue our canon of meaning, our plan of significance, our chart of value-charged purpose. And now at last we can conceive of an exemplar type. They will have the initiative of the hero without their egotistic hubris. They will be as anonymous as the ascetic but without their paralyzing guilt. They will have an even wider circumspection than the greatest humanist but without the humanist's self-limited frame of reference, without their confinement (a) to sensory data as being their only substance and (b) to reason and critical analysis as being their only instrument.

Also, we can now propose and estimate a goal that is not, on the one hand, other-worldly: a nonphysical, nontemporal condition. Nor, on the other hand, is it utopian. That is, it is not simply an extrapolation of quantity, an infinite increase of means, an ever further elaboration of apparatus without any development of the human faculties. As a first step toward conceiving the further evolution now open to man, to us humans of the twentieth century, let us note the extension developments that seem probable to evaluators of the human endowment as research today has been able to estimate it.

In his admirably concise summary of man's specific expression and instrument, his brain, John Pfeiffer (66) remarks that a majority of researchers seem to expect the brain to go on growing. Grey Walter (93), of the Burden Neurological Institute in Bristol, England, believes that areas of the human brain may be now increasing. About this theory of Walter, Pfeiffer makes the evident but significant comment that the enlarged brain case would make its wearer look childlike. We might go further and say they would be infantic. Pfeiffer also remarks that the human brain already uses double the amount of oxygen that is required by an ape's brain, and that one quarter of all the oxygen taken in by the human lung goes to the brain. Four minutes of lack of oxygen from the brain involves the collapse and ruin of its highest centers.

The brain, the instrument of the mind, seems to be asserting an evolutionary right: as it is the largest unspecialized mass of tissue in the body, it can be the growing edge of the life process. This need not mean degeneracy of the rest of the organism. The brain needs the entire physical apparatus to keep itself going and growing. What this does seem to propose is that the brain, as the instrument of thought, the culminant expression of feeling, and the psychosomatic fulcrum of development, should be expected to throw its decisive weight in favor of rendering the entire physique as generalized as itself. In other words, this spearhead of evolution (and especially of human advance) must aim at ever further development and fulfillment of this law of the survival of—and, we may add, the dominance of—the unspecialized.

Epilogue

As Grey Walter has pointed out, the sense of touch seems to be almost independent of the brain's control and ordering; and he adds, as illustration, that the reproductive process seems to proceed on its own, disregardful of the mind that receives the tactilely conveyed messages but can do little if anything about them, unless, as he stimulatingly suggests, we should train our mind tactually. Indeed, this has been explored by the German studies in haptics, which derived from studies on the apprehension of their environment by those who were born blind.

But further, we must note that at the beginning of this century, Ivan Bloch (6) drew attention to the fact that the specific sexual sensations are derived from and concentrated-contracted in from that suffused sensory dilation which in this essay I am calling the panaesthetic neotenic psychophysical tonus.

The brain, then, may be extending the further evolution of man. It may be a conative organ, a center that is striving to establish a paidomorphic structure. In and through this structure, it may express itself; it may inform itself in and about its environment, about its fellow body-minds and about its present field. So it may be moved to undertake further enlargements and modifications not only *in* that field but *of* that field. Certainly the brain has already reached such a complexity that man can no longer hope for peace by settling down, any more than an animal with a large stomach can hope to rest by leaving its digestive areas empty. The brain insists that we keep on the go. The younger and more nimble we become, the better we shall satisfy our rider, enjoy the exercise he insists we take with him and, in the process, utterly outstrip any who might, while we were drowsing, have taken our place in the van of life.

This is how the neotenic drive may fulfill itself. First, there may be a minority with sufficient expert knowledge and authentic authority to inhibit violence, to guide the future by the accuracy of their insights, the surety of their forecasts, and to control and liberate education by producing and inculcating a valid contemporary psychophysical morality, a mental-somatic social hygiene. So, at length, a race able to be free might be produced. Then, this minority might become the balancing moiety of humankind; alongside the "Way of the Fathers" there could march not a comparatively exceptional elite but another complementary column in the human procession. These would be neither superathletes nor superascetics. Human life, as it has developed, has produced an increasing variety of response-types. And as the neotenic type or types emerge, we may find a species of humankind that lives its whole life naturally, without ever narrowing down to the no longer necessary confinement of the specific sexual focus and no longer confined, intellectually, to one professional expertism. In fact, this type must emerge in view of the threat posed by the present population explosion.

The widening of apprehension could at last lead to a race which, comprehending the purpose of life and the meaning of time, could complete its history. For the individual can achieve voluntary death as a further liberating birth; and the individual is the epitome of the race (its phylogeny henceforward following his ontogeny). So the race, its physical process completed, could translate itself into another field and transmute itself to function in another medium, at a higher frequency.

In closing, however rash it may seem, honesty suggests that if a researcher believes there is now detectable a clue that runs through history and points to a process that has repeatedly held societies together and reknit them when men had ruptured their intuitive cohesion, then he should indicate how that process may be made to function today—how it may be used to heal our individual and social fissures. If four times the intuitive reactions of man to his outer environment and inner racial depth broke down, and if four times a specific procedure reknit a minority that was sufficient to prevent the temporary failure of nerve that proves fatal—the collapse of society into total anarchy and a-moralism—what now?

Any informed person is now aware that we are in the psychological revolution. This is the last of the four revolutions (the religious, political, economic, and psychological) that comprise that epoch of revolutions which we still call the Modern Age. But more than that, we are aware that with the explication of this psychological and psychiatric revolution, we pass out of the epoch of revolutions. For revolution is the resultant of the trough of the wave (the subconscious intuitive value system) not being kept in balance with its crest: the critical foreconscious directed to accumulate data in regard to the outer world. Discovery of the unconscious integral mind now permits this balance to be re-established. Psychologically, integrally detected values can now be in coordination with critically detected outer data. Revolution (the advance of sense-data knowledge beyond the compositional capacity of the arrested inherited value system) has always been followed by reaction (the retraction to earlier mores and resistance against new data). But now this revolution-reaction breaker or cataclysmic comber conclusion of the social wave process need no longer occur.

Our psychosocial evolution can be resumed in a balanced advance of the intelligence and the emotions. Being the first generation of humans who are both self-conscious and also now aware of the non-self-conscious, we can now educate those implementers of action (the emotions) and so close the fatal gap, in the individual, between their intellect which works by critical reason and their reflexes that are trained by athletic conditioning.

We are also well aware that the progress in psychiatry has not only detected the way whereby the repressed emotional life may be brought to the surface and so given relief. We have added two further important discoveries to our knowledge of ourselves. First, we have learned that there have always been four cardinal turning points at which the human living process, whether that of the race or that of the individual, faces a crisis of change and may be derailed. Secondly, we have come to see that no therapy, no education of the emotions can be sound and lasting if its aim is to return the individual to normalcy and only render him able to submit to the present rapidly collapsing mores. He can be taught to adjust, to make mutual adaptations with his altering society. But he can do so fruitfully, and with a new sanity toward himself and his society, only if the therapy of psychophysical hygiene that he is given is more than curative, more than preventive. It must be developmental.

Already we have seen the results of such a therapy when employed with the first great age group, that of infancy. We are now at the stage when we can see that these processes of development therapy (through education of the emotions) must continue. The subject of juvenile delinquency may be too much colored at present by the time-old prejudices and subconscious jealousies with which elders have always viewed the impetuous young. Today, too, the speed of change, which is far greater than in any other generation, tends to prove that the old were wrong in trying to prevent the young's rapid response to altered circumstances and increased knowledge.

Nevertheless, here is an issue of great acuteness today, and for two reasons. First, the rate of revolt is rising (23). A radio report the other day gave the figure that 50 percent of cars stolen were purloined by boys between ten and seventeen years of age, and that 19 percent of acts of criminal violence were committed by the same age group. The "rebels without a cause" (to use Robert Lindner's title) in this age section are hostile to discipline and suspicious of esprit de corps. As Lindner (56) has pointed out, repression can only increase the pressure and provoke full neurosis and psychosis. J. A. M. Meerloo (61), who was an expert witness of the trials of brainwashed American prisoners of war in Korea, states that the failure of loyalty was caused, basically, by the fact that the soldier who yielded had generally never been given a fully valid, character-convincing instruction in that voluntary and joyful self-giving without which loyalty is only conformity. The enforced service of a conscript is always in conflict with such dedication; and psychology may yet prove that the two are incompatible.

The second reason why some method of training the adolescent emotions is necessary comes from the other direction. "If we don't train adolescent emotions," says the conservational sociologist, "they may wreck our society." The age group psychologist has an equally strong reason for urging that this third great life crisis shall be rightly handled and those in this third birth be helped to achieve a healthy delivery. For the infancy therapist points out, as mentioned earlier in Section II, Chapter 3, that a child toughened by a harsh infancy (if it survives and does not become antisocially psychotic) is more suited to survive in a tough Junior High, and hence go ahead as a callous, self-seeking competitor, than one trained to welcome and to cooperate.

Margaret Mead is today's most influential anthropologist. In her latest and most important study (59), she twice asks this searching question: If the life of the grownup is to be based on self-interest and if friendship must be disowned when personal profit becomes the standard of adult prestige, would not these now mature persons be better adjusted if they had never known the happy carelessness of their early years? "Where ignorance is bliss, 'tis folly to be wise." But conversely, "A sorrow's crown of sorrow is remembering happier things." In a fighting world, he survives best who never heard of peace. Our helping the individual through his first ordeal and initiation (of the full psychophysical birth of some thirty months) may be worse than useless if he is to be exposed to deforming atavistic pressures in childhood and adolescence.[133]

The child is easily bored and as easily contemptuous of convention and finish. He needs action. Theodore Reich writes of the adolescent's subconscious need for compulsion and confession and the demand for punishment. These adolescent needs are not basic; they are symptoms, for they can be analyzed into deeper causative conditions. They are the miscarriage of an innocent constructive urge toward intense, exertional, agonic effort, toward a positive heightening endurance of a tempering process. For adolescence is also a birth that requires, as did the first two births, the rousing of intense latent vitality, which not only drives the craft through the narrows of parturition but also sends it out with an initiative drive.

So as the infant is roused, by play and bright challenge, to go ahead and avoid the lethargic danger of hebephrenic arrest and inertia, the child and the adolescent must also be helped to keep moving and to keep growing. By skilled ordeals in which we may suspect (if the past ordeals are any guide) that increasingly strenuous water exercise such as swimming, diving, and underwater effort would be a central term, the individual in later childhood may experience not only a catharsis, a purging of congested psychophysical pressures. They may also experience anarsis, that further stringing, tautening, and acquisition of muscular tensile tonus and strength whereby they become ready for adolescence.[134]

Education at this third stage (the stage of the ordeal and initiation of air) would probably involve learning a number of the now tested and efficacious yogic breathing exercises. These increase oxygen utilization, keeping the brain at a peak of activity and the bodily circulation high. The corresponding enlargement of the rib cage and convexing of the sternum not only increases lung room but there seems to be some evidence to suggest that it also affects the mass of tissue situated back of the sternum. During early childhood (generally to about the age of six), this mass of tissue acts as the thymus gland and holds in balanced check the ripening of the reproductive organs.[135] It is possible that this gland may be brought again into endocrine action and assist the adolescent in preserving, as long as it is desirable, the panaesthetic dilation before he temporarily enters the phase of specific reproduction.

First maturity in turn would then have its radiant heat therapy treatments. By this still higher form of strenuous stimulation, the executive type would be kept not only releasing his full energy, but acutely vital so as to be able to look forward to the further and higher stage of second maturity with the interest and appetite with which the adolescent looks forward to his oncoming adulthood. To such a person in first maturity, administration would not be the final station. It would be an education toward a still higher experience and more efficacious authority in second maturity, just as athletic achievements and academic ratings and recognitions are not the final station of the adolescent.

The specific treatment for second maturity would be shortwave radiation. It would seem possible that by this means those who have discharged their obligation to life and learned its purpose, might be freed from what today is an all too common blind and desperate clinging to bodily existence. This wretched and irrational fear-cramp seems too often to increase, not lessen, as physical resources become spent. The old could have much to give, but they are commonly shunned because to listen to complaints is always exhausting. And to be with even the secretly frightened is profoundly fatiguing. If, when a person entered second maturity, he began to be given high frequency treatment as a part of advanced adult education and psychophysical hygiene, three highly beneficial consequences seem possible. In the first place, his unspent energies (his frozen assets of vitality) could be released. He might become a person of such extended outlook that his counsel would be sought and his presence would give peace and encouragement instead of misgiving and dismay. Secondly, he himself might become increasingly psychophysically aware not only that his consciousness (his electric field) is distinctly superior to that field's precipitate (the material body) but that this consciousness can be independent.

Thirdly, after some years of such hygienic exercise, he might be able to understand how to detach this essential noncorporeal field, freeing it increasingly from its entropic system. This would lead to an awareness that (like the tree with the leaf) all the essential essence in the outer vehicle has been resumed into its original volatile condition. Then, with an act of intentional initiative, the consciousness principle could discard the unwanted residue.

Appendix A

THE HYBRID PSYCHE

(The transitional blend of heroic mystic and lawful ascetic, which produces (1) the city-state, (2) the nation-state, and (3) the empire-state)

One question remains: How does this historical schema describe and explain, in its psychological diagnosis, the mental energy that produced the ancient civilizations?

Surely, neither the destructive, paranoid hero nor the schizoid, escapist ascetic can account for those achievements in administration, law, economy, and art that the ancient civilizations produced and which, because of their impressiveness, have seemed to most historians to be the highest fruit of humankind's intelligence. If the psychological hypothesis outlined in this study of history is the basic diagnosis of the force that has been shaping humankind, if successive alterations in the human mind are the persistent cause of the changes throughout successive phases of human culture, then under each of these cultural phases we must be able to detect that specific phase of human consciousness that was the cause of that change in culture.

It is true that in a number of cases in history (for example, in the fourth and fifth centuries A.D. in Ireland), there is given evidence that there is a conversional moment in history. The mutation in consciousness, the contraction of the soul on itself, on these occasions took place with spastic speed. For there are records of heroes in the very heat of battle, at the pitch of their paranoid frenzy, being compunction-pierced, of their having a sudden sense that their violation of the natural law, "Thou shalt not kill within thy species," convicted them of murder. They fled headlong from the bloody field, knowing the curse of Cain, and not only forsook the sword but excommunicated themselves from society and abandoned the world, henceforth to live only to die, to expiate their guilt before it would fall upon their souls after death with the pitiless avenging fury that they had dealt out upon their earthly foes.

Nevertheless, this swift reaction from paranoid, childish, homicidal rage over into schizoid, adolescent, mortificatory guilt has certainly not been the only possible path of human development. Take, for example, the classic case of the emperor Asoka (264–227 B.C.). His conversion took place the night after the culminating victory in which he had completed the conquest of all India proper. In a dream, he is walking over the won field and he sees that all the faces of the dead are his own face. And though his conversion compels him personally to adopt the regime of a monk, publicly he retains his administrative and, in fact, his legal punitive powers.

[Asoka] is a psychological hybrid. His private conscience is set on saving his own soul. His public obligation is tied to the discharge of his duties through the exercise of legalized violence. For example, capital punishment is kept in force. Condemned lawbreakers have their date of execution postponed for one day if that date falls on a holy day in the Buddhist calendar. He has not the peacekeeping *mana* power of a priest–king in an hypnocracy. He is an armed executive–emperor. He cannot assure his own royal succession. His son is recorded to have risen against him and to have had militarily to be crushed. Finally, the Buddhist religion, which he made that of the State, endowed and privileged by such patronage (like the Christian church when similarly bought by Constantine), degenerated and modified its teaching. For instance, on the Asoka pillars there is no mention of Nirvana, the one aim of Buddhism, the deliverance from all physical and all individual life in a state that means the disappearance of the whole material world. What is commended and commanded, in these edicts, is a life of good social deeds to be rewarded after death with the conventional paradisal pleasures.

Here, however, we must note that the Indian and the Irish heroes were late.[136] Already there had been, centuries before, that Eurasian-wide outbreak of the private conscience, the desire for personal salvation (compare Karl Jaspers' *The Origin and Goal of History*; Breasted's *The Dawn of Conscience*), the ego guilt that can only conceive of liberation in an escape from all existence.

We must ask what, then, of the proto-hero? When he broke out and blasted the hypnocracies, did he wreck all society and leave only a desolation haunted by life-rejecting eremites? Clearly not: there arose city-states that were not hypnocracies and, more, nations composed of many cities and their reservoir lands, and, in the end, empires with supercapitals, coordinated provinces. What held these congeries together up to the point when varied races lived subject to one imperial law?

The city-states came first and failed first. We see why when we study their psychosocial cohesion. The hero could not continue ruling by the sword, by martial law, by throwing spoil to his gang and holding down, while trying to live off, terror-stricken serfs. For example, the Homeric hero has to marry the daughter of the priest-king he had murdered and she, in turn, carrying out the ancient law of magic, kills him as soon as he is helpless and unarmed: for example, Agamemnon, Homer's King of men, is murdered by Clytemnestra, with the aid of her native lover, Aegisthus. They, in turn, are killed by her son.

The blood feud continues until sacred kingship is replaced by an armed oligarchy alternating with brief spells of democracy. This mutual private convenience holds in uneasy consent-of-advantage the tiny territory where the mobile tribe gang had grounded. These minute groups were so weak in psychic cohesion that they could not extend fibrils of common loyalty to their fellow [compatriots] of the same blood, tongue, mores, and religion.

Neither in Sumeria nor in Greece did the city-states, so vivid in curiosity about the outer world and so ingenious in ordering that world, succeed in making any psychosocial federalization with their companions. On the contrary, in both areas they fought each other till they fell prey to outer forces, which imposed order, though never consent.[137]

In short, the city-state remained psychosocially merely a lakelet, a bright puddle left where the torrent of heroic barbarian invasion, as its force was spent, settled into these sundered pools. Their drama was arrested at tragedy, their art fixed at the age of adolescent athleticism, their religion set at a polytheistic anthropomorphism, their philosophy caught and frozen in skeptical pessimism (for example, the Socratic elenche) on which hard ice there shimmers an other-worldly idealism (Platonism).

The next stage, the nation, did better. We see it, at present, best illustrated by Egypt's record. Here are the first predynastic hypnocracies: the Badarian, Tasian, Gerzean. And here we see the first signs of the attempt to construct social cohesion, to match technical advance in the know-how with an equally advanced concept of the know-why. As there increased the critical mind, which produced improved technics, there had to be answered, more definitely, the newly emerging questions as to values, purposes, goals. The master invention or composition made by the social psychological thinkers in the Realm of Ends was the Abydos mythos. Therein a frame of reference and an avenue of comprehension were provided that would hold an increasingly technicalized and granularized population in a condition of consent, the good goal of each person interpretatively balanced with the good state of the whole society.

The equation held in poise nature, society, and the separate soul. Osiris, the fertile earth whose sister is Isis the moon, has coitus with her while he lies buried, and from this fertilization is born Ra, the sun, who manifests himself as the Light that is righteousness, the Hawk, which is the all-seeing eye, and the reigning Pharaoh, who incarnates as the presiding man-god.

With amazingly sustained ingenuity millennium after millennium, the priesthood extended this right, of the increasing number of those who became self-conscious, to be granted personal immortality. While at the same time they, with a corresponding control, kept the Pharaoh arrested as a priest–king. His nails and hair, his bodily functions—coitus and elimination—and his every activity were all under constant priestly surveillance and control. On

Appendix A

occasion he would break out with a band of the priests' armed guard. But even Thutmose the Third's great venture was no more than a giant raid. Egypt was a holy nation. Its *mana* could be made to endure along the Nile. Its great mythos with its cohesive power was for Egyptians alone. It had no purchase on humankind in general.

What, then, does Egypt show us in regard to psychological evolution, in respect of that great curve of intensifying consciousness which is the invisible field precipitating the five great frames of reference in which and through which humankind has successively lived?

It shows that there have been occasions when the horde leader could be arrested before, having smashed the hypnocracy, his destructive rage of frustration turned in on himself and he went eremite. The destruction of the priest–kingly matriarchate by the Achaean northern invaders in Greece and the Greek Islands (for example, Crete) was thorough enough to leave, as we have seen, only [tiny], mutually repellant, and internally disruptive city-states.[138]

In Egypt, however, the consent-producing, obedience-enforcing mythos was of sufficiently tough elastic to net the fighter and reduce him to the form and function of a priest–king. The retiarius-priest won against the gladiator-king. Still, although Egypt was a nation and it did master the anarchy of city-statism, it could not spread to an empire.

We must ask, then, this question. If heroism, with its mores drawn from the fighting epic, resulted on occasion in the Hellenic city-state, and if that unit was, inevitably, politically unviable and psychologically unstable; if heroism, when it was captured by a priest–kingly myth, was able to be turned into an amalgam of social suggestion (religious hypnosis) and military control and this made a Nile nationalism enduring some three millennia: What is the amalgam that produced empire?

The first empire, the Persian, is made of the military and the *mana* alloy. But as it is to embrace, keep in communication,[139] and in considerable liberty, a number of different nations, Cyrus and his successors are not reduced back to priest–kings. Instead of a king of two natures, there was made a constitution of two authorities, a binary system in which the system of laws was always called the Laws of the Medes and Persians. In this partnership the Medes, though the Persians had conquered them, were nevertheless always mentioned first. For they were the magicians, the society of magic and *mana*.[140]

So the striking power of the Persian military machine was hilted and sheathed in what alone could produce consent, the seer's authority. Meanwhile both partners in the administration of their rule had back of them the Zoroastrian cosmological ethic in which the ruler was the armed servant of Ormuz, the Light of Righteousness, and all this servant's wars are in the name of this Light, and to push back the Darkness Ahriman.

The psychological history of the Roman Empire illustrates the same problem. The Imperator first known as master of the legions cannot sustain his authority with his forces demobilized. Hence, when Julius Caesar crossed the Rubicon into the homeland of Rome with his legions still under arms and so, by breaking the law of security of the government from a general's coup d'état, showing himself wholly dependent on violence, he had to seek for the psychological sanction of kingship. This move being checkmated by assassination, his successor Augustus has to combine with his control of the army the office of chief priest (the Pontifex Maximus), and when the *mana* of Roman religion, too debilitated by militarism, was too weak a cohesive, the master of the legions had to be made a god.

The two offices, still failing to make an amalgam, failing not merely to sanction a lawful peace throughout the empire but even to guarantee the god-general from assassination by his own guards, had to be taken apart. The killing of a commander-in-chief by his staff shakes discipline in the army. A god murdered by the army is a blow to all social cohesion, an open invitation to anarchy. The emperor must (as did Cyrus) find a god above the battle, a ruler of Heaven whose agent on earth is the commander-in-chief. Hence, Constantine's shrewd pact with the Christian church. Its *mana* was just strong enough to make it able not to submit to flat coercion but to hold out until the purchase price offered it power to use the state to destroy its religious rivals while the state, in turn, used it to help crush political revolt.

The end of the empire was, therefore, postponed, its deliquescence extended. For what *mana* the church had was already ascetic, life-denying, society-deserting. The heroic barbarians' relentless invasion steadily encroached, while, internally, bureaucratic corruption debased the currency and ruined credit, and while slave labor under the whip exhausted agriculture.

In the end, as the barbarians now [populated] the legions, inevitably and soon these heroic-level fighters move in with a king of their own kind. The transitional phase between paranoid hero and schizoid ascetic is over. Monasteries and militarists, celibate, anathema-loaded bishops and loose-breeding, sword-wielding chieftains divide loyalty and provoke anarchy. This confusion endures until this alloy of other-worldly dreams for the sensitive, with this-worldly gains for the tough, leads to the uneasy balance of crude, crescent nationalism with decrescent, ghostly cosmopolitanism, that is, the Holy Roman Empire.

At last the psychic conflict is resolved. The inconsistency of a combination of practicality and ideality in which both are compromised is abandoned. Man, seeking for a force more apt than clumsy violence and a relationship subtler and stronger than dogma, therefore concentrated on means and immediacy. And so he finds that not only do his powers multiply but his sense of independence is made clearly conscious and manifest. The modern human, the fully self-conscious individual, depending on reason (measurement), intelligence (choice), experiment, and critical analysis has appeared. The fourth type of consciousness has emerged.[141]

The initial aspect of the first revolution took place in physics (for revolutions always begin in the mind) (42). When the physics of the Church (for example, the Aristotelian geocentricity) was challenged, the ecclesiastical revolution resulted.

The second revolution was when polity (sociology, social heredity, civil law) challenged the traditional law (for example, the theory of the divine right of kings). The result of this was the political revolution.

The third revolution was in economics. The principles of laissez faire, private enterprise, and free trade challenged mercantilism-capitalism. This complex of ideas then found *itself* challenged by biology. Darwinianism, the natural selection idea of evolution, refuted not only the Adam Smith concept of human nature (with its concept that free enterprise would of itself lead to general wealth and happiness) but also struck at the basis of the political revolution: equality of humans.

Today, we are in the psychological revolution, the fourth and last which, of necessity, ends the Modern Age. For now the critical mind seeking objectivity has to turn on itself in order to examine the instrument whereby it attempts to define objects. First, finding that it has confined itself to such an instrument ("There is nothing in the mind unless it is first in the senses"), the human intelligence next arrives at the conclusion that this instrument itself is strictly confined to select and construct electromagnetic impulses (radiation) to yield the impression of an environment in which and on which an animal can subsist. This psychological insight has led to further developments in the method casually called science.

The first phase of science was threefold, a process of definition, abstraction, and experimentation. In the second phase, while the first and third terms were retained, the middle term was altered (39). Instead of abstraction, hypothesis is now employed. Abstraction's aim is to build up a proposition, every step and statement of which is based on an already established finding. But, to produce such a confirmed coherence, a certain number of anomalous findings must be excluded to preserve the symmetry of the resulting pattern, for example, the natural law.

Hypothesis, on the other hand, rejects none of the findings. It incorporates them by extrapolation, by placing them in an open-ended system. Instead, then, of tying itself to the pretentious and brittle idea of natural law, hypothesis in this, the second phase of the scientific method, uses the gauge of probability. By statistically arrived at degrees of probability, it establishes the likelihood that by extending investigation in this direction, the anomalous data will be found able to occupy a station in this flexible and enlarging design and, in turn, the data so incorporated will show whether new findings will come to light.

~~~~~~~~~~~

To summarize the answer to the question of why is not the great civilic epoch of man (the age of the creative city-states, the inventive nation-states, the administrative empire-states—an outburst of external activity and mastery) traceable to a specific phase in man's intensifying

Appendix A

psyche: this controlled outburst was produced by the transitional combination of a couple of these basic psychological phases.

The hero in decline, the ascetic in ascension—in this conjunction was produced a type of mind still longing for the fame of victorious battle but growing aware that looming up behind the hero's projected image of the Gods of Battles was the vision of an uncapricious, indeflectable law. This hybrid consciousness, this transitional psyche had then either to become the servant of this living law, the executive of righteousness (and this is the frame of reference in which the Chinese and the Western empires sought and found sanction) or, in the longer lasting but smaller societies of the nation, the ruler had to be co-natured with the God.

The Roman emperors' flirtation with deity never became a marriage. For if a man is to be dowered with divinity, the inherent God must prove his presence by evidencing his *mana*. And the more the man-master of the legions uses armed violence, the less is it possible to believe he is possessed of any other force. Nothing more thoroughly disproves religion than religious persecution. Egyptian society and the kingship that crowned it lasted longer than any other nation because the Pharaoh was more often and more nearly divine than any emperor, any king, or any pope.

The search for consent, for an uncoercive authority had still to be made by the last supernational empire, that of Napoleon I. When Talleyrand warned that victories won no consent ("You can do anything with bayonets except sit on them") and [also] Napoleon ("My cannon can defeat the Austrians but not their hatred of me"), then the extreme advice of Sieyes, the constitution maker, alone seemed to offer any settlement. Napoleon had sneered that Austria's claim to the manifest of the Holy Roman Empire was to assert a power that was "neither Holy nor Roman nor an Empire!" But he crowned himself (with the Pope present and giving his blessing) Emperor of the West and claimed for his son, by the daughter of the Austrian emperor, the title that the son and heir of the Holy Emperor had by right of birth: the King, not of Paris or Aix-la-Chapelle (Aachen, the capital of Charlemagne), but of Rome.

In spite of all these efforts to represicipitate loyalty, Bonaparte's empire lasted only those dozen years (1800–1812) that marked

Alexander's and Genghis'. Certainly modern humans, Humanic people, could not solve the problem of human cohesion, the issue of a nonviolent cosmopolitanism. And it is clear why this psychological adhesive, this organic binding, is lacking.

For the cosmos that modern cosmopolitan man postulated was a machine, and the only ethic deducible from a cosmo-machine is (as we have seen) that which regards man as a machine and his behavior as not intentional but imprinted, a series of imposed conditioned reflexes. Not only are intention, purpose, and responsibility dismissed, but consciousness itself is denied.

As a historical fact, as the analytic-critical method of the primary form of the science process increased in its capacity to break things down and so to multiply means, plurify power, and accelerate transit, the units of psychosocial consent, the limits of loyalty, of spontaneous cohesion, have as rapidly shrunken. All empires are in ruins, and where the primary scientific method was most forwarded (the states around the North Sea), as indeed had happened before with the first—the Hellenic outburst of science—the wider the thought the more cramped the feeling. Scandinavia is divided in four pieces; the Netherlands into three—and, with Belgium splitting, would, if self-determination was not coerced, be in four, the fourth being the Walloons. Let choose, three nations (Estonia, Latvia, Lithuania) emerged round the southeast of the Baltic. Left free to choose, Alsace and Lorraine would secede from Germany or from France. France itself would be in pieces if a fanatic out of the thirteenth century did not coerce her. Even small anachronisms such as Ireland, fixated on an anarchic past (an angry alloy of guilt-haunted heroes and mortificatory ascetics), has its northeast section, Ulster, seceded from it.

Appendix B

ON FURTHER DIRECTION OF PSYCHOPHYSICAL EVOLUTION

It may seem strange that our present brand of prophets—the authors of our modern apocalypses, the writers of science fiction—have not availed themselves of present biological views as to man's indicated future and the potentialities in him by which he may attain it, although some of them have been biologically informed. The process of neoteny through fetalization and paidomorphy has been recognized for almost a generation. Louis Bolk, the outstanding Dutch anatomist, named the process forty years ago. And the same process was recognized by Max Hilzheimer (45) in his essay "The Dog: the Foetalization of the Wolf." H. G. Wells, one of the great popularizers of science, gathered a worldwide audience with his *Outline of History*. Then in his *The Science of Life*, published about thirty-five years ago, he introduced the lay reading public to Louis Bolk's conception of "man, the foetalization of the ape."

Let us grant that every stage in the advance of life has been due to fetalization; this has been stated in minimal terms by Cope in his "law of the survival of the unspecialized." Let us also grant that with man this process of the neotenic extension of generalized form and function, physique and behavior, has added to the infancy stage (which no reptile has) the stage of childhood; it has added to the fetalistic postbirth stage the stage of the paidomorph. Then we may say, as Haldane had said, that man will now begin, must begin, to add a still further extension of his retention of generalization. In short, the man of tomorrow, the man we must have as the only type that is psychophysically adequate to handle our psycho-chemical powers, must be as much the paidomorph of the man of today as man today is the paidomorph of the apes.

The person of the future who will carry on and keep the social heredity up to date, who will make a constantly expanding interpretation of a constantly expanding knowledge, must have the child's freedom of association and curiosity. He will find delight both in new facts and in making new sense of those facts.

It is out of such a type that a completely contemporary form of the seer can spring. Every epoch of humankind has required and produced this type: the magician of the cave culture, the herald-bard-prophet of the Heroic Epoch, the mystic-contemplative of the Ascetic Age, the scholar-sage of the Humanic Era.[142] No period has been wholly without that specific discerner of standards, that designer of values, that framer of the prestige pattern that directs endeavor, molds enterprise, canalizes energy, shapes behavior, and instructs taste.

Today, our convulsive culture is subconsciously aware of this need. Our very desire to keep young, our pathetic effort to remain juvenile is a symptom of our blind reaction to a deficiency disease caused by the loss of purpose and coordinant drive in the way we now live. Still and all, and certainly in the light of such an interpretation of man's history as I have tried to outline in this discussion, we can propose an aim. We can suggest the type of man who could be the pattern of prestige for this Leptoid Age. However, to suggest a pattern of prestige is not to say that everyone must attain to it. An orchestra cannot be composed solely of first violins. Indeed, the more human life advances, the more it gives rise to variety. And this variegation is strengthening because variety increases the capacity for multiform enquiries and responses.

The pattern of prestige has always been a theme, a leitmotif, around which and on which man, with an ever-growing orchestrational capacity, could compose symphonies out of a constantly enlarging experience. Besides this there is another factor of variety that is perceptible in human history. From earliest times, from the crystallization out of the coconscious, two possible modes of human conduct seem to have been recognized. In the Ascetic Epoch, they were called the Precepts of Universal Obligation and the Counsels of Perfection. The precepts are the five natural moral laws. They are to be observed at least up to the standard of justice by everyone, and up to the standard of equity by those in control of the group's policy.[143] This means that the two basic classes of society, the maintenance men and the inventors, the applied researchers and the pure researchers, the routineers and the pioneers, are in a constant reciprocal relationship—a relationship as close as the lichen symbiosis in which a fungus (which finds its purchase and nourishment on a rock) and an alga (which feeds on air) combine together to form a single living organism.

Future human evolution, therefore, would be marked by three characteristics. First, there will be a tendency for increasing psychophysical generalization of each constituent of human society. Secondly, there will be an increasing tendency toward a racial fanning out into a variety of these unspecialized types. And, thirdly, there will be an increasing width of qualities of consciousness, of apprehension and comprehension. We now have a number of arts, such as music and poetry for the ear; painting, ceramics, and sculpture for the eye; dancing and gymnastics for the body. But we may develop new arts for, say, scent, taste, and touch. We may develop new sciences in sensory detection, extrasensory perception, and integral thought.

In brief, the really possible Utopia would be this world experienced by a psychophysique at full aperture.

Appendix C

ON THE CATACLYSMIC CHARACTER OF THE SUCCESSIVE EPOCH CHANGES

From a study of the places where each of the four epochs in man's history ended, and of the time when each of these epochs ended and its successor rose to power, it would seem that every epoch first begins in a particular area and then spreads until its influence is felt, sooner or later, throughout the Eurasian land mass and in Africa. The Heroic Epoch seems to have taken on its specific pattern of culture (its epic ideals and its phobias, its mobility and its destructiveness, its exercises and its additions) when the hold of the originally coconscious society had become arthritic. That is to say, what had first been unquestioning submission to an immemorial tradition, which had its own millennial growth, was now repression under a rigid penalty-laden social structure.

This hardened legalization of tradition seems to have taken place first in the Near East, where writing and mathematics first emerged. It provoked the mobile-minded to move out onto the new grasslands that were appearing north of the Caucasus, there to cultivate horsemanship, and finally, in the second phase of the Heroic Ages, to depend on a pastoralist rather than an agricultural economy. Therefore, this Heroic culture could, because of its mobility, diffuse itself to the limits of the great Eurasian-African plains.[144]

In turn, the Ascetic movement seems to have arisen in the upper basin of the Ganges about 750 B.C.,[145] and thence to have spread, by a series of missionary waves, west, north, and east. At first, they were disciplinary. In their second phase they were mortificatory. By the time (510 B.C.) that Cyrus, the founder of the Persian Empire, had extended his frontiers to the Indus, Indian asceticism (disciplinary controls of the appetite), quickly to be followed by Indian mortification (the denial of appetites), could spread to the Mediterranean. Thirdly, when in the fifteenth century A.D. the ascetic prestige pattern was challenged, the rise of Humanic man takes place in Italy. In its initial stage of rational and critical individualism, it spread through Europe. In the nineteenth century, humanic rational criticism becomes materialism and materialistic economics. In this form it spread, and is still spreading, throughout the world.

Fourthly, in this century in the arc of culture stretching from Scandinavia (through Germany, Austria, Lombardy, and France) to Britain, the Leptoid, post-objective complex of concepts and praxes has superseded the humanic total individualism. Certainly, the speed of ideational change seems to be spastic, or perhaps one should say mutational. Right back to the sudden rise, on the lower Nile, of the Pharaohonic civilization out of the pre-Dynastic cultures, we note this increasing abruptness of change.

As to the position of the scholar-sage, his lack of authority in the Renaissance, and his extraordinary prestige in China, let us first look at him in the West. Here we can find four reasons for his ineffectiveness: (1) He was purely a literary, concerned with the resuscitation of a dead language: Greek. (2) The Churchmen still claimed all psychological authority. (3) The natural philosophers, the incipient scientists, claimed all authority in the fields of research and experimentation. And (4) the apparatus of scholarship, meanwhile, was totally inept as an instrument whereby to initiate a psychological therapy.

We can account for the Chinese sages' failure to achieve a Renaissance because of their indifference to psychology and their disregard of physics and physiology. The Chinese Heroic Age did enter on an ascetic phase with the introduction of Indian Buddhism. The sage culture, however, kept the alien asceticism in check. Therefore (according to C. C. Chang), in China it is to Taoism and Mahayana Buddhism that we must look for a psychophysical underground that carries on a cryptic practice based on an esoteric doctrine.

Appendix D

ON THE EVIDENCE FOR AN ESOTERIC MYSTERY TRADITION IN THE WEST AND ITS POSTPONEMENT OF SOCIAL DESPAIR

Because of its very nature, the ways of an [esoteric] underground [tradition] are exceedingly difficult to trace. History, it has been said, is documentation. But secret sects keep their records hidden; proscribed heresies destroy theirs. Yet on the Scilly Isles it has been possible to prove that the present Little Archipelago is a series of hilltops (that were left after the original single island submerged) through the discovery that roads starting on one islet, and going under the sea, may be found emerging on another shore on the further side of the sundering strait. So in history, we can make similar tracings.

The rise of the ascetic, life-rejecting religions meant the persecution and repression of the libidinal life-accepting religions. The heroic protoindividual had not liked them. His creed was that of a male fighter who sacrificed the victims of his victories to his warrior God. Blood and flesh were the sacraments fit for a masculine God of Battles. The heroic blood-shedder denounced the gentle religion of the matriarchies and its beliefs and rites: its sacraments of milk and semen, of life foods that were given willingly and not torn from a murdered fellow man. He denounced it as unclean, and often, when looting these industriously wealthy societies, massacred its peaceful practitioners.

But persistent persecution, cruel inquisition, and crueler punishment were the uglier behaviors of the midindividual, whose eroticism was more acute than that of the protoindividual and whose guilt-motivated cruelty was also greater.

It is probably at this point that the mysteries began to be concealed. In the forcing house of the Nile, we know that at a certain time the idols were broken. This is when individualism had developed beyond the protoindividual level in the ruler and his associates. Akhenaten, the weak, has been married to Nefertiti, the strong, blue-eyed daughter of the far northern Mitanni Kings whose steppe religion had rid itself of images. But the statues of the gods were again set up in the swift reaction that followed. However, one former prime favorite was omitted. This was Min, the god of fertility, whose images were phallic. After that, initiation became a specifically secret thing. And it became secret not because, as formerly, the unitive state of mind (the condition of co-consciousness) *cannot* be expressed in the increasingly concrete terms of a language that is becoming one of separative definitions. These states where the new antagonism of mind and body was banished *must* not be spoken about. For the new schizoid dogma rules that spirit must always be at war with its enemy, flesh. Soon then, in the West, there was no place in the open daylight world for the unitive mysteries. Even in India, the original mysteries that refused to be asceticized had, in the end, to be concealed.

India has certainly had an esoteric underground. Since the Muslim invasions in the fourteenth century, Islam, a puritan religion, began to persecute Tantra. And finally Akbar, the great Moghul who controlled a large portion of the peninsula, although he was tolerant of other cults (mainly because Brahmanism had become almost as prudish as Islamism) made persistent drives to stamp out this ancient life religion.

China, too, has had its secret methods in Taoism. Arthur Waley feels sure that back of the gnomic paradoxes of the Tao Te Ching is

Appendix D

a yoga technique of training consciousness by psychophysical exercises. The most famous of its absurdities—those who know don't say and those who say don't know—is not meant to stultify all exchange of knowledge. It is to point out that the Way is not to be found through rational information. Exercises, not propositions, open the mind, [and] permit it to see the way things truly are and to go along that path of illumined understanding (95).

But it was in the West that repression was the most fierce and persecution was set on annihilation of the old religion. The Hebrew prophets ... succeeded in making their ... people believe that the failure of its attempt to become a great power (or even to survive as a territorial nation) was due to the anger of [Yahweh]. He was angry because they worshiped divinity in a life symbol of the phallus: the sacred pillar, which the prophets were always cutting down. The prophets were like most persecuting critics. They were far more effective as denouncers than they were as consistent creative instructors. Some of them, such as Jeremiah, declared that Yahweh never did want blood sacrifices. Behave ethically, they said, and all will turn out well. It didn't. But of course it was possible to say that if only the moral standard had been high enough then it would have. Other prophets (for example, Malachi who concludes the book of the canonized seers) maintain that if the blood sacrifices are kept up then Yahweh will fulfill his promises of national glory for his people. Nevertheless, although the sacrifices were kept going, the Jews lost, for more than two thousand years, the land they coveted.

After the final destruction of Jerusalem under Hadrian, the Jews seemed to have taken to the psychology of the day. They were known, employed, and [at times] feared as magicians. The Cabala is viewed with almost as much disfavor by [some elements of highly observant] Judaism as was the Witch Cult by medieval Catholicism. But these strange texts, containing alchemical–astrological references and purporting to give methods for obtaining power, may refer in cryptic form to psychophysical methods for controlling the emotions and altering consciousness (as we shall see in a moment with contemporary Greek writings of the second century).

Like the ethical Jewish prophets, the Greek moral philosophers also began their thinking with the assumption that the moral law was self-evident and self-rewarding. *Dike*, justice, is of the nature of things; and man, being a reasonable creature, is sensible enough to follow such an advantageous way of life. Protagoras, like Confucius, believed that virtue could be taught; that the emotions were as open to argument and as influenced by logic as was the reason itself. Then a profound change came about.

Until lately, it was generally supposed that the Greeks were "the young, light-hearted masters of the waves," alien to pessimism and despising asceticism. It was thought that although in India the Indo-European culture, after going through the Heroic Age (of the Vedas), arrived at the Ascetic Age, this did not befall the other Aryan culture, that of the Achaean Greeks. We now know that this is untrue. The true Greek Heroic Age, the age that so named itself, was that late Bronze Age (1000 B.C.), which Homer made unforgettable. This age was boyish (as was that of the Vedas) with its boisterous gods. But its unreflective noradrenaline culture, whose one check was shame, not guilt,[146] did not last. The age that succeeded it (the Archaic or Helladic), whose poet was to be Hesiod and which was to be given its final summation in the archaistic drama of Sophocles, has already exchanged shame for guilt and in its inmost conviction is as life-fearing as Buddhism.[147]

With Socrates, what budded as poetic despair and flowered as dramatic tragedy fruits in logical discussion leading toward intellectual skepticism and individual emotional detachment. And with Socrates, we reach a dividing of the ways. He still believes that reason can guide a man so that he will live righteously. He refuses to be initiated into the mysteries. But he finds that he has to listen to a daimon, an inner preterrational voice whose rulings must be obeyed. Further, and most significantly, this arresting conscience is negative. It never tells him what to do; it vetoes what he thought of doing. And he reported that it was totally silent when, at his final crisis, he had to decide whether to flee or to die.

These items in the life of a man who was so largely decisive in causing the division between cosmology and morals, between science and religion, are highly informative. For it would seem that the mysteries offended the good sense (the rationalism) and probably the moral sense (the sexual repression) of a mind that was already sundered into a logical intelligence and an emotional subconscious, and so subject to further psychic inhibitions (the daimon voice). Hence Greek philosophy, instead of trying to understand the irrational and emotional, tried to reject and repress them. And so, cut off from creative integral thought, Greek thought became skeptical. Phaedo, and Pyrrho after him, establish the Eleatic School of complete skepticism, derived from Socrates' *elenchus*.

Though then Socrates is still mainly a rationalist, both his skeptical method of argument and his own awareness of his interior preterrational guide (his daimon) show that thinking persons are becoming aware that there is something in nature and in human nature that may require more insight than common sense (the rational use of the five senses) can provide. Still, they remain individualistic puritans, fearing their dark side and the unlit aspect of nature. So they rejected the mysteries (1) because the mysteries taught (and their practitioners understood intuitively) that that dark side of one's self is dreadful only if repressed; if it is expressed it will add its energy to creative living. (2) Because the mysteries kept the panaesthetic rites going and these were shocking to the rational puritan. Thus the mysteries had to become esoteric.

However, this doubt as to the adequacy of the five senses to provide human nature with sufficient insight was made explicit by Plato, Socrates' pupil, interpreter, and fulfiller. He saw also that such skepticism was doubly perilous. It must excite the mob to one of two evils: either to lynching the enquirer or to personal license. Also, it would paralyze the intelligentsia. As Plato remarked to Phaedo (his fellow pupil under Socrates, and the founder of the school of complete skepticism), he cleared the ground but never built. A razed site only invites erosion. Because he was socially concerned, Plato's own teaching therefore became increasingly esoteric. The wise, The Guardians, must know, not only intellectually but also by direct experience; they must have been initiated. And further, they must be repeatedly refreshed by being given direct knowledge of that intuitive world which is not comprehended in those biological states of mind-body consciousness that are all the unenlightened man can know.

E. R. Dodds (19), in his valuable volume *The Greeks and the Irrational*, traces in Plato's mind this realization that there had to be a secret doctrine and that this esoteric teaching was more than rational information. It had to change conduct, character, and consciousness. For, if it did not, then society would cleave asunder into an ineffective curd-film of rational culture afloat on a sour whey of superstition, with the cream finally being swallowed up in the fermenting sludge. Dodds gives good reason to suppose that Plato in his extremity[148] came across the Pythagoreans in South Italy or Sicily about 390 B.C. From them he borrowed much of their psychophysical system to propose a method of training for that level of character which we now call the unconscious or semiconscious emotional life. Dodds believes that this method of training, or Plato's adaptation of it, is the foundation of the esoteric social structure that Plato describes in *The Republic* and further accentuates in *The Laws*. The Guardians of the State, it seems clear, were to undergo some regime that would do much more than inform their intelligences and confirm their self-assurance. They would be shaped in their "inner man," as Paul of Tarsus puts it. Or in our current language, their semiconscious and subconscious emotional life would be given profound, character-molding suggestion therapy.

That the actual procedure would be kept secret would not have surprised the Greek world or awakened suspicion. The vow of absolute secrecy was always imposed by all the mysteries and, as far as we know, kept by the initiates. Plato, however, seems never to have put his scheme into practice. His mind appears to have been too grandiose. For him, nothing would serve but a recreated oligarchic Athens set in the amber of his eloquence, or a Syracuse over which he would rule through his vicar, the tamed tyrant Dionysius. He was incurably political, high-handedly impatient of experiment and research. That Plato's great mind never rid itself of the pre–Alexandrine Greek dependence on *a priori* argument (and so the fatal disregard of controlled experimentation) accounts partly for his limitations; and, added to his aristocratic contempt for the common people, it goes far to explain his practical failure. However, there was a defeatism in his emotional life. The Pythagorean movement is the rise of asceticism in the West, the appearance of guilt (instead of shame) as the driving force, and the sense that man is a creature who has fallen into a lower world. Empedocles, the Sicilian philosopher

Appendix D

(c. 490–430 B.C.) who certainly was influenced by Pythagorianism, is the first Greek thinker to denounce marriage and all sex. At heart, Plato could hardly feel that it was worthwhile spending one's life in an attempt to understand this misapprehended world through the misshapen instrument of our fallen state of mind. His fastidious puritanism made him regard the two horses of the soul's chariot as being really irreconcilable, and feel that the only hope lay in the white horse drawing the chariot up into heaven while the black one flung itself down into the Pit.

His great pupil and contrast, Aristotle, did make a start toward the experimental psychology that would have no prejudices but only make observations.[149] He was clearly interested in man's non-rational psyche and concerned that, through empiric study, its nature should be understood and its cooperation enlisted. Most unfortunately (and most probably this was the basic reason for the final collapse of Hellenic Roman civilization), Aristotle's proposals for this vital study were never followed up. By 200 B.C., the fatal division had taken place: the natural sciences (special study of the working of the outer world and what Kant called "The Realm of Means") confined themselves to objective phenomena. These students of molar physics naturally accepted, increasingly, the handy hypothesis of mechanism as being in fact the universal law of materialism. And they accepted the even handier and more dubious assumption that our senses, as we use them, present us with a wholly objective world. When from mathematics, physics, and astronomy such scientists went to physiology, the notion that the body also was a machine, or at best a chemical still, could hardly be avoided.

On the other hand, "The Realm of Ends" was left to the professional specialized philosopher who used logic and rhetoric to convince the mind and inspire the emotions. As Dodds (19) remarks, "After Empedocles the seer and the naturalist fell apart."[150] Zeno and Chrysippus are the two thinkers who shape Stoic thought (from 304 to 205 B.C.) and make popular, with all men of character, a pattern of prestige: the Stoic philosopher who was to rule the conscience, and at times the law and legions, of the Roman world. But certainly these vastly influential founding fathers of intellectual nobility have no concept of psychophysical or psychological training. They are simple rationalists[151] and hence, as Toynbee and others have pointed out, at the end the Stoics have a frankly materialistic cosmology.

It was inevitable, therefore, that Neo-Platonism should return to the problem of psychology and to this question: If our present focal length of consciousness gives a highly inaccurate picture of things and an inadequate insight into ourselves, could there be any methods whereby we might apprehend reality more accurately and conduct ourselves better?

Plotinus is, of course, not only an ascetic, not only one who regards this world as being at best a therapeutic prison.[152] He is also an ecstatic. And he values these experiences of ecstasy not only as being much more convincing than argument but as having a much more efficacious effect on character. However, he does not know nor, as far as we can learn, does he investigate in order to know, how these highly desired, transforming states might be regularly obtained.

Plotinus was suspicious of anything that might degenerate into magic. He did not despise method. He thought that music and mathematics were good preparations for philosophy. He certainly wished to explore, but it is surely going beyond our data about him, and the limits which we know he set himself, to say as Friedrich Heinrich Geffcken says, "he investigates." True, he attended a séance, but with almost the aloofness with which Ramakrishna is said to have sat out, in trance, a Tantra performance. It seems more just to say that if specifically ethical philosophy flowered with Socrates and its stoic fruit fully set in the *Meditations* of Marcus Aurelius, then with Plotinus' *Enneads* the condensed and mature kernel was formed from which sprang the tree of medieval monastic contemplation. Socrates served as a soldier-citizen; Marcus Aurelius ruled as a philosopher–Emperor. By Plotinus' time, the thinking world is ready for the cloister where, protected from the raw actualities of social life, the thinker, by contemplation, seeks in trance to make the "flight of the alone to the Alone." Philosophy had come to where it could only teach escape. The natural sciences had for three centuries (200 B.C.–A.D. 100) found increasingly that understanding of nature and power over the environment were obtained by regarding the universe as a vast machine. No wonder that when the only two possible choices seemed to be "flee to the dear fatherland" (heaven) or "clear your

Appendix D

mind of cant: you and all mankind are basically beasts, conscious automata," nearly everyone thought that man is a pawn of fate and that human nature cannot be changed.

And yet society did go on; and though the structure of the state collapsed, a concealed, re-enforcing network of community endured. There was a minority that neither ran away to the desert nor threw away the armor of its soul. Epicurus had probably been right in expressing his contempt for culture. The oxide of pedantry was spreading over the bright intelligence of scholarship. The pursuit of learning regardless of significance was stultifying understanding. His ironic dismissal of natural science unless it can yield knowledge that helps men attain to Ataraxy, the God's eye view of complete objectivity, is also comprehensible.

To put it mildly, to what end (and certainly our age is asking this question) if natural science gives us the power to flash all matter into energy and we are still subject to passions that make us stampede like panic-stricken beasts? The Stoics were even more anxious, and their success in winning politically powerful recruits made them more concerned to have a system that would unfailingly give *apatheia* [and] invulnerability. These keepers of the consciences of proconsuls and emperors actually opposed, and helped largely to get rejected, the heliocentric view of the cosmos for fear that this larger cosmology would disturb their system of arguments, the proofs they adduced for the truth of their philosophy.

Yet we know that their systems of discipline, and those of the Epicureans, were painfully inadequate. Epicureanism sank to be synonymous with hedonism, and Stoicism shrank until it was indistinguishable from despair. But we also know that the men who had to keep law and order going (and to fight a rear action with the military system to prevent the legions from becoming leeches on a citizenry that was losing any right to deserve protection) did find a mystery, a masonry, to hold themselves together.

After the second century A.D., Mithraism is the cult of the decent army man. Its shrines are found all over the Empire, wherever the Legions were encamped. We do know that it used the limited environment, for the initiation took place underground. There was then the grotto-grave: an earth rite. There was also baptism; and to add to what does not seem to have been a real immersion that could produce some degree of shock, there appears to have been, in most cases at least, the *taurobolium*. The postulant was laid in a grave over which were placed hurdles. As he lay underneath, a bull that had been made to kneel on the hurdles was stabbed and its blood poured down over him. Whether this produced temporary suffocation we do not know. There is even a hint of possible fire worship, in that Mithra himself was in origin a lesser Persian god, a being identified with the Sun by a people that already for some centuries were specific fire worshipers. The use of blood and the forgiveness of sins show, however, that this was a guilt religion with puritan morality and repression techniques. Hence, though it could postpone social collapse, the energy was released only by repression, not generated by cocharging. So Mithraism failed and was superseded by a religion that was confessedly other-worldly, with an acuter sense of guilt, a fanatic hate-fear toward all who did not submit to its view of things, and a ... belief in blood as the one defense against eternal damnation. Under Christianity, the Roman Hellenic world sank into night.

At this point, where in the vestiges of a civilization whose intelligence was about to hibernate must we look for the rudiments of a psychology and psychiatry? The place seems to be in the queer tangle of what is known as theurgy. Theurgy was the name for certain practices through which contact with God could be obtained. The word appears to have been chosen by a certain Julian the Theurgist who lived between A.D. 150 and 200. He was quite rightly weary of theologians, people who argued about God. He "worked upon the Divine" and claimed he could manifest That. He was the son of a Chaldean philosopher. Is there any clue given us here, which might suggest why hereabouts could be a possible point where psychophysical methods to contact the subconscious might be detected?

The Chaldeans were the people in whose country (Mesopotamia) astrology had arisen (and so the basis of astronomy had been laid). The great astrological library of Assurbanipal, the Assyrian King of the mid-seventh century B.C., clearly seems to be the basis of all Western and Eastern astrology. Its basic system is even back of Chinese astrology. Astrology did not merely chart the heavens and there read man's inevitable fate. Why seek to know what could not

Appendix D

be prevented? *The Chaldean Oracles*, which this Julian issued,[153] are astrological. But it is astrology mixed, as it would seem was all astrology, with alchemy. Every star had its chemical and psychological counterpart; for example, Mercury is a star and a metal, and mercurial is a temperament. This, of course, seems pathetic or impudent hocus pocus. Still it is strange that a thinker as important in the neo-Platonic tradition as Proclus should have prized such stuff, saying that theurgy can give "the purifying powers of initiation."[154] And Proclus does give at least one reference that shows he was dealing not only with the illusions of sympathetic magic but (and dangerously) with real biochemistry, with drugs that affect the psychophysique. For he remarks that if the eyes are anointed with strychnine (or even other chemicals) they will see visions. Lately, investigation into the odd but constant association of astrology and alchemy has suggested (through research in the middle term, physiology) a solution for this puzzle. Hidden under the oxide of magical superstition, there may be purposely disguised attempts, not always fruitless, to reach the subconscious through psychophysical methods.

In the Indian Hatha Yoga, charts of the body (Part III, Chapter 3), the *chakras,* and lotuses undoubtedly refer to the ductless glands. And all of the Hatha Yoga exercises are directed to arousing them.

The trouble with all such research in the ancient world was threefold: (1) Most of the magic was simply mistaken science. Like should lead to like. But obvious likenesses are often misleading. (2) Some research went off on a tangent seeking not to help everyone to make peace with his own inner nature but to find and exploit, for purposes of investigation into hypnosis and extrasensory perception, young persons who easily dissociated (mediums). (3) All these researchers wanted quick results. They had, unhappy seekers, to be in a hurry. The Western civilized world, with its tolerance of ancient religions and its emergent sciences, was going into coma. The orthodox church was becoming increasingly stringent in its demands and increasingly cruel in punishing any deviations. Proclus had to flee. The Eleusinian mysteries are proscribed and Eleusis closed by Justinian's decree. Henceforward, all research must be underground.

Nevertheless, throughout the Middle Ages we do find occasional references to indicate that an underground did exist. How far the mask of magic was merely a concealment for unorthodox psychophysical investigation and for the employment, however fragmentary, of the five ordeals and initiations, we can never be sure. Nor can we be certain as to how far this mask distorted man's outlook and made him fancy that he could control Nature with spells. However, we can detect two deep currents.

The first is what might be called a back-to-Nature cult. Eusebius, the Church historian who lived when Christianity had risen to imperial power, tells us of the Adamites, a sect that met, literally, underground: a restricted environment. Its members appeared nude at their meetings, maintaining that by grace they had been returned to the primal innocency of unfallen Nature. The Church, having already given up its charitic love feasts (the *agape*) and become ascetic, was highly suspicious of such proceedings. Nevertheless, these methods of panaesthetic cocharging apparently went on.

The Church could not wholly forget its own beginning nor brand these practices as being obviously depraved. At the earliest *agapes* such intense releases were experienced that, as Fr. Alfred Loisy has said, each Eucharist of the Risen Lord had as its regular sequel a Eucharist of the Paraclete. But this first contagion lessened, and in the second phase only special persons, individual *prophetes*, could dissociate. Soon, however, this gift also gave out. Paul had ruled, "I suffer not a woman to speak." Hence there appears the interesting psychic phenomenon of the subintroductae. A *prophetes* (who could no longer go into trance himself) took about with him a young woman whom he hypnotized. From her glossolalia he picked out pertinent passages, passages that were relevant to his message. In the early Christian church, this common occurrence of hypnotic practice (it went on until the time of Cyprian, A.D. c. 200–258) had an interesting addition. The *prophetes* and his medium slept together, sharing the same bed, but coitus must not take place. Some such panaesthetic cocharging seems to have been continued by the Adamites. Increasing asceticism in the Church and loss of all psychological interests among a lay folk that was becoming increasingly barbarian probably brought such practices to a standstill and certainly made it impossible for such a cult to leave records.

Appendix D

In Byzantine history itself, there are one or two references to magical and possibly psychical research. The eleventh-century author, Michael C. Pellus, mentions such matters. The mask of magic certainly bobs about in the background of the theologically obsessed centuries. The only orthodox way of shifting the focus of consciousness was physical self-violence.[155] Hence, any sensation that was not dysphoric was suspect. When the churchmen had time and strength to turn against the various undergrounds that spread beneath the rigid life-rejecting pall of orthodoxy, we know that the two enemies the Church most feared, and so most hated, were the Witch Cult[156] in the north and the Cathars in the south.

The Witch Cult was a simple fertility cult. The legal reports of the witch trials give hints that it may have used a water ordeal. For example, a witch was said to be detectable by her dread of running water, an inability to cross a stream, and also by her power not to drown if thrown into water. (Later, this was naturally misrepresented as the power to float on water.) They also—at least at the midsummer Beltane feast—"went through the fire" by leaping through bonfires, a practice retained in rural Ireland into the nineteenth century. They claimed to be friends of the lightning and they said that Satan appeared in thunderstorms, "glowing, hissing, his fingers shooting sparks"—if you touched him, you received a shock.

Some rude knowledge of respiratory and sensory control (tested by water immersion, fire, and electric shock) seems then to be suggested. Unfortunately, it seems clear that not only did their principal aim become magical power, and mainly for malignant purposes, but the means was thought to be chiefly through the witches being fertilized by the Satan figure. A coven was traditionally composed of ten females and two males (an old devil and a young devil). There were certain Dionysian dances and there are references to vegetable drugs being taken. The women were then fertilized; often, apparently, with a hollow stone phallus, for they frequently told the court that "his" (Satan's) "nature was cold like spring water in me." There is, in this crude procedure, no hint of any methodic raising of the charge of the body to higher vitality, and the mind to an enlarged and extended focus, by panaesthetic dilation and diffusion.

The Church's quarrel with the Cathars in the south was that they were more ascetic than the orthodox. There can be little doubt that this was a life-denying Ascetic movement coming out of the East, passing through Bulgaria and so into South Europe. Their name, Cathars, shows that theirs was a creed of purgation.

The attack of the Church on these two opposite ends of deviation was so ferocious that the two movements disappeared. And there was little if any spirituality, no charity, and not much sincerity in the assault.[157] For the time being "the peace of Tacitus" was established, on the surface, throughout the shattered countryside: *ubi solitudinem faciunt pacem appellant*.

What went on underground? Can it be that this need to make all life a development of consciousness, to be able to treat the seventy-year cycle as being a five-sectioned series of growth stages, is inherent? Further, if this is so, can it be that whenever stimulant is increased (and breakdown does not intervene), then with the dilation being heightened, the subject not only can endure but requires and finds deep relief in confinement and constriction (the limited environment and cerementing)? Heighten the stimulant even further, and when the organism has learned to react to total restriction with passive submission, it is ready to struggle with an intense effort against a powerful, moving, and fluid environment. Heighten again the stimulant and what began as submission, then went on into wrestling with an outer element, now becomes an interior effort to expand. By breath dilation, the rib cage is expanded and the air ordeal raises the psychophysique to a still higher alertness. If the tension can be stepped up once more, then the charged body can endure temperatures which, if the subject were casually relaxed, would have been not merely exhausting and debilitating but destructive. Such temperatures would be actually stimulating and energizing. This would account for the immunity to fire that the maenads and dervishes have when they are at the height of their dance-induced frenzy.

Restriction, catharsis, respiratory dilation, the tonic sting of heat: these four conditions of the ordeal aspect of the four basic mysteries[158] may always be sought and clumsily contrived as the organism, debilitated by *taedium vitae*, dissipated by pointless

Appendix D

repetition of indulgence, or nagged by dull aches and pains, strives to fight back, spur itself out of its entropic morass, and rouse its own unkindled powers. This belief that it is inherent in man to seek these tonic liberations (and that lacking traditional knowledge of the mysteries, he will and must attempt in some wise to achieve a relief, or rather a release) is not without substantiation.

Colin Still's remarkable study of *The Tempest* seems to make it highly probable that a supreme literary genius, belonging to the close of the first quarter of the Modern Age, has left on record in his last play a description of these four stages. If this is so then, as Still indeed believes, the fourfold development of man is a demand as inherent in his postbirth nature as the growth of eyes and ears were inherent in his prebirth nature. In his *The Timeless Theme*, Still (83) has put together the fragmentary data that, as we have seen, permit an outline reconstruction of the mystery rites. He has painstakingly correlated these data (1) with the Western Gnostic semi-esoteric tradition (58), (2) with the Western epic poems of the primary and secondary phases of the Ascetic Age—*The Aeneid* and *The Divine Comedy*, and (3) with the cryptic plays that culminate in *The Tempest*. He presents detailed evidence to show that all these literary works are veiled descriptions of the triple theme: first, that man is a fourfold creature whose elements may be mystically described as being of earth, water, air, and fire: secondly, that this creature may be restored to wholeness and completion by a method that will recover him from his faulting and fractionation: thirdly, that there are specific steps and techniques whereby this fourfold creature may be made to recover his divine status. Still then goes further and indicates that the reintegration of man-the-fourfold is by the four mysteries of his nature being released in him through the ordeals and initiations of earth, water, air, and the double aspect of fire as heat and light.

The tradition of the mysteries, as Still points out, maintains that the consciousness of man has to rise through seven planes. This means that each of the four ordeal initiations has, intercalated between it and the one above, a transitional stress phase. This is symbolized (between the first and second mysteries) by the analogy of what he calls mire, a mixture of earth and water. As earth liquefies, it becomes morass or quicksand, a midstate on which man cannot walk and in which he cannot swim. It will neither bear him on its surface nor let him float in it. And since he can neither rest on it nor ride it, man sinks in it.

In turn, as water vaporizes it becomes mist, neither clear water nor clear air. Again, it cannot be swum in nor may one safely run or fly in it. The pilgrim is lost in it. This would be the transitional stress phase between the second and third mysteries.

As gases combine with the great gas (oxygen) and burn, there is at first no clear light; the air is full of blinding fumes and wavering images. At this level (between the third and fourth mysteries), man is not given vision but fears that he will be consumed; and if he is unprepared, he will be burned. The three transitional stress phases (mire, mist, smoke) are then increasingly severe stress phases because they are phases of transition and therefore of instability. The former state is outgrown. The new one is still not distinct enough to be functioned in.

It will be noticed that in this description of man's growth in consciousness, no place is given to the primary ordeal of birth and infancy, which should have ushered in the first initiation and so been the preliminary stage of the first mystery, the mystery of earth. There is no reference to a conflict as man moves into his primary sensory condition of unreflective physicality, of nonself-conscious bodilyness. Birth is assumed to be a Fall. It is not regarded as being itself a mystery with its two parts of ordeal and initiation. Birth and infancy are not seen as both crisis (a test) and opportunity; a trial followed by an equipment for a task; a perilous offer, the offer to be endued with a restricted, specialized instrument of action (that is, a free-moving, independent body). The taking of a body is not looked on as an inmergence, an incarnation that can be taken well or ill, featly or frustrantly, aptly or mistakenly.

Such an omission of the first mystery indicates that in this great literary tradition of the mysteries, we have a description not of the original basic therapy but of its supplanter. The first great epoch of the mystery psychophysical therapy springs from the time when primal coconscious man had to submit to the sharpening, intensifying, and defining of the focus of his awareness. He had to become objective. With skilled effort, he had to emerge into detachment and immediacy. Trial and error had to become his conscious education. Otherwise his group, repeating with ever more facility its routine solutions, would have sunk—if not into instinct, at least into reflex responses and final answers. This newly separate person must recognize error without dismay; he must remedy faultiness without disgust and treat solutions as being provisional, temporarily useful, but not irrevocably final.

However, as we know, man's growing sense of an awakening self-judgment and his attempt (through a refreshing regression and rebirth therapy, the earth mystery) to prevent society from ankylosing into a gerontocracy[159] saved only a remnant. The main social structure stiffened. Inevitably there followed the heroic disruption; and the violent blunders of that epoch led, in turn, to the further contraction and contortion of consciousness. Self-blame and the desire to be punished took the place of shame seeking revenge; rage reacted into guilt and despair. Life became *ipso facto* disgusting and birth of any sort not a specific concentration but a degradation. As we have seen, such an attitude inevitably fulfilled its own fear and revulsion. Birth did become traumatic, leaving on the child's subconscious a stain of panic and a sense of punitive banishment. The woman was taught, "in sorrow shalt thou conceive." Birth must involve anguish, and after it she is [characterized as] defiled; she must be purified before she is fit to rejoin unpolluted persons.[160]

Not only could such bruised temperaments only look backward, construing any longing for a fuller condition as being proof of a past paradise from which they had been irrevocably exiled by the sin of growth and encapsulation in a body. The body became *ipso facto* a foul prison. The life in the body and the lives of the future generations could only be viewed as at best an arrest, but more likely as a steady degeneration (from the Age of Gold, through Silver, on to Bronze and, finally, Iron). The entering into human existence was in itself a fall, a fatally degrading experience wherein a creature enmeshed in a web of animal passions was penned in a vile, sunless crypt. For this reason Plotinus, as we have seen, forbade the celebration of his birthday. Birth was a disastrous deposition. This outlook is other-worldly for it says that life can only be unmaimed, de-corrupted in a transcendental, fleshless, bodiless state.

Indeed, the great epic poets on whom Still relies (to show that they carried on the account of the mysteries) demonstrate by their own characters and master compositions that they, like Plotinus, were ascetic-pessimistic. Virgil was known for his melancholy. "Thou majestic in thy sadness at the doubtful doom of humankind," remarks his intense admirer, Tennyson. And Maecenas, patron of Virgil and his fellow poet Horace, used to say that when, as his clients, they regularly dined each side of him, "Here I sit between sighs and tears." Dante's character was that of an embittered man, all whose hopes for himself and for humankind were the other side of the grave. That these hopes were of the most moderate, his great work leaves no possible doubt. Virgil (who in his own works had said that it was all too easy to slip into hell and all too difficult to get out again—*"facilis descensus Averno ..."*) in the *Divine Comedy* acts as Dante's guide through the dismal regions. Dante's masterpiece is a romance in which the greater proportion of the human actors end in eternal torment. To call this a *Divine Comedy* indicates, of course, that humankind is a damned species, that this world is so fallen as to be the common launching ground for hell and that every enjoyment and appetite is tainted with mortal sin.

The fact that the exoteric medieval mystery tradition was a degenerate, life-rejecting form of the original life-accepting, life-hopeful mystery therapy is shown by the absence of the preliminary earth mystery in this later account. Hence, too, the further mistake in regard to the fourth mystery, which we must now note in the degenerate life-denying tradition. Because of the first omission of the earth mystery, the fourth mystery (that of fire) is inevitably misunderstood and so its basic efficacy is lacking.

In extracting the fourfold mystery pattern out of *The Tempest*, and from references in the great Ascetic epics, Colin Still, following the basic tradition, rightly divides the fire ordeal initiation into two. But, although (page 23 of *The Timeless Theme*) he owns that the original traditional division is into rainbow (lower fire, prismatic light) and *aether* (fire) and that the rainbow was mistakenly seen as the possible frontier between air and the *aether* of space, yet he maintains that this "use ... of the Rainbow needs no other warrant than the fact that nothing exists in the objective world of nature which could serve

Appendix D

as well [as a simile] in the ... seven-fold scale." It is an "age-old system of *imagery*." In other words, he is saying that the mystery is purely symbolic. At best it is a ritual that pre-typifies the state of the soul after death, a sacramental performance that guarantees a life beyond the grave, free of the flesh.

This use of the rainbow, the symbol of hope after the deluge disaster and re-establishment of diplomatic relationships after all deviationists have been drowned, is further evidence that this ascetic form of the mythos is degenerate. It is more evidence that it stems from the dawn of the Protoindividualistic Age, as the Flood stories do and as also do the stories of a Babel Tower built by men's impious, independent efforts to stand on their own structure above any further inundation.

As it happens, we know that Greek thinkers, watching upper atmospheric conditions, had speculated as to what lay above the common lung-comfortable air of sea level up to timberline height, that region of perpetual snow. This, it appeared, was the home of that uncanny, terrible blue fire that was so awfully, instantly immolating in one blinding, deafening flash: so different from the quiet, licking and cheerful glow of the domesticated red flame of the comforting hearth and the yellow eye of the guiding lamp. The mystery of the two fires, the coarser and the subtler, is then the distinction between molecular, vibratory heat and electric atomic energy.

In the original life-accepting, pre-guilt mythos, there would be, then, five stages or ordeal initiations that we can put in modern psychophysical terms. Between each of these could be fitted the four transitional stress phases delineated by Still and for which he uses the symbols of mire, mist, smoke, and rainbow. This would then give us nine planes of development-growth, through which human consciousness must rise, instead of seven:

(1) The first plane is birth itself; and this is the first ordeal, the first test. Even when there is no trauma, even when the mother's fear-contractions do not physically strain and damage the child, birth must be a severe crisis. For here is the change from the unconscious womb life to sensory separateness and voluntary end-gaining movement. Choice has to be made: to advance or to cling to unconsciousness. So there is conflict between the homeostatic condition,

when growth was so involuntary as to be unconscious, and the new demand to move and seek, try and see, err and correct.

(2) The second plane would be the first transitional stress phase, symbolized by mire, the mixed elements of earth (stability) and water (movement).

(3) However, when the third plane (the second of the five stages) is reached, the new mobile condition of childhood is arrived at. The adjustment to movement is made and the decision to accept initiative is taken. This is the noradrenaline state of early childhood, of looking for heroical adventures. This state, in turn, loses its assurance, conviction, and clarity.

(4) Therefore, this second transitional stress phase (the fourth plane) Colin Still calls the condition of mist. This is the one in which contact is half-lost but vision is only half-won, fleeting, enigmatic. Here, delusions (premature constructions made from new, half-apprehended insights) may betray and temporarily destroy, that is, reduce the consciousness factor back to its primary condition, of the will to be, and make it start again from base.

(5) If, however, on the fifth plane the ordeal of adolescence can be met, if the initiation of air can be gone through with proper aid, then vision does become clear. The adolescent, instead of becoming a fanatic mortifier, a schizophrenic, becomes a person of clear seeing who can adjudge and estimate himself. He can understand his station of service not as being servile but as being the undergoing of a training—a training that will be needed, when he is called on to command, in order that he may understand and value his subordinates and be not only their commander but their guide (the *paidogogos*). He can also be the pattern of prestige that even now acts as leader to those juniors who, in the age group under him, are leaving boyish heroicism and entering on their period of confusion, the transitional stress phase of mist.

(6) The adolescent state of vision in turn enters into the third transitional stress phase, the sixth plane. For this state, Still uses the symbol of smoke, smoky fire. The clear conviction of the well-adjusted adolescent has to be given up for the capacity to sustain wider uncertainties, to accept the compromises of actual administration and the strain of responsibility for directives, the success and rightness of which cannot be assured.

Appendix D

(7) But the transitional stress phase of fume from fire must pass into the seventh plane, the fourth stage of lower fire. And the state of first maturity is reached when the smoke of confusion leads to the clarity of flame. It is here that the later rendering of the tradition of the rebirths (ordeals and initiations of the mysteries) shows most clearly its distortion and devitalization under the mortificatory, life-rejecting mistake of saying that birth into a body was, *ipso facto*, somehow a blunder, a fall into ignorance. By those who held to the doctrine of original sin, it was assumed that a good birth, which would retain knowledge of the purpose for which a human body was taken, was impossible. Therefore the body, being a fallen body, should be shed as soon as possible. It cannot be developed.

Hence, as Colin Still and all ascetic interpreters of the mysteries must hold, the mysteries must be increasingly symbolic. The earth mystery has disappeared. The water rite has become only a sprinkling. Air and fire ("he shall baptize you with the Holy Breath and with Fire," the saying attributed to John the Baptist) are reduced to metaphors.

Nevertheless, as we have seen in Section III, Chapter 4, the fire mystery does still exist. It can be practiced and it is employed as a psychophysical therapy.

(8) Having successfully passed through the initiation of lower fire, the individual now enters the fourth and last transitional stress phase, the eighth plane. This is that iridescent phase (for which Colin Still uses the symbol of the rainbow) in which the mind is dazzled.

(9) Now comes the final ordeal of second maturity. This is the grand climacteric when the individual passes not only from first maturity to second maturity, from office to retirement, but also enters on what Warthin calls the involuntionary curve; it should be named the exvolutionary re-dilation. This ordeal is marked, as are all the ordeals, by the struggle caused by the individual having to make a new choice, by his having to decide to throw his ship onto a new tack. He has to resolve to terminate an activity that has served its purpose but in which he may be caught by the inertia of momentum, the rhythm of routine, of use and wont. He is encompassed by final melancholy. The manic-depressive madness which, as we have seen in Section II, Chapter 4, is the specific psychosis of the total individual,

Humanic man of first maturity, may now also attack in a peculiar, baffling, and distressing form.

For, as this age stage is re-dilational, there comes a return of generalized euphoria. This, as we said in Section III, Chapter 5, is often mistaken as a return of the reproductive phase. It is more precisely, but usually not more understandingly, called the second childhood. It is the recovery of the panaesthetic sensoriness. I have called it (see Section I, Chapter 5) the emergence of the Leptoid condition. It is not a last flash in the pan, a flare of the dying candle. It could be likened to the leap in the womb of the eighth-month embryo as the electric force in it makes it shake with the alerting summons toward the adventure of birth. For now that electric field, which in nine months built up the embryo from a single cell and then kept the whole body in repair for its nine-hundred-month life of five stages, releases itself and sheds the physical husk.

Here, then, is a completed cycle, from implicit potential through explicit actual to potential again. "That which drew from out the boundless deep turns again home." But with no revulsion, no spastic struggle to escape the twisted coil, the muddy vesture of decay. Death can and should be sublimation by a perfect volatilization—conscious, voluntary, timely, apt—the converse and complement of the freely chosen, temporary condensation and focus of birth.

The ninth plane, then, is not only the ordeal of second maturity but the initiation of the finer fire (aether), the electric surge whereby (as described in Section III, Chapter 5) the nervous system, trained to receive high current, rises like a skilled surf-rider and with perfect balance on the shoulder of the comber, is steadily borne far up onto the level beach.

~~~~~~~~~~~

Thus we can see a complete cycle of nine planes through which human consciousness must rise to complete itself. For the ascetic midindividual, not knowing whence he came, ignorant of his entire nature, and made egotistic by guilt, could only regard birth as being a fall from blissful awareness into sinful ignorance. So Plato saw it. Sophocles was briefer but more explicit: "Happy is he who dies young; but only truly blessed is he that never was born."[161] Hence, for the ascetic, life in the body is a labor and a snarl; an unintended collapse,

Appendix D

not an intentionally and temporarily limited concentration; a trap, not a valve. And death is an escape from a load that could not be eliminated by volatilization. The soul, for its own egotistic ease, hopes to escape and enjoy a personal, unencumbered paradise.

The full self-transforming mystery taught that the entire transcendent self, as manifested in the electric field, chose to take a body, and in these two lives out of each of which we must be born (the embryo life and the life in the postwomb experience) to attain a complete awareness of intention and of timeliness. After which it can return to a completely enlightened potentiality.

In addition to the studies of Colin Still, even further evidence has now been brought forward suggesting that there was a traditional underground that preserved, at least in partial form, the original life-accepting religion. There is some reason to believe that at least until the sixteenth century there survived a series of rites that dealt with the body-mind, the soul-flesh unit, as a reciprocant binary system. Fränger (25) gives striking evidence of this in his masterly study of the painter Hieronymus Bosch (1450–1516). Jeroen van Aken (to give him the name he first carried) was a Flemish artist and he had been chiefly remembered by students of art. For he greatly influenced two masters who have been much more popular than he: Peter Brueghel and Lucas Cranach. His own art was considered too grotesque, too satiric, too literary. This, undoubtedly, it is. And as the need to convey a cryptic message (as in *The Tempest*) can distort a design, even when the hidden meaning conforms with public prejudice since the doctrine to be conveyed is ascetic, even more will obvious beauty be sacrificed to secret sense if the doctrine is not only esoteric but heretical.

Much of Bosch's work is plainly satire: bitter sarcasm directed at the corruption of the Church, which claimed to be ascetic but which largely was ruthlessly self-indulgent. However, his masterwork, *The Garden of Earthly Delights*, is the alternative he offers to an asceticism that had failed and become corrupt. This strange picture Philip II of Spain (apparently quite uncomprehendingly) cherished in his austere bedroom at the heart of his grim palace, the Escurial. No one who reads Fränger's learned study can help being convinced that in this enigmatic masterpiece we have an invaluable and (as far as we know) a unique well-shaft down which we can catch sight of the underground river of the original mysteries still going its hidden way when in the upper world the Renaissance had already entered its middle age and the Reformation was at the door.[162]

The picture is in triptych form. The left panel shows Eden. Here, God the Son, the restorative Eternal Love, is presenting Adam (who is just being wakened from a deep sleep) with Eve, the love partner who has just been produced from Adam's side. The paradisal scenery around is inhabited by quaintly monstrous creatures that all carry esoteric significances. The right panel shows a Hell where pride and violence (the robber Knight) and even the cruel hunter are given tit for tat. The reckless gamblers, the gluttonous religious, the pitiless, the rapacious, the greedy are devoured. A hawk-horus-headed monster, symbol of the all-seeing eye set in the mask and armed with the flesh-tearing scimitar-shaped beak of the bird of prey, rends, bolts, and voids his victims through his pierced throne into a cloaca passage.

Yet even this revolting underground sewer has its exit in the great central panel. For since the Cosmos always conceives perfection, not only does the fool (if he perseveres in his folly) become wise but the depraved, through the peristalsis of their passions, are at length discharged out into freedom again. Even the musicians are strung in a strange anguish on gargantuan forms of their instruments. Perhaps this is because they used music as an amusement, as an escape and not as one of the sense-trainers to be in play with the orchestra of all the sense-stimulators through which consciousness, using these channels in balanced harmony, attains to ecstasy. However, these mistaken music-makers are being twisted into the right key. They are on the left of this panel wing, close up against the central panel.

Arriving at the center, then, and beginning at the foot, we find this base crowded with exits, emergence orifices. Down in the left corner is, as it were, the master clue, the esoteric signature. For here we find both the portrait of the artist as an initiate and also the portrait of the Grand Master. This is doubly important. Because the face of the Grand Master, here full of humorous kindly power, is the face of the sardonic monster who stands at Hell's center in a swamp, on legs made of dead trees and with an egglike body through which, as

Appendix D

through a dismal inn on the road to the cloaca, the penitential souls must traverse. There, looking out at us over his shoulder, he grimly satirizes his own purgative predicament by being douched by his own ignorant followers to whom he had taught an inadequate doctrine. Now, in this re-emergence in the central panel, he understands Blake's wisdom: that folly, if endured to the utmost, gives wisdom.

Further up on the median line, we find the principal emergence. Adolescent, transformed males and females are coming up from the purgatory on the backs of giant birds.[163] We see these resuscitated people coming alive in a Paradise of Delights that, at this level, is the good earth of fantastic abundance (for example, strawberries and gooseberries as big as a man's head). Here, too, are unmistakable Tantra pictures of the rousing of Kundalini.

Above this are people diving into pools of water. Here we reach the level of the great *gymkhana* (the mounted dance) in which, astride a number of tamed monsters, the rising humans wind in rhythm. Above this is air through which limpid sky figures that have now become completely boyish, sail effortlessly. Elevated and levitated, they soar to where the flights of birds wing through a heaven of fathomless calm and infinite extent.

There is no other work of art that shows us that this underground of the original, ante-ascetic mystery cycle was still extant down to the sixteenth century. As Fränger points out, this picture (which hung before the fascinated, uncomprehending eyes of the greatest burner of heretics, Philip II) was apparently used as a kind of instructive altarpiece when these secret spiritual descendants of the Adamites met to go through their ritual.

Possibly after the sixteenth century, this psychophysical tradition perished. Even the author of *The Tempest*, though referring to a rite made respectably ascetic, writes enigmatically. Reason was probably a greater corrosive of the rite than dogma. As it is often said in Tao, the far Eastern mystery that has also degenerated largely into magic, the uninformed man "mistakes the finger pointing at the moon for the moon itself." Unless the meaning of the practices is clearly understood; unless the performer knows that under all the names (and as the meaning of all the ritual) is a psychophysical technique aimed at producing a psychophysical change, a shift of sensation and a dilation of comprehension, then the whole procedure degenerates into superstitious conjuring and/or pointless sensuality.

With the renewed interest in psychotherapy of the last two generations, there has developed an empiric approach to the mind-body-group relationship. Freudianism begins the exploration with a free-associating patient listened to by a detached analyst. The Jungian method often makes use of drawing, a release instrument less inhibited than speech. The nondirective therapy of Carl Rogers attempts the less restrained association of a companionship that does not even attempt to explain the subject to himself, extending only the extractive vacuum of a reposeful, sympathetic attention.

J.S. Moreno, however, brings in the social factor even more. His subjects are taught to act out their problems, aided by auxiliary performers. Maxwell Jones, in England, has carried this still further. The therapeutic plays are written, rehearsed, stage managed, and performed. And here we are only one step away from the full rite which (when performed with masks, vestments, and scenery) deals no longer with a personal idiosyncratic accident or episode in the life of an individual but with the race life as it manifests itself in each man. Here, the group therapy of the mysteries could re-emerge, and man could be taught how he may cooperate with the life force as it strives to bring him through the five cardinal stages whereby he may attain to reciprocal knowledge, to a full consciousness of the total process.

Fifty years ago, in his introduction to anthropology (*Anthropology*, Home University Library), R.R. Marett remarked, "Civilized man tries to think out his problems; savage man dances them out." It looks as though human history may have come full circle. With self-conscious man's discovery of the sunken continent of his subconscious, man today may at last understand his amphibian nature and learn how to unite, in binary power, his critical and creative mind, his analytic and integral thought, the intensity of his individual focus with the width, comprehension, and aim of the racial consciousness.

Appendix E

LABORATORY EXPERIMENTS IN LIMITED ENVIRONMENT

In the last couple of years, psychologists have been experimenting with what they generally call the limited environment, and they have been studying its effects on the individual who is thus isolated. The first set of experiments to be done fall into the category of what I have called the mystery of earth, the first ordeal and initiation, a womb and birth-recall experience. The best known of these experiments are described in an article titled, "Cognitive Effects of Decreased Variation to the Sensory Environment," by W. Heron, W. H. Bexton, and D. C. Hebb of McGill University in Montreal (44).

The second set of experiments comes under the second category I have used in this book: the second ordeal and initiation, that of the mystery of water, the cathartic rite of immersion. The best known of these are the experiments of John C. Lilly, formerly of the National Institute of Mental Health, the U.S. Department of Health, Education, and Welfare at Bethesda, Maryland.[164]

The first set of experiments (those of Hebb *et al.*) were carried out with subjects that had been encased, horizontally, in body-enclosing containers. In the second set (those of Lilly), the subject was floated in a tank of running water. (See endnote 63.)

I shall refer first to the second set, because Lilly gives, as a preliminary to the water ordeal, a valuable summary from a good collection of accounts written by men and women explorers who had experienced the strange psychological effects of isolation. The following data throw light on the psychological factors involved in the mystery techniques of changing consciousness. If we consider first Walter Gibson's (34) account (*The Boat*) of exposure in an open boat in the Indian Ocean during World War II, we have Stage 1 of such an ordeal. The boat started adrift with 135 persons aboard. Four survived. To the isolation, which of course was not absolute, were added the appalling hardships of exposure and an agonizing shortage of food and water. As the mortificatory ascetics not infrequently demonstrated, the effect of such deprivation on a powerful physique may be to provoke changes of consciousness before complete physical collapse intervened.

Gibson, however, attributes his survival to a certain psychophysical preparedness: (1) some years of training under a tropical sun, (2) his capacity to become completely passive, (3) a conviction of survival, and (4) a companion sharing his conviction. The first week seems to have been the worst. This last fact is confirmed by Joshua Slocum (the first man to sail around the world alone) and Alain Bombard, a French imitator.

Two other factors make for survival: a capacity to project helpful hallucinations and encouraging conversations with a mascot, and intense love of living things (29). After such an experience, the inner life may have grown so strong that speaking to others is done only very deliberately. In his *Alone*, Admiral Richard Byrd (9) describes the oncoming [of] and immersion in the oceanic feeling. Courtauld, the Greenland explorer who was similarly isolated in a polar winter darkness, tells of the same experience. Christiane Ritter (72) describes spells of sixteen-day-long isolation. She found that the preliminary ordeal resulted in initiation, although she had to resist the impulse to walk out into the snow, as [with] the skin-diver, at depths below one hundred and fifty feet, [who] may be tempted to take off their breathing mask. Most survivors report a new inner sense of security, a new integration on a deep basic level.

But let us turn back to the first, and least strenuous, of the artificial restrictions of environment, the tests carried out at McGill

Appendix E

University by Hebb (44). These are quietly arrestive and, as we said above, to some degree parallel the rites of earth, the burial regression and rebirth. Donald Hebb and his colleagues used university students as their subjects in these experiments. Each subject was given twenty dollars a day to submit to what would seem to common sense to be at worst a boring way of earning money—by doing nothing. All that was to be done was to reduce patterning of stimuli to the lowest possible level, when surely the healthy, young, money-scarce student would fall to sleep, lulled with the thought that they would wake up automatically richer. To induce this approved and lucrative laziness, the subject was laid to rest on a well-sprung bed which was entirely enclosed in an air-conditioned cylinder, a kind of comfortably roofed cradle. Arms and hands had their separate rests in roomy cardboard sleeves. The eyes were completely shielded with ski goggles that admitted a soothing golden light. It might be thought that the subject would feel they were drifting back to a holy innocent's heaven full of repose and so feel shut up in measureless content.

However, the consequences were utterly different. The observer watched through a window and regularly asked the subject how he felt. He was not abandoned. Father was alert by the cradle. And yet after several hours, every subject found it increasingly difficult to carry on any organized directed thinking for any sustained period. Suggestibility was much increased, and an acute desire for action and stimuli developed. There were periods when the subject, trying to satisfy these needs, would thresh about in the box like a hooked fish. Then there usually came on a state between sleep and waking. Consciousness first diffused and then thought grew confused. After twenty-four hours, a number began to quit, finding the condition unendurable, quite unnerved by this mysterious ordeal. Those who hung on for forty-eight hours began to have hallucinations and delusions. The hallucinations were, when they had been present for some time, complete projections: that is, they were three-dimensional, and the subject could study their apparently solid volumes and planes by shifting his eyes and his head. While doing this, the subject could give a detailed description of the various features of these projections. And carrying on a conversation with the director of the experiment, in which he described these phenomena, in no wise reduced his vision of them. Indeed, at first the subjects who stuck it out until the hallucinations came on found these phenomena a relief from the intense frustration of the two days of acute boredom. But nearly all quit after seventy-two hours. One who lasted out for five days did go into a sudden spastic condition that looked like a seizure. The EEGs taken from this subject's head, however, failed to show the extreme spike rhythm given off by the epileptic fit.

In a completely unprepared healthy youngster, then, this very simple preliminary approach to the earth-burial rite seems to have produced keen distress because of two induced experiences. The sense of an oncoming awareness that his assumed identity of body and mind was not so, that his body was not himself, awoke the first alarm. The second alarm followed when the mind itself began to alter its frontiers and the self-consciousness began to be invaded by subconscious images. The first was due to the loosening of the links with our anchor in space, the body. The second came on because now, like an ice floe melting in the sea, the surface mind was first drifting from its position in time and, finally, [was] being threatened with the melting-merging of its separate, defined personality in a coastless ocean of indistinct and apparently undirected awareness.

It is clear that if the students could have been prepared, this experience would have been highly instructive and therapeutic instead of leading to baffling distress. The images are projections of repressed aspects of consciousness that since infancy have been buried beneath the level of self-consciousness, sealed under by the socially imposed personality-mask-shroud. Released now, as the ice-crust of conformity is thawed, they are floating to the surface. For instance, as the controlled clinical experiments in the use of mescaline and lysergic acid go on, it is becoming increasingly clear that whether the experience is instructive and highly beneficial, or humiliating and embarrassing, depends wholly (with sane subjects) on one of two things. Is the subject informed beforehand as to what he is about to go through and then given the medicament by a psychiatrist who understands the therapy and has himself experienced its effect? Or is the subject allowed to enter the condition in ignorance and then badgered or abandoned while he is in it?[165] With informed

Appendix E

and instructed subjects, in the mescaline and lysergic acid experiments there are no hallucinations. With the uninstructed, the hallucinations can be intense, apparently solid, and often highly distressing in their grotesqueness.

Some aftereffects were noticed by the subjects of the McGill experiments with this particular form of restricted environment. For several hours after their release from the closed cradle, they found difficulty in seeing the world around them as they had seen it before. And in some of the subjects, the hallucinations hung on only to fade gradually during the day.

Now, when we consider Lilly's experiments, we can see that in his employment of water immersion, he reproduced an ordeal that went a step beyond the relaxed ease of the limited environment of the air-conditioned container. The McGill experiments were "to reduce patterning of stimuli" to the lowest possible level. The aim of Lilly was to reduce "absolute intensity of all physical stimuli" to this lowest level. The subject (Lilly first experimented on himself) was suspended in a tank of slow-flowing water, the temperature of which was kept at 34.5 C. This is a neutral temperature, and so the skin makes practically no reaction to the water. The body is naked save for a head mask that completely blinds the subject, and a very light harness that tethers him by the shoulders. He floats, totally submerged, and his breathing is kept going by the use of a snorkel that extends above the water level. The only tactile sensation comes from the touch of the mask and the tether–harness. The only sounds that reach him are his own breathing and occasional slight water tremors that come from the pipes of the tank. Lilly employed one other subject besides himself. The longest exposure lasted only three hours. Each subject had a full night's rest previous to this immersion. Each had a set of training dips in order to overcome any apprehension as to possible risks: for example, to see if there was to be any distress in breathing, or any physical discomfort.

For the first three quarters of an hour, spontaneous recollections of events lately experienced fill the mind. This is followed by a sense of pleasant relaxation. Lilly is a mature researcher who is much more likely to appreciate quietude (the fruitful acre of the well-sown mind) than is a tonic, kinaesthetic Canadian student. But by the third hour, tension began to be apparent and to grow. This stimulated action. The muscles began to twitch and slow swimming motions started up so as to obtain a positive feeling from contact with the flowing water. A strangely satisfying contentment came from stroking one finger against another. When this almost reflex movement of sensory self-awareness was inhibited and then resumed, the vividness and intensity of the pleasure was increased in proportion to the length of time that restraint had been exercised. If the inhibition was made absolute, then the tension rose so high that the whole situation became unbearable and the subject would have had to be removed from the tank. Somehow, the self-touching relieved, if only temporarily, the self-generated tension charge. Meanwhile, some of the demand for interest-attention discharge was satisfied by becoming intensely aware of the mask contact and the contact of the suspensory harness until, in turn, these points of awareness in the otherwise nearly total insensibility became almost unbearable. When self-stimulation is inhibited up to a certain point of intensity, then consciousness begins to undergo an interior shift. Directed thinking about actual problems changes into reveries and fantasies that are "highly emotional and personally charged." If this is not resisted, the state can be one of relaxed enjoyment. However, if the fantasy is rejected as well as the tactile detensioning, then the projection of visual imagery takes place.

Lilly says:

> I have seen this once, after a two-and-one-half-hour period. The black curtain in front of the eyes (such as one "sees" in a dark room with eyes closed) gradually opens out into a three-dimensional dark, empty space in front of the body. This phenomenon captures one's interest immediately, and one waits to find out what comes next. Gradually forms of the type sometimes seen in hypnogogic states appear. In this case, they were small, strangely shaped objects with self-luminous borders. A tunnel whose inside "space" seemed to be emitting a blue light then appeared straight ahead. About this time, this experiment was terminated by a

leakage of water into the mask. It turns out that exposures to such conditions train one to be more tolerant of many internal activities—fear lessens with experience and personal integration can be speeded up. But, of course there are pitfalls here to be avoided—the opposite effects may also be accelerated in certain cases.

The aftereffects that Lilly and his fellow experimenter noticed were different from those experienced by the McGill subjects, but not less remarkable. The chief peculiarity after the immersion was an alteration in the sense of time. Apparently, some kind of release from the subconscious strain of clock pressure is obtained and a sense of initiative and freedom, of spare-timedness, is enjoyed. Seemingly, the subject is able to experience the day as though it were being started afresh; he feels a *dawn sense*, as Mencius calls it in one of his most intriguing passages. "The subject feels as though he had just risen from bed," with his energy restored by a good night's sleep. We are told that this happy hangover persists so that the "subject finds he is out of step with the clock for the rest of the day"—almost, it seems, in a state of being ahead of time.

Social intercourse also needs adjustment. The subject has slipped not only from the close grip of time but also from the tight clasp of convention. If he is alone long enough (and here these experiments confirm the experience of solitaries) and the levels of physical stimuli are low enough, the "mind turns inward and then projects outward its own contents and processes; the brain not only stays active, despite the lowered levels of input and output, but accumulates surplus energy to extreme degrees. Apparently even healthy minds act this way in isolation. What this means to psychiatric research is obvious: we have yet to obtain a full, documented picture of the range available to the healthy human adult mind." And if we could have more detailed accounts, the possible applications to brainwashing and its opposite (psychotherapy) would be more evident.

Since the above was written, very considerable progress has been made and increasing interest has been shown in this field of study. Jack Vernon, of Princeton, has made a series of studies with the limited environment wherein the conditions were more rigorous than those of Hebb and his associates. For at Princeton, the subject was put into total darkness and confined in an underground room where sound was reduced to a minimum. The subject, however, had some space in which to move about in his tomb, which was furnished with food, bed, and toilet facilities. The subjects, too, were different from those that were used at McGill. They were not Canadian students, most of whom are used to an outdoor life and a very strenuous climate. The Princeton subjects were all post-graduates, and most of them had graduated in mathematics. In consequence, having minds trained to think about pure abstraction, the loss of a world of outward images and contacts did not at the start embarrass them. It was only later, when they had exhausted the pure mental games they were able to play with themselves, that the void began to be noticeable, strange and, in the end, distressing. Nor did these minds hallucinate.

Two reasons have been given for this; the first is the nature of the men who underwent this ordeal. For instance, lysergic acid was first called, as was mescaline and, later, psilocybin, a hallucinogen. However, I have experimented with all of these, under supervised conditions, and in none of them found that they were hallucinatory. A mathematician or anyone trained in critical methods does not seem to be able to hallucinate. It may be that hallucination is, as is possibly all dreaming itself, a defense against the mind straying too far outside the frontiers of the ego.

The second reason is exterior. It is possible that men hallucinate more easily in a half light, and with vague outlines, than in a total dark. Certainly, study of children who possess eidetic imagination would show that the pictures they see are built up from the use of hints and themes suggested by outer patterns, for example, cracks in a wall.

A study similar to Vernon's has now been under way for some four years at the Army Research Center [in] Monterey, California. There, Meyers and Murphy have been at work on a large-scale study of the effects of the limited environment on recruits. The setup consists of a series of cubicles, lightproof but far from wholly soundproof. In these cubicles, volunteers—and it was interesting how many

Appendix E

applied—are confined. Contact is kept with the experimenters by means of an intercom, and so the subject can ask to be taken out as soon as he desires. His reactions are also being electrically registered all the while. The two outstanding facts that have emerged so far would seem to be that the one man who was able to extend his vigil for several days had been, before being conscripted, a surveyor in Alaska and, therefore, accustomed to being completely by himself, out in the sparsely inhabited arctic, for spells of a week or more. And, secondly, that the time required for these subjects to begin to be disoriented, and often to hallucinate, was surprisingly short, some doing so in a couple of hours or even less.

One of the most significant developments, however, in this inner-outer field comes from a colleague of Lilly. Jay T. Shurley has now been able to set up a type of subterranean baptistery. In the vaults of the Medical School and hospital of the University of Oklahoma, he has had excavated a deep cell. In the upper level sits the observer, with his observational and recording instruments. Then deep below this is a circular enclosed tank, or well. In this the subject, stripped and wearing a face mask, is submerged. In his mouth is a small microphone whereby he may communicate with the recorder-monitor seated above. So he is in a giant womb, floating, respirating through the tubes that come into his face mask. The water temperature is at neutral and he naturally floats, suspended below the surface of the water and above the bottom of the tank, in the attitude of fetal balance. The results from these trials have already proved most promising, and Lilly himself looks forward with hope that these improved methods will greatly enlarge our knowledge of consciousness, the subject's knowledge of the extent of his own mind, and serve to aid not only pure research but also therapy in all its forms: curative, preventive, and developmental.

Such, then, are the remarkable results that have been obtained from even tentative investigation of the psychophysical effects that are yielded by the limited environment. Further research, it seems clear, should lead not only to further understanding of these states but to command of (or perhaps it would be wiser and more accurate to say coordination with) these conditions. The closed cradle or mummy-case procedure has in it the rudiments of the conditioning (activity-suspension and regression) which was traditionally brought about by the first mystery: womb regression, removal of birth trauma, and then rebirth. The total-immersion tank has in it the rudiments of the second mystery, of catharsis and the resolving of the repressed rages of the noradrenaline child. So it seems evident that now we should not only develop these two basic initiations but also seek to investigate in equally modern terms the remaining three. If the sarchophagic experience, when carried through to completion, can promise to rid the psyche of the birth trauma, and if the submersion ordeal-initiation has as its entire goal complete deliverance from the heroic, childish, baffled rage and suicidal shame, then the respiratory rite can lift from the adolescent ascetic his load of guilt.

Here again, as we have seen, the limited environment has begun to be used for the psychophysical therapy of non-respiratory lung aeration. Next, research into radiant heat tolerance and adaptation to the supertonic effects of electric surge therapy and stimulation may complete the sequence.

Certainly, from these initial studies in the limited environments, we already have clear promise that experiment with psychophysical conditioning may profoundly heighten the body's tonus and enlarge, reciprocally, the field of consciousness.

Appendix F

A NOTE ON (a) THE SOURCES OF FEAR AS IT EMERGES IN THE FIVE AGES OF THE HUMAN PSYCHE AND (b) THE WAYS IN WHICH HUMANKIND HAS COPED WITH IT

All creatures have to attain a psycho-environmental frontier.[166] Here runs the axis where the individual's will rocks between confidence and mistrust, adventure and caution, curiosity and dread, exploration and shrinking. The young of every vertebrate large-brained species (and indeed some of the young of lower species such as fish—for example, the stickleback and its parentally cared-for young) begin under parental protection to investigate their surroundings. Curiosity seems able to manifest itself early. This extension of enquiry enlarges its periphery up to that circumference which can be covered by the protectorate of the parent or parents. Beyond that, among the big-brained parents, advance by the young is discouraged, warned against, and often actively censored and forbidden. Up to that time, therefore, expansion is commendable; curiosity is the approved drive. Beyond that frontier, restraint is counselled, discretion commended: caution is the rightful reaction.

From his first psychic epoch, his first stage of consciousness, however empathic may have been his mind with a world panpsychically intuited, coconscious, preindividualized man nevertheless apprehended a penumbral distinction between what later was to be distinguished as "on our side" (this was if not the profane at least the secular, the realm of physical means), and "on that side," the sacred, the religious, the frame of spiritual meaning, the realm of ends. Coconscious man in regard to and toward that immediate realm of manageable things felt "at home." He could treat persons and objects in this area as familiars [and] be in play with them, free of formality or protocol. Toward what lay outside that realm, he must advance with respect, with pious preparedness. He does present himself but not with forwardness. He is before the unknown: in vigil to detect, if he may, some symptom as to whether It is withdrawn in impenetrable aloofness or might show any hint of condescension.

This is the state of mind toward what Otto labeled as "the numinous." Toward this encircling, incomprehensible presence that constantly envelops him, man, from the first, could not feel familiarity. Curiosity (that intellectual love which reaches out beyond the emotional love felt for all our familial domesticities; that desire to be amused by, to handle and collect the odd, the strange; that desire to play with the peculiar and feel the fantastic to be funny, to feel a humorous lightness toward that which does not fit) is a mood that cannot be sustained toward the indefinable vastness which, when it is still, seems abysmal, and when [it is] moving, seems incomprehensible and irresistible.

This reaction, or rather this climate of otherness awareness, does not contract into the seizure of that panic which was the classical Greek's reaction when sensing, out in the wild, that he was confronted with Pan. The sense of knowing one must not go too far and must, indeed, now cease to go farther, is not a reaction toward flight but an order to wait, petitionlessly suppliant on the threshold. That sensation is awe. For the awe-ful is not the horrible. It is an apprehension of Presence which fascinates [both] as and because it pervasively enforces on the fascinated the command that he keep his distance.

There are, then, for the primitive, the cosocial, two worlds: one is his world, the other is the world of *That*. But they are polar, they

Appendix F

are reciprocal. This world, man's world, is for him to manipulate so it will yield him means and powers. That world, the realm of the Numinous, is not for him to operate. It is for him to draw on as it offers him the unexploitable, incomprehensible range in terms of which his purpose can be extended beyond the visible-tangible; his meaning can be enlarged to an infinite goal.

The Heroic Age snapped that tie. It ungeared from its axis this ultimate polarity. Soon, however, faced with the depth, that void which the thrust of the heroes' armed conquest could not penetrate, the fascination of awe was no longer felt, and its place was taken by craven fear.

For a time, the hero attempts to rationalize, condense, and narrow to manageable proportions his ungeared fear, the sense of terror at having overstepped his station and being in trespass on ground sacred to an incomprehensible, unwordable presence. As Dodds has pointed out, and as have all experts on the Heroic Age, the hero tries to control fear by proclaiming that the only thing the brave man fears (for has he not smashed and annihilated the old numinous sacerdocracy?) is shame. His "shame culture" offers him freedom from fear by his demonstrating that he cannot be craven. His honor being established, by the killing of any who question his courage or, indeed, offend his dignity, he holds that he has killed fear itself. The death of a rival, or his own death in such combat, assures him of his society's affirmation of his fearlessness. If, like Ajax in a moment of excessive homicidal frenzy, on recovery he finds he has only killed sheep, and so become ridiculous, he can still rid himself of the fear of mockery by killing himself.

However, this attempt to narrow fear into the manageable, expiatable bounds of shame did not contain the terror of the unseen. Soon it was found that the horror of the avenging Furies haunted the hero whose unbalanced physical violence had torn up the roots of the subconscious reverence of the biological inhibition against murder within one's own species.

Hence the Heroic Age passes inevitably into the Ascetic Epoch. For now it becomes clear to the reflective, self-blaming type of individual (the next degree of self-awareness, the schizoid in contrast to the paranoid) that by killing another, maybe more fear-trapped than himself, he has increased, not lessened his fear. So whereas shame was the contraction and escape by means of which the paranoid hero tried in vain to conquer fear, to hold the invading, pervading sense of the abysmal unknown, the ascetic, instead of trying to tackle and dismiss the panic, attempted to make terms with it.

Instead then of shame, to be flung out by physical courage, the ascetic accepts guilt. And in this term, he can approach to an almost real and temporarily personally effective expiation. For now he is, by accepting his responsibility, entering into a renewed relationship contractually conceived between himself and the encircling "Without." As, however, this Without was, in its full emotional potency (in its power to cause fear and require a defense against its otherwise paralyzing, indefensible awefulness), the unseen intangible, men all too naturally assumed that, as they could not make out what it was up to, and so could not gather what it was telling them to do [or] how it intended them to behave, therefore it was best to abstain from anything that might provoke it.

Further, it seemed reasonable that, as they could not get into direct touch with it or even see it, they must assume it dwelt somewhere beyond their world of bodies, functions, and appetites, and was itself totally inhuman. Hence, only if they were total abstainers from all physical life could they contact this power. Not only would it not communicate with the indulgent: you could only hope when you died (and so presumably, having left the body and the body having fallen to pieces, you passed wholly into the realm of the Without) to be at best lost, more likely nightmared, or thrown back into a new human body to repeat the circuit of ignorant folly, suffering, and death, unless you had made expiation for being an appetitive, reproductive creature.

So as the heroic effort to focus and hold fear had failed; in turn the ascetic attempt to make terms with dread also failed. The hero, unable to feel awe, tried to make dread manageable by defining it as shame and confining it to an ordeal surmountable by physical courage. With one's own bodily death in the wager, and so honor vindicated, fear was presumed to have been killed with the death of one's rival.

The ascetic knows how much deeper and wider lie the roots of fear. He cannot, therefore, confine so shallowly-narrowly the span

Appendix F

and abyss of dread. He goes beyond the frontier of man's working world into the circumambient Beyond: the vast, enveloping, chartless unknown. But he also feels sad, sure that past experience has shown that his overtures cannot secure Its favors in and for his actual physical life, that is, bring him good fortune in his this-worldly affairs. Nor can any appeal even assure that It will abstain from intrusion into his small hard-won territory, his homeland of controlled and ordered livelihood. The ascetic's hope is, in the end, no more than to learn (in the same hard way that the hero learned the irresistible, implacable laws that rule visible nature) how to discover and follow the laws that run invisible and intangible nature.

This in turn taught him that he who renounced was not granted any more protection (freedom from pain and loss) than the unthinking who snatched what he could and enjoyed while he might. There was no more discernible a natural moral law which punished the physically indulgent, than there was evidence of a natural moral law that granted its observers physical rewards or protection from damage. In short, the idea of law as supposed to be manifested in punitive karma (with its accent on punishment and suffering being wholly due to the fact that one had a physical body with its natural appetites) was recognized as being still as anthropomorphically distorted as was the idea of law supposed to be illustrated and indeed confirmed by the repeated experience of good luck.

The fourth stage of man, Humanic man, emerged. Regarding himself as a total individual, surrounded by his equally completely individualized fellows, and all of them contained within a completely unconscious mechanistic cosmos, Renaissance man not only denied that he had a conscience (if he felt its misgivings, he called them hangovers from a disproved anthropomorphic superstition) but that he had any grounds for any sort of fear. "Glory to man in the highest for man is the master of things!"

But as Humanic man was ignorant of his repressed extra-individual consciousness, he could not define and so confront his fear. He could not rationally conceive awe, for reverence was an atavistic impulse rising from a false, disproved teaching. Shame was even more ridiculous, the craven subservience of an uninformed coward challenged by an even less rational bully, boasting his animal muscular strength. Guilt was only another step down into ridiculous objection. The big muscular bully was projected, hoisted into the vacant, harmless sky and given, in exchange for his club, the thunderbolt.

But inevitably, as man gave up these two methods of condensing awe (which had turned into terror that was first reduced to shame and discharged by courage, and next condensed as guilt and expiated by penitence and absolution) terror once more became pervasive, terror that is unmanageable just because it cannot be defined, confronted, and contacted.

Hence, Humanic man has to end. For his specific age—[which] was to complete man's coming of age, the age of the completely rational, analytic, objective individual—has become the age of anxiety, the age of fear, pervasive, indefinable, inexpressible, unmentionable. And fear, for the creature that sees and surfacely feels itself in itself complete, an all-one, is in fact the confession that he is completely alone.

This must end in intensifying isolationism as this modernic man explores the ever-expanding vastness of the macrocosmos shown by his radar telescope, and the hyperintensity of the microcosmos revealed by his hyper-X-ray electron microscope. For as this rack of hypersensory knowledge tears apart the sane, sensual man's world of common sense, man today, forced into postmodernity, finds that he is not merely "a stranger and afraid, in a world I never made." He discovers that there is no one world, made by someone else for something else. He discovers, far more startlingly, that there are as many worlds as there are apprehending systems to apprehend them. He has to face the awe-ful discovery that as his mind grows, he can and must apprehend how large a part he takes in composing his cosmoi. The simple dualism of the macrocosm and the microcosm was but a beginning symptom of his mind's expansion.

Therefore, as there are as many ranges of cosmoi as man can make his mind range, out and in, to apprehend them, so we come to understand Niels Bohr's summary of the meaning of the revolution (or rather mental mutation) which we call the end of Classical Physics: "This," said the late doyen of modern Physics, "means one thing for all of us: the end of the 2,400-year search for objectivity." There

Appendix F

is and can be no rainbow for you when you stand where its onlooker sees it to be touching the earth. Similarly there is no "fact" in itself. The long-hoped-for, basic, atomic, irreducible unit does not and never did exist.

But, conversely, we have simultaneously discovered that we, the field of onlookers, are only one facet of us, the field of finders. "Definition is limitation." But it is also the recognition of the field out of which the find, the fact, has been extracted. Today we are discovering something more than facts. We perceive the continuum out of which we extract them. We explore the setting in which the find, the fact, not merely lies, but functions, performs, exercises, and influences, as an integral feature of an uncircumscribed whole. The atom, we are told, is in a reciprocal-field relationship with the entire macrocosmos.

Finally, this matrix mind of ours, which is in this expanding play with its matrix, the macro-environment, discovers this hyper-environ is far more like the supermind that today we find enfolds our full selves than it is an unconscious machine. At the highest reach of our transpersonal mind, we discover we are in percolative-osmotic, transfusive contact with a hierarchy of integrated mind-circuits. These pass up in ever intensified frequencies and through constantly increased dimensions, going beyond discrimination, definition, and the all-various modalities of time. Such a compelled conviction alone can now deal with *angst*, and all fear, by restoring awe. But in that vision, the human mind, made for ecstasy and infinitude, experiences a reverence which alone can give purpose to every experience and meaningful delight to every act.

~~~~~~~~~~~~

EDITOR'S AFTERWORD

And so, on this luminous high note, Gerald Heard triumphantly concludes his intellectual *tour de force*, his last-ever published written words in book form, heralding his all-embracing vision for humankind in *The Five Ages of Humanity*.

Of interest is Heard's use in his last paragraph above of the phrase "our transpersonal mind"—three years before pioneering psychologist Abraham Maslow, along with Stanislav Grof and Anthony Sutich, coined the term "transpersonal psychology."

In a similar vein, some of Heard's proposed therapeutic modalities have turned out not as fantastic as they may have seemed at the time. Rather, many have proven prescient and foresighted. Some have become commonplace practices in their own right. Several examples are outlined below.

For the Birth stage: Womb- or birth-regression therapy is practiced today. Isolating oneself during spiritual retreat in a cell at a monastic center is commonplace. Spiritual journaling (paralleling Gerald's suggestion, in the context of water-tank immersion, to make a tape recording of oneself) has become routine.

For the Childhood stage: Sensory-deprivation or float tanks are used in our time, as are Jacuzzis and hot tubs, though these latter apparatuses are used primarily for physical, and not so much psychological-growth benefits. Colonic hydrotherapy centers are common.

For the Adolescent stage: In certain studies, carbon dioxide inhalation therapy has been shown to reduce anxiety. Yogic breathing is often taught at hatha yoga centers.

For the First Maturity stage: The use of infrared heat-lamp therapy is widespread among many physical therapy and other medical clinics, as well as acupuncture practitioners.

In addition, "the therapeutic use of the psychedelics," to use Heard's phrase, has met with a resurgence, as Dr. Thomas Armstrong notes in his Foreword. The PBS series *Nova* explored the topic in "Can Psychedelics Cure" from October 2022, as did the 2021 movie *Aware: Glimpses of Consciousness*. Newer studies abound, as well as mainstream media articles from 2021–23 in *The New York Times*, *Science News*, and *The

Washington Post. A September 2022 peer-reviewed study published in *Cureus* noted, "In the past two decades, there has been a recent uptrend in clinical trials of psychedelic drugs. Psychedelic therapies potentially hold much promise for the treatment of psychiatric disorders ..."[167]

It should be emphasized that while Gerald Heard advocated the *therapeutic* use of psychedelics under supervised, clinical conditions to foster spiritual evolution and to promote individual healing and social sanity, he never endorsed and in fact soundly disapproved of their recreational use. He abruptly cut ties with Dr. Timothy Leary and Dr. Richard Alpert after learning of their infamous 1962 "Good Friday Experiment," condemning their actions as irresponsible.

For the Second Maturity stage: Along with those interventions mentioned by Dr. Armstrong, acupuncture treatments are often augmented by the use electro-stimulation to stimulate one's *chi*. This treatment modality is recognized under a bona fide ICD-10 code.

While Heard interpreted *aether* as electricity, we believe this may only partially encompass the full meaning of this theoretical invisible contiguous substratum that acts as an unseen matrix which binds all phenomena in its borderless web. Humans are capable of perceiving an infinitesimal fraction of the electromagnetic (EM) spectrum known as visible light, from approximately 380 to 700 nanometers.[168] This represents a miniscule 0.0035 percent of the entire EM spectrum,[169] which means that humans are unable to see *99.9965 percent* of what is potentially apprehensible in the universe around us. This same principle applies to the theory of the universal element of *aether*, which, though imperceptible, can account for any number of extra-physical occurrences that occur to humans, such as certain psychic phenomena, remote healing, reports of bilocation, the transmission of spiritual blessings, and the implanting of a deep reservoir of transcendent energy during certain spiritual initiations and empowerments.

Finally, Kundalini may be more of a "psychic energy," to use Dr. Armstrong's term, rather than an "electric energy" as described by Heard. Kundalini cannot (yet) be detected by instrumentation, as can, for example, brain waves. "Psychic" appears to more broadly encompass and explain what is meant by Kundalini and its effects. Some form of electricity may indeed be a subtle adjunct to this powerful unseen internal force, but it is likely not its primary attribute.

Tables: Gerald Heard's Fivefold Schema

TABLE 1

Gerald Heard's Fivefold Schema, Part 1					
STAGE	PHASE	AGE GROUP	BREAKDOWN/ DYSFUNCTION	INITIATION	ELEMENT
Pre-individual	Coconscious	Birth (0-2.5)	Birth Trauma	Rebirth	Earth
Proto-individual	Heroic	Childhood (2.5-10)	Dementia praecox becoming Paranoia	Catharsis	Water
Mid-individual	Ascetic	Adolescence (10-17)	Schizophrenia	Inspiration	Air
Total Individual	Humanic	First Maturity (17-50)	Manic Depression	Illumination	Fire
Post-individual	Leptoid	Second Maturity (50+)	Involutional melancholy	Trans-formation	Electricity (Aether)

TABLE 2

STAGE	PRIMARY THERAPEUTIC MODALITIES: THERAPIES TO BE ADMINISTERED IN ADULTHOOD UNDER SUPERVISION	DESIRED OUTCOME
	Gerald Heard's Fivefold Schema, Part 2	
Pre-individual	Rebirthing: reliving the birth experience without trauma. Regression therapy; hypnosis. Lying in isolation booth: making and playing audiotape recording of oneself, augmented with strobe light, sonic vibrations, pleasant odors.	Amelioration of birth trauma. Release of repressed fear.
Proto-individual	Immersing naked body in water tank with breathing apparatus, augmented with strobe light and sonic vibrations. Colonic irrigation.	Reduction of rage and shame. Decrease of pride and impetuousness. Attainment of emotional maturity.
Mid-individual	Breathing exercises. Inhaling gas mixture of carbon dioxide/oxygen.	Freedom from self-hatred and guilt. Restoration of panaesthetic sensory awareness.
Total Individual	Infrared heat-lamp therapy. Therapeutic use of psychedelics under supervision.	Transcendence of limitations of acute sense of individuality. Increase of self-knowledge and self-growth.
Post-individual	Electric-surge treatment.	Freedom from depression, purposelessness, and end-of-life fear. Maturation into seership. Preparation for post-corporeal state.

Glossary

AGONIA: Greek. Literally, a wrestling match. Pain which is used to attain to, and is transmuted into, a heightened consciousness.

AIDOS: Greek. An intuitive sense of decency.

ANARSIS: Greek. As catharsis is relief by purging, by discharge, so anarsis is release by aspiration and fulfillment.

ASKESIS: Greek. Athleticism; used here without the connotation either of competitive athletics or of mortification.

CHUNG-TZU: The gentleman of culture, generosity, and obedience (see the *Analects* of Confucius).

DIKE: Greek. Justice.

FETALIZATION: Louis Bolk's principle that in all mammals the form that survives and succeeds holds on to aspects of its fetal structure outside the womb: for example, the dog is a fetal form of the wolf, man is a fetal form of the ape, and the paidomorph is a fetal form of man.

[*FORECONSCIOUS*: That part of the mind below surface awareness where impressions gather, and where certain contents, such as memories and emotions, are stored.]

HUBRIS: Greek. Overweening pride.

HYPNOCRACY: A society under the control of a kind of hypnotic suggestion (and, therefore, a psychologically inflexible tradition) as to the purpose and conduct of life: for example, the complex street plan of Mohenjo-Daro shows no appreciable change for 1,000 years.

INTEGRAL THOUGHT: A term used by Dr. Sarvepalli Radhakrishnan, the President of India, to describe the opposite or complement of analytic thought.

KUNDALINI: The Yogic term which is interpreted here to mean a power, probably electric in nature, situated in the perineum or at the base of the spine, and capable of being roused (through various exercises) to course upward through the central nervous or through the sympathetic nervous system, thereby triggering the ductless glands, including the pituitary and probably the pineal. The result, presumably, is the highest form of consciousness.

LEPTOID: From Greek *lepsis*, leap: implying an energetic rousing of the aged both to counteract involutional melancholia and to attain awareness of the eliminatory, fifth age of humankind during which the consciousness must prepare for its birth out of the body via the electrical field, which persists after bodily death. [Ed. note: The English translation of the Greek word *lepsis* that most closely approximates Heard's intended meaning of "leap" is "to seize" in the sense of taking hold, i.e., taking hold of the next stage of humankind's evolution.]

LOGOS: Greek. The divine ruling principle, which is immanent or pervasive in all reality.

METACOMEDY: Literally, beyond comedy. A dramatic form, which would go through and beyond the first act of comedy and the second act of tragedy to a third act in which the protagonist, instead of dying encysted in his egotistic consciousness, would go on to experience his preterconsciousness.

METANOIA: Greek. Mutation of consciousness.

METARSIS: As catharsis is relief by purging and anarsis is a relief and release by aspiration, so metarsis is release into a condition beyond, into what Plotinus named "the Yonder."

NEOTENY: Greek. A zoological term meaning the capacity of carrying the larval or child form on into reproductive maturity; also, and especially, of extending the childhood phase of growth, openness, and teachability. See *Embryos and Ancestors* by Sir Gavin de Beer.

NOMOS: Greek. A system of laws governing a specified field: astronomy, and so on.

NORADRENALINE: A secretion of the suprarenals, which causes outward-directed rage, as distinguished from adrenaline that causes inward-directed rage or guilt.

PAIDOMORPH: Latin/Greek. Literally, child-body, a psychophysique not yet committed to the polar differentiation of the sexual opposites.

PANAESTHESIA: Total tactual perception, a natural capacity for total bodily response to stimulation.

PATHEIA: Greek. Pain that has become degenerative; sickness.

[*PATTERN OF PRESTIGE*: A model of excellence that individuals, separately or collectively, emulate and to which they aspire.]

Glossary

PHATIC: A term used by Malinowski, the anthropologist, referring to the charge of emotion that is often carried by a descriptive word.

PRAXIS: Greek. Psychophysical practice or exercise.

[*PRETERCONSCIOUS*: Beyond normal awareness; the paraconscious. Universal consciousness, often intuitively apprehended in elevated spiritual states.]

PSYCHEDELICS: Greek. [Coined by Dr. Humphry Osmond, which he defined as "mind manifesting."] Literally, [revealers] of the psyche. Chemical or vegetable products (for example, lysergic acid, mescaline, psilocybin, and the like), which when taken in an agreeable environment produce heightened awareness.

RAJAS: Sanskrit. Energy.

RELIGIO: Latin. A rite employing all the senses and performed in order to raise its participants to a cohesive, communal awareness of the force that precipitates and guides life in time; literally, a binding back or together. Religion has come to connote merely dogmatic religion.

SATTVA: Sanskrit. Used here to mean comprehension, understanding.

TAMAS: Sanskrit. Inertia.

~~~~~~~~~~~

The development and refinement of psychiatric nomenclature into its present proportions and complexities make it necessary for me to confine myself to as few terms as possible in order to elucidate the correlations I have seen. Therefore, in this psychological interpretation of history, I have used only five categories of mental breakdown. And I define each one as follows:

The trauma of birth:
   That state in which the infant refuses to develop into childhood, clinging to fetal and rudimentary infantile attitudes and behavior.
   That state of rigidity, or ankylosis, which attacked the coconscious societies, arresting all social growth.

Paranoia:
   That state in which the child projects his rage, born of frustration, outward onto others, onto the world.

The berserk rage of the hero-barbarian societies that destroyed the traditional societies and turned the hero into a homicide.

Schizophrenia:
That state in which the adolescent turns his anger and frustration inward, onto himself, when it becomes guilt.
The horror of life that drove Ascetic man to desert society.

Manic-depression:
That state in which the man of first maturity, in a society that lauds aggression, suffers from cyclic moods of provocative elations, leading to reaction into extreme discouragement.
The cyclic madness that makes modern society hopelessly unstable.

Involutional melancholy:
The continuous and increasing mental gloom which, after the climacteric (marked by impotence, poor appetite, and general failure of interests) is an undelusional state of mind in an increasing number of the elderly.
The melancholy that is the harbinger of social despair.

Of the above five states, the first four may appear among later age groups. This, though, is rare and due to the psyche's emotional [arrested development], which had been masked, to emerge in later life.

Bibliography

1. BASTIEN, ADOLF. *Die Voelker des Oestlichen Asien.* (Leipzig: O. Wigan), 1866-71.
2. BEHANAN, K.T. *Yoga.* (New York: The Macmillan Co.), 1937.
3. BENEDICT, RUTH. *Patterns of Culture.* (Boston: Houghton Mifflin Co.), 1959.
4. BERNSTEIN, MOREY. *The Search for Bridey Murphy.* (Garden City: Doubleday & Co., Inc.), 1956.
5. BERRILL, N.J. *Man's Emerging Mind.* (New York: Dodd, Mead & Co.), 1955.
6. BLOCH, IVAN. *The Sexual Life of our Times.* (London: Rebman), 1908.
7. BURY, J.B. *The Idea of Progress.* (New York: Dover Publications, Inc.), 1955.
8. BUTLER, R.A. "Curiosity in Monkeys." *Scientific American*, February 1954.
9. BYRD, RICHARD E. *Alone.* (New York: G. P. Putnam's Sons), 1938.
10. CAIN, ARTHUR H. "Alcoholics Anonymous: Cult or Cure?" *Harper's Magazine*, February 1963.
11. CAMPBELL, JOSEPH. *The Hero with a Thousand Faces.* (New York: Pantheon Books), 1953.
12. CAMPBELL, JOSEPH. *The Masks of God.* (New York: The Viking Press), 1959.
13. CHOLDEN, LOUIS (ed.). *Lysergic Acid, Diethylamide, and Mescaline in Experimental Psychiatry.* (New York: Grune and Stratton), 1956.
14. CHOPRA, R.N., and CHOPRA, G.S. "The present position of hemp-drug addiction in India." *Indian Medical Research Memoirs*: Memoir No. 31, July 1939.
15. COON, CARLETON S. *The Origin of Races.* (New York: Alfred A. Knopf), 1963.
16. COULTON, G.C. *Five Centuries of Religion.* (New York: Cambridge University Press), 1923–50.

17. DAPPER, OLFERT. *Description de l'Afrique*. (Amsterdam: Wolfgang), 1686.
18. DIMOND, SYDNEY GEORGE. *The Psychology of the Methodist Revival*. (New York: Oxford University Press), 1926.
19. DODDS, E. R. *The Greeks and the Irrational*. (Boston: Beacon Press), 1957.
20. EBON, MARTIN. "Firewalking 1956"; TANAGRAS, ANGELO. "Firewalkers of Modern Greece." *Tomorrow*, Vol. 4, No. 4.
21. EISELEY, LOREN. "Fossil Man and Human Evolution." *The Year Book of Anthropology*, 1955.
22. FULLER, CURTIS. "I See by the Papers." *Fate Magazine*, April 1963, p. 22.
23. FINE, BENJAMIN. *1,000,000 Delinquents*. (New York: Harper and Row), 1957.
24. FODOR, NANDOR. *The Search for the Beloved: A Clinical Investigation of the Trauma of Birth and pre-Natal Conditioning*. (New York: Hermitage Press), 1949.
25. FRÄNGER, WILHELM. *The Millennium of Hieronymus Bosch*. (London: Faber and Faber), 1961.
26. FRANKFORT, HENRI. *The Birth of Civilization in the Near East*. (Garden City: Doubleday & Co., Inc.), 1956.
27. FRANKFORT, HENRI. *Ancient Egyptian Religion*. (New York: Columbia University Press), 1948.
28. FUNKENSTEIN, D. H. "The Physiology of Fear and Anger." *Scientific American*, May 1955.
29. GADDIS, THOMAS. *The Birdman of Alcatraz*. (New York: Random House), 1955.
30. GESELL, ARNOLD, FRANCES L. ILG and LOUISE BATES AMES. *Youth: The Years from Ten to Sixteen*. (New York: Harper and Row), 1956.
31. GESELL, ARNOLD, FRANCES L. ILG and LOUISE BATES AMES in collaboration with JANET LEARNED RODELL. *Infant and Child in the Culture of Today*. (New York: Harper and Row), 1943.
32. GESELL, ARNOLD, and FRANCES L. ILG and LOUISE BATES AMES in collaboration with GLENNA E. BULLIS. *The Child from Five to Ten*. (New York: Harper and Row), 1946.

Bibliography

33. GHISELIN, BREWSTER (ed.). *The Creative Process*. (Berkeley: University of California Press), 1954.

34. GIBSON, WALTER. *The Boat*. (Boston: Houghton Mifflin Co.), 1953.

35. GINGERELLI, J., and F.J. KIRKNER (eds.). *The Psychological Variables in Human Cancer: A Symposium*. (Berkeley: University of California Press), 1954.

36. GOMBRICH, E.H. *Art and Illusion*. (New York: Pantheon Books), 1960.

37. GORER, GEOFFREY. *Africa Dances*. (J. Lehmann), 1949.

38. HADAMARD, JACQUES. *An Essay on the Psychology of Invention in the Mathematical Field*. (New York: Dover Publications, Inc.), 1954.

39. HANSON, N.R. *Patterns of Discovery*. (New York: Cambridge University Press), 1958.

40. HEARD, GERALD. *The Human Venture*. (New York: Harper and Row), 1955.

41. HEARD, GERALD. *Man the Master*. (New York: Harper and Row), 1941.

42. HEARD, GERALD. *The Ascent of Humanity*. (New York: Harcourt, Brace & World), 1929.

43. HEARD, GERALD. *The Eternal Gospel*. (New York: Harper and Row), 1946.

44. HERON, W., W.H. BEXTON, and D.C. HEBB. "Cognitive Effects of Decreased Variation to the Sensory Environment." *The American Psychologist*, Vol. 8, No. 8, August 1953.

45. HILZHEIMER, MAX. "The Dog: The Foetalization of the Wolf." *Antiquity*, Vol. VI, No. 24, December 1932.

46. ITTLESON, W.H. *The Ames Demonstrations in Perception*. (Princeton: Princeton University Press), 1952.

47. JAMES, WILLIAM. *The Varieties of Religious Experience*. (New York: The Modern Library, Inc.)

48. JELLINEK, STEFAN. *Dying, Apparent Death and Resuscitation*. (Baltimore: Williams & Wilkins), 1947.

49. KERÉNYI, C. "The Mysteries of the Kabeiroi." *The Mysteries*. (New York: Pantheon Books, Inc.), 1955.

50. KROEBER, A. L. (ed.). *Anthropology Today.* See H. L. MOVIUS, "Old World Prehistory: Paleolithic." (Chicago: University of Chicago Press), 1953.

51. LA BARRE, WESTON. *The Human Animal.* (Chicago: University of Chicago Press), 1954.

52. LANE, EDWARD WILLIAM. *An Account of the Manners and Customs of the Modern Egyptians.* (London: J. Murray), 1860. Fifth Edition.

53. LEVY, GERTRUDE RACHEL. *The Gate of Horn.* (London: Faber and Faber), 1948.

54. LINDAUER, MARTIN. *Communication Among Social Bees.* (Massachusetts: Harvard University Press), 1961.

55. LINDER, ROBERT. *Rebels Without a Cause.* (New York: Grune and Stratton), 1944.

56. LINDNER, ROBERT. *Must You Conform?* (New York: Rinehart), 1956.

57. MACCURDY, JOHN THOMPSON. *War Neuroses.* (New York: Cambridge University Press), 1918.

58. MEAD, GEORGE R. S. *Fragments of a Faith Forgotten.* (New Hyde Park: University Books), 1960.

59. MEAD, MARGARET. *New Lives for Old.* (New York: William Morrow & Co., Inc.), 1956.

60. MEDUNA, L. J. *Carbon Dioxide Therapy.* (Springfield, Illinois: Charles C Thomas), 1958.

61. MEERLOO, JOOST A. M. *Rape of the Mind.* (Cleveland: World Publishing Co.), 1956.

62. MICHAEL, D. N. *Cybernation: The Silent Conquest.* (Santa Barbara: Center for Study of Democratic Institutions), 1962.

63. MORET, ALEXANDRE, and GEORGES DAVY. *From Tribe to Empire.* (New York: Alfred A. Knopf), 1926.

64. MURRAY, MARGARET. *The Witch Cult in Western Europe.* (Oxford: Clarendon Press), 1921.

65. OTTO, WALTER F. "The Meaning of the Eleusinian Mysteries." *The Mysteries.* (New York: Pantheon Books, Inc.), 1955.

66. PFEIFFER, JOHN. *The Human Brain.* (New York: Harper and Row), 1955.

Bibliography

67. PIGGOTT, STUART. *Prehistoric India to 1000 B.C.* (Baltimore: Penguin Books), 1950.
68. RANK, OTTO. *The Trauma of Birth.* (New York: Brunner), 1952.
69. READ, GRANTLY DICK. *Childbirth without Fear.* (New York: Harper and Row), 1959.
70. RELE, VASANT G. *The Mysterious Kundalini.* (Bombay: Taraporevala), 1927.
71. RIBBLE, MARGARET. *The Rights of Infants.* (New York: Columbia University Press), 1950.
72. RITTER, CHRISTIANE. *A Woman in the Polar Night.* (New York: E. P. Dutton & Co. Inc.), 1954.
73. SARGANT, WILLIAM. *The Battle for the Mind.* (Garden City: Doubleday & Co. Inc.), 1957.
74. SCOTT, GEOFFREY. *The Architecture of Humanism.* (Garden City: Doubleday & Company, Inc., Anchor), 1954.
75. SCOTT, JOHN PAUL. "Critical Periods in Behavioral Development." *Science,* November 30, 1962.
76. SEIDENBERG, RODERICK. *Post-Historic Man.* (Boston: Beacon Press), 1957.
77. SELYE, HANS. *The Stress of Life.* (New York: McGraw-Hill), 1956.
78. SIMEONS, A. T. W. *Man's Presumptuous Brain.* (New York: E. P. Dutton & Co. Inc.), 1962.
79. SIMPSON, G. G. *The Meaning of Evolution.* (New Haven: Yale University Press), 1950.
80. SMITH, ADAM. *Wealth of Nations.* (New York: E. P. Dutton & Co. Inc.)
81. STEVENSON, LANG. "Cancer and Atheroma Explained by a Basic Phylogenetic Pattern in Disease." *The Medical Press* (London), June 14, 21, and 28, 1962.
82. STEWARD, J. H. "Cultural Causality and Law: A Trial Formulation of the Development of Early Civilizations." *American Anthropologist,* Vol. 51, pp. 1–27.
83. STILL, COLIN. *The Timeless Theme.* (London: I. Nicholson & Watson, Ltd.), 1936.
84. SUTTIE, IAN D. *The Origins of Love and Hate.* (New York: Julian Press, Inc.), 1952.

85. THOMPSON, W. R., and RONALD MELZACK. "Early Environment." *Scientific American*, January 1956.
86. TOKSVIG, SIGNE. *Emanuel Swedenborg*. (New Haven: Yale University Press), 1948.
87. VETT, CARL. *Seltsame Erlebnisse in einem Derwischkloster*. (Leipzig: Heitz & Co.), 1931.
88. VOEGELIN, ERIC. *New Science of Politics, An Introduction*. The Walgreen Foundation Lectures. (Chicago: Chicago University Press), 1952.
89. VON FRISCH, KARL. *Bees: Their Vision, Chemical Senses and Language*. (Ithaca: Cornell University Press), 1958.
90. VON HAYEK, FRIEDRICH AUGUST. *The Road to Serfdom*. (Chicago: University of Chicago Press), 1945.
91. WALLAS, GRAHAM. *The Art of Thought*. (New York: Harcourt, Brace & World, Inc.), 1926.
92. WALSH, W. H. *Philosophy of History*. (New York: Harper and Row), 1960.
93. WALTER, GREY. *The Living Brain*. (New York: W. W. Norton & Co., Inc.), 1953.
94. WARNECK, JOHANNES GUSTAV. *Die Religion der Batak*. (Göttingen: Vandenhoeck und Ruprecht), 1909.
95. WELCH, HOLMES. *The Parting of the Way*. (Boston: Beacon Press), 1957.
96. WENGER, M. A., K. K. BAGCHI, and K. K. ANAND. "Voluntary Heart and Pulse Control by Yoga Methods." *The International Journal of Parapsychology*, Winter 1962.
97. WHORF, BENJAMIN LEE. *Language, Thought and Reality*. (Cambridge: Technology Press of Massachusetts Institute of Technology), 1956.
98. WOLBERG, LEWIS ROBERT. *Medical Hypnosis*. (New York: Grune and Stratton, Inc.), 1948.
99. ZOTZ, LOTHAR FRIEDRICH. *Altsteinzeitkunde Mitteleuropas*. Stuttgart: Ferdinand Enke Verlag), 1951.

NOTES

[1] "Historia" is the word that Aristotle uses for a science.

[2] "Prehorticultural," to use W. D. Strong's still economic serial classification. See also Carleton S. Coon (15).

[3] See Appendix A, "The Hybrid Psyche."

[4] See also Appendix A.

[5] G. R. Levy (53) points out that even in Paleolithic cave drawings there are pictures of penned cattle.

[6] See Section I, Chapter 2, on the rise of the hero.

[7] E. R. Dodds (19) has called the Greek phase of the Heroic Age "the shame culture." See his *The Greeks and the Irrational*.

[8] Ajax, when he finds that he has slaughtered a flock of sheep thinking that they were men-at-arms, kills himself because he is mocked.

[9] For example, the Shintoistic Meiji revival that was started in Japan in the [1860s], the melodramatics of a Mussolini, and the Wagnerian operatics of a Hitler.

[10] R. N. and G. S. Chopra (14), two authoritative writers on Indian hemp, say that Herodotus tells of hemp apparently being used, as an excitant, by the Scythians: the heroic tribal culture that in the first millennium drove the Cimmerians out from the lands north of the Black Sea. Messrs. Chopra think, therefore, that the Greek *nepenthe* (brought from Thebes in Egypt) must also have been hemp. It is clear, however, that the effects were completely different: *nepenthe* produced sedation and hemp produced excitement.

[11] For example, when Achilles gives the body of Hector back to Priam, and again, when he has killed a kinglet, he does not take the golden armor but, out of *aidos* (a kind of intuitive sense of decency), he buries his victim in it under a cairn mound.

[12] See Appendix A.

[13] Cf. Napoleon's anxious query of Talleyrand: "Power, surely, can never be ridiculous?"

[14] Aeschylus, born in 525 B.C., produced his first play in 499 B.C., and Euripides died in 406 B.C.

[15] For example, Joseph Priestly, the discoverer of oxygen.

[16] See Section I, Chapter 5; Section II, Chapter 5; and Section III, Chapter 5.

[17] For example, see the *Cloud*'s attitude toward the banishment of the sense of sinfulness.

[18] Philip II of Spain, as he lay dying in great misery, came to the conclusion that God was plaguing him because he had not burnt enough heretics, although he had certainly burnt all those he could lay hands on.

[19] In this work, politics is not being considered save insofar as symptoms of frames of mind, states of consciousness, projections of various degrees of self-consciousness. From that point of view, the Jesuit rise and fall was inevitable; its initial success and subsequent failure was natural. It had a skillful technique whereby the ascetic, other-worldly point of view was contemporized into something that looked like humanism: a humanism in which the firmest authority was modernized so as to appear, to the cultured, to be gentlemanly ease. More, the Society itself became an arbiter of taste and an innovator in art. However, this praxis did not arrest individualism or make it nonsecular.

In 1590, Philip II of Spain, of all people, recognizing this fact, complained to Sixtus V, urging the Pope to alter the Society and even give it another name, and the Pope was prepared to do so just before his death. Individual Jesuits inevitably went on playing the most violent politics in spite of the wise and emphatic order of the Fifth General Congregation (1593–94), commanding "severely and strictly" because of past scandals, that no Jesuit touch public affairs in any way, even though he might be invited to do so. Next, they abandoned the excellent and free education that had brought them real renown, devoting themselves to control of the consciences of autocrats. After that they took to trade; and some groups amassed such wealth that in 1741, Pope Benedict XIV had to make special regulations against this scandal. By 1773, Pope Clement XIV had dissolved the order. Resuscitated in 1804 after 31 years and formally re-established in 1814, it is now only a shadow of its original powerful self.

[20] The Jesuits ruined Molinos and the Quietists, who rejected images, any visualistic or auditory aid, and any use of the surface will with its danger of producing Baudouin's psychological "law of reversed effort."

²¹ For example, the Earl of Shaftesbury. [Ed. note: Presumably, Heard meant Lord Shaftesbury, aka Anthony Ashley-Cooper, the 7th Earl of Shaftesbury.]

²² To what degree there must always be considerable latitude in our judgments.

²³ See also Appendix A.

²⁴ *Erewhon* is *nowhere* spelled backward. Butler took the idea from Sir Thomas More, who had coined a word from the Greek "Utopia," which meant nowhere.

²⁵ It would seem from fossil evidence that the social insects' patterns may not have altered since at least the Oligocene Epoch.

²⁶ See also Cope's "law of the survival of the unspecialized."

²⁷ W. R. Thompson and Ronald Melzack (85) discuss the permanent immaturity of dogs that have been sheltered in total isolation for their first seven to ten months.

²⁸ See Grantly Dick Read's (69) *Childbirth Without Fear*, and the further developments in France and Russia in these methods.

²⁹ Indeed, Theodore Reich maintains that the trauma of birth is the largest cause of mental trouble in later life. See also Nandor Fodor (24), and Otto Rank (68).

³⁰ See report on [the] meeting of American Association of Anatomists at Toronto in 1937. Shour reported that the rings can be detected under the microscope after the use of a special stain. Every ninety-six hours a ring is added in the human tooth; one every twenty-four hours in those of lower animals.

³¹ At the present time, according to L. M. Wolberg (98), *Medical Hypnosis Volume 1*, the consensus is that regression actually does produce early behavior in a way that obviates all possibility of simulation.

³² See *The Psychological Variables in Human Cancer*, by J. Gingerelli and F. J. Kirkner (35). See also the equally impressive study titled *Cancer and Atheroma Explained by a Basic Phylogenetic Pattern in Disease*, by Lang Stevenson, M.D., F.R.C.S. (81), Surgeon at Whipps Cross Hospital, Leytonstone (Essex), England. In these reports, the author indicates that one of the causes of neoplasms is a reaction of the organism,

when under psychosomatic shock, of a far earlier evolutionary level in the phylogenetic tree (for example, the crustacean damage reaction of abandoning an assaulted limb and regrowth of a new one on the old site). Cancer can thus be regarded as a surviving power to restore renewal by producing reproductive cells. After the crustacean level, the second completing step, the capacity to build up a new limb, is, however, lost.

[33] "Concepts come before percepts," *Patterns of Discovery* by N. R. Hanson (39). "Nothing can be seen unless it has already been recognized," *Art and Illusion* by E. H. Gombrich (36).

[34] The culture of the Australian Aboriginals may, perhaps, even be called by that too easily used epithet, decadent. [Ed. note: Heard uses the term "decadent" in its anthropological sense, meaning "in decline."] Konrad Lorenz has pointed out, in his study of the dingo (the feral dog of Australia), that these tribes seem to have entered that continent bringing with them the domesticated dog. But the tribes became so weak in enterprise that the animal deserted them and resumed a purely wild life of adjustment to and conquest of its new environment. However, in 1961, an expedition of Melbourne anthropologists did discover an isolated tribe that called themselves the Bindibu and who were living in the Great Sand Desert that is on the border of Northern and Western Australia, some five hundred miles west of Alice Springs. These people were of so low a culture economically that they had no agriculture, nor houses, nor tents. At night they sheltered themselves from the cold (for they wore no clothes and had no weaving or pottery) with heaped windbreaks made of small, withered bushes (like the tumbleweed of the semidesert states in the Western United States), which they piled around the hollows where they slept. In their hunting they used the dingo which, it would seem, they had either never lost touch with, or had reattached to themselves.

[35] Men of later epochs have reverted to such rigidity. The Median Persian Empire prefaced all its laws with the phrase "The Law of the Merles and Persians which cannot be changed." And even the city-state of Megara, neighbor of Athens, had in its constitution that whoever would suggest a change must do so with a noose around his neck. He was to be hanged if he failed to carry his motion.

[36] The delta wave has also been described by Walter as being the wave of oncoming birth effort. It has been given the name—the letter "d" in the Greek alphabet—because of its association with the initial of the four cardinal words of major stress: disease, degeneracy, death, and defense.

[37] See Section I, Chapter 2; and Section II, Chapter 2.

[38] The paidomorph is that form of psychophysique which, for a longer time than ever before, will remain undifferentiated because not yet committed to the polar differentiation of the sexual opposites. See the work of Louis Bolk, the Dutch anatomist, and *The Human Animal* by Weston La Barre (51).

[39] Autopsy studies of males who had died of miscellaneous causes have revealed that from 20 to 46 percent of them had cancer of the prostate. Most of these growths had remained stationary or had regressed and the individuals had lived a normal life span, though actually they had had cancer for twenty or thirty years. The same appears to be true of women. Mass surveys for detection of early uterine cancer show that in only 20 percent of the cases where cancer was found did the tumor grow and require treatment. In the rest, they receded and disappeared. So, the report continues, we are faced with the startling possibility that any cancer that becomes grossly evident and finally kills may actually be an exception. The opinion of this Symposium would suggest that the emotions of the patient are among the forces that influence the course and outcome.

[40] See *Man's Presumptuous Brain* by A. T. W. Simeons (78); see also endnote 32.

[41] In the Middle Ages, suicide was most common among monks (16). Today schizophrenia is the mental disease most often attended by suicide.

[42] At one world-famous institute of technology, the culture cure for this serious deficiency was to give these quite unprepared adolescent minds the task of reading *King Lear*. The Elizabethan tragedy was dismissed by one of the brighter embryo engineers with the comment, "a medieval shot at *Life with Father*."

[43] See *The Psychology of Insanity*.

[44] A useful analogy here is the elimination of the thymus as the child's growth proceeds. The thymus is the gland in the chest that ceases to function as adolescence approaches. Research into the thymus, in these first years of the 1960s, has indicated, however, that although as a growth-activating gland it is in manifest activity up till the age of eight or ten years (after which its growth slows until by fourteen it starts to wither and disappear), it has another use in keeping up the body's immunity. This find suggests that there may be some truth in the Yoga statement that dilational thoracic breathing with the expansion of rib cage and sternum (for the thymus lies just behind the sternum) does reactivate the thymus and add to the health of the practicer.

[45] As Ruth Benedict (3) indicates in her *Patterns of Culture*.

[46] Research in 1962 into the average life expectancy of the high executives in the advertising business showed that it stands at 61 years.

[47] For example, prostatectomy has been raised from being an agonizing exceptional success to an equality with tonsillectomy. Both operations are introductions: one to adolescence and the other to second maturity.

[48] See [*The Future of Industrial Man*] by Peter Drucker.

[49] The well-known psychoanalyst, Andras Angyal, has pointed out that at the root of all neurotic defensive structures there lies the fundamental urge for self-preservation and for the protection of personal integrity.

[50] Some additional and confirmatory evidence on this important point is provided by findings that seem to show that the brain cases of children born by a successful caesarian section are less contracted than those delivered by the natural delivery. See also endnote 52.

[51] The gorilla and the orangutan are *angst* types, while monkeys are almost inexhaustibly curious. (See [reference] (8) in Bibliography.)

[52] H. F. Fleure has pointed out that the sustained openness of the infant's skull and so its unconstricted brain were largely dependent on the availability of cow's milk for a prolonged lactation period and the postponement of the development of the jaws and the jaw muscles

that run up onto the skull: a development that was necessary if a hard, tough, masticatory diet was to be assimilated. And G. R. Levy (53) has observed, in her *The Gate of Horn*, that even in the Paleolithic (Magdalenian) cave drawings, there are pictures of penned and kept cows. See also Kirk's reference to expansion of skull in caesarian-born children in endnote 50.

[53] "Most workers [archaeological excavators] are quite prepared to accept the Solutrean as being due to a diffusion of certain specialized ideas, not to the invasion of new peoples with superior weapons." *Anthropology Today* edited by A. L. Kroeber (50); see especially "Old World Prehistory: Paleolithic," by H. L. Movius. See also Zotz (99).

[54] The response of the melancholic aged to such a drug as Equanil or Miltown is interesting and promising if it is used as an initial and introductory alleviant for anxiety. Like Tolserol and other meprobamates, Miltown is basically a muscle relaxant. The first step is to unfreeze the physique, which is involuntarily shrinking from oncoming decrepitude. After that, however, the subject must be recharged. As always, sedation only gains time for advance to be resumed.

[55] Psychological discoveries made in an ascetic age lead to the volatilization of the advanced out of society, and so to social collapse, for example, India.

[56] See endnote 31.

[57] See Appendix A.

[58] For example, the horror tabus [as characterized] in all the heroical cultures: that is, the woman defiles and is defiled; her menstrual blood is foul and wicked and parturition is filthy.

[59] See above reference to the growth rings in children's teeth in endnote 30.

[60] Army officers, together with white-collar workers, professionals, white men, and city dwellers, all have a higher suicide rate than do conscripts, laborers, artisans, [Black people], and country dwellers.

[61] The IQs of the top Nazis were remarkably high.

[62] For example, Reserpine, Thorazine, Librium, Melleril, Stelazine, and others. And new ones are regularly being developed.

[63] For further details of the Hebb and Lilly work, see Appendix D. Other researchers in this field have been Meyers and Murphy of the Army

Research Project in Monterey, [California]; Jack Vernon at Princeton University; and Jay T. Shurley at the University of Oklahoma. And although they have used variations of the limited environments designed by Hebb and Lilly, their results were the same: a distinct and sometimes profound modification of consciousness.

[64] See Morey Bernstein's account of his experience in "an equalizing chamber which enables the patient to stop breathing," in *The Search for Bridey Murphy*, pages 42-44.

[65] Cf. Yogi practices of breath control.

[66] See previous reference to Grey Walter's *The Living Brain* in Section II, Chapter 3.

[67] It may also be noted here that not only is incense still used in the celebration of the Mass, but the first mention of its use in religious rites occurs in the Egyptian *Book of the Dead*. Here is given an explanation of its meaning which throws some light on its evocative use. We are told that when the worshipers in the dark of the shrine smelled the aroma, they knew that the God was not only present but benign. For the sweat of a friendly man is sweet, and smelling it they felt at peace.

[68] Both of which had a primary and a secondary ordeal and initiation. At Eleusis, these two ordeal initiations were separated by a period of three years.

[69] The Stone Age Australian Aboriginal cultures, when they were discovered, seemed not to have reached that psychic level.

[70] A hypnocracy is a society that is so completely subject to a traditional, comprehensive social suggestion that, as with a hypnotized subject, orders are implicitly obeyed even when the one who gives orders is not present and has neither threatened nor rewarded those who have been given the orders. See Gerald Heard (40).

[71] For example, Genghis Khan, who sprang from a shaman culture, murdered his spiritual overlord and created a destructive empire that vanished with his death. Chaka, the founder of the Zulu militarist empire, did the same thing.

[72] See Appendix D.

[73] The Yoga practices enjoin floating in a stream, with the sphincter held open in order to irrigate the eliminatory area. They knew of no way of total immersion.

[74] See *Chemistry for the New Age*, by Robert H. Carleton, 1954 edition.

[75] Stobaeus quotes an earlier author, "The first state [the ordeal stage of the air and sound mystery] is nothing but errors and uncertainties, laborious wanderings." The misery of amnesia was also indicated and probably induced. As Colin Still has pointed out on page 151 of his *The Timeless Theme*, "the search for the lost child Persephone," which was a central part of the Eleusinian ritual, "is the search for the Lost Word." This is the mantram which, catalytically, not only gives the clue and solves the riddle but actually makes the mind mutate. It is the *Aletheia*: the sudden truth that inevitably comes with the disappearance of the ignorance (the Lethe intoxication), the truth that the illusory personality now perishes (Persephone means "death-bringer") in order that the true eternal self may emerge.

[76] See K. T. Behanan (2), *Yoga*. Behanan is an Indian by birth and a graduate of Yale University on a Sterling Fellowship. To study Yoga, he went back to India where he was trained by a North West Indian Hatha Yogin whose religious name was Kavalyanda. Behanan says that "the main feature of all Yogi varieties of breathing which are claimed to have spiritual value" is the pause between inhalation and exhalation.

[77] See *Emanuel Swedenborg* by Signe Toksvig (86). In his "Spiritual Diary" Swedenborg says, "I sometimes scarcely breathed by inspiration at all for the space of a short hour and merely drew in enough air to keep up the process of thinking."

In his first volume, *Africa Dances*, in which he reports on the psychophysical exercises of several tribes on the West Central Coast of Africa, Geoffrey Gorer (37), the anthropologist, notes that after hearing that the Moll fisher folk, a shore tribe, could remain under water for long periods, he asked one of these divers to demonstrate. Gorer reports that the man dived in and lay down at a considerable depth on the sea floor. He remained down while Gorer kept the time by his watch. After twenty minutes, and with no sign of distress, he came to the surface and asked whether that was a satisfactory demonstration. Gorer, who had watched him all the while through the water, noticed that only on occasion a bubble of air rose from his mouth. When Gorer asked him how this breath retention was managed he remarked, "by fish breathing," which, as Gorer comments, was not informing.

[78] This was the way it was phrased by St. Francis of Assisi and confirmed by Ignatius Loyola.
[79] See work of Szent-Györgyi. See also endnote 44.
[80] *Ibid.*
[81] See the James Lang principle in regard to the effect of attitude on mood. It is also worth observing here that the ... Galla tribes in mid-Africa, which have adopted an aggressive militaristic social pattern, have two main ordeals in their puberty initiation rites for boys. The first is circumcision: a rite that most psychoanalysts now regard as being a substitute for castration, but which may be considered, with more likelihood, to be a callusing of the glans so as to make sexual feeling less peremptory and, therefore, battle-rage the preferred sensation. The second is excision of the nipples. The Galla maintain that these nerve centers make for compassion and that a man, to be sufficiently heartless, must be rendered incapable of such emotions.
[82] The hypnotized person is not simply *inattentive*; he is entirely *attentive* to *one* thing, that is, the hypnotic suggestion.
[83] See *Carbon Dioxide Therapy* by L.J. Meduna (60), who was Professor of Psychiatry at the University of Illinois, College of Medicine, Chicago.
[84] It is important to note here the steady growth, in psychoanalysis, of companionship between the patient and the analyst. Beginning with the extreme of detachment, as shown in the original Freudian attitude toward the analysand, the Jungian method of treatment shifted from having the therapist crouched out of sight and the therapee sprawled on a couch. Now they face each other. In the Carl Rogers nondirective approach, the patient takes the initiative and the analyst listens as though being instructed. In the Moreno psychodrama, several persons act out an issue with the psycho-dramatist serving as a kind of conductor of an unrehearsed, extemporized chorus or play. With Robert Lindner and other pioneers came experiments in identification. Sándor Ferenczi, although he remained true to the basic child-traumatic discovery of Freud, did introduce a loving, inspiring intimacy that restored the relationship of the mysteries, of the hierophant psychopompus to the postulant and neophyte going through his ordeals–initiations.

[85] It is, of course, assumed that he has already been brought successfully through the first and second mystery ordeal-initiations.
[86] See also *Man's Presumptuous Brain* by A. T. W. Simeons (78).
[87] In classical English, aggression is a reprehensible form of conduct, in American English it has become prestigious.
[88] As Warthin of [The University of Michigan at] Ann Arbor calls the second part of the aging process.
[89] Compare La Rochefoucauld: "I have seen men leave love for power, but never leave power for love." [Ed. note: The cynical La Rochefoucauld preceded Edward VIII's abdication by three centuries.]
[90] For example, Konrad Adenauer.
[91] "The climax was a vision." See Walter F. Otto's (65) Bollingen Foundation-sponsored *The Meaning of the Eleusinian Mysteries*.
[92] [That is], going through the water ceremony of washing in the nearby inlet, receiving auditory instruction, and passing through the series of dark sanctuaries and claustrophobic passages.
[93] Tesla often remarked that he actually saw, in the air before him, a picture of the machine he was afterward to construct in the solid.
[94] See *The Art of Thought* by Graham Wallas (91); [see also] *The Creative Process*, edited by Brewster Ghiselin (33).
[95] Note that the psychedelic element of the mushroom has now been synthesized and given the name of psilocybin.
[96] In the animal world, the inability to attend for any length of time is a built-in safeguard necessary for survival. For instance, if a bird in the grip of one of the most powerful of instincts (the nesting instinct) were to become absorbed in what it was doing, it would fall easy prey to its natural enemies, who could then approach it undetected. On the contrary, a nest-building bird will stop every ten or fifteen seconds and scan its horizon 360 degrees.

In humans, this biological leftover, no longer necessary for survival, is a hindrance and is overcome only through great effort and discipline, and the unique human power of being selflessly interested.
[97] See *The Ames Demonstrations in Perception* by W. H. Ittleson (46). See also *Patterns of Discovery* by N. R. Hanson (39), and *Art and Illusion* by E. H. Gombrich (36).
[98] *In eo*, "to go in," is the basic meaning of initiation.

[99] For instance, as we have mentioned earlier, an aged Pharaoh would have himself put through a sham burial and rebirth in order to make his duped subjects believe that he had come out of the womb for a second time and would now live forever.

[100] See Appendix D on the underground tradition, Tantra, Adamites, etc.

[101] See Appendix D on the underground tradition.

[102] See *Fate* magazine, April 1963, page 22, Curtis Fuller's column "I See by the Papers …," paragraph headed "Before 15,000," which is an account of a firewalk (performed by 30 people) in Argentina, and witnessed by 15,000 people, including Armando Vivante, professor of anthropology at the Universities of Buenos Aires and La Plata.

[103] Though the Greeks at Eleusis lost the fire ordeal and initiation as the fourth mystery (or retained it simply as light after darkness), as we have seen, it lingered on in the worship of Dionysus. At Eleusis, even a water initiation was retained only as a bathing preliminary performed in the small bay outside the Temple precincts. So they were puzzled by the Demeter story as it hung on around the great shrine of the Mother and Daughter. This part of the Mother myth therefore split into two versions. In one, the child of King Celeus and his wife Metaneira is called Demophon. Demeter feeds him ambrosia, a preparational rite, and then applies fire to his mortal parts. At this point Queen Metaneira breaks in and Demophon is burned to death. Demeter then takes the younger child, Triptolemus, teaches him all the arts and crafts, and sends him, in a magic chariot, to spread civilization throughout the world. In the other version, this Triptolemus is the only child in the story, and though he is not made immortal (because of his mother's intervention), he became the benefactor of humankind and also the founder of the Eleusinian mysteries.

[104] They often come in order to be healed of complaints, especially paralysis and insanity.

[105] A description given to me by Roger Fry may throw further light on the level of heightened concentration that must be reached before this psychophysical condition is possible. When traveling in North Africa, Professor Fry was permitted to be present at a meeting of a

dervish group in a small mosque. Having been brought in and seated near the conductor, he was able to watch closely how the conductor tested the preparedness of the performers. These dervishes were dancing themselves into dissociation. As they circled round and passed before the conductor, they held out their hands for him to give them, from the heap before him, the lances and knives with which to penetrate their muscles and the hot irons which had been heated to a red-hot pitch in a small brazier. This conductor told Professor Fry that as long as he could see the pupils of their eyes, it was not safe to give them the weapons. But when the pupil was so contracted as to be invisible, then he handed them not only the knives but the red-hot rods which Professor Fry saw the dancers put in their mouths. He could hear the saliva hiss, but there was no wincing and, next day, no scars.

[106] Max Freedom Long reports seeing a film on firewalking that was shown, with an accompanying lecture, on February 21, 1935, by John G. Hill, Professor of Biblical History at the University of Southern California. The place was an island in the Tahiti group, and the fire ordeal was first being used in the medieval legal way: a man charged with a crime was forced to attempt to prove his innocence by being able to walk unscathed along the fire trench. If, as seems clear, preparation and lack of fear are essential to immunity, it is not surprising to learn that he suffered bad burns. Those others, however, who of their own desire went through the trench in order to obtain health were completely uninjured. After the ritual walking was over, Dr. Hill tried putting his own hand within three feet of the rocks. After eleven seconds, the pain was so great that he had to remove his hand. One of Dr. Hill's companions accepted the priest's invitation to make the walk. Even his shoes, which he did not remove, were uninjured though his face was slightly scorched and in the next few days peeled considerably.

It is not uncommon to find, in the popular press, articles by writers who, with considerable satisfaction to themselves, explain how they have found out what really lies behind the ceremony of the fire walk. They describe how they have demonstrated the very simple nature of the apparent immunity to fire. They claim, and there is little doubt they have shown, that they can place and press for a moment or two the palms of their hands or the soles of their feet on a surface sufficiently heated that, if cold water is poured on it, the water turns into steam. Their explanation, they believe, lies in the fact that if the hot plate has a temperature of sufficient height, water coming into contact with it does not immediately pass into steam but granulates into a series of minute globes resembling liquid mercury, and in that state, for a small space of time, these globules run about over the hot surface.

These explainers point out that this can happen with the sweat in the palms of the hands and the soles of the feet, and that it is because for a few moments the skin is so cushioned and insulated that the person walking on a hot iron plate, or one who clasps a piece of hot iron, is not immediately burnt. However, it is clear that this does not explain how (in the case of Dr. Campbell and many others) it is possible for a person to be exposed for some time to the direct heat of a flame. Nor does it explain the equally well authenticated evidence of unprepared persons being burnt when they attempted to walk through a fire trench when others who *were* prepared had done so and emerged unscathed. Something is projected from the skin to protect it, but this does not seem to be the momentary shield provided by globulated droplets of sweat.

This momentary phenomenon of the sweat-shield has been demonstrated since the nineteenth century. Edward, then Prince of Wales and afterward King Edward VII, visited a famous laboratory and watched the chief technician put his hand into a large crucible of molten lead without harm. Edward followed suit and also without harm. Of course, the immersion in the molten lead was only for a moment.

[107] See Appendix D, *The Timeless Theme*, by Colin Still (83).

[108] Focus means "hearth."

[109] In pre–Communist China the great-parent, head of the whole compound, was an honored load that was carried into senility, for care of him guaranteed that those who cared for him would, in turn, be cared for. Under the influence of Buddhism, even in China it was permissible for the head of a house, at the age of sixty and if it was so desired, to leave the highly honored position and retire into a cloister cell.

[110] Already we are finding with schizophrenia and with catatonia that the patient falls into silence and becomes inaccessible because he realizes that even the psychiatrist (not having had the patient's experience and even if there were words in our common language for it) could not understand this condition, which lies outside any "common-sense" category.

[111] That is, insanities in which no lesion or callus of the brain can be found. And according to *The Human Brain* (66) this is the state of 80 percent of the brains of the insane after death, even after a long period of madness.

[112] [These Sanskrit researchers], together with some modern researchers, believe [the thymus] can be activated in maturity by proper exercises. See also endnote 44.

[113] The nerve that ends in the epigastric region.

[114] See page 161 [of] *The Human Brain* by John Pfeiffer (66).

[115] [Certain] Sufis, to attain states of extrasociation, not only practice on the semicircular canals the centrifuge effect by means of the spinning dance but also often take *Cannabis sativa* (hashish) to attain this dilation. They are reported to warn the postulant that as the oncoming proleptic condition, the rising pressure of the experience is felt, the psychophysique will first seek the relief of catastrophic weeping, then the relief of hebephrenic laughter, and finally the detensioning of epileptoid convulsions. And the postulant is instructed that each of these releases must be denied. Then, it is said, the trainee will be able to experience the manifold world around with the flexibility that permits him to compose every event and, living with complete awareness of initiative, know what Milton named "The sober certainty of waking bliss." (See Vett (87), *Seltsame Erlebnisse in einem Derwischkloster*.)

[116] For example, the Paleolithic cave under Montespan shows the imprint of a ritual dance; and there is the picture of the magician in the Cave of the Three Brothers.

[117] For example, the Indus civilization as shown at Harappa and Mohenjo-Daro.

[118] See Robert Barclay's *Apology*: "Without quaking there is no Quakerism."

[119] See the classic study of seizure salvation in William James' (47) *The Varieties of Religious Experience*.

[120] See, particularly, accounts of his visit to the Southern States in the United States.

[121] William Law, for example, who was mainly influenced by the writings of Jacob Boehme.

[122] Howard Fabing, who has studied the bringing on of the conversion at Southern revivals, is certain that the spiritual shock treatment of the final stage of the conversion process brings on some kind of seizure that is not epileptic.

[123] For example, there is an Anonymous for mothers who have borne a [developmentally disabled] child; for parents whose child is dying of cancer; there are a couple for cancer patients themselves; one for epileptics; and one for those persons who get least understanding or sympathy—the heavily overweight, who have to fight an unbalanced appetite for carbohydrates.

[124] It is a proved policy of the AAs never to have any contact, *as a body*, or any specific association with a particular religion, sect, or party. If members desire to return to a religion, they are advised to try again the faith they had failed to make solve their problem. AA exists to help a man stop drinking. He is then free to give his support to any policy or theology he believes to be true.

[125] See "Alcoholics Anonymous: Cult or Cure?" by Arthur H. Cain (10). Even in the latest of these salvage efforts where with a more collective procedure (for example, living together in a hostel for the purpose), a movement called Synanon takes in alcoholics, drug addicts, neurotics, potential suicides, etc. Still the ends are the same: to restore to social circulation, to adjust—not to develop, to grow.

[126] See von Frisch (89), *Bees: Their Vision, Chemical Senses and Language*; and Lindauer (54), *Communication Among Social Bees*.

[127] Referred to in Section III, Chapter 1 on the earth ordeal and initiation of rebirth.

[128] Any reference as to specific instruction of the preborn is here omitted. The evidence, advanced by one therapist, that the fetus can understand language seems unsatisfactory and, considering the fetus'

position and brain capacity, very highly improbable. [Ed. note: Research performed in the decades subsequent to Heard's comment demonstrates otherwise, albeit in very specific and limited ways.]

[129] The milk of the modern mother is often made too acidic by her [at times] anxiety and impatient frustration for the infant to digest.

[130] The man who succeeded St. Francis as head of this organization, Brother Elias, was picked to make a viable corporation out of a waning enthusiasm. He ended by being deposed because of his use of power politics.

[131] See Henri Frankfort (27), *Ancient Egyptian Religion*; and *The Human Venture* by Gerald Heard (40).

[132] For further analysis of significant detail of this mythos, see Appendix D.

[133] In passing, it should be noticed here that delinquency seems to stem from two types: (*a*) a child type that is an exuberant prankster; and (*b*) an adolescent type that, newly equipped with the critical faculty, like a child with a new knife practices on anything that cuts up easily.

[134] The optimum condition to which each ordeal should be raised is called Right Effort. Right Effort is the Sixth Step in the Noble Eightfold Path of Buddhism. It is generally illustrated by the tuning of a stringed instrument, each string of which must be brought to perfect pitch—neither slack nor overtautened, neither sharp nor flat.

[135] See endnote 44.

[136] The five stages of consciousness are gone through by all humans. But, as Carleton Coon has indicated, it is more likely than not that Homo sapiens has emerged out of Homo erectus not once but five times. The starting up of man's social heredity, therefore, could have taken place five times. Therefore, at least five different times men may have emerged from group co-consciousness. And, next, most of these entered the proto-self-consciousness of heroic barbarism, "gangsterics." Some of these types, however, remained arrested in a set balance of inner and outer, of psyche and economy: for example, fossil societies such as were still found in the *culs de sac* of inner Australia and Papua. In turn, some of those in heroicism did not go on into the total individualism of modern humans. ... In short, the phases

of human consciousness are gone through at different times by different social heredities. So while the Roman Empire had by A.D. 200 reached ascetic life rejection, when Patrick, preaching this life-rejecting Romanism, reached Ireland, he found the Irish still in heroism.

[137] See Henri Frankfort (26), *The Birth of Civilization in the Near East*, on the Sumerian stubborn clinging to an autonomy as blind as that of the Hellenic anarchy.

[138] The city-state of Athens shows in its history that an aboriginal element survived in the population, and that syncretism gave some *mana* of consent through the female God Athena and her synoecistic rites.

[139] The first great highway in history is the one that the Persians built from Persepolis to Ephesus, a distance [covering around 2,200] miles.

[140] The Greeks regarded the Persians as more than half magicians by virtue of this partnership.

[141] The Modern Age itself divides into four epochs. Four convulsive revolutions are its specific symptom, and so it should be called the age of revolutions. Now that the age is over, "modern," we can see, is not a descriptive term. These revolutions are caused by the frame of reference (the realm of ends, the subconscious keel or trough of meaning, of know-why) not being kept in balance with (not going along with and so not bearing) the realm of means, the conscious sail or crest of powers. Through the Middle Ages, the political deadlock of priest and king, of secular nation-state and holy church universal, at least allowed some slight adjustment of inherited values with observed data (for example, the relaxation of the tabu of usury, and the ruling as to what was a just rate of interest, and the approval by Pope Clement IV [in] 1266 of Roger Bacon's chemical researches and study of scientific procedure). Indeed, it grows increasingly evident that with the steady infiltration of Arab scientific work, which arose from their study of Aristotle, the eleventh, twelfth, and thirteenth centuries were more open to physical discovery than was the fourteenth. Later scholasticism offered only a rigid syllogistic resistance to discoveries. Hence, the keel was dropped, the matrix left behind. Natural knowledge, study of the outer world, rushed ahead. Knowledge of the inner world was arrested and the old theories denied.

¹⁴² In the West, the scholar becomes the pedant, or at best a specialist, and is despised as an egghead that does not even hatch out atom power. Only in China did this type become authoritative.

¹⁴³ For a detailed analysis and interpretation of the five natural moral laws, see *The Eternal Gospel*, The Ayer Foundation lectures given at Colgate Rochester Seminary by Gerald Heard (43) in 1945.

¹⁴⁴ For example, the Greek heroic figure of the winged horse, Pegasus, is found in high relief on the back of Chinese bronze mirrors.

¹⁴⁵ However, Dodds (19) thinks it may have started with a shamanistic culture on the steppes north of the Oxus Sea. (See Appendix D.) It is true that arctic hysteria may have abetted this ascetic movement among migrant Mongolians, some of whom may have brought the doctrine of denial down to the Indus and Ganges headwaters. (A Mongolian skull was dug up in the ruins of Mohenjo-Daro.) To date, however, it seems somewhat more probable that a heroic culture, having come up against one that was sophisticated and discouraged—for example, the Aryans meeting the Dravidian culture in the Ganges basin—would turn from shame and projected anger to guilt and self-blame, and that some such inner-seer as Gautama (the Kshatriya who, though an Aryan, became a Buddha) would be one of the launchers of the doctrine of denial.

¹⁴⁶ Even *aidos*, as Dodds points out, though it has in it a certain sense of "We are all mortal," has in it even more "What will the neighbors say?"

¹⁴⁷ For instance, the final comment of Sophocles is "Only truly blessed is he that never was born."

¹⁴⁸ Socrates having been killed, [and Plato] himself in voluntary banishment, his thought facing this sphinx question.

¹⁴⁹ See page 239 [of] *The Greeks and the Irrational* by Dodds (19).

¹⁵⁰ See page 146 of *The Greeks and the Irrational* by Dodds (19).

¹⁵¹ See page 239 of *The Greeks and the Irrational* by Dodds (19).

¹⁵² He would not allow his birthday to be observed, remarking that the less said about such a painful date the better.

¹⁵³ It seems that the text was put into hexameters by Julian. Here he is following the Greek oracle tradition, for the free-association outbursts of the Delphic Pythia were worked up into hexameters before being published.

[154] *The Chaldean Oracles* contain a prescription for a fire cult, so the word initiation may have been used precisely for the great fourth mystery.

[155] Chiefly by flagellation, especially among the Celtic Churches. St. Bridget's order (she is called the Mary of the Gaels) is often called the order of the rod.

[156] See Margaret Murray's (64) *The Witch Cult in Western Europe.*

[157] Innocent III was the pope in whose reign the papacy reached the climax of its power; and he it was who launched this crusade against the Cathars which, under the leadership of a brigand land-grabber, de Montfort, devastated a lovely countryside. Yet, as G. C. Coulton (16) points out in his *Five Centuries of Religion*, this pope himself consulted a necromancer.

[158] As we have said, the fifth mystery ordeal-initiation of electricity may well have come in considerably later and, as we shall see in the following pages, Colin Still, tracing the asceticized rendering of the mysteries, can only regard this final mystery as one of intellectual light.

[159] As have the Australian Stone Age cultures of today.

[160] Even in the Anglican Church, the rite of churching the mother of a newly born child continued until this century and may still hang on. The office for this odd social disinfection is still in the prayer book of the Church of England.

[161] Sophocles, who lived to be over ninety, remarked that the one compensation of old age was to be rid of love.

[162] In the latest and definitive study on the Escurial (*The Prado, Madrid*, Abrams, 1956) H. B. Wehle says that Fränger's interpretation of Bosch's work is more reasonable than any before.

[163] Through all of mythology, the bird is associated with the soul and its migratory flight.

[164] See the report of Symposium No. 2 on *Illustrative Strategies for Research on Psychopathology in Mental Health* at the meeting of the Group for the Advancement of Psychiatry held at the Berkeley-Carteret Hotel, Asbury Park, New Jersey, on November 6, 1955.

[165] See *Lysergic Acid, Diethylamide, and Mescaline in Experimental Psychiatry*, edited by Louis Cholden (13). This judgment has been amply confirmed by a wealth of experimental studies made under controlled conditions.

[166] See "Critical Periods in Behavioral Development" by J. P. Scott (senior staff scientist, R. B. Jackson Memorial Laboratory, Bar Harbor, Maine) in *Science*, November 30, 1962, Vol. 138, pp. 949–958.

[167] [Kurtz J S, Patel N A, Gendreau J L, et al., (September 14, 2022), *The Use of Psychedelics in the Treatment of Medical Conditions: An Analysis of Currently Registered Psychedelics Studies in the American Drug Trial Registry*, Cureus 14(9): e29167, licensed under CC BY-SA 4.0.]

[168] [*Visible Light*, https://science.nasa.gov/ems/09_visiblelight, accessed May 2023.]

[169] [*Visible Light: Eye-opening research at NNSA*, https://www.energy.gov/nnsa/articles/visible-light-eye-opening-research-nnsa, accessed May 2023.]

INDEX

Aboriginal, 52, 97, 134, 162, 193, 368, 372
Abydos, 163, 279, 294
Achaeans, 29, 32, 38, 295, 310
Achilles, 28, 39, 44, 365
ad hoc church, 268, 269, 270
Adamites, 318, 331, 376
addiction, 47, 235, 267, 268, 269, 271, 272
adolescence, 11, 80, 91, 103, 105, 108, 119, 120, 121, 128, 129, 131, 133, 134, 135, 140, 141, 148, 151, 206, 208, 209, 220, 233, 287, 326, 370
adolescent, 8, 9, 12, 48, 68, 104, 119, 121, 122, 123, 124, 125, 126, 127, 128, 129, 130, 131, 132, 133, 134, 140, 141, 148, 152, 196, 200, 201, 203, 206, 232, 235, 273, 286, 287, 288, 292, 294, 326, 342, 369, 381
Aeschylus, 40, 43, 45, 365
aether, 13, 159, 161, 198, 239, 248, 324, 328
Age of Gold, 26, 323
Ages of Faith, 64, 126
agonia, 41
air mystery, 192, 194, 196, 197, 200, 202, 218
Ajax, 31, 108, 345, 365
alcohol, 29, 205, 268, 272
alcoholic, 236, 270, 272
Alcoholics Anonymous, 268, 269, 380
alcoholism, 235, 267, 271
anarchy, 12, 43, 64, 81, 84, 106, 123, 182, 219, 262, 284, 295, 296, 297, 382
Angyal, Andras, 370
anodynes, 29, 119, 192

anxiety, 102, 103, 104, 150, 155, 167, 174, 194, 219, 248, 348, 371, 381
apatheia, 315
Apuleius, 193, 211
aqualung, 186
Aristotle, 40, 55, 210, 313, 365, 382
Arnold, Mathew, 79
Art and Illusion, 368, 375
Aryans, 29, 38, 239, 310, 383
Ascetic Epoch, 2, 9, 10, 32, 33, 36, 46, 56, 81, 83, 90, 102, 121, 127, 130, 132, 161, 169, 190, 218, 236, 264, 281, 302, 303, 306, 310, 320, 321, 324, 345, 383
Ascetic phase, 4, 52, 163, 220, 306
asceticism, 33, 38, 39, 40, 46, 52, 53, 64, 67, 119, 121, 123, 124, 126, 144, 154, 159, 160, 264, 306, 310, 312, 318, 329
askesis, 39, 126, 187
Asoka, Emperor, 292
astrology, 62, 316
ataraxia, 173, 315
Athena, 31, 382
Athens, 43, 45, 312, 368, 382
athleticism, 68, 121, 128, 294
Aurelius, Marcus, 314
Australia, 3, 16, 21, 75, 116, 368, 381
autosuggestion, 66, 165, 167, 170, 221, 227
Bacchae, The, 43, 223
Bacon, Roger, 382
barbarian, 16, 17, 84, 294, 297, 318
Baudouin, Charles, 214, 366
Benedict XIV, Pope, 366
birth trauma, 95, 96, 175, 191, 208, 233, 342 (*see also* trauma of birth)
bodiless state, 46, 323
Boehme, Jacob, 266, 380

Bohr, Niels, 61, 348
Bolk, Louis, 80, 263, 273, 301, 369
Book of Judges, 32, 182
Bosch, Hieronymus, 329, 384
Boucher de Perthes, Jacques, 3, 17
Breasted, James Henry, 4, 5, 37, 293
breath control, 194
Buddha, 52, 54, 383
Buddhism, 38, 53, 234, 292, 306, 310, 378, 381
burial, 162, 163, 165, 166, 169, 171, 185, 190, 197, 200, 208, 220, 227, 335, 336, 376
Burt, Cyril, 8, 89, 90
Butler, Samuel, 77, 367
Byrd, Admiral Richard, 334
Campbell, Joseph, 224, 225, 378
cancer, 105, 122, 123, 369, 380
carbon dioxide, 143, 191, 194, 195, 199, 208
Cathars, 319, 320, 384
catharsis, 12, 41, 44, 71, 120, 182, 183, 186, 187, 189, 190, 197, 200, 203, 208, 209, 213, 220, 227, 320, 342
Catholicism, 5, 126, 237, 309
Celeus, King, 279, 376
chakras, 240, 317
Chaldean Oracles, The, 317, 384
Charcot, J.M., 60, 61
childhood, 9, 11, 78, 80, 82, 90, 91, 94, 98, 102, 103, 104, 106, 108, 118, 119, 121, 124, 125, 129, 133, 138, 148, 152, 154, 200, 203, 208, 209, 220, 233, 263, 271, 287, 288, 301, 326, 328
China, 5, 16, 38, 52, 54, 127, 140, 214, 306, 308, 378, 383
Chinese, 37, 72, 88, 194, 204, 234, 299, 306, 316, 383
Christian church, 292, 296, 318
chung tzu, 53

Church of England, 267, 384
city-states, 293, 294, 295, 298, 382
Clement IV, Pope, 382
Clement XIV, Pope, 366
coconscious, 16, 22, 23, 25, 26, 29, 36, 41, 47, 51, 54, 75, 83, 90, 102, 115, 161, 164, 177, 178, 189, 190, 200, 209, 217, 218, 264, 303, 305, 322, 344
colonic irrigation, 184
comedy, 41, 42, 162
Communist, 127, 378
conduct, character, and consciousness, 15, 23, 44, 57, 160, 265, 312
Confucian, 38, 88, 204
Confucius, 37, 54, 310
consciousness, contraction of, 11, 41, 46, 51, 53, 81, 82
consciousness, evolution of, 8, 158
consciousness, field of, 27, 35, 249, 250, 254, 342
consciousness, first stage, 344
consciousness, fourth type, 297
consciousness, growth of, 9, 10, 121, 263, 322
consciousness, levels of, 84, 230, 241
consciousness, mutation of, 270, 291
consciousness, racial, 332
consciousness, states of, 38, 198, 366
Constantine the Great, 292, 296
Constantine, St., 222
continence, 241
convulsions, 84, 120, 379
cooperation, 79, 83, 110, 122, 178, 185, 231, 263, 273, 313
Cope's Law, 274, 301, 367
Counter-Reformation, 64, 68, 69, 72
Cyrus, 295, 296, 306
damnation, eternal, 266, 316

Index

Dante Alighieri, 53, 324
Darwin, Charles, 60, 63, 99, 111
Darwinianism, 62, 77, 107, 297
dawn sense, 339
delta wave, 174, 244, 369
delusions, 192, 195, 326, 335
dementia praecox, 12, 109, 119, 127, 132, 141, 187, 209, 275
Demeter, 45, 164, 211, 213, 226, 279, 376
dervishes, 130, 320, 377
detension, 63, 72, 77, 144, 169, 251, 267, 338, 379
developmental therapy, 158, 227, 246, 250, 278
Dionysus, 29, 30, 223, 376
Divine Comedy, The, 321, 324
Dodds, E.R., 311, 312, 313, 345, 365, 383
Drucker, Peter, 145, 370
earth mystery, 165, 166, 218, 323, 324, 327
Ebon, Martin, 222
ecology, 62, 79, 263
economics, 2, 60, 62, 71, 111, 136, 234, 297, 306
ecstasy, 41, 54, 211, 223, 266, 314, 330, 349
Egypt, 37, 38, 163, 169, 180, 193, 279, 294, 295, 365
Egyptian Book of the Dead, 372
eidetic imagery, 17, 66, 340
Eiseley, Loren, 98
electric current, 156, 253
electric field, 242, 249, 250, 289, 328, 329
electric shock, 240, 246, 247, 248, 249, 250, 319
electric shock therapy, 239, 244, 245, 248
electric surge treatment, 156, 159, 245, 251, 328, 342

electricity, 161, 239, 247, 248, 250, 251, 384
electrocuted hogs, 249
electrocution, 239, 246
Eleusinian mysteries, 45, 164, 167, 178, 191, 226, 317, 373, 375, 376
Eleusis, 45, 191, 193, 210, 213, 226, 279, 317, 372, 376
embryo, 89, 96, 107, 113, 183, 201, 274, 275, 328, 329, 369
Empedocles, 312, 313
empire-state, 298
engineers, 128, 204, 369
Enneads, The, 314
epilepsy, 60, 239, 242, 244
epileptic, 239, 242, 243, 244, 251, 267, 336, 380
Equanil, 212, 371
Eranos Yearbooks, 158, 224
euphoria, 144, 196, 201, 219, 328
Euripides, 40, 43, 223, 365
evolution, further, 121, 172, 282, 283
evolution, human, 79, 131, 152, 262, 263, 273, 280, 303
evolution, psychological, 46, 48, 145, 158, 295
evolution, psychosocial, 8, 26, 218, 285
extrasensory perception, 5, 136, 155, 303, 317
Fabing, Howard, 237, 380
failure of nerve, 10, 48, 83, 124, 238, 284
Ferenczi, Sándor, 374
fertility rites, 23, 210
fetalization, 80, 107, 263, 273, 280, 301
fifth age group, 233
fifth epoch, 73, 84
fifth mystery, 159, 233, 238, 248, 250, 384

389

fifth ordeal, 139, 159, 234, 246
fifth stage, 83, 136, 145, 146, 160, 233, 240
fire ordeal, 248, 324, 376, 377
fire walk, 221, 222, 223, 224, 377
first initiation, 161, 169, 179, 322
first maturity, 9, 11, 12, 91, 103, 104, 121, 123, 128, 129, 131, 132, 133, 134, 135, 136, 137, 138, 140, 144, 149, 150, 151, 154, 155, 202, 204, 207, 208, 209, 210, 212, 216, 217, 219, 230, 231, 232, 234, 235, 237, 238, 273, 288, 327, 328
first mystery, 171, 175, 184, 191, 322, 342
five epochs, 11, 161
five ordeals, 93, 318
five senses, 138, 158, 311
five stages, 91, 103, 113, 139, 158, 159, 325, 326, 328, 381
four age groups, 233, 235
four epochs, 75, 233, 305, 382
four mysteries, 176, 233, 321
four stages, 145, 321
fourth mystery, 208, 217, 233, 324, 376, 384
fourth ordeal, 138, 220, 221
fourth stage, 76, 83, 136, 203, 208, 327, 347
fourth therapy, 203, 205
Fox, George, 265
frame of reference, 64, 65, 114, 154, 189, 233, 241, 244, 281, 294, 299, 382
Francis of Assisi, St., 277, 374, 381
Fränger, Wilhelm, 329, 331, 384
Frankfort, Henri, 163, 381, 382
Frazer, James, 4, 78
French Revolution, 70
Freud, Sigmund, 58, 59, 61, 63, 77, 78, 154, 184, 201, 236, 239, 248, 374

Fromm, Erich, 144
Fry, Roger, 376
Galileo, 64
Ganges River, 306, 383
Garden of Earthly Delights, The, 329
Genghis Kahn, 300, 372
genitalia, 125, 154, 184, 196, 201
geriatrics, 139, 145, 155, 232
Gesell, Arnold, 8, 89, 91, 119
Gnosticism, 5, 321
Goethe, Johann Wolfgang von, 3
Golden Bough, The, 78
Gombrich, E.H., 368, 375
gorilla, 274, 370
Greece, 16, 181, 193, 293, 295
Greeks, 31, 40, 178, 181, 194, 213, 238, 239, 310, 311, 365, 376, 382, 383
Grotius, 1, 2, 69
guilt, 28, 47, 48, 49, 54, 56, 57, 71, 76, 81, 102, 108, 119, 124, 125, 127, 132, 140, 144, 187, 189, 190, 196, 200, 201, 218, 220, 225, 233, 265, 276, 281, 292, 293, 300, 308, 310, 312, 316, 323, 328, 342, 346, 348, 383
Haldane, J.B.S., 134, 136, 274
Hall, Stanley, 8, 89, 90
hallucinations, 192, 334, 335, 337, 340
Harappa, 180, 379
hashish, 379
hatha yoga, 170, 197, 240, 317, 373
heart disease, 204, 206
Hebb, Donald, 111, 171, 333, 335, 340, 371, 372
Hellenic Roman, 72, 83, 88, 167, 193, 232, 313
hemp, Indian, 213, 365
heretics, 10, 331, 366
Hermes, 30
hero, the, 23, 25, 27, 29, 30, 35, 38, 39, 41, 42, 44, 49, 52, 54, 57, 64, 76, 81, 95, 97, 104, 127, 128, 132, 135, 183, 281, 299, 345, 347, 365

Index

Herodotus, 213, 365
Heroic Epoch, 2, 8, 9, 10, 25, 27, 28, 29, 30, 32, 33, 34, 35, 38, 43, 51, 52, 54, 56, 75, 81, 83, 90, 97, 102, 106, 121, 127, 140, 148, 164, 177, 179, 182, 184, 187, 189, 218, 281, 302, 305, 306, 310, 345, 365
heroicism, 40, 125, 126, 137, 218, 326, 381
heroism, 68, 295, 382
Hesiod, 25, 310
Hitler, Adolf, 109, 141, 365
Hobbes, Thomas, 5, 204
Holy Rollers, 265
homeostasis, 122, 123, 185, 325
Homer, 28, 30, 32, 44, 293, 310
homicidal, 28, 105, 109, 119, 133, 182, 187, 292, 345
homicidal rage, 28, 119, 182, 292
Homo erectus, 381
Homo sapiens, 381
Hosea, 22, 37
Human Animal, The, 274, 369
Humanic Epoch, 2, 9, 33, 66, 67, 128, 229, 231, 239, 302
Humanic man, 48, 52, 56, 57, 58, 62, 64, 66, 69, 70, 81, 84, 104, 123, 128, 132, 137, 146, 151, 206, 212, 216, 219, 281, 306, 328, 347, 348
Humanic phase, 52, 53, 57, 68, 73, 130, 134, 214, 219
humanism, 33, 57, 64, 67, 69, 70, 71, 81, 84, 119, 366
humanitarianism, 66, 69, 70, 71, 72, 73, 81
Hume, David, 27, 70
hydrotherapy, 30
hypnocracy, 16, 292, 295, 372
hypnocratic, 2, 25, 180, 264
hypnosis, 61, 95, 169, 171, 172, 198, 214, 228, 295, 317
hypnotic suggestion, 165, 194, 202, 374

Ignatian, 64, 66, 67, 77, 265, 266
Ignatius of Loyola, Saint, 64, 65, 67, 71, 265, 374
Iliad, The, 32, 33, 39
Imitation of Christ, The, 64
India, 37, 38, 48, 52, 165, 169, 184, 194, 221, 224, 292, 308, 310, 371, 373
Indus civilization, 93, 180, 379
infancy, 8, 9, 11, 73, 80, 82, 90, 91, 94, 98, 106, 107, 108, 119, 121, 129, 133, 138, 140, 148, 177, 178, 200, 203, 263, 271, 273, 285, 286, 301, 322, 336
initiation by water, 181, 183
initiation of illumination, 181
Innocent III, Pope, 384
insanity, 11, 83, 109, 132, 135, 168, 209, 235, 238, 267, 376
integral thought, 63, 82, 303, 311, 332
involutional melancholy, 11, 13, 48, 123, 138, 141, 143, 146, 155, 159, 235, 239, 244
Isis, 163, 193, 279, 294
isolation, 52, 83, 134, 138, 171, 173, 221, 334, 339, 367
James, William, 71, 129, 380
Jaspers, Karl, 4, 293
Jellinek, Stefan, 246, 247, 248, 249, 251
Jesuits, 64, 67, 68, 69, 265, 266, 366
Jesus Christ, 223
Jews, the, 237, 309
Judaism, 265, 309
Julian the Theurgist, 316, 317, 383
Julius Caesar, 296
Jungian, 145, 158, 332, 374
juvenile delinquency, 78, 120, 205, 285
Kant, Immanuel, 313
Kelley, Douglas M., 78
Kirsch, Robert R., 160

kundalini, 197, 240, 241, 250, 331
La Barre, Weston, 273, 274, 369
Lao Tzu, 278
Law of Reversed Effort, 214, 366
Law, William, 266, 380
lepsis, 83, 244, 245
Leptoid, 60, 83, 85, 91, 132, 136, 137, 156, 226, 244, 246, 251, 262, 302, 306, 328
Leviathan, 5, 100, 204
Librium, 102, 371
life expectancy, 134, 148, 370
Lilly, John C., 171, 333, 334, 337, 338, 339, 341, 371, 372
limited environment, 170, 171, 172, 173, 185, 200, 315, 320, 333, 337, 340, 341, 342
Lindner, Robert, 286, 374
Living Brain, The, 120, 244, 372
London Society for Psychical Research, 61
Long, Max Freedom, 377
Loomis, Earl, 109, 272
Lorenz, Konrad, 368
lung aeration, 172, 173, 342
lysergic acid, 172, 174, 214, 336, 340
MacCurdy, John Thomas, 105, 252
macrocosmos, 348, 349
magic, 4, 21, 23, 27, 30, 32, 33, 54, 116, 212, 293, 296, 314, 317, 318, 319, 331, 376
magician, 38, 281, 302, 379
Mahabharata, 32
Malthus, T.R., 60, 111
Man's Presumptuous Brain, 369, 375
mana, 292, 295, 296, 299, 382
managers, 128, 204, 211
manic depression, 141
manic-depressive, 11, 12, 48, 83, 110, 132, 134, 135, 137, 138, 143, 144, 206, 228, 327
martial law, 43, 293

McGill University experiments, 334, 337, 339, 340
Mead, Margaret, 286
Meduna, L.J., 199, 374
melancholia, 235, 236, 251, 252
melancholic, 235, 236, 371
Menninger, Karl, 245
mental disease, 155, 206, 238, 239, 369
mescaline, 174, 214, 336, 340
Mesmer, Franz, 198
Mesopotamia, 23, 316
Metaneira, 279, 376
metanoia, 266, 270
Methodist, 178, 266
Metrazol, 243
Michelangelo, 68, 104
microcosmos, 348
Middle Ages, 62, 317, 369, 382
midindividual, 45, 47, 48, 49, 54, 55, 62, 81, 83, 90, 105, 125, 144, 190, 195, 196, 200, 201, 202, 209, 218, 308, 328
midindividualism, 9, 102, 123, 227
midindividualistic, 64, 76
Midindividualistic Epoch, 9, 36
Milton, John, 379
Miltown, 212, 371
miscarriage, 47, 73, 88, 106, 113, 165, 177, 178, 233, 252, 287
Mithraism, 315
Modern Age, 60, 70, 284, 298, 321, 382
Mohenjo-Daro, 180, 379, 383
monkeys, 246, 370
More, Sir Thomas, 367
Moreno, J.S., 332, 374
mortification, 39, 160, 191, 253, 306
mortificatory, 39, 65, 67, 124, 125, 163, 190, 218, 292, 300, 306, 327, 334
Mount Kailas, 239

Index

mushrooms, 214, 375
Mussolini, Benito, 365
mystery of aether, 13
mystery of air, 12, 194, 196, 197
mystery of earth, 11, 170, 322, 333
mystery of fire, 12, 217
mystery of the two fires, 325
mystery of water, 12, 333
mystery tradition, 184, 208, 324
Napoleon, 299, 365
Narcotics Anonymous, 268
nationalism, 72, 84, 126, 295, 297
nation-state, 298, 382
natural law, 43, 292, 298
natural science, 3, 55, 266, 315
Nazis, 78, 120
Near East, 8, 305, 382
Neo-Platonism, 314
neotenic, 108, 112, 121, 128, 133, 134, 136, 140, 147, 153, 197, 201, 202, 264, 274, 277, 279, 280, 283, 301
neoteny, 107, 108, 112, 113, 120, 128, 134, 138, 147, 151, 264, 278, 280, 301
nepenthe, 29, 365
new class, 141, 150, 155, 231, 232, 245
Nicodemus, 147, 151
Nile, 4, 37, 163, 295, 306, 308
nine planes, 325, 326, 327, 328
nitrous oxide, 198, 199
Noble Eightfold Path, 381
nonself-conscious, 82, 85, 140, 160, 262, 322
noradrenaline, 12, 28, 30, 48, 78, 101, 102, 103, 104, 105, 109, 119, 121, 122, 123, 127, 132, 133, 134, 135, 179, 180, 186, 187, 310, 326, 342
Nothing fails like success, 26, 219
numinous, 344, 345
Odyssey, The, 30, 32, 33, 34

Oedipus, 43
old age, 19, 44, 46, 138, 139, 140, 143, 144, 150, 166, 207, 232, 237, 244, 384
oldsters, 143, 150, 231
Oligocene Epoch, 367
OM syllable, 194
ontogeny, 8, 15, 89, 209, 220, 284
Operation successful, patient succumbed, 231
oracle, Greek, 194, 383
orangutan, 370
ordeal by fire, 39, 209, 221
orgasm, 125, 200, 201
Origen, 6
Origin of Species, The, 60
Osiris, 163, 294
other-worldly, 54, 77, 282, 294, 297, 316, 323, 366
other-worldlyism, 52, 125, 140
Otto, Rudolf, 344
Otto, W.F., 164, 375
oxygen, 143, 191, 199, 249, 282, 287, 322, 365
paidomorph, 121, 277, 280, 301, 369
paidomorphy, 80, 107, 138, 147, 151, 263, 278, 280, 301
Paleolithic Period, 3, 7, 18, 20, 162, 193, 230, 365, 371, 379
panaesthetic, 125, 178, 196, 200, 201, 202, 209, 242, 283, 288, 311, 318, 319, 328
Papua, 16, 75, 140, 381
Paraclete, 267, 318
paranoia, 11, 27, 35, 102, 105, 109, 127, 132, 144, 208, 209
paranoic, 29, 218, 236
parturition, 20, 178, 190, 200, 287, 371
patheia, 41
Patrick, Saint, 382
pattern of behavior, 143, 203, 204, 232

pattern of prestige, 28, 32, 34, 35, 39, 41, 43, 49, 53, 128, 136, 140, 235, 250, 264, 302, 313, 326
Patterns of Culture, 221, 370
Paul of Tarsus, 65, 196, 312, 318
Pellus, Michael C., 319
Penfield, Wilder, 173, 242
Pentecostal, 267
Persephone, 164, 166, 193, 211, 226, 373
Persian, 29, 40, 295, 296, 306, 316, 368, 382
Petrie, Sir Flinders, 4
Pfeiffer, John, 237, 273, 274, 282, 379
Pharaoh, 164, 165, 294, 299, 376
Philip II, King, 329, 331, 366
Philoxenia, 31
phylogeny, 8, 15, 89, 158, 209, 220, 284
physics, 61, 62, 76, 297, 306, 313, 348
pineal gland, 194, 240
pituitary gland, 194, 240
Plato, 233, 311, 312, 328, 383
Plotinus, 314, 323, 324
Plutarch, 167, 193, 213
Pontifex Maximus, 296
Post-Humanic Epoch, 229
Post-Humanic individual, 140, 147
postindividual, 59, 84, 136, 140, 147, 156, 160, 167, 175, 232, 235, 245, 250, 254
Postindividual Epoch, 169, 229, 231
Pre-Heroic Epoch, 9, 25, 177
preindividual, 17, 34, 42, 45, 47, 51, 75, 81, 90, 102, 115, 209, 217
preindividualistic, 75, 82, 116, 166, 185
preindividualized, 8, 139, 344
prepuberty, 154, 155
pre-self-conscious, 3, 8, 133
preterconscious, 28, 31, 58, 59, 60, 64, 82, 118, 136, 157, 166, 182, 190, 210, 254
preterconsciousness, 15, 58, 196, 236
preterindividualistic consciousness, 158
preterrational, 56, 264, 310, 311
priest-king, 25, 38, 51, 166, 292, 293, 294, 295
Proclus, 317
prophetes, 318
Protestants, 237
proto-hero, 42, 48, 293
protohistory, 16, 90
protoindividual, 22, 27, 33, 34, 47, 54, 75, 81, 82, 83, 93, 102, 105, 115, 144, 179, 181, 182, 183, 184, 185, 186, 187, 209, 218, 307, 308
protoindividualism, 9, 29, 45, 52, 105, 124, 177, 227
Protoindividualistic Epoch, 9, 32, 325
protoindividualistic stage, 8
psilocybin, 340, 375
psychedelics, 213, 214, 215, 216, 217, 375
psychiatry, 73, 76, 77, 82, 112, 118, 126, 144, 167, 168, 169, 170, 191, 266, 267, 285, 316
psychoanalysis, 170, 267
psychological interpretation of history, 5, 89
psycho-ontogeny, 8, 9
psychophylogeny, 8, 140
psychophysical development, 139, 171, 233, 272
psychophysical education, 121, 227, 273
psychophysical therapy, 156, 187, 221, 322, 327, 342
psychophysique, 12, 121, 123, 151, 154, 183, 250, 271, 303, 317, 320, 369, 379

Index

psychosomatic, 30, 92, 104, 105, 106, 122, 137, 167, 168, 178, 205, 206, 210, 215, 219, 227, 231, 271, 282, 368
psychotherapy, 77, 107, 161, 168, 171, 199, 200, 205, 233, 236, 332, 339
Psychotics Anonymous, 268
puberty, 12, 197, 374
Pythagorianism, 38, 313
Quakerism, 266, 379
Quakers, 265, 266
Quietists, 366
Radhakrishnan, Dr. Sarvepalli, 63
radiant heat therapy, 288
radiation therapy, 228
radiation, infrared, 12, 228
rages, 39, 168, 175, 200, 342
rainbow, 324, 325, 327, 349
rajas, 147, 180
Ramakrishna, 314
Ramayana, 32, 33
Rank, Otto, 367
rationalism, 4, 70, 125, 236, 310
Realm of Ends, 294, 313, 344, 382
rebirth, 96, 162, 165, 169, 172, 177, 183, 189, 190, 197, 200, 208, 220, 269, 323, 335, 342, 376, 380
recapitulate, 54, 103, 105, 108, 128, 140, 145, 162, 209, 220
recapitulation, 9, 15, 113, 118, 131, 157, 158, 170
regression, 92, 161, 166, 167, 169, 171, 172, 173, 185, 200, 203, 208, 209, 227, 233, 323, 335, 342, 367
Reich, Theodore, 287, 367
religions, ancient, 238, 317
Renaissance, 4, 33, 55, 56, 64, 68, 104, 140, 306, 330, 347
Renaissance man, 56, 104, 140, 141, 347
respiration, 172, 186, 194, 195, 196, 198, 227, 246

Revival of Learning, 53, 59
revolution, economic, 60, 77
revolution, first, 297
revolution, fourth, 60, 298
revolution, psychological, 60, 72, 155, 167, 168, 169, 175, 262, 284, 298
revolution, second, 297
revolution, third, 297
revolutions, four, 60, 284, 298, 382
Rhys Davids, Thomas Williams, 38
Ribble, Margaret, 92
rise of conscience, 4, 37
rishi, 182, 234
rite of breathing, 12
rite of burial, 11
rite of immersion, 12, 333
Ritter, Christiane, 334
Rogers, Carl, 332, 374
Roman Empire, 31, 72, 296, 297, 299, 382
routineers, 150, 204, 244, 303
royal jelly, 279, 280
Salvation Army, 267
Sandwith, George, 225
Sanskrit, 32, 180, 182, 194, 234, 239, 240, 241, 250, 251, 277, 379
sarcophagus, 165, 171
Sargant, William, 238
Satan, 319
sattva, 147
Scale of Perfection, The, 64
schizoid, 12, 123, 125, 127, 128, 132, 138, 196, 202, 220, 291, 292, 297, 308, 345
schizophrenia, 11, 83, 105, 127, 132, 134, 141, 156, 196, 200, 208, 209, 369, 379
schizophrenic, 58, 102, 144, 190, 236, 326
Scholastic Period, 54, 130, 135
Scythians, 213, 365

Search for Bridey Murphy, The, 171, 372
second initiation, 179
second maturity, 11, 13, 91, 108, 123, 129, 132, 134, 137, 138, 140, 141, 145, 146, 147, 149, 150, 151, 155, 156, 159, 160, 204, 208, 209, 216, 231, 232, 234, 235, 237, 238, 239, 245, 246, 250, 251, 252, 253, 288, 327, 328, 370
Sed Festival, 170, 180
sedation, 29, 205, 245, 365, 371
sedatives, 30, 192
seers, 30, 48, 153, 159, 160, 182, 204, 279, 309
seership, 29, 153, 155, 156, 164, 233
self-accusing, 54, 197, 202, 203
self-assertive, 22, 27, 34, 36, 39, 48, 52, 54
self-blame, 11, 47, 48, 140, 383
self-blaming, 46, 122, 134, 187, 190, 206, 345
self-conscious, 4, 38, 39, 45, 46, 52, 55, 56, 58, 72, 75, 77, 82, 88, 90, 134, 135, 140, 157, 160, 161, 213, 217, 219, 262, 285, 294, 297, 332
self-consciousness, 5, 9, 10, 11, 15, 26, 32, 36, 39, 42, 43, 44, 45, 49, 54, 55, 64, 69, 76, 77, 78, 83, 91, 94, 104, 105, 124, 132, 136, 157, 184, 200, 205, 207, 218, 219, 229, 230, 234, 264, 336, 366, 381
self-sufficient, 33, 53, 56, 57, 62, 63, 76
Selye, Hans, 104, 205
senile, 139, 231, 232, 378
sensitiveness, 54, 70, 79, 80, 82, 152, 178, 236, 272, 279
sexual, 37, 144, 165, 196, 200, 241, 242, 283, 284, 310, 369, 374
sexual repression, 310
sexuality, 125, 197, 200, 201

Shaftesbury, Earl of, 367
shaman, 153, 181, 182, 221, 251, 263, 267, 372
shame, 27, 28, 47, 56, 57, 69, 76, 81, 102, 108, 119, 124, 127, 132, 189, 310, 312, 323, 342, 345, 346, 348, 365, 383
shame culture, 345, 365
Sheldon, William, 73, 125
Shirokogoroff, S.M., 181, 221, 251
shortwave radiation, 288
Shurley, Jay T., 341, 372
Simpson, G.G., 6, 7
Sixtus V, Pope, 366
sleep, 61, 163, 168, 198, 330, 335, 339
Slocum, Joshua, 334
Smith, Adam, 57, 297
social heredity, 4, 7, 26, 85, 89, 90, 98, 99, 111, 117, 119, 128, 136, 139, 152, 153, 155, 158, 159, 164, 170, 178, 185, 263, 264, 276, 279, 281, 297, 302, 381
Socrates, 310, 311, 314, 383
soma, 29, 30, 213
Sophocles, 40, 43, 310, 328, 383, 384
Southern Methodism, 267
specialist, 111, 383
specialized, 20, 26, 79, 119, 128, 145, 147, 148, 151, 263, 278, 313, 322, 371
Spencer, Herbert, 4
spiral, 2, 26, 34, 81, 82, 83, 87, 90, 102, 147, 149, 157, 202, 207, 230, 262
Spiritual Exercises of St. Ignatius, The, 64, 65, 67, 309
Stalin, Joseph, 141
Still, Colin, 321, 324, 326, 327, 329, 373, 378, 384
stimulants, 192
Stoics, 173, 313, 314, 315

Index

Stone Age, 3, 140, 153, 193, 372, 384
Strong, W.D., 7, 365
subconscious, 2, 30, 33, 67, 69, 92, 95, 117, 123, 166, 167, 172, 184, 199, 205, 218, 219, 231, 265, 271, 277, 284, 285, 287, 311, 312, 316, 317, 323, 332, 336, 339, 345, 382
suffering, 41, 46, 54, 70, 117, 124, 125, 198, 346, 347
suffocation, 92, 316
Sufis, 222, 379
suggestibility, 2, 81, 110, 165, 172, 201, 335
suggestible, 110, 168, 172, 276
suicide, 27, 42, 138, 143, 167, 237, 238, 369, 371
Sullivan, Harry Stack, 144
Sumeria, 16, 293, 382
superconsciousness, 182
suprarenals, 99, 101, 102, 121, 205, 206, 240
suspended animation, 165, 170, 183, 241, 247
Swedenborg, Emanuel, 195, 266, 373
symbiosis, 8, 65, 79, 94, 98, 152, 167, 263, 303
tamas, 147
Tanagras, Admiral Angelo, 222, 223
Tantra, 197, 253, 308, 314, 331, 376
Tao, 20, 308, 331
Tao Te Ching, 308
Taoism, 306, 308
Taoist, 166, 278
teachability, 17, 80, 85, 120, 274
teachable, 87, 263, 276, 277
Teiresias, 30, 31, 33, 34
Tempest, The, 321, 324, 329, 331
Tennyson, Alfred, Lord, 324
theurgy, 316, 317
third mystery, 167, 189, 191, 196, 197, 220

thymus gland, 197, 240, 288, 370, 379
tickling, 92, 201, 275
Timeless Theme, The, 321, 324, 373, 378
Tolserol, 212, 371
tomb, 146, 162, 163, 166, 183, 211, 340
total individual, 55, 56, 57, 63, 66, 82, 90, 123, 132, 136, 137, 144, 151, 155, 206, 207, 208, 211, 220, 231, 264, 327, 347
total individualism, 48, 52, 57, 62, 69, 70, 83, 103, 138, 202, 209, 228, 281, 306, 381
Toynbee, Arnold, 5, 314
tragedy, 16, 32, 33, 38, 39, 40, 41, 42, 43, 44, 108, 111, 147, 162, 164, 186, 187, 294, 310, 369
transitional stress phase, 321, 322, 325, 326, 327
transmute, 183, 245, 248, 279, 284
trauma of birth, 11, 29, 93, 96, 132, 161, 162, 166, 169, 171, 201, 208, 209, 227, 367 (*see also* birth trauma)
Ulysses, 30, 33, 34
umbilical cord, 92, 191
unspecialized, 80, 147, 263, 264, 274, 279, 282, 301, 303, 367
unspent energies, 288
Upanishads, 37
Utopia, 53, 58, 131, 179, 303, 367
utopianism, 63, 71
Vanitas vanitatum, 32, 83, 236
Varieties of Religious Experience, The, 71, 380
Vedānta-sāra, 173, 250
Vernon, Jack, 339, 340, 372
veterine, 11, 13, 159, 231, 237, 273
Vico, Giovanni, 2, 3, 16
Virgil, 324

Waley, Arthur, 37, 308
Walter, Grey, 120, 244, 282, 283, 372
Warthin, Aldred Scott, 139, 327, 375
water immersion, 319, 337
water initiation, 180, 187, 376
water tank, 185, 186, 187, 333, 337, 338, 341, 342
Way of the Fathers, 277, 283
Wealth of Nations, The, 57
Weber, Max, 4
Wells, H.G., 58, 59, 63, 79, 301
Wesley, John, 71, 265, 266, 267
Wesleyanism, 266, 267
Whitehead, Alfred North, 1
Witch Cult, 309, 319
witch doctor, 263, 267
World War, First, 167
World War, Second, 58, 168, 334
Xerxes, 40
X-ray, 170, 204, 348
Yage snuff, 214
Yahweh, 32, 309
Yamabushi sect, 224, 225, 227
yoga, 184, 317, 370, 372, 373
yogic practices, 194, 195, 197, 240, 241, 287
Zeus, 41, 239
Zimmer, Heinrich, 224
Zoroastrian, 296

ABOUT THE AUTHOR

Born in London on October 6, 1889, Henry FitzGerald "Gerald" Heard lived a life that would take many fascinating and fateful turns. Heard spent his university years at Cambridge University's Gonville & Caius College. There, in 1911, he was conferred a Bachelor of Arts degree with Honours in history.

Following Cambridge, Heard worked for Lord Robson of Jesmond, then for Sir Horace Plunkett, founder of the influential Irish Agricultural [later "Co-operative"] Organisation Society. Heard published his first book, *Narcissus*, in 1924, which advanced the revolutionary idea that fashion and architecture provide clues to the evolutionary stages of humankind. In 1929, he produced his second book, *The Ascent of Humanity*, a brilliant, groundbreaking essay on the philosophy of history that was awarded the British Academy's prestigious Hertz Prize.

Heard began his career as a public speaker in 1926, lecturing for three years under the auspices of Oxford University. In 1929, he became literary editor of *The Realist*, a short-lived but significant monthly journal of scientific humanism. There he worked with a distinguished editorial board that included Aldous Huxley, Julian Huxley, and H. G. Wells. Pacifists Heard and Aldous Huxley, associated with the Peace Movement, gave lectures in England in support of their cause during the mid-1930s.

From 1930 to 1934, Heard served as the BBC's first science commentator, commanding a large and regular listening audience with his sparkling fortnightly broadcasts. H. G. Wells said of him, "Heard is the only man I ever listen to on the wireless. He makes human life come alive." The prolific Heard published ten books during the 1930s.

Gerald Heard moved to America, arriving in New York City in April 1937 on the *S.S. Normandie*, accompanied by Aldous Huxley. He traveled throughout the United States, taught for a term at Duke University, and embarked on a lecture tour with Huxley before settling in Southern California in early 1938. The next year he met Swami Prabhavananda, founder of the Vedanta Society of Southern California. Heard subsequently introduced the ecumenical Vedanta philosophy to Huxley, Christopher Isherwood, and other Western notables, which prompted mystery writer Ellery Queen to write, "Gerald Heard is the spiritual godfather of this Western movement."

In 1941, Heard put the larger part of his personal financial resources into building and endowing the pioneering Trabuco College, which advanced comparative religion studies and interfaith practices in a coeducational, semi-monastic setting. Under the spiritual direction of Heard, and 30 years ahead of its time, Trabuco College was discontinued in 1947 and later donated to the Vedanta Society of Southern California. In addition to writing essays, articles, short stories, and delivering more than a hundred lectures, Heard published an astonishing eighteen books during the 1940s.

Alongside his nonfiction writing, Heard wrote several acclaimed mysteries and supernatural fantasies under the pen name H. F. Heard, including *Reply Paid* and *Doppelgangers*. He published two fiction anthologies, *The Great Fog* and *The Lost Cavern*. His bestselling 1941 novel, *A Taste for Honey*, praised by Christopher Morley and Boris Karloff, and listed among the exclusive Haycraft-Queen Cornerstones, was loosely adapted into a movie, 1967's *The Deadly Bees*, the first in the killer-bees genre. (Karloff played Mr. Mycroft in the ABC TV adaptation of *A Taste for Honey*, titled "The Sting of Death," which aired in 1955.) His 1947 whodunit masterpiece, "The President of the United States, Detective" won first prize in the second-annual *Ellery Queen's Mystery Magazine*'s prestigious short-story contest.

About the Author

For the remaining fifteen years of his active life, Heard spent his time and energy in writing, lecturing, research, travel, and making numerous radio and television appearances. He moderated an eight-part series, *Focus on Sanity*, which appeared on CBS television in 1957. He lectured at many of the major colleges and universities in the United States, including Harvard, Cornell, Princeton, and UCLA. He spoke at religious venues as diverse as the Vedanta Society, the First Congregational Church in Akron, Temple Sinai in Beverly Hills, and the Soto Zen Temple in Honolulu. Heard was a behind-the-scenes inspiration and catalyst who spurred many individuals to pivotal accomplishments in their careers. His last book was his 1964 magnum opus *The Five Ages of [Humanity]*, which Robert R. Kirsch, literary critic of the *Los Angeles Times*, praised as "the most important work to date of this challenging and brilliant philosopher, a volume which in scope and daring might be the 'Novum Organum' of the 20th century."

Gerald Heard, influential author, historian, lecturer, and philosopher, whom Rabbi Zalman Schachter-Shalomi referred to as "the repository of the most encompassing cosmology of his generation," succumbed peacefully on August 14, 1971, at his home in Santa Monica, California at the age of eighty-one. For more information, visit www.geraldheard.com.

www.ingramcontent.com/pod-product-compliance
Lightning Source LLC
Chambersburg PA
CBHW040742060526
44119CB00096B/441/J